BETWEEN RIGHTS AND RESPONSIBILITIES

BETWEEN RIGHTS AND RESPONSIBILITIES

A Fundamental Debate

Edited by
Stephan Parmentier
Hans Werdmölder
Michaël Merrigan

intersentia
Cambridge – Antwerp – Portland

Intersentia Ltd
Sheraton House | Castle Park
Cambridge | CB3 0AX | United Kingdom
Tel.: +44 1223 370 170 | Fax: +44 1223 370 169
Email: mail@intersentia.co.uk
www.intersentia.com | www.intersentia.co.uk

Distribution for the UK and Ireland:
NBN International
Airport Business Centre, 10 Thornbury Road
Plymouth, PL6 7PP
United Kingdom
Tel: +44 1752 202 301 | Fax: +44 1752 202 331
Email: orders@nbninternational.com

Distribution for Europe and all other countries:
Intersentia Publishing nv
Groenstraat 31
2640 Mortsel
Belgium
Tel.: +32 3 680 15 50 | Fax: +32 3 658 71 21
Email: mail@intersentia.be

Distribution for the USA and Canada:
International Specialized Book Services
920 NE 58th Ave Suite 300
Portland, OR 97213
USA
Tel.: +1 800 944 6190 (toll free) | Fax: +1 503 280 8832
Email: info@isbs.com

ISBN 978-90-5095-886-8
D/2016/7849/77
NUR 820

British Library Cataloguing in Publication Data. A catalogue record for this book is available from the British Library.

FOREWORD

It is a pleasure for me to write the foreword to this book on rights and responsibilities.

As the editors note in their introduction, the book was inspired by a conference that took place some ten years ago, in Leuven, in the framework of the Summer Course on Human Rights. The Summer Course was organised annually by the University of Leuven and the Dutch Human Rights Research School. With the late Peter Baehr, Cees Flinterman, Hans Werdmölder, Stephan Parmentier, Wouter Vandenhole and others, I was part of the group that was responsible for the organisation of the event. I have the best memories of the many times that we sat together to prepare the course, of the many discussions with colleagues and students during the course, and of the many pleasant encounters with our loyal friends and lecturers from Northwestern University and the University of Notre Dame, Doug Cassel, Steve Sawyer and Barbara Fick. Writing this foreword brings back all these memories.

Michaël Merrigan later joined Stephan Parmentier and Hans Werdmölder as an editor of the book. A bright researcher, he is finishing his PhD research on fundamental duties and responsibilities. As Michael's promoter, I am closely following that research. It will no doubt bring again new insights to the topic covered by this book.

Fundamental responsibilities, and their relationship to fundamental rights, seem to have become more topical than ever. Where the relevance of fundamental rights is questioned, fundamental responsibilities are often presented as an alternative.

In fact, human rights have always been in a close relationship with fundamental responsibilities. In Article 29(1) of the *Universal Declaration on Human Rights*, it is proclaimed that 'everyone has duties to the community in which alone the free and full development of his personality is possible'. It is true that such references are relatively rare in the subsequent international human rights treaties. But perhaps this can be explained by the simple fact that the stated aim of these treaties is to protect the individual against arbitrary action by the state, and that the drafters did not consider it necessary to repeat, in such a context, that the individual also has responsibilities vis-à-vis the state or others.

One could say that an individual's fundamental rights can only be fully understood against the background of his or her fundamental responsibilities. Rights are guaranteed to individuals, but this does not take away the fact that individuals, as members of a given society, also have certain 'membership' obligations. The existence of fundamental responsibilities is an essential feature of a democratic society, in which individuals or groups of individuals must be prepared to make concessions, for the benefit of society as a whole.[1]

These fundamental responsibilities seem to be based, like fundamental rights, on respect for human dignity.

Human rights can be interpreted in such a way that they become counter-productive. The international human rights treaties are based on the idea of a fair balance between individual rights and the general interest or the rights of others. Most human rights can be limited for good cause. It is for those who have to take decisions that can affect the individual situation of citizens, to search for the proper balance. Similarly, fundamental responsibilities should not be given an overbroad meaning. Putting too much emphasis on fundamental responsibilities, for instance by making the enjoyment of inalienable rights dependent on the fulfilment of certain obligations, could lead to a limitation of human rights to a greater extent than is acceptable in a democratic society.[2]

Everything is, therefore, a question of measure.

This book tries to steer the reader 'between' rights and responsibilities. Starting from a general perspective, it moves on to concrete situations where both rights and responsibilities may be relevant. In many contributions, the tension between rights and responsibilities is made tangible. The authors take positions, and try to find the right balance. This is not an easy task, as there is not so much 'hard' material to rely on.

The authors thus contribute to a debate that will continue to go on in Europe and elsewhere. Their contributions can and should enlighten the participants in that debate.

May this book lead to a better understanding of the position of individuals within 'their' society.

Paul Lemmens
Judge, European Court of Human Rights
Professor, KU Leuven

---

1 See ECtHR [GC], 13 February 2003, *Refah Partisi (Welfare Party) and Others v. Turkey*, § 99, ECHR, 2003-II; ECtHR [GC], 16 March 2006, *Zdanoka v. Latvia*, § 100, ECHR, 2006-IV.

2 Compare Article 17 of the European Convention on Human Rights: 'Nothing in this Convention may be interpreted as implying for any State, group or person any right to engage in any activity or perform any act aimed at the destruction of any of the rights and freedoms set forth herein or at their limitation to a greater extent than is provided for in the Convention.'

CONTENTS

ABOUT THE AUTHORS

Douglass Cassel is Professor of Law and Presidential Fellow at Notre Dame Law School in the United States. He is a scholar and practitioner of international human rights and international criminal law, specialising in accountability for gross violations of human rights, transitional justice, comparative regional human rights systems, and business and human rights. He directed Notre Dame's Center for Civil and Human Rights from 2005 to 2011, and previously directed similar centres at DePaul College of Law and Northwestern University School of Law. Among other positions, he is currently president of the board of the Justice Studies Center of the Americas, to which he was elected by the Organization of American States, and serves on the boards of the Lawyers' Committee for Civil Rights under Law and the Inter-American Institute of Human Rights. He was formerly president of the Due Process of Law Foundation (2000–2012).

Barbara J. Fick is Associate Professor of Law at the University of Notre Dame Law School, where she is also a faculty fellow of the Kroc Institute for International Peace Studies and a fellow of the Higgins Labor Studies Program. She was elected to the Executive Board of the US Branch of the International Society for Labor and Social Security Law from 2006–2012, and was a member of the editorial board of the journal International Contributions to Labour Studies from 1994–1998. She has worked as a consultant with the Solidarity Center, AFL-CIO, and USAID in Eastern Europe, Central Asia and the Middle East on issues of international worker rights and the role of trade unions in fostering democratic societies and advancing human rights. She teaches and conducts research in the field of domestic, international and comparative labour and employment law.

René Foqué is Professor emeritus in Legal Philosophy, Legal Theory, European Legal Thinking and Philosophy of Human Rights both at the Faculty of Law of the Catholic University of Leuven and at the Faculty of Law of the Erasmus University in Rotterdam. He teaches at the European Master's Programme in Human Rights and Democratisation of the European Inter-University Centre in Venice, and is the academic coordinator of the Comenius Lectures in Legal Science in Bologna. He is also a correspondent member of the Royal Dutch Academy of Sciences. During the period 2004–2008 he was the chairman of the jury of the International Spinoza Prize. René Foqué's research and publications relate to the following four themes: democracy and the rule of law, the foundations of criminal law and criminology, the theory and philosophy of European and international law, global governance and human rights and legal science in a transdisciplinary context.

Marlies Galenkamp is Associate Professor in Legal Philosophy and Jurisprudence at the Erasmus School of Law of the Erasmus University Rotterdam, The Netherlands. She studied political science and philosophy. In 1993, she defended her PhD thesis on collective rights, *Individualism versus Collectivism. The Concept of Collective Rights* (new edition in 1998, Gouda Quint, Arnhem). Her research focuses on constitutional rights in general and on the freedom of expression and of religion more specifically. Current research topics include the historical-philosophical origins of constitutional rights, conflicts between these rights, and the abuse of rights.

Martin Kuijer is the senior legal adviser on human rights law at the Netherlands Ministry of Security and Justice, where he is *inter alia* responsible for the contribution of the Ministry in cases against the Netherlands before the European Court of Human Rights. He was appointed Professor in Human Rights Law at the VU University of Amsterdam in 2004, since 2006 he has acted as liaison officer on behalf of the Netherlands government for the European Committee for the Prevention of Torture (CPT), he was appointed substitute judge at the Court of Appeal in Arnhem in 2007, and a (substitute) member of the European Commission for Democracy through Law (the 'Venice Commission') in 2015. He has been involved in various programmes on legal system reform and human rights training in Europe, Africa and America. He is a member of the editorial board of the Netherlands law journal for human rights law (*NTM*) and the Netherlands Yearbook of International Law.

Mumba Malila is a Judge of the Supreme Court of Zambia. He holds an LLB degree from the University of Zambia, an LLM degree from Cambridge University and a Certificate in Human Rights from the Rene Cassin International Institute of Human Rights, Strasbourg, France. He has extensive legal practice experience spanning over 25 years as a private legal practitioner, corporation counsel, government lawyer and university lecturer. Malila was a member of the African Commission on Human and Peoples' Rights between 2005 and 2011 and served as the Commission's Vice Chairperson in the last two years of his term as Commissioner. He was also the Chairperson of the African Commission's Working Group on Extractive Industries and Human Rights Violations and served as a member of the Working Group on Indigenous Populations and Communities in Africa, and the Working Group on the Death Penalty. He was until June 2014 the Attorney General for Zambia, a position he served in a record two times under three different Presidents between 2006 and 2009, and between 2011 and 2014. He served as Special Rapporteur on Prisons and Conditions of Detention in Africa between 2005 and 2009.

Michaël Merrigan is a PhD researcher at the KU Leuven Institute for Human Rights and Critical Studies (LIHRICS). He has obtained a Master's degree in Law (KU Leuven), an LLM in Public International Law (Leiden University) and the European Master's Degree (E.MA) in Human Rights and Democratisation (European Inter-University Centre for Human Rights and Democratisation). As a teaching assistant he has taught tutorials at the KU Leuven, the University of Hasselt and in the framework of the European Master's Degree in Human Rights and Democratisation in Venice, Italy. He is currently preparing a PhD thesis on the topic of fundamental rights and responsibilities in a democratic society, under the supervision of Prof. Dr. Paul Lemmens.

Maria del Carmen Patricia Morales studied philosophy at the University of Buenos Aires and Goethe University in Frankfurt. She received her PhD in 1997 at the University of Buenos Aires with her thesis '*Derechos humanos y etica de la responsabilidad solidaria*'. She is visiting professor at the University of Leuven at the Faculty of Arts for the master of Iberoamerican Studies and for the Institute of European Society and Culture. She has been a researcher at Tilburg University on issues of ethics, human rights and sustainable development, at the global and Latin-America level. She also collaborates with the University Blas Pascal in Argentina on issues of human security. At Tilburg University, she became involved in the Earth Charter process and participated in the drafting of the *Declaration of Human Duties and Responsibilities* (1998) and the *Earth Charter* (2000). She is editor of *Indigenous Peoples, Human Rights and Global Interdependence* (1994), *Towards Global Human Rights* (1996), and *Pueblos indigenas, derechos humanos e interdependencia global* (2001) and author of several articles.

Stephan Parmentier is Professor of Sociology of Crime, Law, and Human Rights at the Faculty of Law of the KU Leuven and served as the Head of its Department of Criminal Law and Criminology (2005–2009). He was elected in 2010 as the Secretary-General of the International Society for Criminology (re-elected in 2014) and also serves on the Advisory Board of the Oxford Centre for Criminology and the International Centre for Transitional Justice (New York). Stephan's research and publications relate to human rights violations and international crimes in situations of violent conflict and post-conflict, strategies and mechanisms for justice and peace building, and quality management in the administration of criminal justice. He is the founder and general editor of the international book Series on Transitional Justice (Intersentia, Cambridge/Antwerp) and editor of the Restorative Justice: an International Journal (Hart, Oxford). He carried out field research in Bosnia, Guatemala, Serbia and South Africa.

Wouter Vandenhole teaches human rights and holds the UNICEF Chair in Children's Rights – a joint venture of the University of Antwerp and UNICEF Belgium – at the Faculty of Law of the University of Antwerp (Belgium). He is the spokesperson of the Law and Development Research Group and chaired the European Research Networking Programme GLOTHRO between 2011 and 2016. He has published widely on economic, social and cultural rights, children's rights, transnational human rights obligations and human rights and development. Vandenhole is a founding member of the Flemish Children's Rights Knowledge Centre and co-convener of the international interdisciplinary course on human rights for development (HR4DEV).

W.J.M. van Genugten is Emeritus Professor of International Law at Tilburg University Law School. He still is Extraordinary Professor of International Law at North-West University, South Africa, from which he also holds a doctorate *honoris causa* (2012). Professor van Genugten is the editor-in-Chief of the Netherlands Yearbook of International Law, and chair of various organisations, including the Royal Netherlands Society of International Law and the Knowledge Platform Security and the Rule of law. He is the author of various international publications.

Hans Werdmölder is an anthropologist and criminologist. From 1996 to 2008, he was head of the Research and Graduate Programme of the School for Human Rights Research at the University of Utrecht. In this capacity he was also responsible for the annual Summer Courses on Human Rights, organised in close collaboration with the Law Faculty of the Catholic University of Leuven, Northwestern University and Notre Dame Law School. In the following years, he was senior lecturer at the Roosevelt Academy in Middleburg, senior researcher and advisor at the Institute for Safety and Crisis Management (COT) in The Hague and associate professor in the field of Youth and Safety at Avans Hogeschool. Since 2008 he has been actively involved in a longitudinal research project concerning Moroccan delinquent men in The Netherlands (1982–2012). His latest book *Marokkanen in de marge. Ontspoorde levens van kleine criminelen* was published by Amsterdam University Press in autumn 2015. He is currently affiliated with the department of sociology at the University of Amsterdam.

Jan C.M. Willems is a researcher in children's rights and human development at the Department of International and European Law and the Maastricht Centre for Human Rights of Maastricht University, the Netherlands. Between 2002 and 2009 he was the first Dutch Chair holder on the International Rights of the Child at VU University Amsterdam. He is author and editor of several books and articles on children's rights, early childhood and child abuse and neglect. His main research interests are transgenerational discrimination, or childism (denialism in relation to the failure of states to prevent ill-treatment of children at the hands of their parents or carers), the rights of newborn persons (especially attachment security as a human right), and the structural prevention of child maltreatment (integrated SMECC approach).

INTRODUCTION

Towards an Integrated Vision of Rights and Responsibilities

Stephan Parmentier, Hans Werdmölder and Michaël Merrigan

> 'And so, my fellow Americans: ask not what your country can do for you, ask what you can do for your country. My fellow citizens of the world: ask not what America will do for you, but what together we can do for the freedom of man.'[1]

During his inaugural speech on 20 January 1961, American President John F. Kennedy could not have foreseen that his words would become so famous in the course of the next fifty years. These two sentences have been repeated over and over again, by different people on different occasions, and have also been adapted accordingly. The presidential proclamation that citizens should not limit themselves to claiming benefits and rights from the society they live in, but should also contribute to the development and the well-being of their societies is a very interesting, even provocative one. The core argument, in a nutshell, boils down to the general idea that citizens also have responsibilities, duties and obligations, next to possessing individual rights. In the past half-century this idea has gradually risen to the centre stage of public debate in many western societies, something that Kennedy in the early 1960s could hardly have envisaged.

Some examples of recent debates in several European countries and beyond may illustrate this trend:

- For how long can persons who have lost their job receive unemployment benefits from local or central state agencies, and what kind of responsibility lies with the unemployed themselves? Can they be obliged to search for another job and, if so, under which conditions? Can persons with insufficient

[1] J.F. Kennedy, *Inaugural Address*, Washington DC, 20 January 1961, www.jfklibrary.org/Research/Research-Aids/Ready-Reference/JFK-Quotations/Inaugural-Address.aspx.

professional qualifications who receive benefits be obliged to receive training so as to improve their position on the labour market?
- In what way can public authorities impose obligations on members of non-European linguistic, cultural and religious minorities to comply with the general values and norms of the host country? More specifically, do all citizens have the right to dress the way they wish, or are certain restrictions allowed and on what grounds? Can newcomers, who are dependent on government benefits, be forced to learn the language of the host country and how?
- To what extent can or should the provision (or reimbursement) by the social security system of expensive health care treatments be made dependent on a patient's previous conduct with regard to his or her own health? Under what conditions can old and new beneficiaries of social systems be expected to accept certain duties or held accountable in the case of non-compliance with the rules and regulations?
- What are the moral and legal duties of large-scale economic actors? We can think, for instance, of multinational companies, both in stable States and in situations of violent conflict, and both in relation to the local and national authorities of the host State and in relation to the civilian population. Can they be held responsible for forming alliances with dubious partners that may endanger the rights of individuals and groups?

These are just some salient examples of current-day discussions about the responsibilities, duties and obligations of citizens in modern and post-modern societies. By and large, these debates can be seen as reflective of three important trends. First of all, from a theoretical angle, the debates are broadening the paradigm of human rights that has dominated the development of western societies since World War II. In this sense, they constitute a supplement to the one-sided emphasis on claims and rights that for a long time appears to have neglected the other side of the same coin of human coexistence. Second, from a more practical perspective, the debates also reflect a fundamental shift in social policy that intends to entail more tangible effects and have more impact on the ground. Seen from this perspective, the growing emphasis on duties and obligations is geared to produce effective social change in complex societies. Third, debates about responsibilities, duties and obligations also highlight the (perceived) importance of developing a global ethic. As the Commission on Global Governance held in its famous report 'Our Global Neighbourhood' in 1995, '[o]ver the long run, rights can only be preserved if they are exercised responsibly and with due respect to the reciprocal rights of others.'[2]

We will briefly elaborate on these three major trends, and then present the various chapters contained in this book.

---

2 Commission on Global Governance, *Our Global Neighbourhood*, Oxford: Oxford University Press, 1995, p. 55.

1. FROM RIGHTS TO RESPONSIBILITIES: BROADENING THE PARADIGM

In his book *The Age of Rights*, Louis Henkin, the renowned American legal scholar, coined human rights as 'the paradigm of our time'.[3] For him, human rights have replaced other grand paradigms such as religion and socialism, and constitute a gradual but inevitable emancipation of mankind and of individual people from the shackles of domination and power politics.

Indeed, the rapid development of human rights norms, institutions and procedures in the post-World War II period has been impressive. At all levels of governance, universal (United Nations) and regional (Council of Europe, European Union, Organisation of American States, African Union), as well as national and local, new arrangements of human rights have seen the light of day. This development has gone hand in hand with the rise of an extensive and vibrant civil society that both monitors the application of human rights and contributes to its creation and further refinement.

In the course of the last 25 years, however, the very concept of human rights has come under serious attack. It is argued from various sides that the strong emphasis on the 'culture of claims and rights' has led to an obsession with the rights of individuals, at the expense of attention to groups and communities worldwide and, moreover, at the neglect of responsibilities and duties for all. Over the years, a number of initiatives have therefore been undertaken, including (but certainly not limited to):

- the *Trieste Declaration of Human Duties* by the International Council of Human Duties in 1993;[4]
- the interfaith project *Declaration Toward a Global Ethic* by the Parliament of the World's Religions in 1993;[5]
- the *Universal Declaration of Human Responsibilities*, as launched by a group of former world leaders calling themselves the InterAction Council in 1997;[6]
- the *Declaration on the Responsibilities of the Present Generations Towards Future Generations* adopted by the General Conference of UNESCO in 1997;[7]
- the so-called *Valencia Declaration of Human Duties and Responsibilities* by the High-Level Group chaired by Richard J. Goldstone under the auspices of

[3] L. Henkin, *The Age of Rights*, New York: Columbia University Press, 1990, p. 4.

[4] International Council of Human Duties, *The Trieste Declaration of Human Duties: A Code of Ethics of Shared Responsibilities*, Trieste: University of Trieste, 1993.

[5] Parliament of the World's Religions, *Declaration toward a Global Ethic*, adopted on 4 September 1993 in Chicago, USA.

[6] InterAction Council, *A Universal Declaration of Human Responsibilities*, 1 September 1997.

[7] UNESCO, *Declaration on the Responsibilities of the Present Generations Towards Future Generations*, adopted on 12 November 1997 by the General Conference of UNESCO at its 29th session. Published in UNESCO, *Records of the General Conference, Twenty-ninth Session, Paris, 21 October to 12 November 1997, Volume 1: Resolutions*, Paris: UNESCO, 1998, pp. 69–71.

the City of Valencia and UNESCO, initiated and organised by the Valencia Third Millennium Foundation in 1998;[8]
- *Recommendation 1401* of the Parliamentary Assembly by the Council of Europe on *Education in the Responsibilities of the Individual* in 1999;[9]
- *Resolution 91* on *Responsible Citizenship and Participation in Public Life* by the Congress of Local and Regional Authorities of the Council of Europe in 2000;[10]
- the pre-draft *Declaration on Human Social Responsibilities* of the Special Rapporteur of the UN Commission on Human Rights in 2003;[11] and
- *Resolution 1845* of the Parliamentary Assembly of the Council of Europe on *Fundamental Rights and Responsibilities* in 2011.[12]

It should be noted that the terminology of this broadening paradigm is far from uniform: the notions of 'responsibilities', 'duties' and 'obligations' are frequently used interchangeably as if they were perfect synonyms. However, they refer to very different realities depending on the context in which they are used, i.e. moral, political, cultural, legal, or otherwise.

It is clear that also the underlying reasons for the increased emphasis on responsibilities and the like can be quite different, depending on the origin of the initiative and even within the various groups supporting each proposal. For some, the argument is mostly philosophical, as they advocate a shift from western individualism to non-western visions and cultures of communal thinking and hence defend the concomitant move from rights to responsibilities. Others also draw on culture but in a different way: they argue that some immigrant communities from non-western countries have failed to adapt their language, culture and religion to the values and norms of western States, and therefore insist on the moral and legal duties of the newcomers to integrate in the host society in an appropriate way. Still other arguments are based on the social and economic realities of Europe and other parts of the western world: as the post-war welfare

8 Fundación Valencia Tercer Milenio, *Declaration of Human Duties and Responsibilities*, adopted by the high-level group chaired by Richard J. Goldstone under the auspices of the City of Valencia and UNESCO, initiated and organised by the Valencia Third Millennium Foundation, 1998.

9 Parliamentary Assembly of the Council of Europe, *Recommendation 1401 (1999) on Education in the responsibilities of the individual*, adopted by the Standing Committee, acting on behalf of the Assembly, on 30 March 1999.

10 Congress of Local and Regional Authorities of the Council of Europe, *Resolution 91 (2000) on Responsible Citizenship and Participation in Public Life*, adopted on 24 May 2000.

11 United Nations Commission on Human Rights, *Pre-Draft Declaration on Human Social Responsibilities*, annex to *Promotion and Protection of Human Rights: Human Rights and Human Responsibilities, Final report of the Special Rapporteur, Miguel Alfonso Martinez, on the Study requested by the Commission in its resolution 2000/63, and submitted pursuant to Economic and Social Council decision 2002/277*, 17 March 2003, UN Doc E/CN.4/2003/105.

12 Parliamentary Assembly of the Council of Europe, *Resolution 1845(2011) on Fundamental Rights and Responsibilities*, adopted by the Standing Committee, acting on behalf of the Assembly, on 25 November 2011.

State during the current economic crisis is facing its limits in providing access to goods and services for all citizens according to their needs, these same citizens are called to contribute to the system according to their possibilities. Some arguments even focus on the collective responsibility of the present generations towards future generations regarding the preservation of life on Earth in all its facets.

Whether philosophical, cultural, social, economic or otherwise, the many arguments in our view tend to converge into one major theme, namely the conviction that societies should be construed based on principles of participation and solidarity and not on exclusion and self-centredness. Or put in more general terms, the belief that social cohesion among the various sectors of society should be strengthened and not weakened. For these reasons, individuals, groups, communities and state agencies are called to contribute to the 'common good of all'. These grand themes are very likely to become much more central in public and policy debates, not only in European and western societies but across the globe.

2. FROM AGENDA-SETTING TO IMPLEMENTATION: DEVELOPING AN AGENDA FOR ACTION

The human rights paradigm is also surrounded by a second major debate, possibly even older than the preceding one. Every day again, scholars, policy makers and the public at large can notice that many tensions exist between 'human rights in the books' and 'human rights in action'. This problem is far from new and relates to all kinds of law, because it is always difficult to foresee and manage the tangible effects of lofty political principles and legal standards when turning them into daily policy and practice.

In some cases, however, these tensions have arguably widened into a real gap, as illustrated through the eruption of many violent conflicts in the past decades. Some of these conflicts have been exceptionally cruel in nature and have witnessed the curtailment, violation and even extermination of the same political and legal principles and standards advocated before. In our view, it suffices to highlight the wars in the former Yugoslavia, the genocide in Rwanda and the ongoing violent conflicts in the DR Congo, Syria or Iraq as examples of blatant human rights abuses, but the list is obviously – and unfortunately – much longer.

Whether the tensions between the law on paper and the law in reality are small or large, various strategies may be envisaged to ease them or even to bridge the gaps. For a long time the solution was sought in new and additional forms of legal regulation in order to overcome the shortcomings of previous statutes, laws and court judgments. However, an excessive emphasis on legal instrumentalism is increasingly considered part of the problem and not of the solution. Recent years have therefore witnessed experiments with other than legal strategies of implementing political principles and legal standards in the field of human rights, including educational, social and economic.

Expansion of the paradigm from human rights, on the one hand, to human responsibilities, duties and obligations, on the other hand, will in itself not solve the aforementioned tensions. New arrangements and instruments to steer human and organisational behaviour through individual duties and responsibilities will be confronted with similar problems. Here, too, new strategies will have to be conceived in order to overcome these pitfalls.

3. FROM LEGAL AND PHILOSOPHICAL DISCUSSIONS TO A GROUNDED DEBATE: SOCIALISING THE FORUM

Past and current discussions about human rights and responsibilities can foremost be seen as legal and philosophical in nature, focusing on the legal standards that should apply and their philosophical underpinnings. These debates, therefore, have seldom been 'grounded' in the sense of having been envisaged by and incorporated in the minds and daily practices of common people.

The past and ongoing discussions about asylum seekers, migrants and ethnic minorities in Western Europe are illustrative in this regard. In the 1980s and 1990s, the discussions tended to be dominated by small groups of left-wing intellectuals and technocratic policy makers at closed conferences, and sometimes guided by politically correct consultants, at the neglect of critical individuals raising practical or more fundamental objections. Thirty years later, migration issues have given rise to increasing populism and new right-wing political parties, in several countries like the Netherlands, France, Belgium and Great Britain, and some of those constitute threats to international human rights. Arguably, this limited debate among elites about rights only – and not responsibilities or duties – has not been in the long-term interest of the new citizens either. Asylum seekers and migrants are not always the pitiful or weak persons they are portrayed to be in personal narratives and the media, but also demonstrate considerable strength as survivors of harsh political, social and economic conditions. Many of these reflections gain even more importance in the wake of the unprecedented migration flows that have come to Europe in the course of 2015.

Van Genugten, one of the authors in this book, once gave a lecture arguing that 'human rights are too important to leave to legal professionals only'.[13] In this publication, we, in turn, argue that discussions about rights and responsibilities are too important to leave to intellectuals only. In societies priding themselves in being 'open', both a public forum and a broad social base are indispensable

[13] W.J.M. van Genugten, *Mensenrechten te belangrijk om louter aan juristen over te laten* (lecture in honour of the 78th dies natalis), Tilburg: Universiteit van Tilburg, 2005.

tools for the understanding of rights and responsibilities, as well as for their enforcement. As much as human rights cannot be a 'legal toy' of politically correct and enthusiastic intellectuals only, they have to become the 'toy' of every citizen. Following van Genugten, it can be stated that the study and the enforcement of human rights and responsibilities should be connected to the economic and social development of the countries and regions concerned.[14]

4. INTRODUCING THIS VOLUME

The developments, tensions and discussions mentioned are far from only theoretical or abstract. As can be seen from the concrete examples listed, they bear consequences in everyday life in the 21st century, in a variety of areas like globalisation, multiculturalism, parental relations, terrorism, etc.

This was the main reason why in September 2006 a colloquium was organised at the Faculty of Law of the University of Leuven in order to reflect on these major tendencies and their implications. It constituted part of the Summer Course in Human Rights, a common project of the Leuven Faculty of Law and the Dutch Human Rights Research School, which was organised on an annual basis and without interruption between 1997 and 2009. The two-week intensive courses brought together junior professionals from academia, government service, civil society and legal practice to exchange ideas and deepen their knowledge and skills in the field of human rights. Many of them now occupy important positions in their home countries or elsewhere, as policy makers, educators, civil society activists and entrepreneurs.

All chapters collected in this volume were presented for the first time at the 2006 symposium, and subsequently reworked and fine-tuned over the years. These original pieces are subdivided in two main parts.

Part I presents four chapters that set the scene of the debate about fundamental rights and fundamental responsibilities.

René Foqué notes that, first and foremost, the discussion regarding duties and responsibilities is in need of a conceptual clarification. He argues that responsibility as an ethical concept is a broader and thicker notion than the moral concept of duty or the legal concept of obligation. It is especially this ethical concept, he says, which is the key to overcoming the main pitfalls of our current human rights paradigm, i.e. moral abstraction, ahistorical immobility, and formalism, and which can help us look beyond the constraints of methodological and normative individualism. Foqué also adds a warning, however: the ethical universe underpinning the notion of responsibility cannot simply be translated into legal obligations, as this would undermine the ethical and political dynamism which is vital for a democratic society.

[14] Ibid.

In the article by *Willem van Genugten* the focus is on a moral appeal or accountability to combat the poverty in the world. Van Genugten argues that a real paradigm shift is needed from the side of rich, well-developed countries. This shift, however, entails a moral, not a legally binding obligation. Van Genugten especially focusses on NGOs, which can, in his view, make an important contribution towards making this paradigm shift a reality. In his challenging article, the author hereby refers to the work of the renowned philosopher Thomas Pogge.

Douglas Cassel also sees a fundamental difference between the concept of legal rights and the moral and ethical concepts of duties and responsibilities. He notes that rights can be enforced by national and international authorities, while duties and responsibilities are – and should remain – mere guidelines for individual behaviour. Cassel also points out the dangers of codifying duties and responsibilities into legal language, arguing more specifically in reference to, among other things, the Christian faith that neither 'the poverty of a rights-based morality, nor the perils of a duty-based legality' must be accepted. Rather, the legal dimension and a richer morality should complement each other, in order to guarantee concern for every individual and the community as a whole.

Patricia Morales focuses on the so-called Valencia Declaration of Human Duties and Responsibilities. Morales claims that this formulation of duties and responsibilities not only reinforces existing human rights and, in particular, those enshrined in the UDHR and succeeding international human rights instruments, but that it also supports our awareness of our individual and collective role in realising these rights. In spite of the obvious disregard by so many actors in recent history for any kind of human duties and responsibilities, Morales sees a glimmer of hope as she notes that the language of duties and responsibilities is increasingly being accepted.

In Part II, the implications of an emphasis on responsibilities, duties and obligations are concretised in specific areas and through specific cases.

Wouter Vandenhole focuses on the question whether the human right to social protection and the duty to work are on an equal footing, and how to deal with conflicts that arise in balancing the two. He argues that the human right to social protection, which includes both the right to social security and the right to social assistance, is of a higher normative order than the duty to work, but may nevertheless be subject to limitations. In practice, however, it seems that the right equilibrium has not been struck yet. Vandenhole argues that neo-liberal and active labour market policies may have swung the pendulum too far away from individual human rights protection.

Barbara Fick focuses on trade unions and the responsibility they have in influencing government policies regarding diverse civil, political, social and economic rights. For this, a collaboration between the human rights community and trade unions is required, whereby the human rights community must see to it that governments respect trade union independence and freedom of action, while trade unions should use their potential to promote human rights in a broad way. As yet, Fick argues, this potential regarding trade unions is underappreciated, but it will prove important in our further globalising world.

According to *Marlies Galenkamp*, rights and duties are closely connected to each other. In her contribution, she argues that this view is commonly overlooked in the Dutch debate on constitutional rights. Individuals are considered to have such rights in a rather unqualified way. However, the freedom of expression does not provide the right to offend people in public. In the same vain, freedom of religion does not constitute a *carte blanche* to discriminate homosexuals or to refuse shaking hands with persons of the opposite sex. Fundamental rights, Galenkamp writes, should therefore always be exercised responsibly. When we lose sight of such responsibilities, the dangers of rights abuses are lurking.

Martin Kuijer points at the dilemma faced by national authorities regarding the treatment of terror suspects. On the one hand, authorities are obliged to uphold suspects' fundamental rights while, on the other hand, States have to offer protection to their citizens. Although the article, at first sight, juxtaposes the responsibility of the State, and not that of (groups of) individuals, against individual rights, it does draw our attention to an essential issue, i.e. the importance of balancing communal needs with individual rights. It is this balancing act against which any discussion of individual duties and responsibilities naturally must take place. In the view of Kuijer, the European Court of Human Rights plays the role of a more objective actor, providing an important safety net in judging whether the balance between state security and the rights of terrorist suspects is maintained.

Jan C.M. Willems focuses our attention on the duties of parents regarding the basic needs and rights of their children. In his view, traditional systems of child protection, such as the Committee on the Rights of the Child and the Council of Europe, are not sufficiently equipped to prevent violations of children's rights. Legal specifications and clarifications of both parental responsibilities and the best interests of the child, the author argues, must urgently be made.

Mumba Malila draws our attention to the African human right system and, more specifically, to the duties listed in the African Charter on Human and Peoples' Rights. Malila argues that the Banjul Charter and the duties listed therein represent a unique attempt to enrich the contemporary notion of human rights with elements of traditional African thought. Though he points at the possible legal pitfalls of using duty-language in an unqualified way, he ultimately believes that the African emphasis on duties can both benefit the African continent as a whole and strengthen individual rights protection.

It goes without saying that the ten chapters in this volume cannot answer all the questions posed by the changing realities of rights and responsibilities in today's world, which is undergoing profound changes. But they can shed new light on important problems related to some of the major transformations occurring in European and western societies and the ensuing changes in philosophical, political, social and legal thinking. Indeed, the problems about rights and responsibilities are far from theoretical but grounded in day-to-day realities, as the ongoing debates on globalisation, multiculturalism, terrorism, etc. clearly illustrate. By probing these multilayered and multifaceted issues, the authors in this volume may also contribute to enriching our traditional understandings of human rights and human dignity, and of solidarity and social cohesion in modern societies, both today and in the decades to come.

PART I

FUNDAMENTAL RIGHTS AND FUNDAMENTAL RESPONSIBILITIES: SETTING THE SCENE

HUMAN RIGHTS AND HUMAN RESPONSIBILITIES

Setting the Ethical and the Conceptual Scene

René Foqué

1. INTRODUCTION

We live in 'a time of responsibility', as the French philosopher Jean Greisch once remarked.[1] We are called upon, all the more insistently, to take a stand and to act on that choice in the often complex and confusing circumstances of insecurity, uncertainty, and vulnerability to which our late-modern societies have become subject. These societies find themselves in fact on the seemingly perilous knife-edge of local contexts, on the one hand, and a globalising perspective, on the other.[2] This leaves people uncertain how to give form to their own personal autonomy, and in particular, how to develop their own future.

As a moral basis to law, autonomy actually refers not so much to the choices we make on a daily basis, perfunctorily and without too much reflection, but rather to the specific capacity of an individual person to make deeply reflective choices. Gerald Dworkin, following Harry Frankfurt, calls this latter conception of autonomy 'a second-order capacity of persons to reflect upon their first-order preferences [that first, more superficial notion of autonomy], desires, wishes, and so forth and the capacity to accept or attempt to change these in light of higher-order preferences and values.' He continues 'By exercising such a capacity,

---

1 J. Greisch, 'L'amour du monde et le principe responsabilité', in M. Vacquin (ed.), *La responsabilité. La condition de notre humanité*, Paris: Editions Autrement, 1994, pp. 72–89, 72.

2 In connection herewith R. Robertson introduces the neologism 'glocalisation' on the one hand to highlight the internal tensions in late-modern but also on the other hand to make clear that it concerns two sides of a single process, in which the one appeals to and strengthens the other. See his 'Time–Space and Homogeneity–Heterogeneity', in M. Featherstone, S. Lash and R. Robertson (eds.), *Global Modernities*, London: Sage Publications, 1995, pp. 25–44.

persons define their nature, give meaning and coherence to their lives, and take responsibility for the kind of person they are.'[3]

It is precisely this notion of responsibility, anchored in a strong sense of autonomy and in a robust capacity for reflection, that can give conceptual texture to a number of legislative instruments proposed in the last decennia and designed to re-establish the equilibrium between individual rights and freedoms, and individual duties, obligations, and responsibilities.[4] I deal with just three of these initiatives, since each of them illuminates a specific dimension of the relation between rights and responsibilities.[5]

2. SETTING THE ETHICAL SCENE

2.1. THREE PROPOSALS FOR CHARTERS OF HUMAN RESPONSIBILITIES

In the wake of the 50th anniversary of the *Universal Declaration of Human Rights*, a number of leading former statesmen and politicians gathered under the auspices of the 'InterAction Council' (created in 1983) and proposed a *Universal Declaration of Human Responsibilities*.[6] In the 'Introductory Comment' to their proposal, the authors explain why the time has come to talk about human *responsibilities*. For them, it is not only a matter of a formal balance between freedom and responsibility, but also the development of a substantial ethical base of shared norms and values – of a 'global ethic' – which can be seen to reconcile grand ideologies, religious beliefs, and political views.[7] Concentrating exclusively on individual rights alone, according to the InterAction Council, risks

---

3 G. Dworkin, *The Theory and Practice of Autonomy*, Cambridge/New York: Cambridge University Press, 1988, p. 20; H. Frankfurt, 'Freedom of the Will and the Concept of the Person' (1971) 68 *Journal of Philosophy* 5–20.

4 On the use, without further differentiation, of the terms 'duty', 'obligation', and 'responsibility', see section 2 below.

5 In addition to these three international proposals, there have been a number of regional and local initiatives as well, which also build on similar ethical perspectives to strengthen the link between rights and responsibilities. Coming to mind, among others, are the examples of Australia in the *Victorian Charter of Human Rights and Responsibilities* (on which, see G. Williams, 'The Victorian *Charter of Human Rights and Responsibilities*: Origins and Scope' (2006) 30 *Melbourne University Law Review* 880–905) and of Canada in the *Montréal Charter of Rights and Responsibilities*, ville.montreal.qc.ca/charterofrights.

6 *A Universal Declaration of Human Responsibilities*, New York, InterAction Council, 1 September 1997. This involved a group of some thirty former presidents and prime ministers, among whom were the former Japanese prime minister Takeo Fukuda, former German Chancellor Helmuth Schmidt, the former Australian prime minister Malcolm Fraser, the former Dutch prime minister Dries van Agt, and the former presidents Jimmy Carter, Valéry Giscard d'Estaing, and Mikhail Gorbachev.

7 The driving force behind the project to develop a 'global ethic' are ex-German Chancellor H. Schmidt, *Auf der Suche nach einer öffentlichen Moral*, Stuttgart: Deutsche Verlags-Anstalt, 1998, and the German theologian H. Küng, *Projekt Weltethos*, Munich: Piper Verlag, 1990 and

contributing more to division and conflict than to co-operation and peace. In this initiative of the InterAction Council, the idea of responsibility not only receives a strong ethical weighting; its ethical dimension is also articulated in terms of social and political ethics.

Next, late in 1999 and under the auspices of UNESCO, came the Valencia *Declaration of Human Rights and Responsibilities*, an initiative of a group of 75 independent experts under the chairmanship of Richard Goldstone, a Justice of the Constitutional Court of South Africa and former Prosecutor of the UN International Criminal Tribunals for the former Yugoslavia and for Rwanda. Much attention is given in the Valencia *Declaration* to the newer problems which have arisen in our late-modern societies because of the incredible pace of scientific and technological advances, all of which have not only afforded people more options, but have also made them more vulnerable. In addition to progress in emancipation, there has also been an expansion of – or at least an increasing threat in the direction of – the instrumentalisation of human beings. Respect for human rights and for everyone's dignity (including that of the weakest members of society) brings with it, in particular, a heightened sense of responsibility for those contextual preconditions, the fulfilment of which are required to give effect to, and to fine-tune, that very respect for human rights.[8] Here, too, a strong ethical awareness underlies the argument for a more robust connection between rights and responsibilities.

That ethical awareness pertains not only to the macro-perspective of the 'global ethic', but also to the micro-perspective of concrete relationships among individuals. 'Responsibility' here acquires a strongly relational meaning. Science and technology mean power. But where power is at play, according to the French philosopher Paul Ricoeur, so too is vulnerability. And where vulnerability rules, so responsibility must have its due. Ricoeur even proposes that the essence of responsibility resides in human fragility. In effect, human vulnerability is charged to our care and requires concrete efforts and attention, and not merely an abstract and universal ethics.[9]

Once again with the support of the UN, a number of independent experts within the Swiss-based International Council on Human Rights Policy proposed tying rights (social and economic, in particular) to specific obligations on the part of companies.[10] Here, too, the ambition is strongly macro-ethically inspired. It is a matter of achieving more distributive justice in a world marked by poverty, exploitation, and organised individualism. The stark logic of free-market thinking

H. Küng (ed.), *Ja zum Weltethos. Perspektiven für die Suche nach Orientierung*, Munich: Piper Verlag, 1995.

8 See especially the introduction of R. Goldstone, 'Présentation', in *Déclaration des devoirs et des responsabilités de l'homme*, Valencia: Fundación Valencia Tercer Milenio, 1999, pp. 19–28.

9 P. Ricoeur, *L'unique et le singulier*, Brussels/Liège: Éditions Alice, 1999, p. 49.

10 International Council on Human Rights Policy, *Beyond Voluntarism. Human Rights and the Developing International Legal Obligations of Companies*, Versoix/Geneva, 2002. *Duties sans Frontières. Human Rights and Global Social Justice*, Versoix/Geneva, 2003.

supplies a too meagre conception of social life, and of a world based thereon, in which rights risk being turned away from their normative core and thereby instrumentalised with a view to promoting the individual interests of the strongest market player. Dramatic examples exist, such as the Bhopal affair in Central India in 1984, where, within a period of 16 years *subsequent to* the catastrophe at Union Carbide in Bhopal, more than 16,000 people died as a consequence of the toxic gasses which escaped during that disaster. The international legal order appeared to offer no satisfactory instruments to deal with such risks and disasters. The initiative of the International Council on Human Rights does attempt to answer this normative and legal deficit, by coupling responsibilities to rights. With its proposal, the Council opens an important road that deserves further development. 'In suggesting that human rights arguments can strengthen more familiar appeals to ethics and legitimate self-interest', writes Mary Robinson in her Foreword to its 2003 report, 'it offers additional tools that citizens and officials can use – in richer countries certainly, but in poorer societies too – to generate the dynamic and effective action that will be required if we are to solve the numerous injustices and inequities that afflict our society, and pass on a more fitting rule to future generations.'[11] The ethical character of the link between rights and responsibilities here acquires a clear, future-oriented dimension, one which expressly recognises coming generations as those for whom the responsibilities of today's actors ought to be framed.

To make that possible, ongoing and serious consideration must be given to the experience of disasters, the reality of the socio-economic context in which they became a very real possibility, and the circumstances (howsoever unlikely) in which they occurred. A similar type of learning from past example applies to what the philosopher Hans Jonas called the 'heuristics of fear' ('*Die Heuristik der Furcht*'), by which he means the capacity of problem-detecting reasoning, of not only considering *the probable* but much more broadly *the possible* as well. Thus understood, the 'heuristics of fear' form a necessary instrument for developing an ethics of the future ('*eine Zukunftsethik*') and for mobilising the strongly contextualised and textured sense of obligation it requires.[12]

2.2. CALIBRATING THE BALANCE: THE ETHICAL DIMENSION

These introductory considerations can already serve as the grounds for a number of preliminary and general observations which together can form a programme for further analysis.

---

11 International Council on Human Rights Policy, *Duties sans Frontières. Human Rights and Global Social Justice*, Versoix/Geneva, 2003, IV.

12 H. Jonas, *Das Prinzip Verantwortung. Versuch einer Ethik für die technologische Zivilisation*, (Frankfurt am Main: Suhrkamp, 1984) 61–69.

In the first place there is the proposition that measures which strengthen the bond between rights and obligations rely explicitly on robust ethical intuitions and that these intuitions are strongly determined by the context of our late-modern societies and the perils and uncertainties attendant thereto.

In the second place, it can be established that the ethical dimension of responsibility discussed here, necessarily points to the autonomy of an individual and that such autonomy is always attached to, indeed even finds its very core in, a capacity to think meaningfully in a future- and project-oriented way and to act within the horizon of a conception of the 'general good' (the 'higher-order preferences and values' to which Gerald Dworkin refers).

In the third place, the notions of responsibility and autonomy are articulated as much on the micro- as on the macro-level of society. That gives to both notions a strongly relational character, and a community and political orientation.

In the fourth place, and lastly, the practice of responsibilities and autonomy demand a vigorous and hardy actualisation. They can not come to maturity when both notions remain blanketed under the 'splendid isolation' of a merely abstract universal ethics. Universality of values can only be attained when we choose again and again for them and actively engage them in actual relationships. The political philosopher Michael Walzer uses the term 'reiterative universality', in contrast to 'absolute universality', to illustrate this point.[13] Universality is no quiet, easy tool that comes to us uncomplicated and problem-free from a universal abstract ethics. Instead it demands constant, enduring maintenance, innovative and flexible framing of contexts, and considered choices. To put it another way, when the universality of norms and values is detached from actual, concrete interaction, then universality loses its power of normative expression and its credibility. Seen thus, the protection of universal values – in the sense of *reiterative universality* – is one of the most important mandates behind the unity of *human rights and human responsibilities.*

2.3. RESPONSIBILITY, AUTONOMY, AND THE CAPACITY FOR REFLECTION

Even etymologically, the word 'responsibility' has a strongly relational and dialogic connotation. It refers to the capacity to respond to the way in which we are addressed by a fellow human being, or by a particular situation. 'Responsibility' bears here the meaning of 'answerability'. Our answers also have to fit the actual call confronting us for a response. We are forced to venture out from the safe and noncommittal world of abstract and general values and take a stand in the

[13] M. Walzer, 'Nation and Universe', in his *Thinking Politically. Essays in Political Theory* (selected, edited, and with an Introduction by D. Miller), New Haven/London: Yale University Press, 2007, pp. 183–218.

concrete life-world which we share with others. This life-world is not merely a static '*Umwelt*' (to draw upon the German anthropologist Helmuth Plessner), our 'general surroundings', but also a dynamic '*Mitwelt*', our 'shared environment', at the same time.[14] This '*Mitwelt*' exhorts us over and over again to make use of one of our typically human abilities: the capacity for reflection and of considered choice. Plessner has, without equal, analysed this human mode of existence in a philosophical context. The core piece of that analysis is the ability of human beings to step back from a focus on their own, daily affairs and consider reflexively how their actions bear upon themselves. Plessner terms this, in a most fitting turn of phrase, '*exzentrische Positionalität*' ('excentric positionality').

This excentric positionality of individuals means that they do not merely take a stand in the world, but that they are also conscious of that position and are in a position to reflect on it. In so doing, the individual finds himself soon enough in a tension between an internal world and an external world. The shared environment, the *Mitwelt*, which man shares with others finds its dynamic in this tension. For the *Mitwelt*, it is not so much a matter of an entire ready-made set of meanings, values, norms, and expectations in which a person can live as if it were some completely furnished house which he would never have to leave. The identity of a person is actually not separable from its concrete, indeed its physical, situation in the here and now of history, although at the same time identity is not a simple correspondence with the set of factual moments of a life.[15]

The human capacity for reflection functions as the nexus between the *necessity of having to choose* and the *power of reflecting upon these choices*. Above, we pointed out that autonomy and responsibility directly concern the manner in which a person can question his *first-order preferences* in light of *second-order preferences*. The first are often completely particular and individual in nature, while the second carry a predilection for more reiterative social – and so more universal – values. These latter ones are also just that tension which the Inter-Action Council underlined when it warned against an all too individualistic, particularistic use of (human) rights. Transposed to the terminology of Gerald Dworkin, this would in effect mean that *first order preferences* would overwhelm *second order preferences* such that rights would end up as instruments for the perfecting of absolute and decontextualised individual interests. Were this to come to pass, cohesion in a community would disappear and the fabric of

---

14 H. Plessner, *Die Stufen des Organischen und der Mensch. Einleitung in die philosophische Anthropologie* (1928), Berlin/New York: Walter de Gruyter, 1975, pp. 288–321.

15 '*In diesem Sich-selber-präsent-Sein liegt der Bruch, die "Stelle" möglichen Sich-von-sich-Unterscheidens, die dem Menschen im Zwang zur Wahl und als Macht des Könnens seine besondere Weise des Daseins, die wir die exzentrische genannt haben, anweist*': H. Plessner, 'Zur Anthropologie des Schauspielers' (1948), in his *Zwischen Philosophie und Gesellschaft. Ausgewählte Abhandlungen und Vorträge*, Bern: Francke Verlag, 1953, pp. 180–192. For the relevance of Plessner's anthropology to legal philosophy, see R. Foqué, 'Het recht van de verscheidenheid', in C. De Vries and K. Schuyt (eds.), *De open samenleving en haar vrienden. In discussie met Jan Glastra van Loon*, Amsterdam/Meppel: Boom, 1995, pp. 145–169.

each society would dramatically unravel. 'Those working on this purpose (the *Universal Declaration of Human Responsibilities*) believe,' according to the former Australian prime minister Malcolm Fraser, one of the active members of the Inter-Action Council, 'that a world in which everyone demands rights but do not accept responsibilities, will be an unequal and even dangerous and discordant world.'[16]

Responsibility can be viewed as the giving of an answer in situations which call upon our autonomous, and thus considered, choosing and acting. Our choosing and acting loses its true autonomous nature when it is chained to our immediate wants and desires. By contrast, it gains autonomy when it manages to compose itself in an excentric manner with regard to our direct wants and desires.

In her important study, *A Political Theory of Rights*, Attracta Ingram defines 'the idea of autonomous action as the pursuit of reflectively endorsed preferences.'[17] The indissoluble connection between responsibility, autonomy, and reflection points to the very same principles which form the ethical weighting to, and the range of meaning of, human rights. In both discourses, it is more a matter of a capacity to act in a shared project-oriented social framework.[18] This certainly explains why the proposals undertaken to develop a charter of responsibilities also drew upon the arguments that the application of human rights themselves would also thereby be improved and enriched. But it also explains why these same proposals were strongly criticised as being superfluous and as doing insufficient justice to the compass of those rights by creating a tension with responsibilities.[19]

An autonomy supported by a reflective capacity and an ability to commit to, and realise, plans, represents the basis for *responsibility as answerability*. Ingram and Raz speak of '*significant autonomy*'. People who are brought to act with responsibility by this form of autonomy 'adopt personal projects, develop relationships, and accept commitment to causes, through which their personal integrity and sense of dignity and self-respect are made concrete.'[20] Viewed in this fashion, a compatibility is created in the practice of taking up responsibility, one which the German philosopher Jürgen Habermas defined as *private* and *public*

16 M. Fraser, *A Declaration on Human Responsibilities*, www.interactioncouncil.org/speeches/pfraser981.html.

17 A. Ingram, *A Political Theory of Rights*, Oxford: Clarendon Press, 1994, p. 100.

18 On this there exists in current-day political and legal philosophy a broad consensus. See e.g. J. Rawls, *A Theory of Justice*, Cambridge, Mass.: Harvard University Press, 1971; R. Nozick, *Anarchy, State and Utopia*, Oxford: Basil Blackwell, 1974; A. Ingram, *A Political Theory of Rights*, Oxford: Clarendon Press, 1994; G. Haarscher, *Philosophie des Droits de l'Homme*, Brussels: Éditions de l'Université Libre de Bruxelles, 1993; P. Gérard, *L'Esprit des Droits. Philosophie des droits de l'homme*, Brussels: Publications des Facultés Universitaires Saint-Louis, 2007.

19 See e.g. K. Raes, 'Universele plichten van de mens? De relaties tussen mensenrechten en morele verantwoordelijkheden', in his *Controversiële rechtsfiguren. Rechtsfilosofische excursies over de relaties tussen ethiek en recht*, Ghent: Academia Press, 2001, pp. 347–381.

20 J. Raz, *The Morality of Freedom*, Oxford/New York: Clarendon Press, 1986, p. 154; A. Ingram, *A Political Theory of Rights*, Oxford: Clarendon Press, 1994, pp. 100–101.

autonomy, respectively. Individual self-determination and an active commitment to the public business of the common good thus come to be aligned.[21]

The proposals to create charters of human responsibilities are certainly inspired by the ethical intuitions that form the kernel not only of significant autonomy but also of the compatibility of private and public autonomy, as suggested by Habermas.

2.4. RESPONSIBILITY AND THE HEURISTICS OF FEAR

According to Hans Jonas, we are able to come to some articulation of both forms of autonomy only out of a 'heuristics of fear', namely, the fear that, more and more, we are living in a world which no longer allows sufficient space for the reflection necessary to fund autonomy and responsibility. Such reflection needs space and, above all, time. That has, at its very least, a double aspect.

In the first place, our late-modern society is typified more and more by what can be called the 'tyranny of urgency', as a consequence of the rapid advances in technology.[22] The human mode of existence is marked by a fundamental rift in its relation to time, in its shrinking capacity for planning, and the development of a view shaped by the instantaneousness of 'now', by a culture of immediacy. Every message, every enquiry demands an immediate, and thus (so it is feared) unconsidered reaction. Reflection requires time to develop. Those who are not quick off the mark, often get the feeling that they are losing touch with those in the world who are. The tyranny of urgency hardly contributes to a channelling and moderating of the uncertainty and unease present in our late-modern societies. Quite the contrary. It represents the motive force behind the two, putting them in place and fostering them. An instant reaction is not 'responsibility as answerability'. Instead, the satisfaction of momentary urges takes the place of 'a second-order capacity of persons to reflect upon their first-order preferences, desires, wishes, and so forth and the capacity to accept or attempt to change these in light of higher-order preferences and values.'[23]

It can be said that there is a dissolving of historical consciousness. The capacity of accumulating knowledge through experience risks being side-lined by the immediacy of the moment, with the past, as that treasury of experience and important action contexts, losing its relevance. But even each vision of the future risks imploding into the mere present.[24] In such circumstances, both

21 J. Habermas, *Between Facts and Norms. Contributions to a Discourse Theory of Law and Democracy*, Cambridge, Mass.: The MIT Press, 1998, pp. 84–104.
22 Z. Laïdi, *La tirannie de l'urgence*, Montreal: Éditions Fides, 1999.
23 G. Dworkin, *The Theory and Practice of Autonomy*, Cambridge/New York: Cambridge University Press, 1988.
24 B. Stiegler, *La technique et le temps*, Paris: Galilée, 1996.

reflection and a significant autonomy and responsibility dependent upon the former become problematic.

There is also a second aspect which the tyranny of the immediate seems to reaffirm: the overarching universalisation of a market mentality, which separates itself from the political, ethical, and social dimensions of a society.[25] Even the market itself demands in fact a social dynamic characterised by immediacy – or at least by a narrowing of timeframes. This leads to other, more meagre forms of social recognition and mutual respect. These latter dimensions of a society then fall prey to a transformation into formalised structures of result-oriented egoism.[26]

This potential retreat of the reflective ability, and thus of a culture of autonomous reason and action having an eye to the future, has activated a 'heuristics of fear' which, in turn, paradoxically, has grounded an increasing call to responsibility. By way of explanation in brief, Hans Jonas did not develop his concept of the 'heuristics of fear' as a sort of augury of doom that has humanity paralysed rather than invigorated. Fear in effect tends to blind people to values in a society and to the appeal of a 'long-range ethics'. That sort of fear, i.e. the fear which can be turned to profit in the electoral markets as well as in the capital markets,[27] was not what Jonas had in mind. For him, it was more about a warning against the abstract and over-blown utopias which the Enlightenment's belief in progress naively projected into the present.[28] In effect, it concerned the illusions of an '*avenir radieux*',[29] of glittering prospects, of utopias which were blind to the problems and imperfections of the present.

In his 'heuristics of fear', there is a critique of that sort of Enlightenment thinking. In contrast to such 'fear', Jonas sets the ability to anticipate calamity, to bring to bear a well-developed sense of problem detection, one which could make people aware not only of what was actually likely to happen, but also of the range of the possible, even if this were unlikely to occur. All of this is necessary, according to Jonas, in order to give humanity a future and to engage our responsibility to future generations.

---

25 On which see R. Foqué, 'De actualiteit van Montesquieu's staatkundige erfgoed', in H.D. Tjeenk Willink et al., *Stoelendansen met de macht*, The Hague: Tweede Kamer der Staten-Generaal, 2006, pp. 9–29.

26 S.A. Marglin, *The Dismal Science. How Thinking Like an Economist Undermines Community*, Cambridge, Mass./London: Harvard University Press, 2008. For background within the history of ideas, see J.Z. Muller, *The Mind and the Market. Capitalism in Modern European Thought*, New York: Alfred A. Knopf, 2002.

27 For a compelling analysis of manipulation through fear, see N. Klein, *The Shock Doctrine. The Rise of Disaster Capitalism*, Ottawa/Toronto/New York: Alfred Knopf, 2007.

28 Hans Jonas (see note 12) aims his points of criticism principally at the neo-marxist idealism of E. Bloch, *Das Prinzip Hoffnung*, 3 vols., Frankfurt am Main: Suhrkamp, 1959.

29 The expression is borrowed from A. Zinoviev, *L'avenir radieux*, Lausanne: L'Age d'Homme, 1978, an extremely cynical novel in which the author dismantles in merciless fashion the illusions of a communist ideal state.

2.5. RESPONSIBILITY-IN-CONTEXT

Political and ethical reason needs to be anchored in a critical reflection on memory[30] and on culturally embodied traditions, instead of an uncritical implementing of abstract utopias. That memory comprises in effect the ingredients which can give meaning to our contemporary life-world.[31]

We saw above how the core of responsibility is located in the recognition of an existential fragility. Human existence is marked in its concrete historical form, by what the Dutch author Geert Mak so splendidly described as 'being doomed to vulnerability'.[32] That vulnerability is entrusted to a mutual care and concern in us, so argues Ricoeur.[33] The ethics of responsibility here finds its concrete task: *responsibility as necessary carefulness.*[34]

At issue here is a responsibility-in-context, and plainly not a responsibility as a component of a decontextualised, abstract ethics. The coupling of fundamental rights with fundamental responsibilities can generate a fund of purpose and meaning when it is set in a perspective of context-fed ethical consciousness. The latter has received increasing attention in the past decades under the feminist critique of the abstract ethics of classic Enlightenment reason. Flowing from this critique, by consequence, has been a heightened attention to what may be called an 'ethics of care' view.[35]

In the neo-Kantian tradition,[36] an individual's autonomy in large measure becomes possible through an individual's distancing himself from each concrete, actual situation by use of his rational capacity. Thus can a formal equality be realised because, for example, we can appear to one another as mutually, and fully equal, holders of rights and duties. That also means that we can only stand in the shoes of the other insofar as the other can be abstracted from his own personal history, circumstances, and identity. My own life-story or that of the other loses thereby its ethical relevance. Responsibility is then explained more in terms of an

30 A. Margalit, *The Ethics of Memory*, Cambridge, Mass./London: Harvard University Press, 2002. As a sharp warning against the development of, as it were, a cult of memories: Tzv. Todorov, *Les abus de la mémoire*, Paris: Arléa, 1995.

31 On this see J. Shklar, 'The Liberalism of Fear', in her *Political Thought and Political Thinkers* (edited by S. Hoffmann), Chicago/London: The University of Chicago Press, 1998, pp. 3–20; M. Walzer, 'On Negative Politics', in B. Yack, *Liberalism Without Illusions. Essays on Liberal Theory and the Political Vision of Judith Shklar*, Chicago/London: The University of Chicago Press, 1996, pp. 17–24.

32 '*Gedoemd zijn tot kwetsbaarheid*': G. Mak, *Gedoemd tot kwetsbaarheid*, Amsterdam/Antwerp: Atlas, 2005.

33 P. Ricoeur, *L'unique et le singulier*, Brussels/Liège: Éditions Alice, 1999.

34 The expression comes from Michael Walzer, in an interview on occasion of being awarded the 2008 *International Spinoza Prize*. See H. Verrijn Stuart, R. Foqué and W. Witteveen, 'De grenzen van recht en politiek. Een gesprek met Michael Walzer', in M. Walzer, *Grenzeloze rechtvaardigheid*, Amsterdam: Boom, 2008.

35 A. Van Heijst, *Menslievende zorg. Een ethische kijk op professionaliteit*, Kampen: Uitgeverij Klement, 2005.

36 On the Kantian ethics based on a morality of duty, see further section 3.2 in this chapter.

abstract autonomy and therefore no longer has any direct access to the existential fragility of a concrete Other.

A clear application of such a conception of ethical consciousness is to be found in the theory of moral development of Lawrence Kohlberg.[37] According to Kohlberg, ethical consciousness comes into being only after the last 'postconventional stage' of moral development, when the individual, on becoming an adult, is able to abstract from all possible moral convention and from concrete situations which are characterised by mutual, personal relationships among people. From the feminist vision of the growth of ethical consciousness has come sharp criticism against this uncompromising type of abstract ethics. In particular, the trail-blazing work of Carol Gilligan has had a decisive influence.[38] The relevance of her critique of the abstract ethics of Kohlberg and others extends well beyond the boundaries of a strictly feminist ethics, and creates at the same time an opening into an ethics of care and into the conception of responsibility-in-context as developed therein. The world of female experience reveals just how much an ethical consciousness is fed by personal relations and by the contact which issues from such personal relations as mutual care and concern. Gilligan and others are also of the opinion that an abstract ethics relegates the world of female experience to the private sphere and isolates it from the publicly shared discourse of a society. That which applies to the world of female experience in Gilligan's work also applies – we might say – to late-modern humankind in general.

A decontextualised view of responsibility ignores the fact that responsibility often refers to a collection of feelings which are called upon precisely in those concrete dealings with others. The English philosopher, Peter Strawson, called these feelings aptly 'reactive attitudes'. These are reactions to circumstances and events, to the appeals and claims made by others, such as gratitude, bitterness, revenge, forgiveness, friendship, love, sympathy, disappointment, solidarity, and such like. 'In the absence of *any* forms of these attitudes, it is doubtful,' says Strawson, 'whether we should have anything that *we* could find intelligible as a system of human relationships, as human society.'[39] This approach recalls the same insights and the same concerns expressed by the authors of the aforementioned proposals for a Charter of Human Responsibilities.[40] The conception of responsibility at issue in these proposals is one of responsibility-in-context.

---

37 L. Kohlberg, 'From *Is* to *Ought*: How to Commit the Naturalistic Fallacy and Get Away with It in the Study of Moral Development', in his *The Philosophy of Moral Development. Moral Stages and the Idea of Justice*, San Francisco/Cambridge/New York: Harper & Row, 1981, pp. 101–189.

38 C. Gilligan, *In a Different Voice. Psychological Theory and Women's Development*, Cambridge, Mass./London: Harvard University Press, 1982.

39 P. Strawson, *Freedom and Resentment and Other Essays,* London: Methuen, 1974, pp. 1–26.

40 See e.g. M. Fraser, *A Declaration on Human Responsibilities*, www.interactioncouncil.org/speeches/pfraser981.html.

2.6. ANOTHER COSMOPOLITANISM

Classic modern cosmopolitanism bears a Kantian signature. It builds upon an abstract ethics in international relations. The cosmopolitan perspective comes into focus through the ability of its agents to abstract from their respective culturally and historically defined identities. Rights and responsibilities here draw their meaning from their decontextualised, abstract and absolute universality.

A conception of responsibility-in-context draws its meaning, however, as we have suggested above, from its embodiment in concrete situations, and from a viewpoint of 'reiterative universalism' (Walzer's term).[41] This type of perspective can open the way to what Seyla Benhabib in her 2004 Tanner Lectures at Berkeley called 'another cosmopolitanism'.[42] In the context of international relations as well, its actors borrow their identity from their cultural and social background. This will play into determining the ethical content of their dealings with one another. Reciprocal responsibilities are in effect given by the tenuousness of everyone's culturally anchored customs and historical memory and experience. 'Political actors,' says Benhabib, 'need bounded communities – whether they be cities, regions, states or transnational institutions – within which they can establish mechanisms of representation, accountability, participation and deliberation. For the majority of human beings, these institutions are not only sites, in the sense of *spaces* (*des lieux*), but also *places*, that is, sites of attachment and sites of memory (*lieux de mémoires*).'[43] Institutions are not empty formal structures. Quite the contrary, they are bearers of worlds of historical experiences and cultural value orientations.[44]

Cosmopolitan law – in human rights terms, but also in terms of responsibilities – should be considered as a *sui generis* legal order. The practice of international relations and the actual contexts in which these relations develop, offer us a unique laboratory in which we can follow the growth of an international, cosmopolitan legal order step by step. Benhabib, in her Tanner Lectures, offers a theoretical framework to comprehend that growth process in itself. It is not about a vertical, top-down structured process from abstract universality to concrete applicability, but rather a bottom-up process where claims to universality continuously seek legitimation. Hence, this legal order remains at once *sui generis*, and yet also dependent on national, regional, and even local processes of political will formation. General legal principles in which rights and responsibilities can also be grounded in a cosmopolitan perspective, can only be

---

[41] Ibid.

[42] S. Benhabib, *Another Cosmopolitanism. The Berkeley Tanner Lectures*, Oxford/New York: Oxford University Press, 2005.

[43] Ibid., p. 169.

[44] A.C. Zijderveld, *Institutionalisering. Een studie over het methodologisch dilemma der sociale wetenschappen*, Meppel: Boom, 1974, and his *De samenleving als schouwspel*, 's Gravenhage: Vuga Uitgeverij, 1987, pp. 71–132.

articulated in a manner which Benhabib calls 'jurisgenerative politics', which she contrasts with both legal positivism and natural law. 'Jurisgenerative politics is a model that permits us to think of creative interventions that mediate between universal norms and the will of democratic majorities. On the one hand, the 'rights claims' that frame democratic politics, must be viewed as transcending the specific enactments of democratic majorities under specific circumstances; on the other hand, such democratic majorities *reiterate* these principles and incorporate them into democratic will-formation processes through argument, contestation, revision and rejection.'[45]

The proposals for a *Charter of Human Responsibilities* addressed above can be seen as contributing to the development of 'another cosmopolitanism', to the degree they can be interpreted from the perspective of ethical intuitions which rest upon 'significant autonomy' and a strongly developed capacity for reflection on the concrete circumstances of the human condition. Universality for such a cosmopolitanism is not a calm, passive thing, but represents a form of 'reiterative universalism' that must continuously draw for its effect upon an active 'responsibility as answerability'.

3. SETTING THE CONCEPTUAL SCENE

3.1. RESPONSIBILITY AS A HIDDEN ASPECT OF HUMAN RIGHTS

Despite the strong ethical intuitions underpinning the various proposals for creating a *Charter of Human Responsibilities*, and notwithstanding a repeated affirmation of a strong bond between rights and responsibilities, the issue of responsibility still receives meagre consideration in human rights discourse. Recognition of this fact formed the basis for a stimulating 2004 conference in Brussels. The title of the conference and of its proceedings, published a year later, left no room for misunderstanding: *La responsabilité, face cachée des droits de l'homme.*[46]

The most important reason why responsibility is still to be considered as the hidden aspect of human rights lies in the fact that the idea of responsibility lacks conceptual clarity and precision. How might this conceptual deficit be overcome?

As a first proposition, the term 'responsibility' sits amidst two others, namely, 'duty' and 'obligation'. One bears the responsibility to act, or has the duty or obligation to act or refrain from acting in a certain way. What is the difference

45 S. Benhabib, *Another Cosmopolitanism. The Berkeley Tanner Lectures*, Oxford/New York: Oxford University Press, 2005, p. 49.

46 'Responsibility: The Hidden Face of Human Rights': H. Dumont, F. Ost and S. Van Drooghenbroeck (eds.), *La responsabilité, face cachée des droits de l'homme*, Brussels: Bruylant, 2005.

here in meaning among responsibility, duty, and obligation? Often the three are used interchangeably, as if they are synonyms. Hence, for example, Douglas Hodgson proposes, without further critical comment, that, 'The term "duty" will be used interchangeably with the terms "obligation" and "responsibility" since their meanings are largely synonymous.'[47] For that matter, the same is the case for the commentary and explanatory notes found in the *InterAction Council* and the *Valencia Declaration*, as wells as in the draft from the *International Council on Human Rights Policy*. A similar conclusion can be drawn from the more regional initiatives in Canada and Australia. The comments of the former German Chancellor, Helmuth Schmidt, on the German translation of the *Universal Declaration of Human Responsibilities* of the *InterAction Council*, are illustrative. There he noted that he ultimately came to prefer the word '*Pflichten*' ('duties'); while the German words '*Verantwortungen*' or '*Verantwortlichkeiten*' ('responsibilities') were likely closer to the original text, he, however, considered the word '*Pflicht*' to be clearer. And, in the end, according to Schmidt, this shows, all the more, how strongly responsibilities and duties seem truly to coincide.[48]

This equation of duties, obligations, and responsibilities creates a conceptual confusion because they each have different connotations.[49] 'Obligation' is a term with a more legal weight. It belongs rather to the idiom of a 'rule-book model'[50] of society that is effected via techniques of compulsion and coercion in law. Obligations have the logical structure of rules: they are binary in character. They are applicable only in an 'all-or-nothing fashion'.[51]

'Duty' is a term with a more moral connotation. This is to say that it refers to a rather legalistic and strongly abstract conception of morality, as described aptly by Judith Shklar. 'It is the ethical attitude that holds moral conduct to be a matter of rule following, and moral relationships to consist of duties and rights determined by rules.'[52] This means that duties are the moral equivalent of legal obligations. Both have the same logical structure of binary application, in the 'all-or-nothing fashion'.[53]

---

47 D. Hodgson, *Individual Duty within a Human Rights Discourse*, Aldershot/Burlington: Ashgate Publishing Company, 2003, p. 2.

48 H. Schmidt, *Auf der Suche nach einer öffentlichen Moral*, Stuttgart: Deutsche Verlags-Anstalt, 1998, p. 259.

49 In the same sense, see the conclusions of F. Tulkens, 'Pour une approche dialectique des droits et des responsabilités. Conclusions', in H. Dumont, F. Ost and S. Van Drooghenbroeck (eds.), *La responsabilité, face cachée des droits de l'homme*, Brussels: Bruylant, 2005, pp. 523–536. Even in the strongly analytic work of W. Hohfeld, *Fundamental Legal Conceptions* (edited by W. Lock), New Haven: Yale University Press, 1924, the same confusion seems present.

50 R. Dworkin, *Law's Empire*, Cambridge, Mass./London: Harvard University Press, 1986, p. 210.

51 R. Dworkin, *Taking Rights Seriously*, Cambridge, Mass./London: Harvard University Press, 1977, p. 24.

52 J. Shklar, *Legalism. Law, Morals and Political Trials*, Cambridge, Mass./London: Harvard University Press, 1964, p. 1.

53 A.J. Simmons, *Moral Principles and Political Obligations*, Princeton/New Jersey: Princeton University Press, 1979, pp. 7–28.

'Responsibility' is a more ethically laden term, as discussed at length above. It has an entirely different logical structure, one which is not binary in nature, but instead represents the object of personal choices and considerations. Responsibility is not a matter of regularity of rule application, but of the capacity for finding adequate dialogical answers to constantly changing worlds of experience and to more or less historically institutionalised patterns of behaviour.

3.2. KANT'S ABSTRACT MORAL DUTY

One of the most foundational – and certainly one of the most influential – forms of a morality of duty is found in the ethical theory of Immanuel Kant. He worked out that idea in his *Critique of Practical Reason* (1788) and his *Groundwork for the Metaphysics of Morals* (1785), where he explained the three formulations of his renowned categorical imperative.[54] With the categorical imperative, he provided the modern discourse of human rights with an absolute and universalistic base.

The first formulation of the categorical imperative reads as follows: 'Act only on that maxim through which you can at the same time will that it should become a universal law.'[55] Kant places the duty on people to act autonomously and to respect the right and the obligation of everyone to do the same. Two observations are of importance here.

In the first place, there is Kant's insight that moral behaviour is more a question of volition than of desire. 'An action from duty has its moral worth *not in the purpose* to be attained by it but in the maxim in accordance with which it is decided upon, and therefore does not depend upon the realization of the object of the action but merely upon the *principle of volition* in accordance with which the action is done without regard for any object of the faculty of desire.'[56]

A second observation concerns the legalistic character of his morality of duty: 'Duty is the necessity of an action from respect for law.'[57]

Let us now examine the second formulation of the categorical imperative. It reads as follows: 'So act that you use humanity, whether in your own person or in the person of any other, always at the same time as an end, never merely as a means.'[58] This second version refers to the absolute prohibition of an uncompromising instrumentalisation of oneself or of another. Kant considers this as an absolute and *a priori* duty for every human being. 'This principle of humanity, and in general of every rational nature, *as an end in itself* (which is the

[54] Both works are reproduced in I. Kant, *Practical Philosophy* (translated and edited by M.J. Gregor), in *The Cambridge Edition of the Works of Immanuel Kant* (general editors: P. Guyer and A.W. Wood), Cambridge/New York: Cambridge University Press, 1996, pp. 133–271 and 37–108 respectively.

[55] I. Kant, Groundwork, ibid., p. 73.

[56] Ibid., p. 55.

[57] Ibid.

[58] Ibid., p. 80.

supreme limiting condition of the freedom of action of every human being) is not borrowed from experience,' says Kant. And subsequently he sets this proposition in greater relief when he writes, 'Humanity is represented ... not as an object that we of ourselves actually make our end, but as an objective end that, whatever ends we may have, ought as law to constitute the supreme limiting condition for all subjective ends, so that the principle must arise from pure reason.'[59]

In the third formulation of the categorical imperative, the meaning of the autonomy of the person is again defined in no uncertain terms, as 'the will of every rational being as a will giving universal law.'[60]

It is clear that Kant has provided with the three interconnected formulations of the categorical imperative a robust philosophical basis for human rights. Rights, for Kant, are grounded in moral duties having a universal tenor.

There is also a rather less persuasive perspective connected to the Kantian universal morality of duties. The categorical imperative for Kant has a universal character, one which is an expression of pure reason, and not borrowed from experience. Therein lies precisely its *a priori* character. A moral duty, such as that at issue in the categorical imperative, is conceived as *unconditional*, while a hypothetical imperative is *conditional* – conditioned namely by concrete purposes to and objectives for action which I can choose freely. By way of example, my task of studying human rights can be conditioned, for instance, by my desire to work for an NGO or international organisation at a later date. This is a completely different issue than respect for human dignity. That may never be a matter of free, contextualised choice, according to Kant, but is instead a moral duty with an unconditional *a priori* character. Hence it can never be conditioned by concrete experiences, neither mine nor those of others. Moreover it is completely independent of cultural and historical contingencies.

The moral concept of 'duty' is defined by contrast to the emotional or strategic impulses which a person may have. Duty is founded in the principle of volition, often coming up against the seductive temptations of my own desires. An autonomous person, in the context of this morality of duty, is an agent who wills and acts out of a well-developed sense of duty.

3.3. CRITICISING THE KANTIAN MORALITY OF DUTY: RETHINKING THE ETHICAL PERSPECTIVE

One of the most damning critiques of the abstract and *a priori* character of the Kantian morality of duty is provided by Hannah Arendt in the famous last chapter of Part Two to her *Origins of Totalitarianism*. She accuses that conception of morality of lacking any concrete institutional and cultural texturing. That is all

59 Ibid., p. 81.
60 Ibid.

the more the case, says Arendt, when the morality of human rights is concerned, as well as an effective respect for human dignity in concrete historical contexts.

'The survivors of the extermination camps,' writes Arendt, 'the inmates of concentration and internment camps, and even the comparatively happy stateless people could see that the abstract nakedness of being nothing but human was their greatest danger ... It seems that a man who is nothing but a man has lost the very qualities which make it possible for other people to treat him as a fellow-man.' Arendt's conclusion is clear and uncompromising: 'The very phrase "human rights" became for all concerned – victims, persecutors, and onlookers alike – the evidence of hopeless idealism and fumbling feeble-minded hypocrisy.'[61]

Arendt's criticism of the forms of hopeless idealism and hypocrisy is an equally sharp criticism of the Kantian morality of duty, one which deserves serious consideration. That morality of duty indeed renders responsibility a hidden facet of human rights, dominated as it is by an abstract and universal morality. Thus, human rights remain thereby isolated in a theoretical concept insulated from every actual human form of existence.

Hegel often criticised Kant's very abstract, formalistic, and legalistic morality of duty, because Kant's hasty exclusive concern for purity of will ultimately could be reduced to 'a preaching of duty for duty's sake'. 'Hegel's response to the abstract character of Kantian morality is to stress that moral duty has a history and that to conceive it as something apart from social and political circumstances is to misconceive it. Such anti-historical theories are false because they simply fail to grasp the nature of human diversity in all of its details.'[62]

Alisdair MacIntyre, in his *Short History of Ethics*, formulates the anti-Kantian position as follows. 'Moral concepts are embodied in and are partially constitutive of forms of social life.'[63] Hegel introduced here the term '*Sittlichkeit*' ('ethical life') in contrast to the term '*Moralität*' ('morality'). The Hegelian idea of *Sittlichkeit*, of ethics, refers to more or less institutionalised forms of value-oriented behavioural practices, as well as the means by which the ideal of a just society is embodied in a concrete social 'habitus', in the manners and customs of the people. A similar ethics forms the seedbed for our actions and our responsibilities which serve now and in the future to give form to the common good.

The concept of 'the ethical' pertains to the dynamic character of a historically positioned way of life, of culturally embodied practices dealing with suffering, humiliation, and pain; but also with a view of happiness and of the good society in which each individual person can develop self-respect in a context of more or less institutionalised forms of mutual recognition. That means the 'ethical life' of

61 H. Arendt, *The Origins of Totalitarianism* (1951), London: André Deutsch, 1986, pp. 300 and 269 respectively.

62 S.B. Smith, *Hegel's Critique of Liberalism. Rights in Context*, Chicago/London: The University of Chicago Press, 1989, p. 71.

63 A.McIntyre, *A Short History of Ethics*, London: Routledge & Kegan Paul, 1967, p. 1.

a society carries in itself the experiences and practices which allow each person the capacity for respect of another, based on their own self-respect.[64]

Thus conceived, the ideal of human dignity can be freed from the isolation of an abstract moral formalism, and can then serve as the basis for not so much a moral duty as for an ethical responsibility. Responsibility is a notion which belongs to a contextualised and a culturally and politically modulated ethics. In this way, the notion of responsibility differentiates itself from the moral notion of duty and from the formal-legalistic notion of obligation.

3.4. HUMAN RIGHTS AND HUMAN RESPONSIBILITIES

Human rights discourse is of recent vintage. It developed as a counter-weight to the formation of the large unitary state in Europe, and thereby possesses right from the start a strongly critical bent against power. Human rights produced the idiom in which, in modern times, the ideal of the good society came to be expressed.[65] That ideal is no longer to be derived 'top-down' from a natural law universe of *a priori* values and norms, but is now seen instead as a human work-in-progress. The ideal of the good society is one always in the making, because it is entrusted to an active citizenship and to the innovative powers of citizens acting as autonomous moral agents. It has a thoroughly *reiterative* nature.

Connected herewith is the observation that the notion of responsibility is also of recent date. In light of what has been said above, this may come as no great surprise. It appears for the first time in the middle decades of the 18th century and thereafter developed as a central category for reflection on our ethical consciousness. The double etymological background to the term can illuminate this further.[66]

As noted above, the term 'responsibility' refers to the verb '*respondere*', to the ability to give an answer: responsibility as answerability.[67] This means that responsibility must not be coupled to an abstract subjectivity, as the moral agent is conceived in the Kantian morality of duty. Responsibility, on the contrary, belongs to a context of concrete inter-subjectivity and possesses thereby a dialogical character, because it represents an answer to the appeal of another. That, however,

---

64 A. Honneth, *The Struggle for Recognition. The Moral Grammar of Social Conflicts* (translated by Joel Anderson), Cambridge/Oxford: Polity Press, 1995, pp. 119–120.

65 G.A. Van der Wal, 'De mensenrechten, idee en geestelijke wortels', in his *Recht met reden. Verzamelde opstellen* (edited by and with a foreword of R. Foqué), Deventer: Kluwer, 2003, pp. 147–163.

66 F. Ost and S. Van Drooghenbroeck, 'La responsabilité, face cachée des droits de l'homme', in H. Dumont, F. Ost and S. Van Drooghenbroeck (eds.), *La responsabilité, face cachée des droits de l'homme*, Brussels: Bruylant, 2005, p. 19. The authors follow here the incisive analysis of Michel Villey and of Jean-Louis Genard: M. Villey, 'Esquisse historique sur le mot "responsable" (1977) 22 *Archives de Philosophie du Droit* 49–51; J.-L. Genard, *La grammaire de la responsabilité*, Paris: Les Éditions du Cerf, 1999, pp. 31–35.

67 See above, in an ethical perspective, section 2.3.

does not detract from the fact that an actual taking up of responsibility also contains in effect a conscious, reflected choice and an affirmation of the unicity and singularity of the acting and reflecting person. This singularity and the very personal character of the choices to be made resonate in a second etymological background to the term 'responsibility', as analysed by Villey and Genard. In classic Roman law, a '*sponsor*' is a debtor held to the performance of a certain act. A '*re-sponsor*' is one who guarantees the debts of another. The *re-sponsor* is responsible for fulfilment of the obligations of another, if future circumstances should so require. It is a matter here of a very personal commitment which is undertaken in all freedom.

This double etymological background suggests an important conclusion regarding the meaning of the concept of responsibility. In that concept, two dimensions of our acting ethically are linked. The one is the dimension of inter-subjectivity and dialogue, and the other is that unique subjectivity which is expressed in the singular character of personal reflections and choices. This connection cannot obtain in the abstract, but must be modulated by concrete life experiences and institutionalised behaviour.

It is precisely in the nexus where inter-subjectivity and subjectivity encounter each other that the ethical meaning of responsibility unfolds. In the first place, responsibility involves an active care and concern for my human dignity and that of the other. In the second place, and simultaneously, responsibility also involves an active care and concern for a shared practice of 'carefulness', of shared ethical intuitions, institutions, experiences, and practices of respect and mutual recognition. Responsible citizens know by experience that they must have care and concern for the realisation of a decent society. That is to say, 'a society whose institutions do not humiliate people'.[68]

Finally, the notion of responsibility belongs to the domain of human action. Responsibility refers to the human capacity to give one's actions an innovative character. Hannah Arendt repeatedly emphasised this in her impressive study of the human condition. 'To act in its most general sense, means to take an initiative, to begin, to set something into motion (which is the original meaning of the Latin "*agere*")'. In their actions, 'men show who they are, reveal actively their unique personal identities,' observes Arendt.[69]

In his actions, an individual person can contribute to the revelation of his personal identity by taking responsibility for what he does, and does not do. This means that a person only becomes a holder of rights and responsibilities not only when he possesses the capacity to decide and to act, but also when he is able to account, in his own life-story, for his actions and decisions: 'responsibility

68 A. Margalit, *The Decent Society* (translated by Naomi Goldblum), Cambridge, Mass./London: Harvard University Press, 1996, p. 1.

69 H. Arendt, *The Human Condition*, Chicago/London: The University of Chicago Press, 1958, pp. 177–179.

as imputability'.[70] Responsibility, imputability, and accountability reflect one another in the concrete life-story of an individual.[71]

This ethical dimension of responsibility seems to remain the hidden face of human rights, because our human rights discourse does not express sufficiently the nexus of intersubjectivity and dialogue, on the one hand, and personal commitment and concern, on the other hand. It has already often been said that our human rights discourse appears to remain too individualistic in its thinking and practice. The notion of individualism – as the dominant characteristic of our contemporary human rights discourse – should be understood both in its methodological and in its normative sense. Methodological individualism (the leading paradigm in modern social sciences) contends that human behaviour in a social context and social phenomena should only be explained with reference to, and in terms of, atomistic individuals. Normative individualism (the leading paradigm in modern legal scholarship) insists that our moral and legal concepts should ultimately be referred to in terms of individual rights, obligations, and interests. Responsibility, as the hidden face of human rights, can confront human rights with the conceptual and ethical deficits of both their methodological and their normative individualisms. Responsibility – referring to action and concern – can make us sensitive to the inter-subjective and dialogical structure, within which and only within which, our very personal and individual actions and choices can find their ethical relevance.

In the practice of human rights, the Kantian and the more Hegelian positions do not have to exclude each other. On the one hand, the focus on universality, on a certain cosmopolitan perspective, outlined by Kant, remains very crucial in not excluding any person from ethical concern, and thus in not disconnecting human rights from ethical responsibility as their hidden face. On the other hand, the focus on concrete forms of institutionalisation and of historical forms of embodiment of this ethical concern in (in what are very often local or regional) practices of '*Sittlichkeit*', of ethical life, can protect human rights against legal formalism and positivistic self-referentiality.[72] This more Hegelian perspective is equally important and relevant. A moderate form of 'another cosmopolitanism' and an open form of local, national, or regional practices, norms, and institutions have to go hand in hand.

---

70 P. Ricoeur in connection with this speaks also of a 'narrative identity' in contrast to the concept of 'abstract identity', which is found in the Cartesian tradition as much as the Kantian one. See his 'Who is the Subject of Rights?', in his *The Just* (translated by D. Pellauer), Chicago/London: The University of Chicago Press, 2000, pp. 1–10.

71 This reveals just how much responsibility involves the dimension of a past of choices made and completed actions, as well as a future-oriented dimension which adverts to the purposiveness of our actions and decisions. For more on this theme, see P. Ricoeur, 'Le juste entre le légal et le bon', in his *Lectures 1: Autour du politique*, Paris: Éditions du Seuil, 1991, pp. 176–195.

72 For a sceptic's view on the increasingly self-referential character of human rights, see M. Koskenniemi, 'The Effects of Rights on Political Culture', in P. Alston (ed.), *The EU and Human Rights*, Oxford/New York: Oxford University Press, 1999, pp. 99–116.

4. CONCLUSIONS

4.1. THE NEED FOR CONCEPTUAL CLARITY

My first conclusion would be as follows. Responsibility is a broader, and, at the same time, thicker notion than the ideas of obligation or duty. It is of utmost importance for our human rights practices to make a very clear conceptual distinction between the three ideas of duty, obligation, and responsibility. The very notion of responsibility can avoid the pitfalls of moral abstraction, of a-historical immobility, and formalism. At the same time, it can free our minds from the narrowness of both methodological and normative individualism. As the hidden face of human rights, responsibilities refer to the ethical concern which has to inspire all our actions and practices. The addressees of these responsibilities are both the individual citizens and the national and supra-national authorities. The idea of a society based upon a strong intertwinement of human rights and responsibilities, inspired by our ambition of not excluding any person from ethical concern, is an idea that combines respect for individual autonomy, for moral agency, and for human dignity, with the need for social order, for a shared and strongly embodied and culturally embedded ethical life of the community and for an effective legal order.

4.2. THE ETHICAL AND THE CONCEPTUAL HAVE TO MEET EACH OTHER IN A POLITICAL CONTEXT

The foregoing analysis of the ethical meaning of the concept 'responsibility' implied at the same time a search for a phenomenological foundation. That foundation finds its starting point, not in an abstract morality of duty, but in the fundamental human need to be able to live in a decent society. It encompasses, according to Ricoeur, 'the desire to live well with and for others in just institutions.'[73] It is not an issue here of pure will, as with Kant, but of the culturally and politically embodied desires of people. Thus viewed, responsibility always relates to what may be wished for in concrete circumstances and contexts. There is, thus, a political justification, at its foundation, for the priority of the ethical over abstract morality. Indeed, it is precisely in the context of a democratic political order that a free hand ought to be given to personal convictions, but also to communal care and concern for the development and maintenance of those institutions which a decent society requires.

[73] P. Ricoeur, *Oneself as Another* (translated by K. Blamey), Chicago/London: The University of Chicago Press, 1992, p. 239.

4.3. DO NOT TRANSFORM THE ETHICAL LIFE OF A SOCIETY IN TERMS OF LEGAL OBLIGATIONS

A last conclusion, one which follows from the arguments for a clear distinction among the three concepts of duty, obligation, and responsibility, is the warning (which can never be emphasised too much) not to immediately juridicise ethical responsibility in terms of obligations and duties. Should that nevertheless occur, then it would deprive our society of every ethical and political dynamic. There is reason to fear that all the proposals aimed at casting responsibilities, just like rights, in the quasi-legal mould of formal Declarations or Charters (which require an effective means of application), create at the very least the illusion that a juridification of the ethical dimension is desirable, and even possible. A society which thinks that it can function with its legal obligations on automatic pilot deprives its citizens of their capacity for reflection and action. Then, the call for more responsibility may well end up as an unintended 'self-destructive prophecy'.

RIGHTS, RESPONSIBILITIES AND DUTIES FOR THE CIVIL SOCIETY

Moral Challenges Put Forward by the Millennium Development Goals*

Willem van Genugten

1. INTRODUCTION

Human rights lawyers and human rights activists often hesitate or even hate to talk about human responsibilities and obligations (hereafter summarised as 'duties'). This is the case for obvious reasons, which can best be understood in light of the very beginning of the history of human rights, relating to the protection of human beings against the abuse of power by States. Talking too much about duties of human beings (and their societal organisations) would be a nice 'playing card' in the hands of authoritarian governments, whether they are communist left, military right or religiously fundamentalist. In daily global reality one could and can find a lot of support for that fear. Think of the camps in the former Soviet Union and of today's developments in countries like North Korea and Iran. Also think of the grounds upon which in countries like China freedom of expression is dealt with: one is allowed to say everything, as long as it fits into the interests and views of the communist party.

Despite this, there might be good grounds to talk about human duties, alongside rights. This chapter addresses these duties of human beings and their non-governmental organisations towards other human beings and the world society as a whole. The focus will be upon a basically moral appeal connected to forms of accountability, and not upon new legally binding obligations. Further to that, the focus will be upon one selected issue: the need to realise the Millennium Development Goals (MDGs) and the human rights related thereto. Is the MDG reality 'ordering' us to rethink the notion of duties for not only States but for individuals and their organisations as well?

* The final update of this research was done in 2011.

2. A FEW HISTORICAL REMARKS

Before entering into the question whether or not the MDGs raise the need to sharpen the notion of human duties in the context of human rights, it might be good to observe that already during the 1946–1948 negotiations on the Universal Declaration of Human Rights (UDHR) the issue of duties was discussed time and again. Already during the very first meeting of the drafting committee, it was proposed to formulate as a core principle of the Declaration 'that man does not have rights only', but also 'owes duties to the society of which he forms part'. The first Article of the first Draft UDHR presented by the UN secretariat was simply devoted to duties:

> 'Every one owes a duty of loyalty to his State and to the (international society) United Nations. He must accept his just share of responsibility for the performance of such social duties and his share of such common sacrifices as may contribute to the common good.'[1]

For the present chapter, it is sufficient to refer to the final results of the 1946–1948 negotiations on the UDHR: Article 29(1), which states that '[e]veryone has duties to the community in which alone the free and full development of his personality is possible', followed by the clause that such limitations to human rights should be determined by law, 'solely for the purpose of securing due recognition and respects for the rights and freedoms of others and of meeting the just requirements of morality, public order and the general welfare of in a democratic society' (Article 29(2)). The Article should be read in the light of the Declaration as a whole, and should especially be seen in conjunction with Article 30, which states that nothing in the Declaration 'may be interpreted as implying for any State, group or person any right to engage in any activity or to perform any act aimed at the destruction of any of the rights and freedoms set forth herein.' For Western human rights lawyers this is a well-known way of thinking: talk about social responsibilities and make sure that the limitations posed upon individuals are (a) determined by law and (b) 'doubly locked' by guaranteeing that in case of clashes between human rights and duties, the starting point is with the rights, not the duties. It is a way of thinking which over decades has been applied by human rights' supervisory committees and courts and which has proven its great value.

Given the quotes taken from the UDHR, one can say that the late 1940s did not show a ban on talking about duties within the human rights framework. One can easily observe that the core reason for that was the historical background against which the UDHR had to be developed: how to avoid such a social,

1 Quotes taken from (and examples of other draft articles to be found in): E.-I.A. Daes, *Freedom of the Individual under Law: an Analysis of Article 29 of the Universal Declaration of Human Rights*, New York: United Nations, 1990, pp. 17–19.

economic and security disaster as World War II, leading to gross violations of the rights of peoples and individual human beings, taking place again? It is clear that the drafters of the UDHR not only wanted to touch upon the duties of States and the community of States as a whole to prevent this from happening again, but also upon duties for individuals as well as for their organisations towards one another and to the society at large. See especially the Preamble of the UDHR: the Declaration is to be seen as

> 'a common standard of achievement for all peoples and all nations, to the end that *every individual* and *every organ of society*, keeping this Declaration constantly in mind, *shall* strive by teaching and education to promote respect for these rights and freedoms and by progressive measures, national and international, to secure their universal and effective recognition and observance'.[2]

The wish to avoid a WWII-like situation in the future called for an all-embracing talk on duties, individuals and their organisations included.

3. THE PRESENT WAY OF LOOKING AT DUTIES

It would be easy to mention hundreds of duty-related issues already incorporated in the human rights discourse and application of human rights standards, whether it is the duty to act 'in the interest of the child' or the limitations to the freedom of speech, as for instance worded in Article 10 of the European Convention on Human Rights or Article 19 of the International Covenant on Civil and Political Rights. Both Articles use the words 'duties and responsibilities' that one has to bear in mind when making use of one's freedom of speech, and state that limitations have to be prescribed by law. In a Western lawyer's mind and in legal models like the ones used in, for instance, the Netherlands, Belgium, and the USA, the underlying concept is quite simple: it is up to the (national and/ or international) legislator to decide what limitations are allowed, and plaintiffs should go to court if in concrete cases they think the limits of the limitations are neglected. That's, all in all, a workable model. We should keep in mind, however, that in many countries this might be an overestimation of what laws and courts can do, if available at all. I will come back to that.

It is also obvious that human rights documents are full of duties for States. In more recent times, however, also the notion of duties to be fulfilled by non-state actors has been given quite some attention, conceptually as well as practically.[3] One subsector in the field of non-state actors relates to the business community,

---

2 UDHR, Preamble, final paragraph. Emphasis added.

3 See, among many sources, P. Alston, *Non-State Actors and Human Rights*, Oxford: Oxford University Press, 2005; A. Clapham, *Human Rights Obligations of Non-State Actors*, Oxford: Oxford University Press, 2006. For those who read Dutch: C. Flinterman and W. van Genugten

the discussion on which was given a boost by the adoption in June 2011 of the UN Guiding Principles on Business and Human Rights ('the Ruggie Principles'). That non-state actor segment, however, will not be discussed here. The focus will be on the conglomerate of all kinds of non-governmental organisations (NGOs), together called 'civil society'. As of now, there seem to be about 65,000 civil society organisations in over 300 countries and territories, in every field of human endeavour.[4] In international human rights matters, such organisations have gradually witnessed a role change from being one of the driving forces behind the adoption of international human rights conventions and other human rights instruments, to being active in making the norms in these instruments become reality. That role is fully accepted in the human rights field, and is by now gradually expanding to other fields as well.[5]

But are these NGOs addressed in terms of duties they should have to fulfil? The answer is positive as far as their ways of behaviour and performing is concerned – they should provide reliable facts, be held accountable for what they are doing in practice with the money entrusted to them, and so on – but clearly negative when it comes to their contribution to the core notion behind the UDHR, that is, the need to fully realise human rights for every human being world wide. Despite the wording chosen in the Preamble of the UDHR – see above – it is clear that NGOs are neither responsible nor obliged to realise human rights for all, as is the case with States. NGOs are seen as important actors, even more so: they are seen as indispensable actors who are called upon to do their very best, so to say, but their contributions are not evaluated in terms of the (legal) duty to fulfil human rights obligations. To a great extent, NGOs take on board what they themselves like to do.

These NGOs are therefore sometimes confronted with criticism as regards their specific approach and, more fundamentally, as regards their legitimacy. Let me mention three issues. First, the causes to which NGOs dedicate themselves are often characterised by normative dilemmas that require various public interests and values to be balanced against each other. However, by their very nature, many NGOs, especially the single issue organisations, do not appear to be well equipped for dealing with such dilemmas: any particular NGO's fundamental objectives and mission impose upon it a bias that would make it nearly impossible to detect and solve dilemmas in cases at issue. Second, NGOs lack democratic legitimisation. Although many NGOs can boast extensive membership support, these members cannot therefore exercise control in the way voters can as a result

(eds.), *Niet-statelijke actoren en de rechten van de mens: gevestigde waarden, nieuwe wegen*, The Hague: Boom Juridische Uitgevers, 2003.

4 See Union of International Associations, *Yearbook of International Organizations Online*, www.uia.be/yearbook. According to the website of the Union of International Associations, the number of organisations includes 'dormant or inactive organisations'.

5 See, for instance, Advisory Council on International Affairs, *The Role of NGOs and the Private Sector in International Relations*, The Hague, October 2006. The report was prepared under the chairmanship of the present author.

of the democratic rules of government composition under public law. It is even doubtful whether members themselves actually think of their membership in terms of representation at all. It is often very unclear why they have decided to join an NGO. Is it because of the organisation's mission or is it because of other benefits, such as discounts on purchases or admission tickets, and so on? Is membership perhaps simply the result of an insistent NGO's successful marketing strategy in recruiting (new) members? Not unimportantly: many human rights NGOs are mainly active in (developing) countries where they have virtually no membership at all. Third, one can observe an unbalanced distribution of internationally operating NGOs over the world. On the whole, it is still mainly NGOs from the affluent North, with its liberal-democratic tradition, that tend to denounce human rights abuses committed in developing countries. In doing so, they do not always properly appraise the underlying causes of human rights violations, such as government corruption, lack of means and manpower to implement and enforce legislation, and cultural differences between communities. The solutions proposed by these NGOs to prevent human rights violations therefore sometimes lack sagacious judgment.[6]

These are only a few ways of discussing the legitimacy of NGOs, the underlying issue being the quest for establishing a solid foundation for their activities. As the philosopher Michael Edwards observed, legitimacy is generally understood

> 'as having the right to be and to do something in society, a sense that an organization is lawful, proper, admissible and justified in doing what it does and saying what it says, and that it continues to enjoy the support of an identifiable constituency.'[7]

Commonplace conceptions of NGO legitimacy, if they go beyond the mere recognition of their factual role at all, often boil down to what might be called an appeal to substantial moral criteria. A justification of NGO activities in terms of substantial moral criteria is a justification that refers to the degree to which a certain person or organisation's activity aspires to values and ideals, such as human rights, helping people in distress, and so on, and to what extent such activities are effective in practice. In that case, one looks more at aspiration and performance than at membership criteria and the like.

Having said this about their legitimacy, it might be good to return to the (positive) roles assigned to NGOs in today's international arena. The present-day views of their tasks is clearly formulated in the 2004 innovative and trendsetting

---

6 These points are taken from W.J.M. van Genugten, R.A.J. van Gestel, J.E.J. Prins and A.H. Vedder, *NGO's als 'nieuwe toezichthouders' op de naleving van mensenrechten door multinationale ondernemingen*, The Hague: Boom Juridische Uitgevers, 2004.

7 M. Edwards, 'Legitimacy and Values in NGOs and Voluntary Organizations: Some Sceptical Thoughts', in D. Lewis (ed.), *International Perspectives on Voluntary Action: Reshaping the Third Sector*. London: Earthscan, 1999, p. 258.

report of the UN Panel of Eminent Persons on United Nations – Civil Society Relations (named after its chair: the 'Cardoso report').[8] The report states amongst other things that the involvement of a diverse range of actors, including those from civil society, creates an opportunity 'to harness new capacities and diverse experience to address some of the most exacting challenges the world faces today', while the UN is also confronted with 'the challenge of balancing its unique intergovernmental characteristic with being open to work with new actors in a profound way'.[9] In addition, the report notes that the way the multilateral agenda is set has changed considerably. While in the past 'Governments would come together to discuss a new issue until there was a sufficient consensus for an intergovernmental resolution, which then led to action by Governments and intergovernmental organizations', today it is increasingly likely 'that a civil society movement and a crescendo of public opinion will bring a new issue to global attention and that initial action on new issues will be taken through multi-constituency coalitions of Governments, civil society and others.'[10] Since 2004, the manifold roles of civil society in relation to the equally manifold tasks of the United Nations have been expanded and clarified further, their roles being recognised as indispensable in many cases. Thus they move from 'being accepted' to being 'co-constituents' and 'partners'. In words used by the UN itself in May 2012, describing the topic 'UN and Civil Society':

> 'The United Nations is both a participant in and a witness to an increasingly global civil society. More and more, non-governmental organizations (NGOs) and other civil society organizations (CSOs) are UN system partners and valuable UN links to civil society. CSOs play a key role at major United Nations Conferences and are indispensable partners for UN efforts at the country level. NGOs are consulted on UN policy and programme matters. The UN organizes and hosts, on a regular basis, briefings, meetings and conferences for NGO representatives who are accredited to UN offices, programmes and agencies.'[11]

It is a telling quote, sending a variety of signals to the outside world, which as such is composed of players with a variety of views on civil society organisations. In addition, it can be observed that the wording the UN is using while describing the position of the civil society in the larger UN framework is time and again revised. It shows that the role of civil society in the UN will always be moving.

This way of presenting initiatives taken by NGOs is in line with a State-oriented approach to international decision-making and with the somewhat classical division of roles within that spectrum of tasks. In short, NGOs are seen

8 Report *We the peoples: civil society, the United Nations and global governance*, UN Doc. A/58/817, 11 June 2004.

9 Ibid., p. 7 (quotes are taken from the very good executive summary of the report).

10 Ibid.

11 See www.un.org/en/civilsociety/index.shtml.

as complementary providers of information, as 'early warning organisations', sometimes even as the conscience of mankind, while for these reasons they are given the honorary title of co-constituencies of the international public order, but again they are not seen as duty-bearers in relation to the 'end-product' (that is, the worldwide realisation of human rights for all).

Again, this approach is perhaps, and as far as I am concerned most likely, founded on good grounds, and such grounds should not be discarded easily. This is most probably what the Cardoso panel had in mind, when it held hat 'the unique role of the United Nations as an intergovernmental forum is vitally important and must be protected at all costs' and that 'the most powerful case for reaching out beyond its constituency of central Governments and enhancing dialogue and cooperation with civil society is that doing so will make the United Nations more effective.'[12] NGOs are seen as sub-contractors, who can make the UN more effective, while embracing a plurality of constituencies creates support which governments of their own might never be able to create. Subcontracting thereby means that NGOs offer and use their specific capacities to carry out public tasks or, the other way round, that States even ask NGOs to conduct such tasks, thereby investing tax money in NGO activities and holding the NGOs accountable for the way that public money has been used. This type of approach, together with granting bigger roles to NGOs in the international arena more in general as well, is sometimes called a paradigm-shift. The Cardoso panel for instance does so, based upon the arguments that the new approach to NGOs makes the UN 'become an outward-looking organisation', 'embrace a plurality of constituencies', 'connect the local with the global' and 'help strengthen democracy for the twenty-first century'.[13] Having said that, one can also observe, however, that the core of the classical paradigm is still 'alive and kicking'.

4. MORAL DUTIES FOR INDIVIDUALS AND THEIR ORGANISATIONS?

What kind of problems faced by our world today may justify thinking in terms of more far-reaching duties for individuals and their organisations? One could think of issues such as the prevention of religion-driven terrorist attacks. Formulated in terms of duties for individuals and their organisations: how about the duty to respect the lives of others, the duty to refrain from hate speech, the duty to respect the existence of a diversity of religions?

Having said that, I would like to focus here upon another issue: the field covered by the eight Millennium Development Goals (MDGs). In short: eradicate extreme poverty and hunger; achieve universal primary education; promote

12 Ibid., pp. 7 and 8.

13 Ibid., pp. 8–9.

gender equality and empower women; reduce child mortality; improve maternal health; combat HIV/AIDS, malaria and other diseases; ensure environmental sustainability; develop a Global Partnership for Development.[14] Behind these formulations, one can find a lot of miserable, human rights related facts. For instance, the fact that about one billion people in the world live on less than one US dollar a day, while almost half the world – over 3 billion people – can spend less than 2.50 US dollars a day.[15] Moreover, it is estimated that at least 80% of humanity still lives on less than 10 US dollars a day.[16] In addition to these figures, it should be observed that poverty goes far beyond low income levels. Poverty also means, in the words of the former Millennium Project lead by the economist Jeffrey Sachs, 'having to walk more than one mile everyday simply to collect water and firewood', and 'suffering diseases that were eradicated from rich countries decades ago'.[17] That's a harsh reality at the beginning of another new millennium. The numbers are constantly changing, while the exact impact of the present economic and financial crisis still has to be measured. But having said that, it is clear already at first sight that the fulfilment of the MDGs is simply outreaching the capacities and capabilities of States and their intergovernmental organisations. And the implication of that would be: if one wants to deal with the MDGs effectively, one will have to find new ways alongside the existing ones. Simultaneously, one has to keep in mind that the realisation of the MDGs is maybe not so much outreaching the capacities and capabilities of States, but rather shows the limits of their political will to find real solutions.

The focus on the States' political will as a starting point addresses the right actors, but to my mind it is naive as well. Isn't the lack of political will always present due to diverging interests, isn't it a core characteristic of international organisations that by far most of their time is devoted to finding common ground, which often, however, is not found at all and only leads to a 'consensus' on the level of the common lowest denominator (be it standards or supervisory instruments chosen)? That (lack of a real) consensus is often used as a pretext behind which one can comfortably hide. As a matter of fact, what is called the 'International Community of States' – being a label that idealistically embraces such notions as 'common goals to fight for' and 'joining forces in the fight against global injustice' etc. – is in many ways not so much more than an 'International Gathering of States', replacing, for instance, the methods of immediately starting wars against one another by the duty to talk first. Over-exaggerating? Indeed.

---

14 'Millennium Declaration', adopted at the Millennium Summit of the General Assembly of the United Nations; UN Doc. A/RES/55/2, 18 September 2000.

15 See www.unmillenniumproject.org/facts/index.htm, and www.globalissues.org/issue/2/causes-of-poverty.

16 See www.globalissues.org/article/26/poverty-facts-and-stats.

17 Ibid. Since January 2007, the Millennium Project's work is incorporated into the MDG Support Group of the United Nations Development Program.

True? I am afraid so, at least to a large extent. And this despite everything the international community is doing right, as well. But is that enough?

To my mind the MDGs, or structural patterns of poverty and the like, ask for an approach that transcends the level of the present instrumental way of thinking about possible solutions. Have a look at a relatively simple – that is to say, clearly defined and to a large extent technical – issue such as the right to clean water, being a central issue in several MDGs. The topic was the core issue of the 2006 *Human Development Report*.[18] The report addresses, amongst other things, the question of the 'prospects for the world achieving the water and sanitation Millennium Development Goal'. The Report states the following:

> 'The global aggregate picture is mixed. With strong progress in high population countries such as China and India, the world is on track for halving the share of people without access to water, but off track on sanitation. The problem with this global aggregation is that it masks large differences between regions and countries. Disaggregation to a regional level shows less positive results … On current trends some regions will miss the water and sanitation target. Sub-Saharan Africa will miss the water target by a full generation and the sanitation target by more than two generations. South Asia will miss the sanitation target by four years, and the Arab States will miss the water target by 27 years. Looking beyond the regional picture to the national level reveals further cause for concern. Because the Millennium Development Goals are for everyone, it is country-level performance that counts – and current performance falls far short of the level required:
> - Water: 55 countries are off track, and the target will be missed by about 234.5 million people, with a total of 800 million people still lacking access to water.
> - Sanitation: 74 countries are off track, and the target will be missed by 430 million people, with 2.1 billion still lacking access to sanitation.'[19]

In 2010, the UN General Assembly adopted a resolution on 'The Human Right to Water and Sanitation'. The Resolution states that the General Assembly is '*[d]eeply concerned* that approximately 884 million people lack access to safe drinking water and that more than 2.6 billion do not have access to basic sanitation, and alarmed that approximately 1.5 million children under 5 years of age die and 443 million school days are lost each year as a result of water- and sanitation-related diseases'.[20] The 2006 and 2010 figures do by and large overlap.

While the *Human Development Report 2006* is full of appeals upon national States and the global community of States to fulfil their (human rights) obligations in this specific field, it also observes that:

18 United Nations Development Programme, *Human Development Report 2006*, New York, 2006.
19 Ibid., pp. 56–57.
20 A/RES/64/292, 3 August 2010.

> 'in many countries progress in water and sanitation has been driven from below. Local and municipal governments and service providers have developed practical strategies for tackling inequalities in access. Communities have not waited passively for government help. The rural poor, women's organizations and associations of urban slum dwellers have mobilized their own resources. In some cases that mobilization has met with indifference, or even hostility. In others new partnerships have emerged between governments and people, with community initiative being scaled up.'[21]

The way UNDP presents the issue still fits into the classical scheme of dividing responsibilities and obligations, including its analysis of work done at the grass-roots level by local communities and local organisations in order to make international promises a daily reality. And indeed, what would that daily reality really consist of, when local people and communities would *not* take the initiative and would *not* see it as their own responsibility to try to survive? Again, that 'own responsibility' would not free the national States nor the international community of States from their responsibilities and obligations to do their utmost, to set the right priorities, and so on, but this way their tasks are backed up by other actors.

But do we need an additional way of thinking? Broadening the issue again to the MDGs in full, we are touching upon a series of extremely urgent, global problems nobody can escape. The underlying moral argument has been touched upon by many, but the best elaboration to my mind has been presented by Thomas Pogge, professor of Political Philosophy at Columbia University. In his 2002 *World Poverty and Human Rights* he argues that at least

> 'the more privileged and influential citizens of the more powerful and approximately democratic countries bear ... a collective responsibility for their governments' role in designing and imposing [the present] global order and for their governments' failure to reform it toward greater human rights fulfilment'.[22]

The core of his argument is that, in doing so, individual human beings from these countries do neglect 'positive obligations', following from human rights:

> '[The] distinction between the negative duty not to harm and the positive duty to help is morally significant. In the context of understanding what human rights are it is a very important distinction. In my view, somebody is a human rights violator only when he or she actively harms others or contributes to harming them. Human rights, this very minimal notion of what human beings owe one another, do not require that people benefit or rescue or protect each other. They merely require that we not harm others. However, with regard to poverty, even this very

21 Ibid., p. 63.

22 T. Pogge, *World Poverty and Human Rights*, Cambridge: Polity Press, 2002, pp. 172–173. Also see the second revised edition of the book (2007).

> minimal demand is arguably widely unfulfilled today, since the rich countries and their citizens collectively harm many in the poor countries through the global economic order they impose.'[23]

In several other articles Pogge discusses similar duties for international (human rights) NGOs as well. His argument has many facets. One such argument is that citizens do have moral duties, but because it is difficult to practically fulfil them, 'we cooperate with others', for instance politically, 'trying to get our governments and corporations to do less harm and more good in poor countries', or 'by supporting international non-governmental organizations (INGOs) that offer to pool money we give them and to make such funds effective toward human rights, development, and/or humanitarian goals.'[24] This scheme starts from a classical approach, that is to say: individuals and their organisations address 'their' governments, and emphasise the need to find practical arrangements and to join forces with instrumental roles for NGOs. According to Pogge, however, that is not enough. For that reason he constructs extra moral obligations for individuals and for (international) NGOs as well. In relation to individuals he touches upon the need to elect 'the right politicians' and to let them do 'what they should do'. In the words of the late legal philosopher John Rawls, such behaviour would require at the level of individuals the presence of two moral powers: 'A capacity for a sense of justice and a capacity for a conception of the good', while it is also assumed that 'each citizen has, at any time, a conception of the good compatible with a comprehensive religious, philosophical, or moral doctrine'.[25] Without by now entering into a discussion of the sense of reality of Rawls' views,[26] one can argue that he touches upon two (moral) capacities that are indeed indispensable to the fulfilment of the duties addressed in this chapter. Without such a starting point of moral awareness the rest would be void.

In his paper on 'Moral Priorities for International Human Rights NGOs', Pogge elaborates upon morality aspects of decision-making by NGOs, for instance when they have to decide how to spend their funds: 'To put it bluntly, an INGO must often make decisions that will certainly lead to many deaths because spending one's very limited funds on trying to protect some is tantamount to

23 See A. Pinzani, interviewing T. Pogge, 'Global Justice as Moral Issue', *ethic@*, Florianópolis, vol. 4, no. 1, June 2005, p. 3.

24 T. Pogge, 'Moral Priorities for International Human Rights NGOs', www.etikk.no/globaljustice/papers/GJ2003_Thomas_Pogge_Moral_Priorities_for_International_Human_Rights_NGOs.doc, p. 2.

25 J. Rawls, *The Law of Peoples*, Cambridge, Mass./London: Harvard University Press, 1999, p. 92.

26 For those who read Dutch, see my 'De houdbaarheidsdatum van Rawls' praktische uitweidingen', in 'The Law of Peoples' (2001) 2 *Rechtsfilosofie & Rechtsheorie* 183–193. In the same volume, pp. 194–206: T. Pogge, 'Rawls en de echte wereld: zijn fatsoen en bijstand voldoende?', translation of 'Rawls on International Justice' (2001) 51/203 *The Philosophical Quarterly* 246–253. Also see: www.columbia.edu/~tp6/index.html.

leaving others to their fate.'[27] Linking the wishes of individual members to the performance of their organisations, Pogge observes that 'we trust that this INGO has developed carefully formulated moral priorities governing how the collected money should be spent'.[28] But that same trust also confronts INGOs 'with a second, still awesome responsibility': 'They must not let their contributors down by setting the wrong moral priorities, by funding infeasible or counterproductive projects, or by frittering money away through carelessness and corruption.'[29] In addition to that, 'an INGO is not merely an actor in its own right, but also an agent and trustee for its contributors; it must then reflect not merely on its own moral responsibilities, but also on its contributors' moral responsibilities, which these contributors entrust it with discharging.'[30] It has already been discussed.

Having said that, Pogge comes to four 'moral considerations' for international NGOs to take into account:

> '(A) Other things (including cost) being equal, it is morally more important to protect a person from greater serious harm than from lesser.
> (B) Other things (including cost) being equal, it is morally more important to protect persons from harm the more such harm they would otherwise be suffering.
> (C) Other things (including cost) being equal, it is morally more important to achieve some given harm protection for more persons than for fewer. Here aggregate harm protection is a linear function of the number of persons protected. Generally, the moral value of several harm reductions is the sum of their moral values.
> (D) Other things (including harm protection) being equal, an INGO should choose cheaper candidate projects over more expensive ones. More specifically, the choiceworthiness of candidate projects is inversely proportional to their cost.'[31]

The core reason to quote Thomas Pogge extensively is because of his clear elaboration upon the fundamental moral grounds that should lead NGOs while being involved in the worldwide fight against poverty and while working on poverty related issues. This is a way of looking at NGOs which is often overlooked and cannot be missed in a chapter on 'duties'. At the same time it must be observed that a morality-driven approach is not necessarily linked to 'generosity' and 'benevolence', and other forms of one-way traffic, based on the model of the (rich) West giving and the (poor) South receiving. At the beginning of the present

[27] T. Pogge, 'Moral Priorities for International Human Rights NGOs', www.etikk.no/globaljustice/papers/GJ2003_Thomas_Pogge_Moral_Priorities_for_International_Human_Rights_NGOs.doc, p. 3.
[28] Ibid., p. 4.
[29] Ibid.
[30] Ibid., p. 5.
[31] Ibid., pp. 6–15.

Millennium, it is largely agreed upon that such a one-sided approach creates dependency from donors and the like, and is not a good way to realise structural improvements, to put it mildly.[32]

Back to the morality-driven approach, it is clear that in daily practice it will not be easy to apply such a principle consequently. Nevertheless, it is to my mind a relevant way of looking at NGO behaviour, framing the expectations one might have of them. This is also the case, given – at least often – their own claims, be it incorporated in their charters or statutes or as words in documents with which they apply for governmental money to be spend for the realisation of (human rights related) development goals. These claims then serve as part of the measuring standards that can be used for a critical evaluation of their more concrete projects.

Another way of looking at NGOs and their daily projects might be considering them as strengthening the 'natural community' communitarians are sometimes talking about. That concept includes voluntary associations, charities, parental groups, and neighbourhoods and so on as 'institutions' or bodies that fill in gaps which are left by States, on purpose or because of lack of capacity and the like and fits large groups of NGOs as well. One of the central notions in the communitarian approach – despite a huge variety of views communitarians represent as well – is being against an over-estimation of (the desirability and power of) individualism and relates to looking for another way of organising societies, in order to solve problems which in a State and in an individual-oriented model cannot be solved.[33]

It would be beyond the scope of this article to fundamentally discuss the added value of the communitarian approach, but let me give one quote from the study *A Human Rights-Based Approach to Development*, relating to an evaluation of the activities of four Dutch NGOs working in Africa in the field of human rights and development with, amongst other things, Dutch governmental money.[34] As to 'working in an African context', the report concludes that 'it has again become clear that the existence of communities … plays a major role in the structure of Southern African countries', including the roles fulfilled by the leaders of these

---

32 See for instance R. Dowden, *Africa: Altered States, Ordinary Miracles*, London: Portobello Books, 2008; A. de Waal, *Famine that Kills: Darfur, Sudan*, Oxford: Clarendon Press, 1989 (revised edition, 2005); P. Collier, *The Bottom Billion; Why the Poorest Countries Are Failing and What Can Be Done About it*, Oxford: Oxford University Press, 2008; D. Moyo, *Dead Aid; Why Aid Is Not Working and How There Is a Better Way for Africa*, New York: Farrar, Straus and Giroux Publishers, 2009; B. Berendsen (ed.), *Common Goods in a Divided World*, Amsterdam: KIT Publishers, 2011. And for those who read Dutch: Wetenschappelijke Raad voor het Regeringsbeleid, *Minder pretentie, meer ambitie; Ontwikkelingshulp die verschil maakt*, Amsterdam: Amsterdam University Press, 2010.

33 See for instance: A. Etzioni, *From Empire to Community: A New Approach to International Relations*, New York: Palgrave Macmillan, 2004. For an interesting overview of the history of and recent developments within communitarianism see http://plato.stanford.edu/entries/communitarianism.

34 W. van Genugten, A. Meijknecht, H. Moors and W. Vandenhole, *A Human Rights-Based Approach to Development*, Tilburg: Tilburg University, March 2006, www.iva.nl/forceDL.php?filename=pubPDF1442.pdf.

communities, and that the 'local communities are often seen as one of the entities within which rights have to be realised, but also as instruments in the manifold struggles for the further realisation of these rights':

> 'In order to change human rights and poverty practices at the community level, one often relies upon – or has no alternative but to rely upon – the chiefs of these communities, or upon, for instance, grass roots groups of women. They are the indispensable 'vehicles' for passing the message to the really lowest organisational level.'[35]

To my mind, the quote illustrates and reflects in a practical sense the notions communitarians are talking about.

A third way of looking at NGOs might be to see their activities as work or even an industry, and to think in terms of markets upon which NGOs are in competition with other NGOs. NGOs with a sense of responsibility will be prepared to accept accountability for matters such as: how do they acquire their funding? How do they design their governance structure and their self-supervision mechanisms? How do they practice transparency as to the rules of the game they intend to play? Developing such accountability mechanisms can, at least to some extent, be left to the market, knowing that competing NGOs will 'tackle' them, in case the figures presented are not reliable or if results are claimed that cannot be claimed at all.

Whatever these schematic typologies might be, it is clear that there is a huge variety of NGOs, some being more (directly) morality-driven than others. But diverse or not, it is also clear that without the activities of such groups in the long run neither society nor the globe will be able to survive.

5. CONCLUDING REMARKS

Worldwide, individuals and especially their organisations/NGOs are involved in trying to practice elements of the MDGs. States will simply not be able or willing to effectively tackle all MDG-problems. Bringing in other actors is then an issue of effectiveness as well as morality, as discussed in this chapter. It is clear that the core of the obligations rests with the national States as well as with the international community of States. But it is also clear that that model falls short of a sense of reality, given the interests of individual States, given some less positive characteristics of the world 'community' of States, and, above all, given the huge problems presented by, *inter alia*, the MDGs.

Finally, it is sometimes said that linking the realisation of the MDGs to the notion of moral duties for everyone is a matter of moral panic. My reaction to

[35] Ibid., p. 10.

that is that we should keep in mind the word 'moral' and forget about the word 'panic'. The problems are huge, no doubt, and do indeed require a response driven by human rights and morality, leading to the formulation and acceptance of legal and moral duties for 'every individual and every organ in society' (Preamble UDHR). 'Panic', however, sounds too much like 'a non-arguable moral flight forward' and that, to my mind, is not the case.

STEERING CLEAR OF THE TWIN SHOALS OF A RIGHTS-BASED MORALITY AND A DUTY-BASED LEGALITY

Douglass Cassel

In considering the extent to which human rights must be matched by human responsibilities, we might begin by asking, responsibilities of whom? International law imposes manifold duties on *States* to respect, ensure and fulfil human rights.[1] It places duties on non-state organisations as well.[2] For example, international labour law calls on *business corporations* not to employ forced labour,[3] while international humanitarian law binds armed *guerrilla groups* not to attack civilians.[4]

This essay focuses on a particular class of duty bearers: individual human beings as they relate to one another and to society at the community, national and international levels. In the terms suggested by René Foqué in this volume, the first two parts of this essay argue that morally-based 'duties' and ethically-based 'responsibilities' are and should be more demanding than mere reciprocal respect for rights. The essay then goes on to contend that these higher moral and ethical standards cannot safely or feasibly be incorporated in what Foqué calls legally-based 'obligations'.[5]

1 e.g. United Nations Human Rights Committee, General Comment No. 31 [80] Nature of the General Legal Obligation Imposed on States Parties to the Covenant, 26 May 2004, CCPR/C/21/Rev.1/Add.13. (General Comments), paras. 5–8.

2 See generally A. Clapham, *Human Rights Obligations of Non-State Actors*, Oxford, 2006.

3 e.g. Organization for Economic Cooperation and Development, *Guidelines for Multinational Enterprises*, part IV, www.oecd.org/daf/investment/guidelines.

4 e.g. Protocol Additional to the Geneva Conventions of 12 August 1949, and relating to the Protection of Victims of Non-International Armed Conflicts (Protocol II), 8 June 1977, entered into force, 7 December 1978, Art. 1.1.

5 R. Foqué, 'Human Rights and Human Responsibilities: Setting the Ethical and the Conceptual Scene', in this volume, text at notes 46–53.

1. THE POVERTY OF A RIGHTS-BASED MORALITY

Before considering individual obligations in a legal sense, I prefer to begin from an ethical or religious perspective. An erudite philosopher once suggested (or quipped) that human rights were the 'new secular religion' of the 20th century.[6] That might be true in much of western Europe, especially if one were to read the Universal Declaration of Human Rights[7] in its original, communitarian understanding, balancing rights with duties in an integral vision of how best to organise society in order to enrich human development and happiness.[8] However, if human rights are understood through the interpretative lens more prevalent in practice over the last sixty years – as entitlements of individuals[9] – then it diminishes the divine to elevate human rights to the theological plane.

A society based on rights-claims alone is not in and of itself a moral society. As commonly articulated in the form of individual entitlements, human rights can be exercised in ways which are inherently selfish. Human rights speak of *my* rights, *my* entitlements, *my* legal space, *my* dignity, *my* body, *my* privacy, and so on. Of course, in a world where the individual is often assaulted by State brutality or repression, these entitlements indeed have their urgency. They must be recognised, cherished and safeguarded. By themselves, however, they do not suffice to construct a moral society. They do not convey the full dimension of the relationship between the individual and the other, whether that other is another individual or a collectivity of other persons. As the eminent theologian Hans Küng insists: 'No rights without responsibilities!'[10]

The necessity of a concept of responsibility, moreover, has been recognised at least since the dawn of western human rights commitments during the Enlightenment. As Küng reminds us,

> '[T]his concern is by no means new, but goes back to the "founding period" of human rights. The demand was already made in the debate about human rights in the French Revolutionary Parliament of 1789: If one proclaims a Declaration of Human *Rights* one should combine it with a Declaration of Human *Responsibilities*. ... Nearly half of the Revolutionary Parliament who voted for the Declaration of Human Rights voted also for a proclamation of human responsibilities'.[11]

6 J. Maritain, *Man and the State*, 1951, pp. 110–111.

7 UNGA Res. 217 A (III), 10 Dec. 1948.

8 See generally M.A. Glendon, '*Propter Honoris Respectum*: Knowing the Universal Declaration of Human Rights' (1998) 73 *Notre Dame L. Rev.* 1153.

9 A typical formulation asserts, 'Human rights are also grounded in positive law theory, according to which rights are entitlements of individuals and groups that are affirmed and protected by the laws of an organized society, whether national or international.' C. Easley, S. Marks and R. Morgan, 'The Challenge and Place of International Human Rights in Public Health' (2001) 91 *Am. J. Public Health* 1922–1925.

10 Hans Küng, *Global Ethics and Human Responsibilities*, 2005, www.scu.edu/ethics/practicing/focusareas/global_ethics/laughlin-lectures/global-ethic-human-responsibility.html.

11 Ibid.

Küng further reminds us that during the drafting of the Universal Declaration of Human Rights in the late 1940s, Mahatma Gandhi, who was consulted about the Declaration, wrote that '[t]he Ganges of rights originates in the Himalayan of responsibilities'.[12]

To a degree, even the classic, individualistic articulation of modern international human rights recognises this truth. But only up to a point. Human rights treaties and jurisprudence enjoin us to respect the rights of others[13] and to be tolerant of physical differences (race, gender, etc.)[14] and of divergent views (on politics, religion, etc.).[15] At most, however, this classic conceptualisation calls for mutual tolerance and respect. In safeguarding free expression, for instance, human rights teaches that – however much I may despise both you and what you say[16] – I must respect your right to say it (within broad limits; I need not accept defamation, for example).[17] In other words, I do not care for you in the least, but I will neither silence you nor step on you.

Is this the best we can hope for among members of the human family?

2. A RELIGIOUS PERSPECTIVE

Not if we look to religion. No major religion embraces so parched a perspective on how human beings should treat each other. In fact, not a legalistic and minimalist concept of 'rights', but a much more comprehensive concept of 'love' can be said to be central to the major faiths and belief systems of this world, including, for example, Buddhism, the Baha'i faith, Confucianism, Judaism, Hinduism, Christianity and Islam.[18]

---

12 Ibid.

13 e.g. International Covenant on Civil and Political Rights, UNGA Res. 2200A (XXI), 16 December 1966, entered into force, 23 March 1976 (ICCPR), Art. 19(3), which provides that the exercise of the right to freedom of expression 'carries with it special duties and responsibilities. It may therefore be subject to certain restrictions, but these shall only be such as are provided by law and are necessary: (a) For respect of the rights or reputations of others; …'.

14 e.g. International Convention on the Elimination of all Forms of Racial Discrimination, UNGA Res. 2106 (XX), 21 December 1965, entered into force 4 January 1969.

15 e.g. Declaration on the Elimination of All Forms of Intolerance and of Discrimination Based on Religion or Belief, UNGA Res. 36/55, 25 November 1981. The European Court of Human Rights broadly interprets freedom of expression in light of the 'demands of that pluralism, tolerance and broadmindedness without which there is no "democratic society" …': ECtHR, *Lingens v. Austria*, App. No. 9815/82, Judgment of 8 July 1986, para. 41.

16 e.g. ibid. (freedom of expression protects not only favorable or indifferent ideas, but also those that 'offend, shock or disturb').

17 Ibid., para. 42.

18 See, for example, the summary prepared by Stephen M. Apatow, on the web page of the Interfaith News Network, www.humanitarian.net/interfaith/studycenter/Omnia_vincit_amor.

Consequently, the concepts of individual duty and individual responsibility – not individual rights – take centre stage.[19] Two decades ago the Parliament of the World's Religions recognised the following as a 'minimal *fundamental consensus*': 'Every form of egoism should be rejected: All selfishness, whether individual or collective ... Self-determination and self-realisation are thoroughly legitimate so long as they are not separated from human self-responsibility and global responsibility, that is, from responsibility for fellow humans and for the planet Earth.'[20]

In Christian faith, for instance, the teaching of Jesus Christ is far more ambitious than a mere rights-claims approach. Christ calls on us to love one another.[21] What is required is not merely to tolerate, not merely to respect the rights of others, but to endeavour to *love* them – to open and extend one's heart with empathy and affection, to care for others as much as for oneself.[22]

For most of us, it is difficult to live up to that ideal: how many of us can find it in our hearts to love, for example, a terrorist? Yet Christian teaching challenges us to love even our enemies[23] and to distinguish the evil from the evildoer.[24]

The poverty of a morality based merely on rights-claims can be illustrated with respect to any human right. Consider, for example, the most fundamental human right: the right to life. Human rights law protects my right to live by prohibiting arbitrary deprivation of my life by the State.[25] But it imposes no duty to sacrifice my own or anyone else's life.[26] In contrast, Christian morality, like

19 See for example P.G. Lauren, *The Evolution of International Human Rights: Visions Seen*, Philadelphia: University of Pennsylvania Press, 2011, pp. 6–11; D. Hodgson, *Individual Duty within a Human Rights Discourse*, Aldershot: Ashgate Publishing, 2003, pp. 41–60.

20 Parliament of the World's Religions, *Declaration Toward a Global Ethic*, 4 September 1993, Chicago, pp. 3, 7; *accord*, Pope Francis, Encyclical, *Laudato Si'*, 2015, para. 208 ('Disinterested concern for others, and the rejection of every form of self-centeredness and self-absorption, are essential if we truly wish to care for our brothers and sisters and for the natural environment').

21 Gospel of Matthew 22: 37–40.

22 Gospel of Matthew 22: 39. In his Encyclical *Pacem in Terris*, 11 April 1963, para. 35, Pope John XXIII taught, '[h]uman society, as We here picture it, demands that men be guided by justice, respect the rights of others and do their duty. It demands, too, that they be animated by such love as will make them feel the needs of others as their own, and induce them to share their goods with others ...'.

23 Jesus taught that we should love our enemies and pray for those who persecute us. Gospel of Matthew, 5:44.

24 e.g. *Pacem in Terris*, Encyclical of Pope John XXIII, 11 April 1963, para. 158 ('It is always perfectly justifiable to distinguish between error as such and the person who falls into error – even in the case of men who err regarding the truth or are led astray as a result of their inadequate knowledge, in matters either of religion or of the highest ethical standards. A man who has fallen into error does not cease to be a man. He never forfeits his personal dignity ...').

25 ICCPR, Art. 6(1); European Convention on Human Rights (ECHR), Art. 2.

26 e.g. Rome Statute of the International Criminal Court, 17 July 1998, entered into force 1 July 2002, Art. 31(1)(d) (no criminal responsibility for an act 'caused by duress resulting from a threat of imminent death or of continuing or imminent serious bodily harm against that person or another person, and the person acts necessarily and reasonably to avoid this threat, provided that the person does not intend to cause a greater harm than the one sought to be avoided').

other religious traditions, is much richer and far more ambitious: Christ teaches that there is no greater love than to lay down one's life for another.[27]

In fact, the actual practice of human rights often surpasses its minimalist doctrine. One regularly meets human right defenders, in all parts of the world, who are prepared to lay down their lives for others. All too many, in fact, have done so. The conditions in which human rights defenders in many countries live and work are often difficult and dangerous.[28] By their behaviour, then, human rights defenders recognise the poverty of a rights-based morality. Even though they have every right to huddle for safety in their homes or to flee to another country, they instead venture forth, at risk of life and limb, to defend the rights of others. By their practice they proclaim that human rights are indispensable, but not sufficient, as the ethical foundation of a humane world.

Human responsibilities are thus embedded, not only in religious and ethical traditions,[29] but also in the instinctual reactions of many human rights defenders to evil. But should human responsibilities also be codified internationally in quasi-legal declarations or legally binding treaties?

3. AFFIRMATIVE DUTIES IN INTERNATIONAL HUMAN RIGHTS INSTRUMENTS

Duties are articulated most prominently and affirmatively in three of the international instruments recognising a broad range of human rights.[30] Two are Declarations, both dating from 1948, neither meant to be legally binding at the time: the Universal Declaration of Human Rights,[31] and the American

27 Gospel of John, 15:13.

28 e.g. United Nations Human Rights Council, *Report of the Special Rapporteur on the situation of human rights defenders, Observations on communications transmitted to Governments and replies received*, UN Doc. A/HRC/28/63/Add.1, 4 March 2015.

29 For ethical perspectives on human responsibilities, see generally the chapter contributed by René Foqué in this volume, 'Human Rights and Human Responsibilities: Setting the Ethical and the Conceptual Scene'.

30 These are not the only ones. See also e.g. League of Arab States, *Arab Charter on Human Rights*, 22 May 2004, reprinted in (2005) 12 *Int'l Hum. Rts. Rep.* 893, entry into force 15 March 2008, Art. 1(3) (Charter aims include: 'To prepare the new generations in Arab States for a free and responsible life in a civil society that is characterized by solidarity, founded on a balance between awareness of rights and respect for obligations, ...'); Association of Southeast Asian Nations, *ASEAN Human Rights Declaration*, 19 November 2012, www.asean.org/news/asean-statement-communiques/item/asean-human-rights-declaration, Art. 6 ('The enjoyment of human rights and fundamental freedoms must be balanced with the performance of corresponding duties as every person has responsibilities to all other individuals, the community and the society where one lives ...'); *Cairo Declaration on Human Rights in Islam*, 5 August 1990, UN GAOR, World Conf. on Hum. Rts., 4th Sess., Agenda Item 5, UN Doc. A/CONF.157/PC/62/Add.18 (1993) (English translation), Art. 1(a) ('All men are equal in terms of basic human dignity and basic obligations and responsibilities').

31 UNGA Res. 217 A (III), 10 December 1948.

Declaration of the Rights and Duties of Man.[32] The third is a treaty adopted in 1981: the African Charter of Human and Peoples' Rights.[33]

3.1. UNIVERSAL DECLARATION OF HUMAN RIGHTS

The Universal Declaration of Human Rights articulates human responsibilities only in a brief, general way. Echoing the concept of *fraternité* from the French Revolution,[34] Article 1 proclaims that all human beings 'should act towards one another in a spirit of brotherhood.' Article 29(1) implicitly recognises that rights and responsibilities are mutually dependent, stating that '[e]veryone has duties to the community in which alone the free and full development of his personality is possible.' These philosophical statements serve mainly as interpretive guides for the more specific rights set forth in the Declaration.[35] In contrast, both the American Declaration and the African Charter more specifically enumerate human responsibilities.

3.2. AMERICAN DECLARATION OF THE RIGHTS AND DUTIES OF MAN

The American Declaration – adopted six months prior to final approval of the Universal Declaration by the United Nations General Assembly[36] – joins a stronger philosophical emphasis on duties with an explicit listing of certain basic duties.

The philosophical emphasis is reflected in the Preamble, five of whose six paragraphs concern duties. After an initial paragraph proclaiming universal dignity and rights, the second preambular paragraph makes clear that duties are essential concomitants of rights. It states that '[t]he fulfillment of duty by each individual is a prerequisite to the rights of all. Rights and duties are interrelated in every social and political activity of man. While rights exalt individual liberty, duties express the dignity of that liberty.' The third paragraph relates legal to moral duties, explaining that '[d]uties of a juridical nature presuppose others of a moral nature which support them in principle and constitute their basis.'

---

32 Res. XXX, Final Act of the Ninth International Conference of American States, Bogotá, Colombia, 30 March–2 May 1948, p. 38 (PAU 1948).

33 Adopted 27 June 1981, OAU Doc. CAB/LEG/67/3 rev. 5, 21 ILM 58 (1982), entered into force 21 October 1986.

34 Even today, article 2 of the 1958 Constitution of France states in part, '*La devise de la République est 'Liberté, Egalité, Fraternité*'.

35 See M.A. Glendon, '*Propter Honoris Respectum*: Knowing the Universal Declaration of Human Rights' (1998) 73 *Notre Dame L. Rev.* 1153, 1168–1169.

36 The American Declaration was adopted in May 1948, and the Universal Declaration in December 1948.

Both these paragraphs may be viewed as universally applicable philosophical statements. The remaining three paragraphs, in contrast, reflect the distinctively Christian religious heritage of the Americas. They ground duties in the supreme goal of 'spiritual development,' as expressed through culture and moral conduct.[37]

Chapter 2 of the Declaration lists certain basic duties. Most broadly, Article 29 states, '[i]t is the duty of the individual so to conduct himself in relation to others that each and every one may fully form and develop his personality.' Without going so far as the religious injunction to love one another, this goes perhaps as far as one might expect an intergovernmental declaration to go in promoting social solidarity. While lacking the clarity and precision needed to be useful in practice, it is at worst innocuous and at best inspirational.

The remaining duties are more specific. They assert the duties of parents toward their children and of children toward parents;[38] the duty of 'every person' to acquire education, to vote, to obey the law, to cooperate in regard to social security and welfare, to pay taxes, to work, and to refrain from unlawful political activities in other countries;[39] and the duty of every 'able-bodied' person to perform military or alternative service and to hold public office when elected.[40] Some of these – such as the duties to obey the law and to pay taxes – articulate obligations that are legally enforceable in most countries. Others are by nature not likely to be deemed justiciable. Core aspects of the duty to respect one's parents cannot be legislatively defined or judicially enforced. Nor can the duty to treat others so that they may fully develop their personalities.

The American Declaration was not thought to be legally binding at the time of its adoption.[41] Thus the drafters were free to list both moral and legal duties. Although the Declaration has subsequently acquired legally enforceable status (as an 'authoritative interpretation' of the freedoms referred to in the Charter of the Organisation of American States),[42] the Declaration's duties have rarely if ever been treated as independent sources of legal obligation.[43] Hence there is little or no risk of mischievous interpretations of some of the more vaguely worded duties.

37 These paragraphs state: 'Inasmuch as spiritual development is the supreme end of human existence and the highest expression thereof, it is the duty of man to serve that end with all his strength and resources'; 'Since culture is the highest social and historical expression of that spiritual development, it is the duty of man to preserve, practice and foster culture by every means within his power'; 'And, since moral conduct constitutes the noblest flowering of culture, it is the duty of every man always to hold it in high respect.'

38 Art. 30.

39 Arts. 31–33 and 35–38.

40 Art. 34.

41 IACtHR, Advisory Opinion OC-10/89, *Interpretation of the American Declaration of the Rights and Duties of Man within the Framework of Article 64 of the American Convention on Human Rights*, 14 July 1989, Series A, no. 10, para. 34.

42 Ibid., paras. 42, 43 and 45.

43 No examples of such treatment appear, for example, in a lengthy compilation of Commission decisions published in 1994. See *Inter-American Commission of Human Rights: Individual Case Resolutions* (1994) 10 *Am. J. Int'l L. & Policy* 27.

3.3. AFRICAN CHARTER OF HUMAN AND PEOPLES' RIGHTS

The same cannot be said of the African Charter on Human and Peoples' Rights. Some aspects of the African Charter are similar to the American Declaration. Philosophically, the Preamble to the Charter states succinctly that 'the enjoyment of rights and freedoms also implies the performance of duties on the part of everyone.' Like the American Declaration, the Charter declares the duty of respect within the family, the duty to work and the duty to pay taxes.[44]

But the full catalogue of duties in the African Charter is distinctive, reflecting its immediate post-colonial origins. One duty is a salutary response to the legacy of Africa's victimisation by racism and slavery: the duty of everyone to 'respect and consider his fellow beings without discrimination, and to maintain relations aimed at promoting, safeguarding and reinforcing mutual respect and tolerance.'[45]

The Charter sets forth additional duties, however, which add up to a nationalist, statist, regionalist and collectivist agenda. They include the duties of 'every individual':

- to 'family and society, the State and other legally recognised communities and the international community';[46]
- to the 'national community, by placing one's physical and intellectual abilities at its service';[47]
- to the 'security of the State';[48]
- to 'social and national solidarity, particularly when the latter is threatened';[49]
- to the national independence and territorial integrity of one's country and to its defence;[50]
- to 'positive African cultural values' and the 'moral well-being of society';[51] and
- to 'promotion and achievement of African unity'.[52]

Taken together, these duties might be interpreted to justify draconian restrictions on human rights to free expression, association and assembly.[53] Peaceful political dissent in Robert Mugabe's Zimbabwe, for example, might be repressed on the purported ground that it threatens 'social and national solidarity'.

---

44 Arts. 29(1) and 29(6).
45 Art. 28.
46 Art. 27(1).
47 Art. 29(2).
48 Art. 29(3).
49 Art. 29(4).
50 Art. 29(5).
51 Art. 29(7).
52 Art. 29(8).
53 M. wa Mutua, 'The Banjul Charter and the African Cultural Fingerprint: An Evaluation of the Language of Duties' (1995) 35 *Va. J. Int'l L.* 339, 359, 372–374.

Thankfully, the African Commission on Human Rights has not interpreted these duties in such a restrictive manner; on the contrary.[54] Although at least one prominent scholar argues in defence of the inclusion of duties in the Charter,[55] on its face the African Charter illustrates the potential risks to rights posed by broadly worded enumerations of duties.

4. DUTIES AS RESTRICTIONS ON RIGHTS

To some extent the risk that broadly worded duties may be interpreted to justify severe restrictions on rights is unavoidable in international human rights law. Even without including a catalogue of duties, the European Convention on Human Rights (like other comprehensive human rights treaties)[56] permits restrictions on rights to private and family life, and to home and correspondence, in the interests of:

- national security;
- public safety or economic well-being;
- prevention of disorder or crime;
- protection of health or morals; and
- protection of the rights and freedoms of others.[57]

The Convention authorises restrictions on similar grounds of the rights to free expression, assembly, association and manifestation of religion.[58] And all Convention rights are subject to the general restriction that they may not be used to destroy rights or to limit them more than allowed by the Convention.[59] Such grounds of restriction are not formulated in the language of duty. Nonetheless, in effect they reflect duties: to cooperate in safeguarding national security and public safety, to respect the rights of others, and so on.

Even so, there are important differences between affirmative statements of duty, as in the African Charter, and the duties implicit in grounds for restricting rights, as in the European Convention. First, restrictions on rights can be imposed only when rights are actually or potentially exercised, whereas affirmatively

54 e.g. *Constitutional Rights Project et al. v. Nigeria*, Comm. Nos. 140/94, 141/94, and 145/95, Decision of 15 November 1999, paras. 40–44. See generally M. Evans and R. Murray (eds.), *The African Charter on Human and Peoples' Rights: The System in Practice*, 1986–2006, 2nd ed., 2008.

55 M. wa Mutua, 'The Banjul Charter and the African Cultural Fingerprint: An Evaluation of the Language of Duties' (1995) 35 *Va. J. Int'l L.* 339, 359–380.

56 ICCPR, Arts. 12(3), 18(3), 19(3), 21 and 22(2); American Convention on Human Rights, OAS T.S. B-32, 22 November 1969, entered into force 18 July 1978, Arts. 12(3), 13(2), 15, 16(2), 21(2), 22(3) and 30.

57 Art. 8(2).

58 Arts. 9(2), 10(2) and 11(2).

59 Art. 17.

asserted duties may be enforced even against passive citizens, leaving no room for escape. Restrictions on freedom of assembly, for example, are sometimes imposed by democratic societies in the interest of public order. But an affirmative duty to contribute to national solidarity might be invoked by authoritarian regimes to compel otherwise passive citizens to join pro-government assemblies. Secondly, restrictions on rights are also less likely than affirmative duties to be judicially interpreted to justify broad restrictions on rights. The general rule in instruments like the European Convention is to guarantee rights; restrictions are exceptions to the rule, and must be specially justified. With regard to many rights, the European Convention reflects this general rule by expressly requiring that restrictions be 'necessary in a democratic society'.[60] The European Court of Human Rights interprets this requirement to impose tests for both ends and means: restrictions on rights must be necessary to meet a 'pressing social need,' and must do so only by narrowly tailored, 'proportional' means.[61] The Inter-American Court of Human Rights imposes similar tests.[62] In contrast, the affirmative statements of both rights and duties in the African Charter might be read to give them equal juridical status, thus shifting the balance against rights.

In reality, of course, given the indeterminacy of the language, whether in the grounds for restrictions of rights, or in the formulation of duties, what matters most is the value orientation of those who interpret the language. Just as the European Court of Human Rights narrowly interprets the permissible grounds of restrictions of rights, so, too, the African Commission on Human Rights narrowly interprets the extent to which African Charter rights may be restricted in service of African Charter duties.

5. CODIFICATIONS OF DUTIES

Problems similar to those suggested by the African Charter arise, in more across-the-board fashion, in comprehensive Declarations of human responsibilities. One scholar identifies at least a dozen such Declarations.[63] They are not without scholarly supporters.[64] However, while such Declarations may be ethically and morally admirable, from a legal standpoint they are often too vague to

60 Arts. 8(2), 9(2), 10(2) and 11(2).

61 e.g. *Observer and Guardian v. UK*, App. No. 13585/88, Judgment of 26 November 1991, A216, para. 59(c) and (d).

62 e.g. IACtHR, Advisory Opinion OC-5/85, *Compulsory Membership in an Association Prescribed by Law for the Practice of Journalism (Arts. 13 and 29 American Convention on Human Rights)*, 13 November 1985, Series A No. 5, para. 46.

63 S. McGregor, 'Human Responsibility Movement Initiatives: A Comparative Analysis' (2013) 7 *In Factis Pax* 1, 7 and n. 38.

64 Ibid.; S. McGregor, 'Augmenting Human Rights with Human Responsibilities', *Global Education Magazine*, 10 December 2013; K. Suter, 'The Quest for Human Responsibilities to Complement Human Rights' (2010) 26 *Medicine, Conflict and Survival* 201; see also L. Kostakidis-Lianos and G. Williams, 'Bills of Responsibilities: Is one needed to counter the

be practically useful, too minimalist to be elevating or too ambitious to be enforced, and ultimately too prone to abuse through opportunistically repressive interpretations of vague language.[65]

One problem in giving legal weight to such declarations is that some duties they assert are too vacuous to be useful in practice. An extreme example is found in the Universal Declaration of Human Responsibilities, proposed by the InterAction Council in September 1997.[66] Article 3 of that document declares that '[e]veryone has a responsibility to promote good and avoid evil in all things.' As an ethical proposition one could hardly disagree. But as a statement intended to carry any sort of legal weight, what – in substance – does it mean? Humankind has debated what is 'good' at least since the time of Aristotle. Without more specific guidance, this would add nothing to the law.

In fairness one must point out that the sponsors of the Universal Declaration of Human Responsibilities disclaim any intention to treat it as a legal document. They explicitly stated that:

> 'Legal codification is impossible in moral attitudes like truthfulness and fairness. It [The Declaration] aims at voluntarily taking responsibility. The Responsibilities Declaration is morally rather than legally binding. All these are the question of conscience and not the question of law. The Declaration appeals to the ethical impetus of individuals.'[67]

Nonetheless, lest others over time seek to treat the Declaration as a document setting forth legal obligations (as has happened with the Universal Declaration of Human Rights), its deficiencies as a potential articulation of legally binding norms are worth noting.

In addition to legally impractical invocations of good and evil, a second problem is a tendency to reach too low. Some duties are expressed in too minimalist a fashion to contribute much to human solidarity. For instance, Article 4 of the same proposed Universal Declaration declares, '[w]hat you do not wish to be done to yourself, do not do to others'. Aside from its inherent vagueness, this negative statement of the golden rule is a far cry from the positive version: 'do unto others as you would have them do unto you'. It equates to 'do not abuse others', a standard far lower than 'treat them as well as you would wish to be treated.'

"excesses" of the ACT Human Rights Act 2004?' (2005) 30 *Alternative Law J.* 58, 62 (criticising failed Australian Bill of Responsibilities, but supporting continued debate).

65 See generally J. Knox, 'Horizontal Human Rights Law' (2008) 102 *Am. J. Int'l Law* 1; Amnesty International, *Muddying the waters: The Draft Universal Declaration of Human Responsibilities: No Complement to Human Rights* [IOR 40/02/98] (1998).

66 See www.interactioncouncil.org/universal-declaration-human-responsibilities.

67 *Dissemination of the Universal Declaration of Human Responsibilities*, 1998, para. 14, http://interactioncouncil.org/dissemination-of-the-universal-declaration-of-human-responsibilities.

A third problem is the opposite: some ethical injunctions aim too high to be meaningfully enforced. Article 8 of the aforesaid Declaration, for example, exhorts, '[e]very person has a responsibility to behave with integrity, honesty and fairness.' Again setting aside the vagueness, this may be a noble ideal, but how many of us can always live up to it? Would any of us want government enforcers to monitor our compliance?

A final – and the most serious – problem is the potential for abuse by repressive regimes or rulers. Consider, for example, Article 12 of the pre-Draft Declaration of Human Social Responsibilities, issued by the United Nations Special Rapporteur on 'Human Rights and Human Responsibilities' in 2003.[68] Article 12 declares that every person has the duty to exercise his or her rights with due respect 'for the security of his or her society and the morality prevailing in it'. Such language might be used to justify violations of civil liberties in the 'war on terrorism', or assaults on the dignity of gay people by virtue of the 'prevailing' morality in many societies.

One might respond that restrictions on rights for reasons of security and morality are already permitted by international human rights law. But as noted in the preceding section, restrictions on rights are generally interpreted narrowly by human rights courts and commissions. In contrast, the duties stated in the pre-draft Declaration are declared to enjoy 'equal value' with rights.[69] Asserting an 'unbreakable link' between rights and duties, the Preamble explicitly rejects any 'insistence on favouring the rights of the individual.'[70] This approach would appear to justify far greater restrictions on rights than currently allowed.

The European Union Presidency responded by rejecting the pre-draft Declaration. While accepting that 'members of any society have responsibilities towards each other, towards the community and towards a democratic society,' the EU rightly repudiates the 'idea that a State can determine which rights an individual can enjoy in return for the exercise of responsibilities'.[71] Perhaps in consequence, after showing some interest by a close vote in 2004,[72] the UN Commission on Human Rights in 2005 requested the Special Rapporteur to redraft the pre-Draft Declaration,[73] in light of criticisms received mainly from

68 UN Human Rights Commission, Sub-commission on the Promotion and Protection of Human Rights, *Final Report of the Special Rapporteur on Human Rights and Responsibilities*, UN Doc. E/CN.4/2003/105/Annex I.

69 Pre-Draft Declaration, Art. 5.

70 8th and 9th preambular paragraphs.

71 EU Presidency Statement – Human Rights and Human Responsibilities – ECOSOC, 22 July 2004, http://eu-un.europa.eu/articles/es/article_3700_es.htm.

72 On 21 April 2004, by Decision 2004/117, adopted by a vote of 26–25 with two abstentions, the Commission requested the High Commissioner for Human Rights to disseminate the pre-Draft Declaration for comment. UN Commission on Human Rights, *Report on the 60th Session*, UN Doc. E/2004/23 and E/CN.4/2004/127, p. 333.

73 On 20 April 2005, the Commission, by a vote of 26–25 with one abstention, requested the Special Rapporteur to prepare a 'new initial version of the pre-draft declaration', taking into

European states.[74] In 2006 (its last session before going out of existence) the Commission appears to have abandoned the effort altogether.[75]

One might object to the foregoing critique by noting that the examples of duties and codifications relied upon are selective, and that a more carefully crafted declaration of responsibilities might avoid posing a threat to human rights.[76] Perhaps so. But the discussion here focuses on two leading recent draft Declarations and on some of their key provisions. There is reason to be sceptical that artful drafting can avoid the kinds of problems they illustrate.

6. 'HORIZONTAL' VERSUS 'VERTICAL' DUTIES

In evaluating Declarations of human responsibilities, US scholar John Knox distinguishes between 'horizontal' and 'vertical' duties.[77] In his argument, horizontal duties are owed directly by individuals to others, thus presenting relatively little risk of being converted into instruments of State repression. In contrast, vertical duties are owed by individuals to the State, indirectly to protect other persons. However, because they open the door to broad or arbitrary interpretations by State authorities, Declarations of vertical duties pose a risk of justifying State repression.[78]

account the comments received. UN Commission on Human Rights, *Report on the 61st Session*, UN Doc. E/2005/23 and E/CN.4/2005/135, p. 344.

74 After circulating the pre-Draft Declaration for comment, the High Commissioner for Human Rights received 27 replies from governments, two from inter-governmental organisations (including the European Commission) and one from Amnesty International. Most of the commenting governments were European. Apparently all but two commenting governments (Russia and Cuba) opposed the pre-Draft Declaration, mainly on the ground that it would undermine human rights by making their enjoyment conditional on fulfillment of duties. Report of the Office of the High Commissioner for Human Rights, *Compilation of the essential aspects of replies received on the pre-draft declaration on human social responsibilities*, UN Doc. E/CN.4/2005/99, 7 February 2005.

75 When the Commission ceased to exist in 2006, the thematic mandate on human rights and human responsibilities was not among those mandates it referred to the new Human Rights Council. UN Commission on Human Rights, *Report on the 62nd Session*, UN Doc. E/2006/23 and E/CN.4/2006/122, pp. 1–4.

76 A lawyerlike effort is the *Declaration of Responsibilities and Human Duties*, adopted in 2002 by a group of prominent persons chaired by Judge Richard Goldstone, under the auspices of the City of Valencia and UNESCO, http://globalization.icaap.org/content/v2.2/declare.html. Article 1 of the Declaration carefully distinguishes between 'duty', defined to mean an 'ethical or moral obligation', and 'responsibility', defined to mean an 'obligation that is legally binding under existing international law.' Most of the legally binding 'responsibilities' in the Declaration fall on States and other entities, while most references to individuals in the Declaration concern only their ethical 'duties'. Moreover, because the foregoing definition of legally binding 'responsibilities' includes only '*existing*' legal obligations, the Declaration does not purport to create any *new* legal obligations for individuals.

77 J. Knox, 'Horizontal Human Rights Law' (2008) 102 *Am. J. Int'l Law* 1–2.

78 Ibid., p. 20 ('Oppressive governments have regularly sought language setting out duties on individuals to serve as a pretext for restricting their rights').

The distinction is valid in the sense that statements of vertical duties are more easily prone to State abuse than are statements of horizontal duties. This can be illustrated by, for example, the Declaration of Responsibilities and Human Duties, adopted in 2002 by a group of luminaries chaired by Judge Richard Goldstone, under the authority of UNESCO and the City of Valencia, Spain.[79] The Declaration distinguishes between ethical or moral 'duties' and legally binding 'responsibilities.'[80] The horizontal legal responsibilities it imposes on individuals seem, at first, unobjectionable. For example, the Declaration recognises horizontal responsibilities of individuals not to commit, condone or support slavery, torture or enforced disappearances.[81] In contrast, the vertical duties it imposes – 'not to condone, support or participate in any manner in the commission of crime'[82] – invite abuse. They allow no exception, whether for unjust laws, or for laws which are just in and of themselves but which support unjust regimes. They would condemn, for example, the national liberation struggle against the Apartheid regime in South Africa, or sit-ins by the civil rights movement in the USA in the 1960s.

Yet even the Declaration's well-intentioned affirmations of horizontal duties are not risk-free. Consider its injunction that individuals have a legally binding responsibility not to 'condone' torture. Might that not legitimise overbroad prosecutions of human rights defenders for 'justification' of terrorism, as were conducted in the 1990s by the Fujimori regime in Peru?[83]

Granted, any law can be abused. But sweeping declarations that individuals have legally binding, human responsibilities – especially vertical, but even horizontal responsibilities – inherently risk dignifying State repression of human rights.

7. CONCLUSION

To the extent that declarations of human responsibilities aspire to legal – as opposed to ethical – status, they pose a significant risk of hindering, rather than promoting, morally admirable conduct. They add little of substance to ensure performance of moral duty, while exposing hard-won human rights guarantees to the danger of abusive restrictions and conditions.

This conclusion need not counsel complacency in accepting current articulations of human rights as comprehensive ethical guides. While rights must be legally guaranteed, their articulation as law also sends an ethical message. To

---

79 *Declaration of Responsibilities and Human Duties*, 2002.

80 Ibid., Art. 1(a) and (b).

81 Ibid., Arts. 23(2), 24(2) and 25(2).

82 Ibid., Art. 14(4).

83 See e.g. IACtHR, *Provisional Measures, Chipoco Case*, Decision of 27 January 1993, www.corteidh.or.cr/docs/medidas/chipoco_se_02_ing.pdf.

the extent this message exalts only individual entitlements, without due regard for individual responsibilities, it is one-sided.

We must accept neither the poverty of a rights-based morality, nor the perils of a duty-based legality. While ensuring rights in law, we must also teach the need for a richer and more ambitious morality, one based on more than minimally acceptable tolerance of other people. What Christians and members of many faiths call love, others may prefer to call empathy, compassion or solidarity. By whatever name, a rich and fulfilling morality respects the self, but strives to care as much for the other and for the community as well.

HUMAN DUTIES AND RESPONSIBILITIES FOR THE REINFORCEMENT OF HUMAN RIGHTS

The Declaration of Human Duties and Responsibilities (1998)

Patricia Morales*

'The Declaration under discussion here not only represents an inaugural announcement, but also a formal undertaking'
Norberto Bobbio

The aim of this chapter is to offer a contribution to the discussion on the moral and legal interrelation of rights, duties and responsibilities, inspired by the unique approach of the *Valencia Declaration of Human Duties and Responsibilities*[1] (DHDR) (1998). This declaration attempted, for the first time, to comprehensively reveal the role and importance of duties and responsibilities contained in our human rights systems and to identify their bearers. This chapter is intended as an overview of the various provisions in the declaration. I will also make reference to other initiatives appealing to global responsibility, such as, for instance, the *UN Millennium Declaration* (2000) and the UN's *The Future We Want* (2012).

In this chapter, the DHDR will be considered in light of the *Universal Declaration of Human Rights* (UDHR) (1948) and also as an inspired input to

* I am very grateful to Prof. Stephan Parmentier, University of Leuven, and Prof. Paul Lemmens, University of Leuven, for the opportunity to take part in the Conference on Fundamental Rights and Responsibilities back in 2006. I also thank Justice Richard Goldstone for his enormous talent to comprehend the human condition as well as the instruments needed for the protection of the dignity and rights of all members of the human family. Last but not least, I would like to thank Karl-Otto Apel and Ricardo Maliandi for their enormous efforts in rethinking the pillars for a universal ethics in the light of our interdependent world. This article is not intended as a legal analysis of the complex problem of rights, duties and responsibilities and their interplay. Rather, it is the account of a privileged witness to the drafting of the 'Declaration of Human Duties and Responsibilities'.

1 R. Goldstone, *Declaration of Human Duties and Responsibilities, Background Documents*, Valencia: Fundación Valencia Tercer Milenio, 1998, pp. 29 ff.

succeeding statements. The UDHR has, since its adoption, played an essential role in the promotion and protection of human rights worldwide. Today it can be held to constitute the moral core of international, regional and national law, hereby exceeding its original purpose.

The DHDR was written on the occasion of the 50th anniversary of the UDHR, under the auspices of UNESCO and the UN High Commissioner of Human Rights. The goal of this new document was to strengthen the implementation of human rights. The approach of the DHDR is, however, decidedly different from that of traditional human rights documents. Rather than focusing on individual rights, it formulates a number of duties and responsibilities which are deemed essential in light of our global interdependence. Its preamble states categorically:

> 'The effective enjoyment and implementation of human rights and fundamental freedoms is inextricably linked to the assumption of the duties and responsibilities implicit in those rights'.[2]

The DHDR's drafting process was inspired by the need for a transition from a 'formal equality' to a 'substantial equality', with a shared concern for the situation of millions of ignored and marginalised people in our globalised world: 'the recognition of human rights is insufficient … [I]f such rights are to be realized it is necessary that they are enforceable … There must be a duty on all relevant authorities and individuals to enforce those rights.'[3] This perspective was shared by the Italian philosopher Norberto Bobbio, who also supported the text of the DHDR. Bobbio established an interesting comparison between the transition from 'moral rights' to 'legal rights' and the need to transform 'moral duties' into 'legal duties'.[4]

As one of the participants of the Valencia group and an ardent believer in the value of this declaration as a guidance for individual and collective human action in the light of human rights, I believe that it would be beneficial to society in general and to decision-makers, jurists, scientists and other specialists in particular, to put this declaration in the spotlight one more time and frame it within the wider debate on rights, duties and responsibilities.

Continuing the legacy of the UDHR and subsequent human rights instruments, the point of departure of the DHDR is the shared concern among the drafters regarding what they perceive to be the lack of political will to enforce human rights around the world. Moreover, the DHDR specifically aims to take

2 Preamble DHDR.

3 See Justice R. Goldstone, 'Human Rights, Duties and Responsibilities', Interview by Patricia Morales in M.K. Tolba (ed.), *Our Fragile World, Challenges and Opportunities for Sustainable Development*, Oxford: UNESCO-EOLSS, Eolss Publishers, 2001, vol I, III, pp. l-lii.

4 See N. Bobbio, *Declaration*, p. 98. Bobbio holds that 'the same problem valid for rights in the strong sense of the term, i.e., the transformation of "moral rights" into "legal rights", is also valid for duties as concerns their passage from "moral duties" to "legal duties"'.

into account the new challenges in the field of human rights protection brought by technological advances and globalisation. The DHDR does this by translating these challenges into the language of duties and responsibilities.[5]

The value of the DHDR can be best appreciated when we review its 41 articles and compare its content with the 'traditional' human rights formulations as found in the UDHR, as well as in a number of other initiatives such as *The Future We Want*,[6] the *UN Millennium Declaration*,[7] the *Rome Statute*,[8] *the Global Compact*,[9] and several UNESCO declarations and conventions.

1. THE DUTIES AND RESPONSIBILITIES OF THE DHDR

In Article 1 DHDR, 'duty' and 'responsibility' are defined for the purpose of the Declaration: 'duty' means an ethical or moral obligation, and 'responsibility' constitutes an obligation that is legally binding under existing international law.

The DHDR tries to explain, in detail, the complexity of the exercise of duties and responsibilities. The bearers of these duties and responsibilities are all the members of the global community, who have collective as well as individual duties and responsibilities. These include the duty to promote the universal observance of human rights and fundamental freedoms. 'Global community' refers both to States and to non-State actors. It includes international, regional and sub-regional intergovernmental organisations, non-governmental organisations, public and private sector (trans)national corporations, other entities of civil society, peoples, communities and individuals taken as a collective.

The DHDR reflects this myriad of actors that have to be mutually supportive bearers of duties and responsibilities. This is a vastly different approach than adopted by, for instance, the *UN Millennium Declaration* (*MD*). This international document written by and for governments is focused primarily on the duties and responsibilities of States.[10]

5 Para. 16 of the preamble reads as follows: 'Recognising the changes that new technologies, scientific development and the process of globalisation have brought about, and aware of the need to address their impact upon and potential consequences for human rights and fundamental freedoms'.

6 *The Future We Want*, 2012, adopted by the General Assembly in New York on 27 July 2012 (A/RES/66/288).

7 *UN Millennium Declaration*, adopted by the UN General Assembly in New York on 8 September 2000 (A/RES/55/2), www.un.org/millennium/declaration/ares552e.pdf.

8 *Rome Statute of the International Criminal Court*, 1998, adopted by the UN General Assembly in New York on 17 July 1998.

9 See the list of the 10 principles of the *UN Global Compact (1999)*, www.unglobalcompact.org/what-is-gc/mission/principles.

10 UN Millennium Declaration: 'We [heads of State and Government] recognize that, in addition to our separate responsibilities to our individual societies, we have a collective responsibility to uphold the principles of human dignity, equality and equity at the global level. As leaders we have a duty therefore to all the world's people ...' (I. Values and principles, § 2).

Article 2 DHDR focuses on the bearers of duties and responsibilities, as it holds that:

> 'Members of the global community have collective, as well as individual duties and responsibilities, to promote universal respect for and observance of human rights and fundamental freedoms ...'

This declaration considers the existence of collective responsibilities inside the limits set out by universally recognised rights, and the equitably distributed accountability which implicitly follows from them. The DHDR simultaneously addresses the responsibilities of individuals and groups. It states:

> 'As the holders of human rights and fundamental freedoms, all individuals, peoples and communities in the exercise of their rights and freedoms, have the duty and responsibility to respect those of others, and a duty to strive for the promotion and observance thereof'.[11]

This statement clearly builds upon Article 29 UDHR, which reiterates the interrelation of duties, responsibilities and rights. This interrelation was later also entailed in the International Covenants of 1966.[12]

1.1. THE RIGHT TO LIFE AND HUMAN SECURITY

Most of the titles of the DHDR's chapters proclaim a right or fundamental freedom that will be the thematic focus of the related duties and responsibilities listed in the respective section. Chapter 2 begins the list of duties and responsibilities with the right to life and human security. These rights need to be secured for the present and also future generations in the awareness that for the first time in human history the survival of humankind is in peril due to human action. This article clearly matches Article 3 UDHR, which protects everyone's right to life, liberty and security of person. The related DHDR chapter draws our attention to the issue of intergenerational responsibility.

Article 3 DHDR is dedicated to the duty and responsibility to protect the life of every member of the human family and to ensure the survival of both present and future generations. This entails the need 'to take reasonable steps to help others whose lives are threatened, or who are in extreme distress or

---

11 Art. 2(7) DHDR.

12 See both the preambles of the *International Covenant on Economic, Social and Cultural Rights*, 1966, www.ohchr.org/EN/ProfessionalInterest/Pages/CESCR.aspx and of the *International Covenant on Civil and Political Rights*, 1966, www.ohchr.org/en/professionalinterest/pages/ccpr.aspx.

need'.[13] A key element of the formulation of the DHDR has been the present duty and responsibility for the potential consequences of our actions for future generations. Federico Mayor, Director-General of UNESCO at the time of the drafting of the DHDR, summarised it correctly when he held that '[t]he rights of these future generations are the duties of present generations'.[14] Therefore, the right to peace and the right to live in a balanced ecological environment have to be recognised and guaranteed as well. In this context, also the *Earth Charter*,[15] a declaration of principles for a sustainable world, deserves mentioning, as it emphasises the urgency of identifying a shared responsibility of care towards the whole community 'of life', including the well-being of human family. The papal encyclical *Laudato si'* strengthens this universal responsibility towards the Earth and the community of life.[16]

Article 4 DHDR proclaims the duty and responsibility to promote collective security and a culture of peace for all members of the global community. War and conflict prevention, international peace, global security and cooperation are all needed for this purpose. The responsibility of States, according to Chapter 7 of the UN Charter, is underlined and also their duty strengthening mediation, conflict prevention and post-conflict peace-building mechanisms and peace-keeping capacities.

Article 5 DHDR is dedicated to the duty and responsibility to promote rapid and effective disarmament in the interest of peace. This duty and responsibility primarily befalls States, as they have the capacity to reduce military expenditure in favour of human development. Together with non-State actors, States must carry out nuclear disarmament, cease any production or use of chemical and biological weapons and stop the use of landmines.

The duty to intervene in order to prevent gross human rights violations is stated in Article 6 DHDR. Examples of gross human rights violations include the acts of genocide, crimes against humanity, war crimes and other systematic human rights abuses. It is mainly States which are in charge of preventing and also punishing such violations, and there is also a collective duty on behalf of States to intervene in cases where individual States fail to prevent such abuses. Chapter 7 of the UN Charter remains the basic framework underpinning this responsibility. The definition of gross human rights violations and the call for

---

13 Art. 3 DHDR.

14 Message from Federico Mayor Zaragoza, then Director General of UNESCO, for the inaugural session of the First Congress on *Human Duties and Responsibilities in the Third Millennium Valencia*, 28 January 1998.

15 Earth Charter International, *Earth Charter*, adopted on 29 June 2000 in The Hague, www.earthcharterinaction.org/content/pages/Read-the-Charter.html.

16 Pope Francis, *Laudato si'*, Rome 2015, w2.vatican.va/content/francesco/en/encyclicals/documents/papa-francesco_20150524_enciclica-laudato-si.html.

prevention and punishment in this DHDR chapter were inspired by the text of the Rome Statute,[17] which was adopted some months before the DHDR was finalised.

Article 7 DHDR proclaims the duty and responsibility to respect, unconditionally and in all circumstances, international humanitarian law in times of armed conflict. This body of law, all too commonly infringed, entails obligations both for government forces and insurgents, including the obligation to refrain from committing acts of genocide, crimes against humanity, and war crimes.

Article 8 DHDR refers to the duty and responsibility of humanitarian assistance and intervention to those in need. In a globalised world with millions of displaced people, it entails at least the provision of adequate food, shelter, health care and other essential requirements necessary for survival, in order to ensure the right to life for everyone in the world.

Article 9 DHDR concludes this chapter with the duty and responsibility to protect and promote a safe, stable and healthy environment. This entails respect, protection and preservation of the uniqueness and diversity of all forms of life. An adequate use of resources – one which avoids excessive exploitation and consumption – and collaborative scientific research and exchange of information are required. This article can be connected to the global environmental agreements from the Kyoto Protocol[18] to the UN Conference on Climate Change in Paris in 2015, which aim to reduce greenhouse gas emissions world-wide, and to effectuate an urgent change of attitude towards the environment. This duty towards the present and future generations has been supported by a broad scientific consensus on the existence of climate change and the responsibility of human beings in this process.[19]

1.2. HUMAN SECURITY AND AN EQUITABLE INTERNATIONAL ORDER

Article 10 DHDR emphasises the duty and responsibility to promote an equitable international order for the universal enjoyment of sustainable human, economic, social, cultural, political, scientific and technological development. It also aims at promoting an equitable participation in the decision-making processes for an

---

[17] *Rome Statute of the International Criminal Court*, Rome 17 July 1998, entered into force on 1 July 2002, www.icc-cpi.int/nr/rdonlyres/ea9aeff7-5752-4f84-be94-0a655eb30e16/0/rome_statute_english.pdf.

[18] *Kyoto Protocol*, Kyoto 1998, entered into force in 2005, http://unfccc.int/resource/docs/convkp/kpeng.pdf.

[19] See the Intergovernmental Panel on Climate Change, *Climate Change 2014 Synthesis Report*, www.ipcc.ch/pdf/assessment-report/ar5/syr/SYR_AR5_FINAL_full.pdf.

interdependent and technologically well-equipped world, providing an extensive vision of the general formulation of Article 28 UDHR, which reads as follows:

> 'Everyone is entitled to a social and international order in which the rights and freedoms set forth in this Declaration can be fully realized'.

The DHDR statements are categorical:

> 'Economic policies and development should not be pursued at the expense of human rights or social development',[20]
>
> 'Economic and social development shall not be pursued at the expense of the environment and natural resources',[21] and
>
> 'As sovereign and equal members of the international community, all States have the right to participate fully, equitably and effectively in international and global institutions and decision-making processes ...'[22]

Around the same time as the drafting of the DHDR, the UN Millennium Development Goals set an influential agenda for a global partnership to fight poverty, establishing shared goals for a better world by 2015. Their fulfilment is measurable indicated by a progress at quantitative level. This year a new Agenda for sustainable development will be adopted by the UN. Although the MDGs were not accomplished, the awareness of shared and differentiated responsibility and the call for a global solidarity have increased significantly.

Article 11 DHDR enunciates the duty to alleviate usurious debt that would endanger human lives and impede economic and social development.

This Chapter continues with Article 12 DHDR, which is dedicated to the duty and responsibility to promote safe, responsible and equitable scientific and technological development for the benefit of all humankind. The UNESCO spirit[23] of encouraging intellectual and moral solidarity is emphasised, and the article in particular takes into account the condition of the scientifically less advanced States. Article 12 has been well-received by the scientific community. The capacity of science to remain neutral in the face of ethical dilemmas has increasingly proven to be an illusion, especially areas such as genetics or

---

20 Art. 10(6) DHDR.

21 Art. 10(7) DHDR.

22 Art. 10(8) DHDR.

23 See *UNESCO Constitution*, London, 1945, Preamble, http://portal.unesco.org/en/ev.php-URL_ID=15244&URL_DO=DO_TOPIC&URL_SECTION=201.html, and the subsequent UNESCO international documents on science and technology, and information and communication, and the creation of the UNESCO Ethics of Science and Technology Programme in 1998 with the establishment of the World Commission on the Ethics of Scientific Knowledge and Technology (COMEST).

cybernetics. The approach advocated by the DHDR therefore makes reference to various UNESCO initiatives regarding ethics in bioscience.[24]

Article 13 DHDR enunciates duties and responsibilities of public and private sector corporations, indicating as common criteria the respect for sovereignty of host countries and simultaneously the full respect and promotion of universal human rights and international labour standards. With a view to an ethical code for corporations and to the promotion of a more sustainable and inclusive global economy, the then UN General Secretary, Kofi Annan, proposed the *Global Compact*, an international initiative which brings together companies with UN agencies, labour organisations and civil society in order to support universal environmental and social principles. This initiative was launched in 2000.

Article 14 DHDR enunciates the duty and responsibility to prevent and punish international and organised crime as a shared task of the members of the global community. This article entails the same innovative approach towards global cooperation that can also be found in the Rome Statute.[25] It calls for efforts to be undertaken in order to combat international and transnational crimes and to assist international criminal tribunals.

Article 15 DHDR proclaims the duty and responsibility to eradicate corruption and build an ethical society in both the public and private sectors, through the implementation of codes of conduct and training programmes, and by promoting accountability and public awareness of the harm caused by corruption. This emphasis on codes of conduct was also encouraged by the Global Compact, in particular for the private sector.

1.3. MEANINGFUL PARTICIPATION IN PUBLIC AFFAIRS

Article 16 DHDR expresses the duty and responsibility to ensure meaningful participation in public affairs, to ensure that the authority of government is based upon the will of the people and on the rule of law. This responsibility is clearly connected to the universal right found in article 21 UDHR to take part in the government of one's country, directly or through freely chosen representatives at the local, national and global levels.

[24] *UNESCO Universal Declaration on Bioethics and Human Rights*, October 2005, http://portal.unesco.org/en/ev.php-URL_ID=31058&URL_DO=DO_TOPIC&URL_SECTION=201.html, and the *UNESCO International Declaration on Human Genetic Data*, Paris, 2003, http://portal.unesco.org/en/ev.php-URL_ID=17720&URL_DO=DO_TOPIC&URL_SECTION=201.html.

[25] Rome Statute, Part 2.

1.4. FREEDOM OF OPINION, EXPRESSION, ASSEMBLY, ASSOCIATION AND RELIGION

Following Article 19 UDHR on the right to freedom of opinion and expression, Article 17 DHDR reformulates this right as a duty and responsibility to respect and ensure freedom of opinion, expression, and the media. It requires, *inter alia*, that the pursuit of truth is unhindered, and it condemns any degrading treatment of individuals and the presentation of violence as entertainment.

Article 18 DHDR establishes duties and responsibilities concerning information and communications technologies with the aim of ensuring universal access to basic communication and information infrastructure and services. Similarly, UNESCO has already made a recommendation on information promoting universal access to cyberspace.[26]

Complementing article 20 UDHR on the right to freedom of peaceful assembly and association, Article 19 DHDR enunciates the duty and responsibility to take all necessary steps to ensure the substantive realisation of the rights to freedom of assembly and freedom of association.

Finally, Article 20 DHDR, following Article 18 UDHR on the right to freedom of thought, conscience and religion, formulates the related duty and responsibility to respect and ensure freedom of religion, belief and conscience, and the right to adhere or not adhere to a religion or belief.

1.5. THE RIGHT TO PERSONAL AND PHYSICAL INTEGRITY

Article 21 DHDR focuses on the duty and responsibility to respect and ensure the physical, psychological and personal integrity of all members of the human family in all circumstances, including in situations of armed conflict. It reformulates Articles 10–12 UDHR, which are dedicated to the right to personal integrity and the right to respect for privacy.

Article 22 DHDR enunciates the duty and responsibility to take all necessary measures to respect and ensure the right to personal liberty and physical security. The primary duty and responsibility in this field lies with the State, which has to prevent arbitrary arrest and detention and ensure that all arrests and detentions are carried out in accordance with universally recognised standards of fairness and due process.

---

[26] See *UNESCO Recommendation concerning the Promotion and Use of Multilingualism and Universal Access to Cyberspace*, October 2003, www.unesco.org/new/fileadmin/MULTIMEDIA/HQ/CI/CI/pdf/official_documents/Eng%20-%20Recommendation%20concerning%20the%20Promotion%20and%20Use%20of%20Multilingualism%20and%20Universal%20Access%20to%20Cyberspace.pdf.

Article 23 DHDR emphasises the duty and responsibility to prohibit, prevent and punish slavery, institutions and practices similar to slavery, and slave-like practices including child prostitution, child exploitation, enforced prostitution, debt bondage, serfdom, and other forms of enforced labour inconsistent with international law. States are required to establish effective controls to prevent the illegal trafficking of persons and to create greater public awareness through education regarding human rights abuses associated with such practices. Article 4 UDHR states that:

> 'No one shall be held in slavery or servitude; slavery and the slave trade shall be prohibited in all their forms'.

Today slavery is still not eradicated from the world, although universally condemned.

Article 24 DHDR enunciates the duty and responsibility to condemn torture and to take all necessary measures to prevent torture, cruel, inhuman and degrading treatment or punishment. It requires States to declare criminal and punish all acts of torture, cruel and inhuman and degrading treatment or punishment and to enforce strict controls over places and conditions of custody of persons deprived of their liberty. This duty can be connected to Article 5 UDHR: 'No one shall be subjected to torture or to cruel, inhuman or degrading treatment or punishment'.

Article 25 DHDR proclaims the duty and responsibility to condemn and to prevent and eradicate enforced disappearances. It requires States to declare as criminal and to punish all acts of forced disappearance, to ensure that persons deprived of their liberty are only held in officially recognised places of detention, and that they have adequate access to judicial officers, legal representation, medical personnel and family members during their detention.

1.6. IN SEARCH OF EQUALITY

Chapter 7 DHDR deals with the principle of equality. In a similar approach, UNESCO adopted two notable documents promoting cultural diversity, i.e. the *UNESCO Universal Declaration on Cultural Diversity*[27] (2001) and the *Convention on the Protection and Promotion of the Diversity of Cultural Expressions* (2005).[28]

Article 26 DHDR enunciates the general duty to respect, ensure and promote the right to equal treatment and to eradicate discrimination in all its forms.

27 *UNESCO Universal Declaration on Cultural Diversity*, Paris, 2001, http://portal.unesco.org/en/ev.php-URL_ID=13179&URL_DO=DO_TOPIC&URL_SECTION=201.html.

28 *UNESCO Convention on the Protection and Promotion of the Diversity of Cultural Expressions*, Paris, 2005, http://portal.unesco.org/en/ev.php-URL_ID=31038&URL_DO=DO_TOPIC&URL_SECTION=201.html.

Article 27 DHDR states the duty and responsibility of States to respect and ensure the substantive equality of every member of the human family, not only to ensure equality before the law, but also to take positive action to prevent direct or indirect discrimination.

Article 28 DHDR proclaims the duty and responsibility to ensure substantive racial and religious equality. This includes the duty to ensure the effective enjoyment of all human rights and fundamental freedoms without discrimination on the basis of race, religion or ethnicity, and to condemn all forms of racial and religious discrimination and respect racial, ethnic and religious diversity; promoting equal opportunities for all.

Article 29 DHDR formulates the duty and responsibility to ensure sex and gender equality as well as the recognition of women's rights as human rights. In particular, States have to ensure the effective enjoyment of all human rights and fundamental freedoms without discrimination on the basis of sex or gender and to promote equality in the representation and participation of women in public and political life. They also have to strive for the eradication of cultural, religious and social practices which discriminate against women and for the economic empowerment and the recognition of the full legal capacity of women.

Article 30 DHDR is dedicated to the duty and responsibility to ensure the substantive equality of persons with a disability, and to ensure the enjoyment and exercise of all human rights and fundamental freedoms without discrimination on the basis of disability.

Some progress towards the accomplishment of this duty can be observed at the international level. In March 2006, the *UN Programme on Disability*[29] led to the establishment of the Secretariat for the *Convention on the Rights of Persons with Disabilities.*

1.7. PROTECTION OF MINORITIES AND INDIGENOUS PEOPLES

The aim of Chapter 8 is to emphasise the need for protection of minorities and indigenous peoples. Both the global community and individual States are considered by this Declaration to have a responsibility, collectively as well as individually, to ensure the rights of these vulnerable groups.

Article 31 DHDR formulates the duty and responsibility to respect and protect the existence, identity and rights of national, ethnic, religious and linguistic minorities, with States having the primary duty and responsibility to take adequate measures. The aforementioned efforts of UNESCO regarding the

[29] *UN Convention on the Rights of Persons with Disabilities*, www.un.org/disabilities/convention/conventionfull.shtml.

protection of cultural diversity and cultural expressions are a good example of a way to fulfil this duty.

Article 32 DHDR enunciates the duty and responsibility to respect, protect and promote the rights of indigenous peoples, in particular their right to preserve, maintain and develop their identities and to protect their means of livelihood. Indigenous rights are protected in many different ways at the national level, but it was felt there was a strong need for the international community to also assume a collectively responsibility.

Finally, in 2007, the UN General Assembly adopted the UN Declaration of the Rights of Indigenous Peoples, in order to protect these rights universally.

1.8. RIGHTS OF THE CHILD AND THE ELDERLY

Chapter 9 deals with the implementation of the principle of equality, with a special focus on the primary responsibility of States towards children and the elderly.

Article 33 DHDR emphasises the duty and responsibility to respect, protect and promote the rights of the child, following the rights contained in the almost universally ratified *UN Convention on the Right of the Child* (1989).[30] Its main point of departure is the realisation that, in spite of the wide acceptance of this convention, millions of children today are still innocent victims of armed conflict, extreme poverty and hunger.

Article 34 DHDR is dedicated to the duty and responsibility to promote and enforce the rights and wellbeing of the elderly. It aims at ensuring the full and effective enjoyment by elderly people of all human rights and fundamental freedoms without discrimination on the basis of age, calls for the respect and promotion of the well-being, dignity and physical and personal integrity of the elderly. Although major efforts have been undertaken by the United Nations, including the International Year of Older Persons (1999) and the formulation of UN Principles addressing the independence, participation, care, self-fulfilment and dignity of older persons, there is until now no recognised framework for securing the rights of the elderly. Therefore, the DHDR constitutes a very interesting contribution towards the enforcement of such rights.

1.9. RIGHT TO WORK, QUALITY OF LIFE AND STANDARD OF LIVING

Chapter 10 DHDR complements the system of duties and responsibilities related to the rights to work, quality of life and standard of living. To this purpose, the

30 *UN Convention on the Right of the Child*, New York, 1989, www.ohchr.org/en/professionalinterest/pages/crc.aspx.

DHDR takes into account the responsibility of States and as well as the shared responsibility of the world community in the context of an increasing global interdependence.

Article 35 DHDR formulates the duty and responsibility to promote the right to justly remunerated work, and can as such be linked to Article 23 UDHR.[31] Article 35 DHDR proposes a number of measures, including the adoption of policies designed to promote productive work, to ensure employment security – in particular protection against arbitrary or unfair dismissal – and to ensure equality of opportunity and conditions of work.

Article 36 DHDR emphasises the duty and responsibility to promote quality of life and an adequate standard of living for all. The DHDR reiterates the shared responsibility for eradicating extreme poverty in the world, especially in view of finite natural resources. Similarly, but with a more pragmatic approach, the *Millennium Development Goals* (2000)[32] constituted an inter-governmental agreement on the progressive and global realisation of human rights. Today, international cooperation is dedicated to consolidate a post-2015 development agenda for ending poverty. However, it is regrettable that the MDGs have been only partially met, in particular taking into account that the gap between poor and rich people has significantly increased.[33]

1.10. RIGHT TO EDUCATION, ARTS AND CULTURE

The right to education, particularly in the first years of a child's life, can only be made effective when someone takes responsibility, be it the government, family or the local community. An effective right to education is closely connected to other issues, such as the prohibition of child labour in all its forms, the appropriate allocation of resources and poverty alleviation.

Chapter 11 DHDR is dedicated to the formulation of duties and responsibilities regarding the promotion of education, arts and culture. These issues are, of course, central to the activities of UNESCO, which has established programmes such as 'education for all' and various instruments for securing adequate conditions for education and artistic and cultural activities.

Article 37 DHDR enunciates the duty and responsibility to promote and enforce the right to education, taking into account that illiteracy still affects millions of people in developing countries.

Article 38 DHDR emphasises the duty and responsibility of States and the global community to foster arts and culture and the global community.

---

31 Art. 23 DHDR.

32 *UN Millennium Declaration*, adopted on 8 September 2000 in New York, www.un.org/millennium/declaration/ares552e.htm.

33 *UN The Millennium Development Goals Report 2015*, www.un.org/millenniumgoals/2015_MDG_Report/pdf/MDG%202015%20rev%20(July%201).pdf.

1.11. RIGHT TO A REMEDY

The DHDR concludes with Chapter 12, which is dedicated to the right to a remedy where a human right or fundamental freedom is threatened or has been violated.

Following Article 8 UDHR, Article 39 DHDR proclaims the duty and responsibility, primarily of States, to provide for and to enforce effective national judicial, administrative, legislative and other remedies.

Article 40 proposes the duty to monitor and implement the Declaration of Human Duties and Responsibilities, by suggesting the establishment of tripartite councils composed by the State, civil society and private sector representatives.

Article 41 DHDR, finally, concludes with a non-derogation clause which states:

> 'Nothing in this Declaration shall be interpreted as impairing or restricting the rights contained in the Universal Declaration of Human Rights and other international and regional human rights instruments.'

2. SOLIDARITY AS THE ROAD TO FULFILLING THE RESPONSIBILITIES AND DUTIES FOR HUMAN RIGHTS

The rights of the French and American Revolutions were conceived as universal. Yet we seem to have inherited a moral deficit as regards the formulation of duties and responsibilities. The lack of attention devoted to them has inhibited the universal enjoyment of rights.[34] Since the end of the 18th century, the principle of responsibility between the individual and society was extended to morality and politics. 'Solidarity' assumed a political place alongside 'fraternity' after the French Revolution. In Article XXI of the revised *Declaration of Human Rights* of 1793, the notion of solidarity appeared as a 'public assistance' that is a 'sacred obligation' of society that would pay a subsistence to unfortunate citizens. The concept of solidarity, as noted by Kurt Bayertz, has the historical problem of 'not being defined in a binding manner'.[35] Due to this theoretical deficit, 'solidarity' implies merely a moral obligation to act, i.e. something that is commendable but not binding.

Jürgen Habermas noted that in the field of morality, solidarity is the 'reverse side' of justice. Solidarity complements justice by expressing human concern. Morally valid norms would be those 'which could find acceptance by all those concerned as participants in a practical discourse.'[36]

---

34 K. Bayertz (ed.), *Solidarity*, Dordrecht: Kluwer Academic Publishers, 1999, p. 3 ff.

35 Ibid., p. 3.

36 J. Habermas, 'Justice and Solidarity', in M. Kelly (ed.), *Hermeneutics and Critical Theory in Ethics and Politics*, Cambridge: MIT Press, 1990, pp. 32 ff.

The concept of solidarity as a mediating tool is clearly visible in the *Declaration on the Responsibilities of the Present Generations towards Future Generations*[37] (UNESCO 1997) in which the principle of solidarity is understood in the light of the fraternity of the human family within a specific temporal dimension. The Declaration asserts 'the necessity for establishing new, equitable and global links of partnership and intra-generational solidarity', and promotes 'inter-generational solidarity for the perpetuation of humankind'.

Progressively, the human community is making efforts towards the recognition of not only human rights, but also of the responsibilities necessary for realising these rights. Slavery, colonialism, oppression and domination of women and children, and disregard of the rights of vulnerable peoples were officially condemned. Yet extreme poverty persists, and pollution is threatening the future of humankind. Today, we have the unique opportunity to radically define our assumptions about duties and responsibilities both through an intra-generational and inter-generational perspective as well as, in the radical sense proclaimed by the geographer Aziz Ab'Saber, with an aim towards the continuation of humanity against a much farther horizon.[38]

3. FINAL REMARKS

The formulation of duties and responsibilities, such as in the DHDR, theoretically reinforces not only the proclamation of human rights and, in particular, those enshrined in the UDHR and succeeding international human rights instruments, but it also supports the awareness of our individual and collective role in the realisation of these rights.

The DHDR remains a relevant document today, and it has received positive feedback from the scientific community, political leaders, social actors, representatives of NGOs and of UN Agencies, being used as educational and legal source.

The UN Conference on Sustainable Development in Rio (2012) was the biggest conference of the United Nations ever with the participation of the governments and the major groups from civil society. However, the international community could renew only partially the commitments made in Rio 1992 after reflecting on the poor achievements in the following years. Its final document, *The Future We Want*, reiterates the commitments of the previous conferences with the authority of a broad consensus and the weakness of a non-binding character. In my opinion, *The Future We Want* shows that the global discourse is starting to contain a permanent reference to human duties and responsibilities, recognising

37 Available online at http://unesdoc.unesco.org/images/0011/001102/110220e.pdf#page=75; see also: F. Mayor (ed.), *Letters to Future Generations*, Paris: UNESCO Publishing, 1999.

38 Aziz Nacib Ab'Saber, *A Obra de Aziz Nacib Ab'Saber (2010)*, São Paulo: BECA (588 pp. and CD); see in particular the chapter 'Artigos'.

the rights of the most vulnerable peoples, the demands for the eradication of poverty and the aspiration to safeguard future generations. However, it remains urgent to complement the many good intentions with meaningful actions. We have to work together to turn this moment into a historical moment of transition. The establishment of the human rights legal framework was also not without its difficulties, entailing a long and often slow process. Now, in the 21st century, we can work together on the next step in this process, one that includes duties and responsibilities.

For the first time in history, the international community is starting to be aware of its responsibility towards future generations. We can speak, in the words of the philosopher Karl-Otto Apel, of an urgent answer needed to the '*homo faber*' by the '*homo sapiens*', 'providing a novel order of things based on a global ethics of responsibility'.[39] On the roots of Kant and at the same time Max Weber, Apel has developed the pillars for a 'common universally valid foundation of an ethics of justice, solidarity, and co-responsibility', trying to meet the challenges of the global problems of humankind as a whole, problems of peaceful co-existence of the different cultures … and problems of responsible cooperation between different nations'.[40]

It is often held that we are now living in the 'Anthropocene', an epoch in which human action is having an increasingly drastic impact on the planet. Because of this tremendous impact on both the planet and humankind, our responsibility must be said to have also increased. We must make an effort to find new answers to these challenges. I would suggest that we are invited to enter also into a kind of 'Sophocene' (*sophia* = wisdom), where human beings for the first time in history engage in a deliberate effort – as limited and chaotic as it may be – to refrain from egocentrism and to go beyond our own self-interest. What we are witnessing, and what the DHDR attempts to encapsulate, are only the first steps.

39 K.-O. Apel, *The Response of Discourse Ethics to the Moral Challenge of the Human Situation as Such and Especially Today*, Leuven: Peeters Publishers, 2002, p. 22.

40 K.-O. Apel, 'How to Ground a Universalistic Ethics of Co-responsibility for the Effects of Collective Actions and Activities?' (1993) 52(2) *Philosophica* 10.

PART II

RIGHTS AND RESPONSIBILITIES IN SPECIFIC CONTEXTS

HUMAN RIGHTS IN A GLOBALISING ECONOMY

Is the Right to Social Protection Qualified by a Duty to Work?

Wouter VANDENHOLE

1. INTRODUCTION

Socio-economic human rights, including the right to social protection,[1] have been facing multiple ideological challenges in the past two decades. A first challenge comes from the neo-liberal ideological pressures which the European social security systems have experienced, together with growing concerns over financial sustainability. This challenge has been compounded by the financial and economic crises since 2008.[2] A second challenge originates from a cultural relativist debate, often but not exclusively in terms of Asian or African values, which has resulted in a competing discourse on human responsibilities and duties.[3] The cultural relativist debate challenges human rights more in general, but mainly questions civil and political rights. Somehow in line with cultural relativism, there has been an attempt also at establishing a new global ethic which human responsibilities are central to.

As far as the right to social protection is concerned, the first challenge, that is the neo-liberal one with its emphasis on the individualisation of responsibility

---

1 Social protection is used as an overall term covering both social security and social assistance.

2 See e.g. ECSR, *Conclusions* 2009 (General introduction), 12–13. A. Nolan (ed.), *Economic and Social Rights after the Global Financial Crisis*, Cambridge: Cambridge University Press, 2014.

3 As Ghai has pointed out, 'in the 1980s and 1990s "Asian values" seemed to fit in with the imperatives of globalization, with their emphasis on minimal State welfare, limited trade union rights, reliance on family, and restricted political participation.' (Y. Ghai, 'Rights, Social Justice, and Globalization in East Asia', in J. Bauer and D. Bell (eds.), *The East Asian Challenge for Human Rights*, Cambridge: Cambridge University Press, 1999, p. 262.

for social risks,[4] is far more serious than the second one. Neo-liberal policies in Europe, in a context of increasing financial difficulties of social security systems, have confronted the human rights monitoring bodies with restrictive policies and practices in the field of social protection, and necessitated them to cautiously balance economic and social realities with human rights standards. The question that inevitably lurks is whether they have not too much accommodated neo-liberalism to the detriment of high human rights standards.

In what follows, brief attention will be given first to the cultural relativist critique and to proposals for a new global ethic based on human responsibilities. The remaining of the chapter will focus on the neo-liberal challenge, as it has emerged in policies and practices. In particular, we will examine how the right to social protection relates to a duty to work. While some attention will be given to the International Covenant on Economic, Social and Cultural Rights (ICESCR) and the ILO Conventions, the main focus will be on the (Revised) European Social Charter ((R)ESC). It will be argued that while an obligation to work may well exist, it does not enjoy the same legal status as the human right to social protection and its composite rights. The human right to social protection can only be subjected to limitations arising from the non-fulfilment of an obligation to work if the legality, legitimacy and proportionality tests are met, i.e. when there is a legal basis, a legitimate aim is pursued and the means used can be shown to be proportional to the achievement of that aim.

An approach in which duties for the individual are given the same legal status as human rights is not justifiable. The right to social protection and the duty to work do not carry equal weight, nor should they. The human right to social protection is of a qualitatively different nature, as well as of a higher legal status. The rationale of human rights is that they protect the individual from the State: it is an instrument of empowerment against the much more powerful State. Notwithstanding developments which may have taken away an important degree of power from the State, such as the process of economic globalisation, in relation to the individual, the State remains a disproportionately powerful player. Human rights law should therefore continue to focus on protection and empowerment of the individual against the State (in addition to other powerful actors).[5] Secondly, the duty rhetoric is to be approached with caution, for it has often if not always been abused by States and governments to justify extraordinary encroachments on human rights.[6] Thirdly, and more in particular with regard

[4] L. Lamarche, 'The Right to Social Security in the International Covenant on Economic, Social and Cultural Rights', in A. Chapman and S. Russell (eds.), *Core Obligations: Building a Framework for Economic, Social and Cultural Rights*, Antwerp: Intersentia, 2002, p. 96.

[5] For a more elaborate discussion, see e.g. W. Vandenhole, G.E. Türkelli and R. Hammonds, 'Reconceptualizing Human Rights Duty-Bearers', in A. Mihr and M. Gibney (eds.), *The SAGE Handbook of Human Rights*, Los Angeles: Sage, 2014, pp. 1031–1046.

[6] Compare International Council on Human Rights Policy, *Taking Duties Seriously: Duties in International Human Rights Law – A Commentary*, p. 2: 'in many cases those in power have used the language of duty and obligation to suppress human rights.'

to the right to social protection, those who are eligible to social security and social assistance benefits may not be able to work, such as those suffering from industrial diseases, those responsible for children or the elderly. So while human rights law aims to protect and empower the weakest sections of the population in particular, they may be hit hardest by any measure purporting to activate them. In a broader context, measures to make beneficiaries of health or educational services contribute financially, e.g. through the introduction of user fees for basic education and basic health care, tend to have a disproportionately adverse impact on the weakest groups in society. It was a most welcome development that in the Millennium Development Project, the abolition of user fees was put forward as a quick win intervention.[7]

The above does not mean that the right to social protection and its composite rights are absolute and impose unchecked obligations on the State. Limitations are allowed if they can be reasonably justified, do not threaten the essence of the right and are not in violation of other rights, in particular the right to work, which includes the right to freely choose one's work.

On a methodological note, the analysis of the European Committee of Social Rights' (ECSR) case law is based on the conclusions taken under the reporting system, for lack of complaints over the issue so far.[8] Strictly speaking, only decisions of non-conformity with the (R)ESC may amount to treaty interpretation proper. Moreover, conclusions of non-conformity have been rather few in number so far. The ECSR seems to prefer to increase pressure on States by requiring more detailed information on withdrawal of unemployment benefits in case of refusal to accept a job offer, than by finding non-observance of the Charter. The analysis made here includes therefore also the questions put to States, while a decision on conformity was deferred. These questions, and the accompanying comments on the treaty standards made by the ECSR, contain strong indications as to how and which policies and practices may be judged in non-conformity with the Charter in the years to come.

2. CULTURAL RELATIVISM AND HUMAN RESPONSIBILITIES

Human duties or responsibilities are not completely unknown to the human rights discourse.[9] The Universal Declaration of Human Rights (UDHR) contains

7 For a more elaborate discussion, see W. Vandenhole, 'EU and Development: Extraterritorial Obligations under the International Covenant on Economic, Social and Cultural Rights', in M.E. Salomon, A. Tostensen and W. Vandenhole (eds.), *Casting the Net Wider: Human Rights, Development and New Duty-Bearers*, Antwerp: Intersentia, 2007, pp. 103–104.

8 The Committee has dealt with retrogressive measures and restrictions of the right to social security in the aftermath of the financial and economic crises since 2008, see *infra* nn. 60–61.

9 For a more extensive discussion, ibid.

a long list of human rights, civil, political, economic and social. In the final but one Article, it provides that '[e]veryone has duties to the community in which alone the free and full development of his personality is possible'. The second paragraph adds that in the exercise of the rights and freedoms, 'everyone shall be subject only to such limitations as are determined by law solely for the purpose of securing due recognition and respect for the rights and freedoms of others and of meeting the just requirements of morality, public order and the general welfare in a democratic society.' Article 29 UDHR thus clarifies that the rights enumerated should not be seen as absolute rights of individuals, in disregard of the rights of other individuals or of the legitimate concerns of the community one lives in. Limitations are subject however to conditions of legality, legitimacy and proportionality. Article 30 UDHR warns moreover that '[n]othing in this Declaration may be interpreted as implying for any State, group or person any right to engage in any activity or to perform any act aimed at the destruction of any of the rights and freedoms set forth herein.' The general reference to duties to the community in the UDHR is to be seen in connection with the possibility of imposing limitations and is checked by the prohibition to interpret the provision on duties as implying a right to destroy any of the rights provided for.

An explicit reference to social security is made in Article 22 UDHR. However, what was in fact meant was social *justice* rather than social security.[10] Article 25(1) UDHR guarantees the right to *security* in the event of unemployment, sickness, disability, widowhood, old age or other lack of livelihood in circumstances beyond his control. In the draft submitted by the American Law Institute back in 1945, a reference to the obligation of the individual to co-operate with the State according to his powers in the promotion of his own social security was included.[11] Similarly, Cassin believed that greater importance was to be given to actions by individuals and groups within society than to action by the State.[12] In the end, no reference to duties was included in this provision however.

The Preambles of both the ICESCR and the International Covenant on Civil and Political rights explicitly refer to duties and responsibility of the individual. It reads:

> 'Realizing that the individual, having duties to other individuals and to the community to which he belongs, is under a responsibility to strive for the promotion and observance of the rights recognized in the present Covenant ...'

Emphasis is on the responsibility for the individual to 'strive for the promotion and observance' of economic, social and cultural rights. This responsibility originates from his 'duties to other individuals and to the community to which he belongs.'

---

10 B.-A. Andreassen, 'Article 22', in G. Alfredsson and A. Eide (eds.), *The Universal Declaration of Human Rights*, The Hague: Kluwer, 1999, p. 475.

11 Ibid., pp. 464–465.

12 Ibid., p. 469.

In the operative part, no reference to duties or responsibility was included, only a general limitation clause, allowing for 'limitations as are determined by law only in so far as this may be compatible with the nature of these rights and solely for the purpose of promoting the general welfare in a democratic society' (Article 4 ICESCR).[13]

The African Charter on Human and Peoples' Rights is the international human rights treaty that contains the most explicit and elaborate duty-language in a separate chapter. Chapter 2 of the African Charter contains three Articles on duties. In accordance with Article 27(1), each individual has duties towards his family and society, the State and other legally recognised communities and the international community. This is followed by a provision in which it is made clear that the rights and freedoms of each individual are to be exercised with due regard to the rights of others, collective security, morality and common interest. Article 28 contains a 'duty to respect and consider his fellow beings without discrimination, and to maintain relations aimed at promoting, safeguarding and reinforcing mutual respect and tolerance.' Article 29 of the African Charter enumerates duties which emanate from being a good family member (*inter alia* to maintain one's parents in case of need), a good citizen and a good African *inter alia* by placing one's physical and intellectual abilities at the service of the national community, by preserving and strengthening social solidarity, by working to the best of his abilities and competence, and by paying taxes imposed by law in the interest of the society. The Charter does not clarify how to balance the rights and duties enumerated.

With the exception of the African Charter, duties only find their way in human rights discourse through the possibility of limitations. These limitations are to be interpreted restrictively, and need to meet conditions of legality, legitimacy and proportionality. Clearly, duties are not at the same normative level as human rights.

The references in human rights instruments to responsibilities and duties teach us that individual rights are seldom absolute, and may have to be balanced with duties and responsibilities for the common good. Individual rights are thereby not fundamentally challenged are compromised, but simply put into perspective.

The cultural relativist critique of human rights, and its counter-emphasis on human duties and responsibilities, aims to be, *in principle*, of a qualitatively different order.[14] Human duties in a cultural relativist perspective potentially

---

13 For further clarification of the meaning of this limitation clause, see e.g. ICECSR Committee, General Comment No. 14 (2000), *The Right to Highest Attainable Standard of Health (Article 12 of the ICECSR)*, UN Doc. E/C.12/2000/4, paras. 28–29.

14 See e.g. B. Ibhawoh, 'Cultural Relativism and Human Rights : Reconsidering the Africanist Discourse' (2001) 19 *NQHR* 43–62; J. Bauer and D. Bell (eds.), *The East Asian Challenge for Human Rights*, Cambridge: Cambridge University Press, 1999; M. Freeman, 'Human Rights and Real Cultures: Towards a Dialogue on "Asian values"' (1998) 16 *NQHR* 25–39.

constitute a competing normative order for human rights. Human rights are fundamentally questioned, for they are often believed to promote an excessive individualism.

Instruments in which human responsibilities are proclaimed tend to be of a much more moderate nature. A Universal Declaration on Human Responsibilities was proposed by the InterAction Council in 1997. This Declaration refers to a new global ethic in which rights and responsibilities are given equal importance, in order to address global problems. The Declaration aims at 'balancing freedom with responsibility'. It does not purport to question the validity of the human rights framework, as Article 19 testifies:

> 'Nothing in this Declaration may be interpreted as implying for any State, group or person any right to engage in any activity or to perform any act aimed at the destruction of any of the responsibilities, rights and freedoms set forth in this Declaration and in the Universal Declaration of Human Rights of 1948.'

A highly controversial pre-draft Declaration on Human Social Responsibilities contains a specific provision on the obligation to work (Article 24):

> 'Every person has the right and the duty to work to the degree permitted by his or her physical and intellectual capacities, not only as the effective way of guaranteeing his or her family's necessities, but as his or her contribution to the development of the society in which he or she lives.'[15]

The duty to work is held towards one's family and one's society, and is qualified by one's physical and intellectual capacities. The *rationale* for the work on human social responsibilities is the belief

> 'that the current globalization requires the creation of new extralegal perspectives based on morality, human solidarity and equity ... and the adding of a more visible global ethical perspective – humanist, pluralist and expressing solidarity – to what already exists in international practical actions in this matter'

and that

> 'an essential element of this new ethical perspective will be the creation and encouragement of a generalized awareness that the individual not only has rights that give a legal framework to his freedom but also duties towards the society in

[15] Annex: Pre-draft Declaration Human Responsibilities to *Human Rights and Human Responsibilities – Final Report of the Special Rapporteur, Miguel Alfonso Martínez, on the Study Requested by the Commission in its Resolution 2000/63, and submitted pursuant to Economic and Social Council decision 2002/277*, UN Doc. E/CN.4.2003/105.

> which he or she lives that reinforces his or her own freedom, and that there exists an unbreakable link between one and the other.'

It is moreover argued

> 'that the insistence on favouring the rights of the individual leads to conflicts, divisions and interminable disputes, and that the neglect of individual responsibilities can endanger freedom and prevent hundreds of millions of human beings from realizing their rights.'[16]

Nonetheless, the preambular paragraphs four and five emphasise the importance of the human rights framework, and final Article 29 provides that 'nothing in the Declaration can be interpreted as diminishing the purposes and principles of the United Nations, nor the obligations and duties freely contracted by States in other pertinent instruments of international law in the field of human rights.'

Three conclusions can be drawn. First, text proposals on human responsibilities do not question the importance of human rights law, but rather seek to balance human rights law with moral duties or responsibilities. No priority is accorded to duties over rights. Second, as far as the moral duty to work is concerned, this duty is not presented as an absolute one. Rather, it is qualified by the capacities of the duty-holder. Finally, duties are held towards the family and the community, not towards the State. To the extent that the right to social security is sought to be qualified or limited by a duty to work, this will only be possible if the duty can be justified by reference to the needs of the community, not those of the State.

All in all, *in practice* at least, the cultural relativist approach and the proposals to elaborate a global ethics emphasising human duties have not been able to seriously question the right to social protection. Financial constraints and neo-liberal policies and practices on the other hand have had a much more real and felt impact on the right to social protection. In what follows, the financial and ideological challenges to the right to social protection, in particular by favouring duties for rights-holders, will be examined in more detail.

3. THE NEO-LIBERAL CHALLENGE: BALANCING THE RIGHT TO SOCIAL PROTECTION AND THE DUTY TO WORK

The ageing of the population, compounded by the financial and economic crises since 2008, amongst other factors, has led to growing financial deficits in social protection benefits. Ideologically speaking, the rise of neo-liberal doctrine in social policy-making has led to cutting back on public expenditure growth as

16 Ibid., preambular paras. 7–9.

well as to privatisation and marketisation of the State,[17] resulting in the demise of the social welfare State as traditionally understood.

Given the fiscal challenges and the dominant ideological discourse, European governments have taken measures, in varying degrees, to maintain the financial viability of their social protection systems, *inter alia* by emphasising personal responsibility and the duty to actively contribute to the maintenance of the social security system. States have thus made the entitlement to social protection, in the field of both social security and social assistance, more and more conditional on the willingness to (seek) work, sometimes regardless of qualifications or professional experience, working conditions or personal circumstances. In the words of the Governmental Committee of the European Social Charter:[18]

> 'In general terms, States (have) to consider the different functions of the social security system: those related to protection and those related to activation and motivation. There (is) widespread acceptance today that greater emphasis (is) to be placed on the latter in order to help address the situation on the labour market and the problems relating to the funding of the system.'[19]

In principle, the objective of preserving the social protection system is a highly legitimate one, and the means chosen (i.e. activation of the persons concerned and avoiding benefit dependence) are in conformity with human rights obligations. Even more, the avoidance of benefit dependence is itself a human rights obligation under the right to social assistance (Article 13 of the (R)ESC). In the view of the ECSR, States are to elaborate an integrated strategy of poverty alleviation and empowerment of individuals so as to avoid creating dependency on benefits. Core elements of such a strategy include employment opportunities, and vocational training and re-training.[20] Similarly, the International Labour Organisation (ILO) has recognised the 'need to reform existing systems with a view to adopting innovative ways to cover risks more effectively and to remove potential disincentives to job creation and job seeking.'[21] A potential disincentive is the unemployment trap, whereby unemployed people do not feel like moving

---

17 See e.g. H. Stocke, 'What Is Left of State Responsibility? Turning State Obligations into State Responsibility in the Field of Economic, Social and Cultural Rights', in M. Scheinin and M. Suksi (eds.), *Human Rights in Development Yearbook 2002: Empowerment, Participation, Accountability and Non-Discrimimation: Operationalising a Human Rights-Based Approach to Development*, Leiden: Martinus Nijhoff, 2005, pp. 41–50 in particular.

18 The Governmental Committee, composed of representatives of the States parties, considers findings of non-compliance of the expert committee, the European Committee of Social Rights. It may invite the Committee of Ministers to address a recommendation to the State concerned if it is not convinced that that State will remedy the situation.

19 Governmental Committee of the European Social Charter, *Report Concerning Conclusions XVII-1*, Strasbourg, 8 April 2005, T-SG (2004) 25, para. 184 (Poland).

20 European Committee of Social Rights, *Conclusions XIV-1*, para. 54.

21 ILO committee on Employment and Social Policy, Geneva, March 2003, Doc. GB.286/ESP/1(Rev.), para. 36.

from unemployment benefits to employment. The unemployment trap is believed to remain a considerable challenge in many Member States of the European Union.[22]

In reply to the criticism that pure income replacement policies might entail disincentives to work once unemployment is of longer duration, the ILO has introduced the concept of Active Labour Market Policies (ALMPs). ALMPs are one of the ten core elements of the ILO's Global Employment Agenda. The meaning of ALMPs has been explained as follows:

> '"Passive" policies are those that are concerned with providing replacement income during periods of joblessness or job search; active policies concern labour market integration. Indeed, active support for labour market integration is the main thrust of ALMPs. Broadly speaking then, passive policies correspond to social transfers that are not conditional upon joining a training or work programme, though they usually include job search provisions that are increasingly enforced and which correspond to an active element in passive policies.'[23]

The crucial question is how far the activation measures can go.[24] Is someone only eligible for social protection benefits if he actively seeks for work and accepts any job opportunity? Can only the enjoyment *of the right to social security*, or more in particular the enjoyment of the right to unemployment benefits, rather than the enjoyment of the right to social protection generally speaking, be made conditional on the acceptance of work?[25] Can or should such conditionality be absolute or qualified, i.e. subject to limitations? Answers to these questions depend in part on the moral and/or legal status that is attributed to the duty to work. Does the duty to work enjoy the same moral and/or legal status as the right to social protection or one of its composite rights? In other words, are the normative frameworks of human rights and duties of equal moral and/or legal status? Alternatively, is the duty to work part of the human rights normative framework? If that is the case, is the right to social protection or its composite rights to social security and social

---

22 *Jobs, Jobs, Jobs, Creating More Employment in Europe – Report of the Employment Taskforce Chaired by Wim Kok*, November 2003, p. 33, http://ec.europa.eu/employment_social/employment_strategy/pdf/etf_en.pdf. The European Heads of State and Government established the Employment Taskforce in response to concerns that Europe was failing to tackle effectively the significant employment challenges it faces.

23 ILO committee on Employment and Social Policy, *Active Labour Market Policies*, Geneva, November 2003, Doc. GB.288/ESP/2, para. 11.

24 On the topic of human rights and activation policies for the unemployed more generally, see D. Dumont, 'Que peuvent les droits de l'homme face aux politiques de retour à l'emploi autoritaires?' (2013) *European Journal of Human Rights* 741–745; E. Dermine, 'Activation Policies for the Unemployed and the International Human Rights Case Law on the Prohibition of Forced Labour' (2013) *European Journal of Human Rights* 746–776; J.-M. Bonvin and E. Moachon, 'Droit au travail et responsabilité individuelle dans les États sociaux contemporains. Une analyse en termes de capabilités des politiques d'activation des personnes sans emploi' (2013) *European Journal of Human Rights* 777–803.

25 For the terminology of social protection, social security, social assistance, see below.

assistance *paralleled* by a duty to work, or is that duty subordinated to the right? In the latter case, the right to social protection and its composite rights cannot be unconditionally restricted by the duty to work, but only be limited under certain conditions. In what follows, we seek to answer these questions by analysing the authoritative interpretation of the right to social protection by treaty monitoring bodies.

3.1. INTERNATIONAL COVENANT ON ECONOMIC, SOCIAL AND CULTURAL RIGHTS

The 1966 International Covenant on Economic, Social and Cultural Rights (ICESCR) is the global core treaty on economic, social and cultural rights. Article 6(1) of the ICESCR guarantees the right to freely chosen work:

> 'The States Parties to the present Covenant recognize the right to work, which includes the right of everyone to the opportunity to gain his living by work which he freely chooses or accepts, and will take appropriate steps to safeguard this right.'

In the ICESCR Committee's view, the right to work 'includes the right of every human being to decide freely to accept or choose work. This implies not being forced in any way whatsoever to exercise or engage in employment.'[26] Such an interpretation seems to amount to recognition of a right not to work at all.[27] In case a right not to work exists, it is hard to imagine that one could claim at the same time a right to social security or social assistance, for in principle, only *involuntary* unemployment is protected. At the same time, an unqualified duty to work was clearly excluded by the drafters: the term 'accepts' is believed to cover the right to accept or refuse an offer of employment.[28] It therefore seems preferable to construct the freedom to work in light of the principle of proportionality.[29] This is also the way the ILO Committee of Experts on the Application of Conventions and Recommendations (CEACR) and the ECSR have construed the freedom to work (see below). Even if the right to freely accept or choose work is not absolute, the duty to respect this right means that no unreasonable limitations can be

---

26 ICECSR Committee, General Comment No. 18 (2005), *The Right to Work (Article 6 of the ICECSR)*, UN Doc. E/C.12/GC/18, para. 6.

27 Craven has pointed out that while the liberty not to work at all may have been intended by the drafters initially, subsequent rephrasing and Statements show concerns for the 'legitimization of "social parasitism"' and references to a duty to work. He argues that 'on a textual analysis there is no clear right not to work.' See M. Craven, *The International Covenant on Economic, Social and Cultural Rights – A Perspective on its Development*, Oxford: Clarendon, 1995, pp. 198 and 224.

28 Ibid., p. 199.

29 K. Drzewicki, 'The Right to Work and Rights in Work', in A. Eide, C. Krause and A. Rosas (eds.), *Economic, Social and Cultural Rights. A Textbook*, Dordrecht/Boston/London: Martinus Nijhoff, 2001, p. 233.

imposed, making it difficult to expect an unemployed person to accept *any* work offered.

Article 9 of the ICESCR protects the right to social security. It reads:

> 'The States Parties to the present Covenant recognize the right of everyone to social security, including social insurance.'

This very short and deliberately[30] general provision offers little guidance. In an attempt to grasp the basic notion of social security, the Lebanese representative argued during the drafting process that 'man, being essentially a social being, had duties towards society, but that society also had duties towards him, when through no fault of his own, he was unable to play his full part in life.'[31] The question is whether these duties of society are subject to limitations, or put more in terms of the Lebanese definition, whether an unemployed person who refuses a job could be blamed for that ('a fault of his own'), and therefore be refused social protection benefits.

In its 2007 General Comment on the right to social security, the ICESCR Committee argues that the 'withdrawal, reduction or suspension of benefits should be circumscribed, based on grounds that are reasonable, subject to due process, and provided for in national law.'[32] In footnote 19, explicit reference is made to ILO Convention No. 168, which defines the specific circumstances in which withdrawal, reduction or suspension of unemployment benefits is permitted. As will be seen below, this ILO Convention restricts withdrawals of unemployment benefits to cases in which a *suitable* job has been refused.

Withdrawing social protection benefits in case of job refusal has been introduced in Europe in the context of the introduction of labour activation policy measures. Article 2 ICESCR contains a general obligation of progressive realisation, which has been understood to exclude in principle retrogressive measures. In the words of the ICESCR Committee:

> 'There is a strong presumption that retrogressive measures taken in relation to the right to social security are prohibited under the Covenant. If any deliberately retrogressive measures are taken, the State party has the burden of proving that they have been introduced after the most careful consideration of all alternatives and that they are duly justified by reference to the totality of the rights provided for

[30] The drafters believed that 'it was for the specialized agencies to give economic, social and cultural rights their practical and detailed expression', as aptly summed up by the Yugoslavian representative (UN Doc. E/CN.4/SR.220, 13). See also the Greek representative's statement that there was 'a very marked tendency in the Economic and Social Council and the General Assembly to make reservations with regard to the detailed definition of economic and social rights' (UN Doc. E/CN.4/SR.221, 14).

[31] UN Doc. E/CN.4/SR.221, 11.

[32] ICECSR Committee, General Comment No. 19 (2007), *The Right to Social Security (Article 9)*, UN Doc. E/C.12/GC/19, para. 24.

in the Covenant, in the context of the full use of the maximum available resources of the State party.'[33]

In earlier general comments, the prohibition of retrogressive measures without proper justification had been understood as that the need to preserve an absolute minimum, or the minimum essential levels or core obligations. Retrogressive measures incompatible with the core obligations were considered to be *prima facie* violations. In other words, no justification could be invoked for retrogressive measures incompatible with the core obligations.[34] In line with these earlier general comments, the complete withdrawal of all social protection benefits for an indefinite period of time in case of job refusal would have been considered as a violation of the core obligations, and therefore an impermissible retrogressive measure. Unfortunately, the Committee in its General Comment on the right to social security has reverted to its 1990 position that the obligation to observe core obligations too is qualified by the maximum available resources, thereby lowering considerably the standard to be met by States.[35]

3.2. ILO CONVENTION NO. 168 ON EMPLOYMENT PROMOTION AND PROTECTION AGAINST UNEMPLOYMENT (1988) AND THE EUROPEAN CODE OF SOCIAL SECURITY

ILO Convention No. 168 on Employment Promotion and Protection against Unemployment (1988) is not a human rights treaty.[36] Moreover, it has only been ratified by eight States[37] and can therefore hardly be considered as a broadly accepted and authoritative instrument to interpret the right to social security as it pertains to unemployment benefits. However, the ECSR *de facto* applies the standards of this Convention in its examination of reports, and extends thereby quite considerably its scope of application in practice.

---

33 Ibid., para. 42. In the same paragraph, the Committee clarifies how it will assess in concreto deliberately retrogressive measures.

34 See e.g. ICECSR Committee, General Comment No. 14 (2000), *The Right to Highest Attainable Standard of Health (Article 12 of the ICECSR)*, UN Doc. E/C.12/2000/4, para. 48.

35 ICECSR Committee, General Comment No. 3 (1990), *The Nature of States Parties Obligations (Art. 2, para. 1)*, para. 10. For a commending comment, see M. Langford and J.A. King, 'Committee on Economic, Social and Cultural Rights. Past, Present and Future', in M. Langford (ed.), *Social Rights Jurisprudence. Emerging Trends in International and Comparative Law*, Cambridge: Cambridge University Press, 2008, p. 493.

36 This and other ILO Conventions tend to be situated more and more in a rights based approach to social security, though, see CEACR, *Report III (1B) & Add. – General Survey concerning social security instruments in light of the 2008 Declaration on Social Justice for a Fair Globalization*, March 2011, www.ilo.org/ilc/ILCSessions/100thSession/reports/reports-submitted/WCMS_152602/lang--en/index.htm.

37 Next to three Nordic countries, Norway, Sweden and Finland, also Albania, Belgium, Brazil, Romania and Switzerland.

Convention No. 168 allows for withdrawal, reduction or suspension of unemployment benefits under specific conditions. A distinction is made between voluntary and involuntary unemployment. The latter is protected. Freely chosen employment is stressed. The Convention clearly stems from an era in which the unemployment benefits trap was already well-known.[38] In Article 2 of the Convention, States parties commit themselves to seeking to ensure that 'their systems of protection against unemployment, and in particular the methods of providing unemployment benefit, contribute to the promotion of full, productive and freely chosen employment, and are not such as to discourage employers from offering and workers from seeking productive employment'. It offers nevertheless a good level of protection against the withdrawal of unemployment benefits in case of refusal to accept employment. Withdrawal of benefits can only in case of refusal to accept *suitable* employment. A list of criteria for assessing suitability of employment is offered:

> 'In assessing the suitability of employment, account shall be taken, in particular, under prescribed conditions and to an appropriate extent, of the age of unemployed persons, their length of service in their former occupation, their acquired experience, the length of their period of unemployment, the labour market situation, the impact of the employment in question on their personal and family situation and whether the employment is vacant as a direct result of a stoppage of work due to an on-going labour dispute.'[39]

The CEACR for a long time only adopted direct requests with regard to this Convention. This changed in 2007, when the Committee issued its first observation with regard to Norway.[40] Confronted with the substitution of the rule that a person could be disqualified from receiving unemployment benefit for having refused 'suitable employment' by the more restrictive concept of withdrawing the

38 Lamarche submits that the Convention represents a 'paradigmatic change in social security', for it allows 'the right to an income replacement measure [to] be superseded by employment strategies aimed at shortening the stay on unemployment and encouraging the acceptance of work' (L. Lamarche, 'The Right to Social Security in the International Covenant on Economic, Social and Cultural Rights', in A. Chapman and S. Russell (eds.), *Core Obligations: Building a Framework for Economic, Social and Cultural Rights*, Antwerp: Intersentia, 2002, p. 109). She is very critical of this Convention, which she believes 'is essentially aimed at transforming the function of national unemployment regimes and not at protecting or guaranteeing replacement income to the unemployed.' Lamarche also submits that Convention No. 168 'departs from traditional ILO social security conventions, whose goal is continual improvement of the economic protection provided by social security regimes' (ibid., 110).

39 Article 21(2).

40 The CEACR makes two kinds of comments: observations and direct requests. Observations contain comments on fundamental questions raised by the application of a particular convention by a State. Direct requests relate to more technical questions or requests for further information (www.ilo.org/global/standards/applying-and-promoting-international-labour-standards/committee-of-experts-on-the-application-of-conventions-and-recommendations/lang--en/index.htm).

benefit for refusing employment 'without any reasonable grounds', the CEACR made the following comments. First, it pointed out that Convention No. 168 purported 'precisely (to offer) unemployed persons protection from the obligation to take up any job which is not suitable.'[41] Secondly, Article 21(1) specifies that the entitlement to the unemployment benefit may be withdrawn or suspended only when the person concerned refuses to accept *suitable* employment. The Committee therefore wanted to know whether and to what extent, in assessing the reasons advanced for a job refusal leading to the withdrawal of the benefit, account was taken in practice of the criteria of suitability of employment laid down in Article 21(2). It also wanted to know whether at least during an initial period of unemployment, consideration was given 'to his skills, qualification, acquired experience and length of service in his former occupation, as well as to his personal and family situation in case the job offered implies change of residence.' In the view of the Committee, disregard by the employment market service of the jobseeker's competence in judging the reasonableness of his or her refusal to accept the employment offered, had shifted the task of finding quality jobs suited to the theoretical and practical competence of the jobseekers from the employment market service on to the jobseekers themselves to become primarily their own responsibility.[42] The Norwegian government was asked to reconsider the question 'with a view to ensuring that, in all cases covered by art. 10, para. 1 of the Convention in relation to art. 21, unemployment benefit is paid at least during the initial duration of unemployment specified in Article 19, paragraph 2(a)'.[43] In subsequent observations, the Committee has in particular emphasised the need of offering the unemployed protection against the obligation to take up any job *during an initial 26-week period* of unemployment.[44]

As confirmed by questions put to other States parties, not only qualifications and professional experience, but *all* criteria of suitability of employment foreseen by the Convention are to be taken into account.[45] The CEACR therefore seems

41 Article 10(1) reads: 'The contingencies covered shall include, under prescribed conditions, full unemployment defined as the loss of earnings due to inability to obtain *suitable* employment with due regard to the provisions of Article 21, paragraph 2, in the case of a person capable of working, available for work and actually seeking work' (emphasis added).

42 CEACR, *Direct Request concerning Convention No. 168, Employment Promotion and Protection against Unemployment, Norway*, 2000, para. 1, www.ilo.org/dyn/normlex.

43 CEACR, *Direct Request concerning Convention No. 168, Employment Promotion and Protection against Unemployment, Norway*, 2000, para. 1, www.ilo.org/dyn/normlex. A similar concern was expressed with regard to Sweden, where sanctions for refusing an unsuitable job seemed to apply after 20 calendar weeks, whereas the Convention provides for 26 calendar weeks of initial protection, see CEACR, *Direct Request concerning Convention No. 168, Employment Promotion and Protection against Unemployment, Sweden*, 2008, www.ilo.org/dyn/normlex.

44 CEACR, *Observation concerning Convention No. 168, Employment Promotion and Protection against Unemployment, Norway*, 2007 and 2008, www.ilo.org/dyn/normlex.

45 See e.g. CEACR, *Direct Request concerning Convention No. 168, Employment Promotion and Protection against Unemployment, Brazil*, 1999 and 2013; CEACR, *Direct Request concerning Convention No. 168, Employment Promotion and Protection against Unemployment, Romania*, 1998, www.ilo.org/dyn/normlex.

to apply a stricter test than the ECSR, which focuses almost exclusively on the criterion of qualifications and experience.

The question has also arisen whether it is compatible with Convention No. 168 to provide for the withdrawal of the entitlement to an unemployment benefit if the insured person, without any reasonable grounds, refuses to seek income from the creation of a self-employed activity during the benefit period. In the view of the Committee, 'the aim of the law appears to consist in compelling unemployed persons who have the capacity of doing so, to move from formal employment into self-employment, under the threat of the withdrawal of the unemployment benefit at the discretion of the employment market service officials.' As self-employed persons were not covered by the Norwegian unemployment protection scheme, this meant that they were automatically pushed outside the scope of that scheme. Where the self-employment activity failed, a person who initially enjoyed the protection against unemployment would find himself in the situation of having been deprived of that protection by the institute of unemployment benefit itself. The Committee considered, hypothetically ('to the extent that this may be the case'), that:

> 'such method of providing unemployment benefit could not be deemed compatible with the Convention, which, on the contrary, aims at extending unemployment protection progressively to additional categories of persons by, inter alia, bringing previously self-employed persons under the coverage of the unemployment protection scheme (Article 26). As designed by the Convention, unemployment benefit is intended to serve as a transitional wage replacement to help unemployed persons to return to suitable employment carrying full rights to unemployment protection and other social security benefits (Articles 10 and 14), but not to direct them into self-employment where they are likely to lose any of those rights. Read together with these provisions of the Convention, Article 20 therefore would not permit to withdraw unemployment benefit on the ground that the person concerned refused to earn income from self-employment instead of from suitable employment.'[46]

The Committee also recalled that the employment promoted by an activation policy designed to promote full and productive employment in the broadest sense, using all appropriate means, including social security, should be freely chosen: 'By implication, the principle of the free choice of employment should also extend to such other forms of productive activities which society deems necessary to promote through its labour market policy.' It emphasised that the element of compulsion, 'exercised through the threat of the withdrawal of the entitlement to unemployment benefit in case of refusal to earn income from self-employment, could be hardly reconciled with the requirement that social security means in

[46] CEACR, *Direct Request concerning Convention No. 168, Employment Promotion and Protection against Unemployment, Norway*, 2000, para. 2, www.ilo.org/dyn/normlex.

general and the methods of providing unemployment benefit in particular should contribute to the promotion of freely chosen employment (Articles 7 and 2 of the Convention).'[47]

Interestingly, the CEACR does not rely on human rights arguments, but rather on arguments of sound labour market policy to justify its comments, such as 'the most effective utilization … of human resources potential'[48] and the avoidance of 'a lowering of the skills level of the national workforce and the substantial reduction of the employment opportunities for unskilled workers at the low end, pushing them into long-term unemployment and exclusion', thereby creating labour market imbalances and inefficiencies and situations of underutilisation of the human resources potential.[49]

The CEACR also assists in monitoring implementation of the European Code of Social Security (1964),[50] which is together with its Protocol and the Revised Code (1990)[51] one of the 'basic standard-setting instruments of the Council of Europe in the field of social security'.[52] The (Revised) European Code of Social Security defines unemployment in terms of the absence or suspension of earnings due to the inability to find *suitable* work, not just any work (Article 20 Code, Article 19 Revised Code). Article 19(2) of the Revised Code offers a list of criteria to establish suitability, which are broadly similar to the ones in ILO Convention No. 168.[53]

3.3. (REVISED) EUROPEAN SOCIAL CHARTER

The European Social Charter is the core treaty on social rights within the Council of Europe. It was first adopted in 1961, and revised in 1996.[54] The right to social security is guaranteed in Article 12 of the RESC. It reads:

---

47 Ibid.

48 CEACR, *Direct Request concerning Convention No. 168, Employment Promotion and Protection against Unemployment, Norway*, 1999, www.ilo.org/dyn/normlex.

49 CEACR, *Individual Direct Request concerning Convention No. 168, Employment Promotion and Protection against Unemployment, Norway, 2000*, para. 1, www.ilo.org/dyn/normlex.

50 Ratified by 21 States.

51 Only ratified by the Netherlands in 2009 so far.

52 J. Nickless, *European Code of Social Security: Short Guide*, Strasbourg: Council of Europe Publishing, 2002, p. 5.

53 i.e. the age of the unemployed person, the length of his service in his previous occupation, his experience, the duration of his unemployment, the State of the labour market and the employment's impact on his personal and family circumstances.

54 The European Social Charter has been ratified by 27 Member States of the Council of Europe. The Revised European Social Charter (RESC) contains the provisions of the ESC and the 1988 Protocol, and adds a number of new or strengthened substantive provisions. It has been ratified by 33 Member States of the Council of Europe. The 1996 RESC is meant to gradually replace the 1961 Charter. Monitoring of both Charters is exercised by the European Committee of Social Rights (ECSR). All Conclusions referred to in the subsequent footnotes can be found at http://hudoc.esc.coe.int/eng.

'With a view to ensuring the effective exercise of the right to social security, the Parties undertake:

1 to establish or maintain a system of social security;
2 to maintain the social security system at a satisfactory level at least equal to that necessary for the ratification of the European Code of Social Security;
3 to endeavour to raise progressively the system of social security to a higher level;
4 to take steps, by the conclusion of appropriate bilateral and multilateral agreements or by other means, and subject to the conditions laid down in such agreements, in order to ensure:
    a equal treatment with their own nationals of the nationals of other Parties in respect of social security rights, including the retention of benefits arising out of social security legislation, whatever movements the persons protected may undertake between the territories of the Parties;
    b the granting, maintenance and resumption of social security rights by such means as the accumulation of insurance or employment periods completed under the legislation of each of the Parties.'

Article 12 RESC is one of the 'hard-core'[55] provisions, that is one of the articles every State party is obliged to accept a minimum number of.[56] The first paragraph establishes the principle of the institution or the maintenance of a system of social security. The second paragraph defines a minimum level. This minimum level differs in the 1961 and 1996 version: the former refers to ILO Convention No. 102, the latter to the European Code of Social Security. The difference between the two reference instruments lies in the minimum requirements with regard to the number of parts that are to be accepted for the ratification of the respective instruments (i.e. three for the ILO Convention, six for the European Code). The third paragraph of Article 12 RESC contains an undertaking to progressively raise the system of social security to a higher level. The final paragraph encourages measures to ensure equality of treatment between nationals of different Member States as well as the granting, maintenance and resumption of social security rights in other Member States.[57]

For our purposes, the undertaking in Article 12(3) RESC to raise progressively the system of social security to a higher level is of particular importance. The Committee has emphasised from the beginning that it requires States 'to make a continuous effort to bring their social security systems progressively to a higher level.'[58] Its control in respect of this paragraph is stricter than in respect of the first

55 ECSR, *General Considerations on Certain Areas Covered by the Charter: Social Protection, Conclusions XIII-4*, Strasbourg: Council of Europe Publishing, 1996, p. 35.

56 The (R)ESC is based on an à la carte system in which States choose which Articles or paragraphs they are bound by. Under the ESC, States are to accept at least 5 of the 7 hard core Articles (Art. 20(1) ESC). Under the RESC, States are to accept at least six out of nine hard-core Articles (Art. A, part III RESC).

57 See ECSR, *Conclusions I* 1969–70, p. 62.

58 Ibid., pp. 62 and 200.

two paragraphs.[59] In light of a perceived tendency to make legislation and practice more *restrictive*, rather than expansive, for demographic, economic and financial reasons, the ECSR adopted a general observation on this paragraph in 1996.

In the wake of the financial and economic crises since 2008, the ECSR has dealt with complaints about restrictive changes to the Greek social security system. In a complaint about a very restricted entitlement to social security for young workers under an apprentice contract, it defined the limits to limitations to the right to social security:

> 'The Committee recognizes that it may be necessary to introduce measures to consolidate public finances in times of economic crisis, in order to ensure the maintenance and sustainability of the existing social security system. However, any such measures should not undermine the core framework of a national social security system or deny individuals the opportunity to enjoy the protection it offers against serious social and economic risk. Therefore, any changes to a social security system must maintain in place a sufficiently extensive system of compulsory social security and refrain from excluding entire categories of workers from the social protection offered by this system ... The Committee considers that financial consolidation measures which fail to respect these limits constitute retrogressive steps which cannot be deemed to be in conformity with Article 12 § 3.'[60]

With regard to reforms of pension schemes it held:

> '[T]he Committee has explicitly considered that restrictions or limitations to rights in the area of social security were compatible with the Charter in so far as they appeared necessary to ensure the maintenance of a given system of social security ... and did not prevent members of society from continuing to enjoy effective protection against social and economic risks.[61]

A reasonable justification not only requires a legitimate objective (i.e. the maintenance of a given social security system), but also proportionality ('necessary') between the measures taken and the objective pursued (compare Article 31 of the Charter on restrictions). The Committee has put forward five criteria to assess compatibility of restrictions to the right to social security: (1) the nature of the changes; (2) the reasons given for the changes and the extent of the changes; (3) the necessity of the changes and their adequacy to achieve the aims

59 Ibid., p. 40.

60 ECSR, 23 May 2012, No. 66/2011, *General Federation of employees of the national electric power corporation (GENOP-DEI) and Confederation of Greek Civil Servants' Trade Unions (ADEDY) v Greece*, para. 47.

61 ECSR, 7 December 2012, No. 76/2012, *Federation of employed pensioners of Greece (IKA-ETAM) v Greece*, para. 71.

pursued; (4) accompanying measures of social assistance taken for those who end up in a situation of need following the changes; and (5) the results obtained.[62]

Article 13 (R)ESC guarantees the right to social and medical assistance. In the view of the ECSR, it is one of the Charter's originalities to 'enshrine not only the right to social security but also the right to social and medical assistance.'[63] Although the Committee recognises the 'highly controversial' nature of the dichotomy between social security and social assistance, it takes nevertheless the division into account, for the respective provisions in the Charter contain different undertakings for States.[64] Benefits are qualified as social assistance (in contradistinction to social security) if 'individual need is the main criterion for eligibility, without any requirement of affiliation to a social security scheme aimed to cover a particular risk, or any requirement of professional activity or payment of contributions.' Social security on the other hand includes 'contributory, non-contributory and combined allowances related to certain risks ... and are not intended to compensate for a potential state of need which could result from the risk itself'.[65]

Another provision that might be relevant to assess whether and to what extent the right to social security can be qualified by a duty to work, is Article 1(2) of the (R)ESC. It reads:

> 'With a view to ensuring the effective exercise of the right to work, the Parties undertake: ...
>
> 2 to protect effectively the right of the worker to earn his living in an occupation freely entered upon;'

Article 1(2) thus guarantees the right to free choice of employment. The ECSR has in fact examined measures of suspension or withdrawal of social security benefits in case of refusal to accept a job under both Article 12 and Article 1 (R)ESC. Before turning to the conclusions of the Committee, a closer look will be had at the measures introduced by the States parties in recent years.

The positions of States parties can roughly be brought under one of the following categories:

(1) a job can at all times be refused if it is not suitable or unreasonable;
(2) a job that is not suitable can be refused during an initial period; or
(3) a job can never be refused.

During the 2013 reporting cycle, it appeared that the following five States parties (as compared to eight in the 2006 cycle) maintained a system in which a job offer

62 Ibid., para. 72.
63 ECSR, *supra* note 55, p. 35.
64 Ibid., p. 36.
65 Ibid., p. 36.

could always be refused if it was not suitable or reasonable: Armenia, Cyprus, France,[66] Iceland and Moldova. Criteria to assess suitability included a person's qualifications and skills, experience, age, physical aptitude and health, family situation, level of remuneration, working conditions, and travel time, cost of transport or possibility of finding accommodation.

At least four States (as compared to six in the 2006 cycle) allowed unemployed persons to refuse an unsuitable or unreasonable job offer during an initial period: Austria, Belgium (with the exception of occupations in which employment opportunities are very limited), Finland and Iceland. After that initial period, the criteria of suitability or reasonableness could be relaxed with regard to the correspondence of the job offer with the training, qualifications and occupational background of the jobseeker, or more generally. The initial period was usually of a minimum of three to six months. The Committee asked 13 States to clarify whether there was a reasonable initial period during which an unsuitable job could be refused.

A minority of Member States, i.e. Denmark,[67] Norway[68] and Sweden,[69] have operated a system in which a job not matching with qualifications and previous occupation cannot be refused without losing unemployment benefits or facing a reduction in benefits, even not during an initial period of unemployment.

The ECSR has shown a growing interest in the issue of reducing, suspending or withdrawing unemployment benefits in case of job refusal. In 1995, and to our knowledge for the first time, the issue was raised with regard to one State only (i.e. Belgium). In subsequent years, attention was paid to it with regard to less than five States (three in 1997; four in 1999; two in 2001; one in 2002). The Committee took a real interest in 2004, when the issue was examined in the conclusions of eight countries, and systematised its queries about it in 2006. In the 2009 review cycle, the Committee followed up on the issue with a substantial number of States, but refrained from finding any situation of non-conformity, also in cases in which it had done so previously, e.g. Denmark and Germany.[70] In the 2013 review cycle, it touched on the issue with regard to 25 States, and asked from more than half of them for more information on a reasonable initial period during which an unemployed person could refuse a job or a training offer not matching his/her

66 With regard to France, this was already clear in the 2006 cycle, see ECSR, *Conclusions* 2006 (France).

67 ECSR, *Conclusions XVIII-1* (Denmark).

68 ECSR, *Conclusions* 2006 (Norway).

69 ECSR, *Conclusions* 2013 (Sweden), p. 21. Sweden considered however the reintroduction of a 100 days reasonable initial period.

70 ECSR, *Conclusions* 2009 (Belgium), p. 130; (Bulgaria), p. 168; (Cyprus), p. 198; (Finland), p. 258; (France), pp. 307–308; (Italy), pp. 414–415; (Lithuania), pp. 466–467; (Malta), p. 502; (Moldova), p. 542; (Netherlands), pp. 575–576; (Norway), pp. 612–613; (Romania), pp. 698–699; (Sweden), p. 769; ESCR, *Conclusions XIX-2* (2009): (Denmark), pp. 141–142; (Germany), pp. 180–181; (Greece), p. 220; (Hungary), p. 257; (Iceland), p. 279; (Poland), p. 360; (Slovak Republic), p. 389; (Spain), p. 426.

previous skills without losing his/her unemployment benefits.[71] The ECSR found two situations of non-conformity.

Initially, the ECSR examined the loss of benefits for refusal to accept a job under the right to work, and more in particular the right to freely chosen work. Next to issues of forced labour and eradication of all forms of discrimination in employment, it examined (after a while under a separate heading of 'Other aspects of the right to earn one's living in an occupation freely entered upon') the suspension or withdrawal of benefits. After having raised the issue also under the right to social security,[72] or both under the right to work and the right to social security with regard to some States,[73] the Committee as of 2006 has examined the issue exclusively under the right to social security and social assistance.[74]

The ECSR has never criticised the withdrawal of unemployment benefits in cases of refusal to work, to search for a job, or to undergo training after a reasonable initial period,[75] unless criminal sanctions were applied.[76] Clearly, the Committee does not reject activation measures or Active Labour Market Policies (ALMPs). Under the (R)ESC, States are allowed to sanction beneficiaries of the social security system who refuse to accept a *suitable* job. The definitions of what a suitable, reasonable or appropriate job offer constitutes vary considerably, and it would be good for the Committee to indicate what the minimal elements of a suitable, respectively a reasonable or appropriate job offer are. In our view, crucial elements of a suitable job are: qualifications and occupational experience; whether the job would unduly restrict the future prospects of a person in pursuing his/her (original) occupation;[77] family situation; working conditions and remuneration; and travel distance.

States can also oblige beneficiaries of unemployment benefits to accept *any* job, regardless of qualification and experience, but here some limitations apply. First, this can only been done after a 'reasonable' initial period has lapsed, during which an unemployed person's qualification and professional experience are

---

71 ESCR, *Conclusions* 2013 (Montenegro), p. 20.

72 See e.g. ECSR, *Conclusions XV-1* (Norway), p. 441.

73 e.g. ECSR, *Conclusions XVII-1* (Czech Republic), vol. 1, pp. 93 and 104.

74 See e.g. for Belgium, with regard to which it raised the issue three times under Article 1(2) (ECSR, *Conclusions XVII-1*, vol. 1, p. 59; *Conclusions XIV-1*, 102–104; *Conclusions XIII-4*, pp. 329–330), before dealing with it exclusively under Art. 12 in 2006 (*Conclusions XVIII-1*), albeit it with reference to its earlier treatment under Art. 1(2).

75 ECSR, *Conclusions XVII-1* (Czech Republic), vol. 1, p. 93. Compare *Conclusions XVIII-1* (Poland).

76 Articles 198 and 199 of the Danish Criminal Code (repealed in 1999) laid down penalties for idleness or insufficient means of subsistence for which the persons concerned was held responsible. The Committee considered that the situation in Denmark was not in conformity with Article 1(2) of the Charter with respect to the prohibition of forced labour as long as these provisions had not been repealed (see ECSR, *Conclusions XV-1* (Denmark), vol. 2, pp. 139–140).

77 ECSR, *Second Addendum to conclusions XV-1* (Germany), p. 18.

to be taken into account.[78] For the ECSR, this goes to the heart of the right to unemployment benefits itself:

> 'Under Article 12, the Committee considers that one of the aims of an unemployment benefit system is to offer unemployed persons adequate protection during at least an initial period of unemployment from the obligation to take up any job irrespective of their occupational field, with a view to giving them the opportunity of finding a job which is suitable taking into account their individual preferences, skills and qualifications.'[79]

An obligation to accept any reasonable job from the first day of unemployment is believed 'to undermine the adequate coverage of the unemployment risk for which every worker has contributed during his working activity.'[80] In the view of the Committee, three months is a reasonable initial period. Depending on the other conditions, it initially held three months to be too short in the case of Denmark.[81] On the other hand, considering employment in *another occupation* reasonable after 100 days of claiming unemployment benefits was accepted to be in conformity with the Charter.[82] Similarly, to require an unemployed person after three months to broaden his/her job search 'unless he/she has a clear chance of finding work in his/her own field of experience in the near future', was deemed acceptable under the Charter.[83] In the 2013 reporting cycle, it has itself suggested a three-month period as reasonable. The longer the period of unemployment, the less fully an unemployed person's qualifications and experience need to be taken into account.

Secondly, a right to appeal to an independent body against decisions on the suitability of the employment and on the length of suspensions is to be provided for.[84] Thirdly, in terms of sanctions, the Committee has not excluded the permanent withdrawal of the unemployment benefit following the refusal of a job, but has asked whether that would be the case,[85] as well as whether that person would qualify for social assistance.[86] Finally, the economic and social

---

78 ECSR, *Conclusions XVII-1* (Czech Republic), vol. 1, p. 93: 'It considers that full compliance with the right to earn one's living in an occupation freely entered upon entails a reasonable initial period when job seekers can refuse offers of employment that do not match their qualifications and experience ... without risking the suspension of their unemployment benefits.' Compare ECSR, *Conclusions 2009* and *Conclusions XIX-2*, where the Committee has repeated this principle with regard to many States under review.

79 ECSR, *Conclusions XVIII-1* (Denmark).

80 Ibid.

81 ECSR, *Conclusions XVI-1* (Denmark), vol. 1, pp. 169–170.

82 ECSR, *Conclusions XVIII-1* (Austria).

83 ECSR, *Conclusions 2006* (Ireland).

84 ECSR, *Conclusions XIV-1* (Belgium), pp. 102–104; ECSR, *Conclusions XV-1* (Denmark), vol. 2, pp. 139–140. Compare ECSR, *Conclusions 2009* and *Conclusions XIX-2*.

85 ECSR, *Conclusions XV-1* (Denmark), vol. 2, pp. 139–140.

86 ECSR, *Conclusions XV-1* (Italy), vol. 2, p. 357.

context is to be taken into account in order to assess the proportionality of a measure: in a situation close to full employment and of economic growth very stringent measures will be difficult to defend.

Based on the foregoing, the Committee has so far found only five instances of non-conformity. In most cases, it preferred to ask more detailed information. Information requested typically deals with the number of suspended cases and their duration, questions for clarification of the grounds and modalities of suspension, whether and which avenues for appeal are available, and in the 2013 cycle, whether there was an reasonable initial period during which an unsuitable or unreasonable job offer could be refused.

In Norway, unemployed persons were to accept a job regardless of their skills, qualification or prior occupational experience, or of their personal and family situation when the proposed job entailed a change of residence. While the Committee acknowledged that 'the introduction of measures enabling the social security system to contribute actively to combating unemployment and to the re-settlement of unemployed persons in economic life form(ed) part of the objectives of the social protection policy of the Norwegian Government', and that these objectives were not in themselves incompatible with Article 12(3), it considered that:

> 'in a situation close to full employment and of economic growth … the adoption of measures which are so restrictive is not proportionate to the objectives pursued and does not come within the range of adaptations of the social security systems permissible under Article 12 para. 3.'[87]

The Committee concluded that the development of the situation in Norway was not in conformity with Article 12(3) of the ESC.

In its 2006 conclusions, the Committee held that Norwegian legislation was not in conformity with Article 12(1) of the revised Charter since there was no reasonable initial period during which the unemployed could refuse a job not matching with his previous occupation and skills without losing his unemployment benefits. It justified its conclusion by referring to the nature of social security itself: the lack of an initial period 'undermine[d] the adequate coverage of the unemployment risk for which every worker ha[d] contributed during his working activity.'[88] In 2009, it no longer found a situation of non-conformity following clarification by the government that during the first three months of unemployment, responsibility for finding a job lay with the jobseekers themselves, which meant that it was in fact themselves who determined the suitability of the potential job.[89]

87 ECSR, *Conclusions XV-1* (Norway), p. 441.
88 ECSR, *Conclusions* 2006 (Norway).
89 ECSR, *Conclusions* 2009 (Norway), pp. 612–613.

In Denmark, unemployed persons were to take any reasonable job from the first day of employment. Reasonable work was any work that the individual is able to perform. The Committee considered that this was not in conformity with the Charter 'since there (was) no reasonable initial period during which the unemployed may refuse a job not matching with his previous occupation and skills without losing his unemployment benefits.'[90]

Seriously stringent legislation that was initially considered to be in conformity with the ESC applied in Germany. Under German legislation, in principle any job was assumed a suitable job. Exceptions were the physical or mental inability to perform the work; if it would unduly restrict the future prospects of a person in pursuing his/her (original) occupation; or if other important grounds could be invoked, such as the raising of a child, responsibilities towards a household or care for a relative. The raising of children was not taken into account when the children were over three years and when appropriate day care facilities were available. The following elements could not alone lead to a job being considered not suitable: that the job did not correspond to the previous occupational activity of the person; that the job was of low value in view of the person's education; that the geographical distance to the place of work was greater than to the previous place of work; or that the working terms and conditions were less favourable than in the previous job. Notwithstanding the stringent measures, the Committee concluded that the situation was in conformity with Article 1(2) of the Charter with respect to the prohibition of forced labour.[91] The availability of appeal to an independent body seemed to be an important factor in the decision of conformity. Moreover, the measures described applied under social assistance law, not under social security law. However, in 2006, the Committee concluded that the legislation was not in conformity with the Charter as there was no reasonable initial period during which an unemployed could refuse a job not matching previous occupation and skills. In the Committee's view, this legislation undermined the adequate coverage of the unemployment risk for which every worker had contributed during his working activity.[92]

In the 2013 cycle, it found situations of non-conformity in the Netherlands and Romania, mainly because they had not responded to the Committee's request for information under the 2009 cycle, so that it had not been established by the States concerned that there was a reasonable initial period.[93]

The Committee has shed a light on the acceptability of linking willingness to seek work or the acceptance of a job offer with *social assistance* too. Since its 2006 conclusions with regard to Luxembourg, it has accepted that it is in principle:

---

90 ECSR, *Conclusions XVIII-1* (Denmark), p. 275.

91 ECSR, *Second Addendum to Conclusions XV-1* (Germany), p. 18.

92 ECSR, *Conclusions XVIII-1* (Germany), pp. 309–310.

93 ESCR, *Conclusions* 2013 (Netherlands), p. 22; (Romania), p. 26.

> 'compatible with Article 13 to establish a link between social assistance and willingness to seek work or undertake vocational training, so long as the conditions are reasonable and fully consistent with the objective of providing a long-lasting solution to the individual's problems. However, reducing or suspending social assistance benefits is only compatible with the Charter if this does not deprive the individual concerned of means of subsistence … There must also be a right of appeal against any decision to suspend or reduce benefits'.[94]

Under the Luxembourg Guaranteed Minimum Income Act, as amended in 2004, applicants for the Guaranteed Minimum Income (GMI) had to be available for employment and be ready to accept any job offered by the employment office.[95] If a person lost his entitlement to GMI, he *could* receive benefits under the Emergency Residence Act. There was however no legal claim to it. The Committee therefore concluded that 'the withdrawal of social assistance for reasons such as refusal to accept a job offer … may amount to a total deprivation of the person concerned of his/her means of subsistence as there are no sufficient legal guarantees for other types of assistance'.[96] So clearly, an unconditional link between the right to social assistance and an obligation to work is incompatible with the Charter. Conditions such as the willingness to seek employment or to receive vocational training must be reasonable and consistent with the aim pursued (i.e. to find a lasting solution to the individual's problems), and the reduction of the level of social assistance benefits should not go under a certain minimum level needed for subsistence.[97] In case of withdrawal of a particular type of social assistance, there must be sufficient legal guarantees for other types of assistance.[98]

States are thus confronted with two sets of principles under Article 13, between which a certain tension may exist. On the one hand, the Committee has argued that social assistance should not be understood in the narrow sense of the payment of a subsistence allowance. Rather,

> 'the system of social assistance must embrace an integrated strategy of alleviation of poverty and empowerment of individuals to regain their place as full members of society, through the means most appropriate to their personal circumstances, wishes and ability, and customary in the society where they live. In most cases,

94 ECSR, *Conclusions XVIII-1* (Luxembourg). Compare ECSR, *Conclusions XIV-1, General Introduction*, p. 52, para. 56; ESCR, *Conclusions* 2013 (Serbia), p. 25.

95 ECSR, *Conclusions XVIII-1* (Luxembourg).

96 ECSR, *Conclusions XIX-2* (Luxembourg), p. 334. The same standard of 'deprivation of means of subsistence' was applied in the 2013 reporting cycle, see e.g. ECSR, *Conclusions* 2013 (United Kingdom), p. 20; (Malta), p. 30.

97 ECSR, *Conclusions XIX-2* (Czech Republic), p. 107. The Committee concluded in a similar vein that the situation in Romania was not in conformity with the Charter because 'it had not been established that the possibility of withdrawal of assistance in response to the failure to undertake community work [did] not amount to a complete deprivation of means of subsistence for the person concerned'; see ECSR, *Conclusions 2009* (Romania), p. 707.

98 ECSR, *Conclusions XIX-2* (Luxembourg), p. 334.

> employment opportunities, together with vocational training or re-training, constitute the core element in any such strategy.'[99]

Central to the right to social assistance are job opportunities and vocational training. On the other hand, States should be careful in making social assistance benefits conditional upon readiness of accepting job offers and/or training.

The Committee has also scrutinised legislative provisions under which persons who had deliberately reduced or abandoned their paid employment, who had been dismissed for serious misconduct or who had lost *unemployment benefit* (i.e. a social security benefit) for refusing to accept a position offered by the employment office, were not entitled to a social assistance benefit either. The Committee submitted, in accordance with its established case law, that individual need should be the only condition for entitlement to social assistance and that the only ground for refusing, suspending or reducing such assistance is that adequate resources are available. It then concluded 'that the link made between dismissal for serious misconduct and the right to social assistance (was) not in conformity with Article 13 § 1.'[100] It is unclear whether the Committee meant that all three grounds for non-entitlement were not in conformity (i.e. deliberate reduction or abandonment of paid employment; dismissal for serious misconduct; and loss of unemployment benefit for refusing to accept a position offered by the employment office), or only the particular ground of dismissal for serious misconduct. While the Committee only referred to the latter ground explicitly, it did not offer any arguments why the other two grounds for non-entitlement would be acceptable notwithstanding the general principle that the only ground for refusing, suspending or reducing social assistance is that adequate resources are available so that an individual is not deprived of his or her means of subsistence.

In conclusion, while acknowledging economic, financial and demographic challenges to the systems of social security in Europe, the ECSR has only accepted reforms, including making social security and social assistance benefits conditional upon the willingness to (seek) work, to the extent that they do not threaten the essence of the rights to social security and social assistance. Central to an adequate coverage of the unemployment risk under the right to social security is a reasonable initial period during which the unemployed can refuse a job not matching with their previous occupation and skills without losing their unemployment benefits. The right to social assistance is characterised by the fact that individual need is the only condition for entitlement to social assistance. The only ground for refusing, suspending or reducing such assistance is that adequate resources are available. Moreover, under both rights a safety net is to be provided for. In case an unemployed person is denied an unemployment benefit, he must be eligible for a social assistance benefit. If someone is denied a social assistance

99 ECSR, *Conclusions XIV-1* (General Introduction), p. 52, para. 54.

100 ECSR, *Conclusions XVIII-1* (Luxembourg).

benefit, this should not deprive him of his means of subsistence. Finally, the right-character of the rights to social security and to social assistance should not be trembled upon: appeal to an independent body against any job offer or refusal/suspension of benefits is to be provided for. So neither an unjustified refusal to (seek) work on the part of the beneficiary of social security/social assistance benefits, nor an unconditional linkage between the acceptance of a job offer and eligibility to social security/social assistance benefits on the part of States can find support in the (R)ESC.

Whereas an increased emphasis on individual responsibility is not rejected per se, it does not in any way lower the obligations of the State nor the corresponding individual rights of the rights-holders. In another context, that of the encouragement of volunteer work in the provision of social welfare services by States parties, for the elderly, the disabled and children, the ECSR has made clear that it has no difficulty with increasing the 'individual's sense of responsibility within the community', but that final responsibility rests with the State.[101]

The European Court of Human Rights has so far not taken position on making social protection conditional on the willingness to (seek) work.[102] The Court has brought rights to social security and social welfare benefits within the ambit of the right to property. Social security rights are protected under the right to property, regardless of the fact whether contributions have been paid.[103] Although it has maintained that 'Article 1 of Protocol No. 1 does not include a right to acquire property … [and that it] places no restriction on the Contracting State's freedom to decide whether or not to have in place any form of social security scheme, or to choose the type or amount of benefits to provide under any such scheme',[104] it has also held that if a State 'has in force legislation providing for the payment as of right of a welfare benefit – whether conditional or not on the prior payment of contributions – that legislation must be regarded as generating a proprietary interest falling within the ambit of Article 1 of Protocol No. 1 for persons satisfying its requirements.'[105] In the event of a complaint about the violation of the right to property in regard to a social security or social assistance benefit which has been provided for as of right, the Court will therefore have to examine whether the applicant satisfies the requirements for the benefit. It remains to be seen whether the Court would be prepared to examine also the reasonableness of the requirements. Only then might the Court be able to offer

---

101 See L. Samuel, *Fundamental Social Rights – Case Law of the European Social Charter*, Strasbourg: Council of Europe Publishing, 2002, p. 335.

102 On the ECHR and social security, see M. Cousins, *The European Convention on Human Rights and Social Security Law*, Antwerp: Intersentia, 2008; A.G. Heredero, *Social security as a human right. The protection afforded by the European Convention on Human Rights*, Strasbourg: Council of Europe Publishing, 2007.

103 ECtHR (GC) (adm) 6 July 2005, *Steck v. UK*, paras. 50–53.

104 Ibid., para. 54; ECtHR (GC) 12 April 2006, *Steck v. UK*, para. 53.

105 ECtHR (GC) (adm) 6 July 2005, *Steck v. UK*, para. 54.

individual redress for the withdrawal of social protection benefits for refusal to accept *any* job offered, regardless of suitability.

4. CONCLUSIONS

Central to this chapter is the question whether the human right to social protection and the duty to work are on an equal footing, and how to resolve any conflict that may arise between them. In our view, the human right to social protection (including both the right to social security and the right to social assistance) is of a higher normative order than the duty to work. No convincing arguments have been put forward so far to change this hierarchy between human rights and duties.

Human rights are seldom absolute, though. The right to social protection is no exception: it may be subject to limitations, provided a reasonable justification can be given. In relation to a duty to work, this means that a withdrawal of social protection benefits is only permissible if the person concerned refuses a *suitable* job offer. Suitability is to be defined in light of qualifications and experience, wage and working conditions and family situation. An appeal to an independent body to challenge the suitability of a job offer and the withdrawal of benefits should be available. Whereas flexibility in interpreting the suitability of a job may increase the longer a person receives social protection benefits, at least during a reasonable initial period suitability should be assessed quite strictly.

In the context of the (R)ESC, the withdrawal of *social security* benefits has mainly been examined in light of the obligation to progressively raise the level of the system of social security (Article 12(3) (R)ESC). In light of the latter provision, it is submitted that the ECSR may well have accommodated too much neo-liberalism and active labour market policies, and downplayed too much human rights standards. Not only has it accepted retrogressive measures, while the Charter only provides for progressive measures, it has also defined the reasonable initial period during which an unemployed should be entitled to refuse an unsuitable job quite short, and it has mainly if not exclusively focused on qualifications and experience, while downplaying the other criteria for suitability. Nonetheless, it has also shown some firmness, in that it insists on basic protection. In case an unemployed person is denied an unemployment benefit, he must be eligible for a social assistance benefit. With regard to the right to *social assistance*, the ECSR has rightly emphasised that sanctions for job refusal should never deprive a person of his means of subsistence.

Finally, the duty to work and to contribute to the system of solidarity is to take duly into account ability: the duty to work applies first and foremost to those in a position to do so.

HUMAN RIGHTS IN A GLOBALISING ECONOMY

Rights and Responsibilities of Trade Unions

Barbara J. FICK

1. INTRODUCTION

In addressing the role of trade unions in the local, national and international economy, many commentators, both within the labour movement as well as outside, tend to focus quite narrowly on the role of unions in organising and representing workers in the workplace. This is not surprising given that the fundamental objective of the trade union movement is to ensure the social and economic well-being of workers, and a common experience affecting that well-being is what happens in the workplace. Thus union activity aimed at improving wages and working conditions obviously serves to achieve that fundamental objective.

But workers' social and economic well-being is not solely affected by what occurs within the workplace, and trade unions have a role in influencing government policies on economic and social issues generally, and in working to insure political and civil rights. Not only is this role consistent with the fundamental objectives of the trade union movement, it is a responsibility[1] which unions assume as the beneficiary of the rights to association, assembly and free speech.

[1] I am using the term 'responsibility' in the sense in which René Foqué defines it in his chapter in this volume, i.e. an ethically based concern inspiring action with respect to issues involving the welfare of others.

2. UNIONS AS BENEFICIARIES OF HUMAN RIGHTS PROTECTION

The Universal Declaration of Human Rights recognises as a basic human right the right to freedom of association,[2] and in particular the right to form and join trade unions.[3] Other international and regional instruments recognising the right to association also specifically mention the right to form trade unions.[4] Unions have benefited from the protections accorded by these and other international instruments in securing their ability to freely operate to protect worker interests.

The right to association, however, is not only a good in itself, i.e. as an individual freedom to form human relationships, but is also a means to achieving other goods;[5] in the case of trade unions it also provides a means of ensuring the social and economic well-being of workers. It is this instrumental aspect of freedom of association which encompasses the obligation to use that freedom in ways that will advance human rights and dignity for the community as a whole.

This instrumental responsibility has been directly addressed in the 1998 UN Declaration on the Right and Responsibility of Individuals, Groups and Organs of Society to Promote and Protect Universally Recognized Rights and Fundamental Freedoms (UN Declaration).[6] Article 18 sets out the responsibility of groups and non-governmental organisations (NGOs) to promote human rights and contribute to the promotion and advancement of democratic societies, institutions and processes.

---

2 Universal Declaration of Human Rights Art. 20, GA Res. 217A, at 71, UN Doc. A/810 (1948).

3 Ibid., Art. 23(4).

4 See, e.g., International Covenant on Civil and Political Rights, Art. 22, 19 December 1966, 999 *UNTS* 171 (entered into force 23 March 1976); International Covenant on Economic, Social and Cultural Rights, Art. 8, 16 December 1966, 993 *UNTS* 3 (entered into force 3 January 1976); European Convention for the Protection of Human Rights and Fundamental Freedoms, Art. 11, 4 November 1950, *Europ. T.S.* No. 5, 213 *UNTS* 221 (entered into force 3 September 1953); American Declaration of the Rights and Duties of Man, Art. XXII, *OAS Official Rec.* OEA/Ser.L./V./11.23, Doc. 21, rev. 6 (1948); Arab Charter on Human Rights, Arts. 28 and 29, 15 September 1994, reprinted in 18 *Hum. Rts. L.J.* 151 (1997).

5 See, e.g., *Roberts v. U.S. Jaycees*, 468, U.S. 609, 617–618 (1984): 'Our decisions have referred to constitutionally protected 'freedom of association' in two distinct senses. In one line of decisions, the Court has concluded that choices to enter into and maintain certain intimate human relationships must be secured against undue intrusion by the State because of the role of such relationships in safeguarding the individual freedom that is central to our constitutional scheme. In this respect, freedom of association receives protection as a fundamental element of personal liberty. In another set of decisions, the Court has recognized a right to associate for the purpose of engaging in those activities protected by the First Amendment – speech, assembly, petition for the redress of grievances, and the exercise of religion. The Constitution guarantees freedom of association of this kind as an indispensable means of preserving other individual liberties.'

6 Declaration on the Right and Responsibility of Individuals, Groups and Organs of Society to Promote and Protect Universally Recognized Human Rights and Fundamental Freedoms, GA Res. 53/144, UN Doc. A/RES/53/144 (8 March 1999).

3. THE 'TRADITIONAL' ROLE OF TRADE UNIONS

In discussing the role of trade unions, a preliminary matter of definition may be useful. Trade unions are organisations whose membership includes workers and whose purpose, in whole or in part, is to represent the workers in dealing with employers relating to workplace issues, and to promote and defend the interests of workers. In order to effectively pursue these objectives the structure of a trade union should be democratic, responsive to the interests of the workers, and free from government control and interference. This definition applies to the majority of trade unions in the world, although some unions labour under government control (e.g. China, and the Democratic People's Republic of Korea), or are subject to excessive government interference (e.g. Madagascar, Iran or Zimbabwe), which limits their effectiveness both in promoting and defending worker rights as well as in fulfilling their broader responsibility in promoting human rights generally.

Even when viewing trade union activities within the narrow perspective of their mission to represent worker interests in the workplace, the issues with which they deal fall squarely within the sphere of human rights defined as economic rights. Thus, negotiating with both employers and governments to improve wages, safety and health at work, social security protections and job security puts unions squarely in the forefront of promoting basic human economic rights as defined in, *inter alia*, the Universal Declaration of Human Rights,[7] the International Covenant on Economic, Social and Cultural Rights,[8] and the American Declaration of the Rights and Duties of Man.[9] But even within their traditional role, unions have never limited themselves to purely 'economic' issues.

A brief look at some of the International Labour Organisation (ILO) Conventions suggests the breadth of interests relating to protecting worker rights. While the majority of the Conventions do address workplace issues, there are also Conventions dealing with social policy,[10] the rights of migrant workers,[11] as well

---

7 Universal Declaration of Human Rights, *supra* note 2, at Arts. 22 (right to social security), 23 (right to work) and 24 (reasonable limitations on hours of work).

8 International Covenant on Economic, Social and Cultural Rights, *supra* note 4, Arts. 7 (right to fair wages and safe and healthful working conditions) and 9 (right to social security).

9 American Declaration of the Rights and Duties of Man, *supra* note 4, Arts. XIV (right to work and fair remuneration) and XVI (right to social security).

10 International Labour Organisation Convention (No. 117) Social Policy (Basic Aims and Standards) Convention, adopted 22 June 1962, 494 *UNTS* 249. In explaining the rationale behind the adoption of this Convention, the preamble states that 'steps should be taken by appropriate international, regional and national measures to promote improvement in such fields as public health, housing, nutrition, education, the welfare of children, the status of women, conditions of employment'.

11 International Labour Organisation Convention (No. 143) Migrant Workers (Supplementary Provisions) Convention, adopted 24 June 1975, 1120 *UNTS* 323. Art. 1 requires that States 'respect the basic human rights of all migrant workers.'

as the very first international instrument dealing with the rights of indigenous peoples.[12]

The broad scope of interests encompassed by the trade union movement was apparent from the early days of the industrial revolution. Samuel Gompers, the first president of the American Federation of Labor and one of the architects of the International Labour Organisation at the Versailles Peace Conference, delivered an address entitled 'What Does Labor Want?' before the International Labour Congress held in Chicago Illinois in 1893. His answer was: 'We want more schoolhouses and less jails; more books and less arsenals; more learning and less vice; more constant work and less crime; more leisure and less greed; more justice and less revenge; in fact more of the opportunities to cultivate our better natures, to make manhood more noble, womanhood more beautiful and childhood more happy and bright.'[13]

Separate from an interest in promoting economic and social goods for society as a whole, the trade union movement also has a role in promoting and maintaining democratic conditions in society, i.e. civil and political rights. The 1970 *ILO Resolution Concerning Trade Union Rights and Their Relation to Civil Liberties*[14] recognises that without the assurance of fundamental civil and political rights, the ability of trade unions to achieve their objectives is severely hampered. Moreover, 'by developing countervailing power trade unions can prevent or check cronyism … and in this way they contribute to good governance. An empirical cross-country study using data from the period 1985–1994 showed that freedom of association is correlated with reduced corruption. … Evidence was also found of a positive statistical relationship between labour standards, democracy and political freedom.'[15]

Thus, it can be seen that trade unions have both a self-interest in promoting the economic, social and political rights of workers in the workplace and in the

---

[12] International Labour Organisation Convention (No. 107) Indigenous and Tribal Populations Convention, adopted 26 June 1957, 328 *UNTS* 247. This Convention requires States to 'promot[e] the social, economic and cultural development of these populations and rais[e] their standard of living' (Art. 2(2)(b)); to give priority in economic development plans to the improvement of the conditions of life and work and level of education of the populations concerned' (Art. 6); to allow indigenous populations 'to retain their own customs and institutions where these are not incompatible with the national legal system' (Art. 7(2)); and to recognise '[t]he right of ownership, collective or individual, of the members of the populations concerned over the lands which these populations traditionally occupy' (Art. 11) This Convention was subsequently revised by International Labour Organisation Convention (No. 169) Indigenous and Tribal Peoples Convention, adopted 27 June 1989, 281 *ILM* 1382.

[13] Address by Samuel Gompers before the International Labour Congress, Chicago, Ill. (September 1893) as quoted by T.R. Donahue, 'The Role of and Challenges Facing Unions in the 1940s and the 1980s – A Comparison' (1984) 52 *Fordham L. Rev.* 1062, 1063.

[14] Resolution Concerning Trade Union Rights and Their Relation to Civil Liberties preamble, Int'l Labour Conf., 54th Sess., Record of Proceedings 733 (1970): 'without national independence and political liberty full and genuine trade union rights could not exist.'

[15] W. Sengenberger, *Globalization and Social Progress: The Role and Impact of International Labour Standards,* 2002, p. 58.

broader society, as well as a responsibility under the UN Declaration to protect and promote the broad range of human rights.

4. THE IMPORTANCE FOR UNIONS TO PERFORM A BROADER ROLE

Trade unions are ideally situated to deal not only with local and national problems but also those created by the globalising economy. The structure of the trade union movement provides a ready mechanism for addressing issues at all levels of society. Local unions are affiliated with national labour organisations, which themselves band together to form national federations. In turn, most national federations are members of international confederations. This structure facilitates communication from the local to the regional to the national and finally international arena. These relationships are well-established and enjoy a long tradition of collaboration on trade union issues.

For example, from 1949 until 2006, the largest international confederation was the International Confederation of Free Trade Unions (ICFTU), with 241 affiliated unions in 156 countries and a membership of 155 million workers.[16] It operated regional offices in Africa, Asia and the Pacific and the Americas. On 1 November 2006, the ICFTU merged with the World Confederation of Labour (the second largest international confederation) to create a new international confederation – the International Trade Union Confederation (ITUC). This new body consists of 309 national affiliates representing 175 million workers in 161 countries. It maintains its predecessor's regional presence in Africa, Asia and the Pacific and the Americas.[17]

An example of a national federation is the American Federation of Labor-Congress of Industrial Organizations (AFL-CIO) established in 1955, with 56 affiliated unions representing 12.5 million workers.[18] The AFL-CIO, through its international arm, Solidarity Center, maintains 20 regional offices throughout Africa, South and Central America, Asia, Eastern Europe and the Middle East.[19] Thus, the trade union movement is well-positioned geographically to contest authority in the local, national and global settings.

With grass-roots actors on the ground in local and national union structures, unions are in a good position to perform monitoring and intelligence-gathering roles concerning human rights issues. Their relationships with employers, and

---

16 See www.icftu.org/displaydocument.asp?DocType=Overview&Index=990916422&Language=EN.

17 See www.ituc-csi.org/ IMG/pdf/no_7_-_list-affiliates_03co_may_2014-2/pdf.

18 The AFL-CIO is the result of a merger between the American Federation of Labor, founded in 1886, and the Congress for Industrial Organization, founded in 1935. See www.aflcio.org/About?AFL-CIO-Unions.

19 See www.solidaritycenter.org/where-we-work/.

in particular multi-national corporations (MNCs) (which latter group can often be major figures in abetting human rights violations, as is evidenced by the allegations of Unocal involvement in the use of forced labour in Myanmar[20] or the alleged use of the military by Royal Dutch Shell to protect its oil facilities in Nigeria resulting in violence against the Ogoni people)[21] provide an opportunity to prevent and punish corporate wrongdoing. Their role as representative of workers who are also voters allows for exerting pressure on governments to improve political, social and economic rights. Their relationship with their members and workers provides an ongoing opportunity for education on social and political issues.

Lederach, in his work on conflict transformation and peace-building, speaks of an intermediate level of actors within a societal pyramid who are strategically placed to provide an infrastructure for resolving conflict. He identifies three levels of players: the top-level which is composed of the elite political, military and economic leaders; the bottom level which is the grass-roots of society with local leadership; and the mid-range leadership of primary networks of groups and institutions which exist within the society, such as heads of national religious institutions, academic institutions or highly visible civil society organisations.[22]

In his work of attempting to reconcile differences and resolve conflict, he found that working solely with the top-level leadership presents the problem of implementation: they may agree to a solution but can they ensure implementation or acceptance at the grass-roots level? Focusing on the grass roots can be problematic as there is no systematic means for grass-roots work to impact the top level and there is often no connection between different grass-roots organisations to ensure wide-spread coherent agreement at the local level. Lederach views the top and grass-roots level initiatives as occurring largely in isolation from each other and identified a need to link these two levels.

> '[I]f one relied exclusively on the highest level of actor, the peace process often was not able to translate itself downward in the society with a sense of broad-based support and the potential for implementation. On the other hand, if the process remained completely local, it was often incapable of generating change beyond local concerns. The "middle-out" idea, adding an intermediate level in the pyramid, emerged as a way of locating a set of actors that was able to link

---

20 See e.g. allegations relating to corporate involvement in forced labour in *Doe v. Unocal Corp.*, 110 F.Supp.2d 1294 (C.D. Cal. 2000) and ICFTU, *Letter to the Committee of Experts on the Application of Conventions and Recommendations: Burma, Forced Labour Convention, 1930 (Convention No. 29)*(14 October 2002), www.icftu.org/displaydocument.asp?Index=991216572.

21 See Wiwa v. Royal Dutch Petroleum Co., 226 F.3d 88 (2000). The case was subsequently settled in 2009 for $11 million.

22 J.P. Lederach, *Building Peace*, 1997.

vertically (up and down the society through one or another form of network) and horizontally (across the lines of division in the conflict).'[23]

While Lederach's work is mainly concerned with resolving violent conflict, his paradigm is useful for dealing with any type of societal conflict. In terms of identifying potential mid-level 'mediators', national trade unions and trade union federations clearly fit the role. The leaders of these organisations have access to both governmental elites (via the Ministry of Labour and their connections to labour-based political parties) and economic elites (via their collective bargaining role with business leaders). Having assumed their leadership positions through either direct or indirect democratic process, trade union leaders have access to, and influence on, their grass-roots constituency. Finally, they cut across the potential isolation of groups at the grass-roots level. The local union affiliates of a national trade union are geographically located throughout a society and cut across demographic lines. Thus, trade unions have the capacity for both horizontal and vertical interaction, fulfilling Lederach's requirements of actors 'who connect at both levels of leadership and bridge the divisions. These are considered to be strategic agents of change within the society.'[24]

Moreover, many human rights problems – from environmental damage to child labour – are created by the actions of MNCs, many of whom are susceptible to pressure from trade unions. The Global Union Federations[25] have capitalised on their relationships with MNCs to, *inter alia*, create contractual obligations (called International Framework Agreements) on the part of MNCs to observe ILO core labour standards[26] at all their locations. Many of these International Framework Agreements include not only the core labour standards but also requirements for decent wages and working conditions. Some of the more recent agreements even contain clauses whereby the MNC agrees to require its suppliers and business partners to similarly observe core labour standards. There are over 100 framework agreements covering such diverse groups of MNCs as DaimlerChrysler (automobile manufacturing), AngloGold (gold mining and

23 J.P. Lederach, *From Resolution to Transformative Peacebuilding* in *From the Ground Up* (edited by C. Sampson and J.P. Lederach), 2000, p. 53.

24 J.P. Lederach, *supra* note 22, p. 117.

25 Global Union Federations are international organisations comprised of national trade unions within specific industrial or occupational sectors. For example, the International Metalworkers' Federation is composed of 200 national unions which represent workers in the metal industry.

26 In 1998 the ILO adopted the Declaration on Fundamental Principles and Rights at Work recognising four core labour standards: freedom of association and right to collective bargaining; the elimination of forced labour; the elimination of child labour; and the elimination of discrimination in employment and occupation. International Labour Organisation, Declaration of Fundamental Principles and Rights at Work, 37 *ILM* 1233 (1998).

exploration), Ikea (retail home furnishings), Accor (hotels and tourism), and Danone (food industry).[27]

The trade union movement is thus well-placed within the local, national and international scene to effectively promote the human rights agenda both at the governmental and corporate level.

5. ARE TRADE UNIONS FULFILLING THEIR RESPONSIBILITY?

The answer to that question is an equivocal 'to some degree'. Certainly on the international level, the trade union movement has been active on many different human rights issues. At its 1988 World Congress, the ICFTU stated that its mission was to influence international economic and social policy, to promote peace, security and disarmament, and to protect and promote trade union and other basic human rights. The ICFTU regularly engaged with both the World Bank and the International Monetary Fund, *inter alia*, to advocate greater global equity and financial stability, to pressure these institutions to drop harmful conditions on loans to developing countries and to mobilise support for debt cancellation. It also called for the international financial institutions to implement a decent work agenda to achieve sustainable poverty reduction.

The ICFTU worked with its affiliate unions to promote peace and reconciliation within divided countries and societies. It worked with its Greek and Turkish affiliates in Cyprus to bridge the divide between north and south, bringing together trade unionists from both sides of the island to discuss freedom of movement and a single model of employment as well as the possibilities for reunification.[28] The ICFTU sponsored meetings between its Palestinian and Israeli affiliates to promote joint cooperation on economic and social issues.[29] The ICFTU's global campaign to eliminate child labour included working with both trade unions and NGOs at the local and regional levels to support broadening educational opportunities as one measure for reducing child labour.[30]

Since the merger in 2006, the ITUC (successor to the ICFTU) has carried forward the ICFTU's human rights initiatives. The Constitution of the ITUC

---

27 For a list of International Framework Agreements, see global-unions.org/framework-agreements.html.

28 ICFTU Online, *Cypriot Union Leaders Join for Peace* (19 February 2004), www.icftu.org/displaydocument.asp?Index=991218975&Language=EN; ICFTU Online, *Cypriot Trade Unions Push for a Just and Permanent Solution* (11 July 2002), www.icftu.org/displaydocument.asp?Index=991216346&Language=EN.

29 See e.g. ICFTU Online, *Israeli and Palestinian Trade Union Centres Meet to Develop Cooperation Agreement* (14 April 2005), www.icftu.org/displaydocument.asp?Index=991221502&Language=EN.

30 18th World Congress of the ICFTU, *Congress Statement: Campaigning for an End to Child Labour*, www.icftu.org/displaydocument.asp?Index=991209288&Language=EN.

commits the organisation 'to promote and to act for the protection of democracy everywhere ... [i]t shall defend everywhere collective rights and individual liberties, including freedom of thought, expression and assembly.'[31] The ITUC is, *inter alia*, continuing its predecessor's global campaign to eliminate child labour.[32] Additionally, under the ITUC umbrella, Histradrut (the Israeli national trade union centre) and the Palestinian General Federation of Trade Unions signed an agreement on 8 August 2008 protecting the rights of Palestinian workers employed by Israeli companies.[33] During the Russian incursion into Georgia in August 2008, ITUC worked with its Georgian and Russian affiliates to assess humanitarian needs and launched an appeal to help meet the needs of those affected by the conflict.[34]

Many national trade union organisations have also worked to promote peace and human rights. After the genocide, the Confederation of Trade Unions of Rwanda established a social pharmacy system to enable workers to obtain medicine at reasonable prices, and a cooperative store system where workers who had not been paid could receive loans and stock up on provisions. It also developed a micro-financing bank to help kick-start the economy.[35] In an attempt to begin healing the ethnic divisions caused by the Bosnian War, the Trade Union Federation of the Republika Srpska and the Trade Union Federation of Bosnia-Herzegovina created a multi-ethnic trade union in the Brcko district.[36] In 2003 the South African Clothing and Textile Workers' Union established five union-based voluntary HIV testing and counselling centres.[37] Solidarity Center has worked with the Indian National Trade Union Congress on a pilot program to reduce HIV/AIDS transmission through training workshops and distribution of materials to unions, management and NGOs.[38]

More recently, a Chinese ship attempted to deliver its cargo of arms and ammunition to the Mugabe regime in Zimbabwe during the interim period between the 29 March 2008 presidential election and the scheduled run-off on 27 June 2008. The ship docked at the port of Durban, South Africa. Fearful that these weapons could be used against Mugabe's political opponents, the South African transport workers union (SATAWU) refused to unload the ship or to transport any cargo by truck overland to Zimbabwe. When the ship left

---

31 ITUC, Constitution: Declaration of Principles at 5, www.ituc-csi.org/IMG/pdf/Const-ENG_2WC.pdf.

32 See ITUC, Union View #18 (May 2010), www.ituc-csi.org/child-labour-enough.html.

33 See www.ituc-csi.org/spip.php?article2334.

34 See www.ituc-csi.org/spip.php?article2349.

35 ICFTU, *Spotlight Interview with Eric Manzi* (2 October 2003), www.icftu.org/displaydocument.asp?Index=991218486&Language=EN.

36 Agreement of 23 May 2000 between the Trade Union Federation of the Republika Srpska and the Trade Union Federation of Bosnia-Herzegovina regarding the Brcko district, on file with the author.

37 Solidarity Center, *2003–2004 Annual Report*, p. 13, www.solidaritycenter.org/content.asp?pl=910&sl=910&contentid=911.

38 Ibid.

the Durban port, SATAWU contacted its union counterparts in other African ports to alert them that the vessel may attempt to unload its cargo elsewhere. The International Transport Workers' Federation (the global union federation with which SATAWU is affiliated) mobilised its union affiliates in Mozambique, Angola and Namibia, receiving assurances that they would also refuse to unload the ship. Eventually the freighter returned to China.[39]

In many countries, however, trade unions at both the local and national level are reluctant to step beyond their roles in the workplace to challenge their governments and other leaders regarding broader social, economic and political issues. This is sometimes the result of fear, sometimes lack of resources, but often the result of the leaders' too narrow vision as to the role of their organisation. More work needs to be done on capacity building to develop the ability of these unions to fulfil their responsibility to the larger society as required by the UN Declaration.

6. THE WAY AHEAD

Over the last twenty years there has been a growing realisation among all segments of the NGO community, including trade unions, of the importance of working together to protect human rights in a globalising society. The annual World Social Summit is one concrete manifestation of this realisation. But there is clearly more bridge building that can be done – not just to talk about common problems but to actively work together to deal with them.

Local and regional trade union groups are a valuable source of 'on the ground' intelligence about local problems and situations. They can provide data to human rights lawyers and NGOs in support of their work. Closer collaboration is needed between human rights groups and trade unions in monitoring government compliance with human rights standards, initiating and supporting litigation on behalf of third parties whose rights have been violated, and pressuring MNCs to uphold human rights in their business dealings, whether it be concerns for the environment, accessibility to their pharmaceutical products or treatment of their workers. Human rights NGOs can work with local trade unions in helping to build the latter's capacity to use their position within society to promote and protect the broad range of human rights.

The human rights community also needs to work with trade unions to insure government respect for trade union independence. Trade unions controlled by the government (as in China), or subject to government repression (as in Belarus), or harassed by government officials (as in Zimbabwe) are unable to effectively

39 See e.g. C. Dugger, 'Zimbabwe Arms Shipped by China Spark an Uproar', *New York Times*, 19 April 2008, A1; J. Moyo and N. Tolsi, 'Arms Ship Turns Tail', *Mail & Guardian Online*, 25 April 2008, www.mg.co.za/article/2008-04-25-arms-ship-turns-tail.

perform their fundamental objective of ensuring the economic and social well-being of workers much less their responsibility under the UN Declaration to promote and protect basic human rights. This collaboration thus needs to be a two-way street: with unions working to promote the broad spectrum of human rights, and human rights groups working with unions to ensure union independence and freedom of action.

Confronting human rights problems in a globalising economy requires a strong connection between international and local actors. The trade union movement is an ideally situated, but underutilised, actor which can play a major role in contesting global authority and ensuring respect for human rights.

FUNDAMENTAL RIGHTS AND RESPONSIBILITIES WITHIN A MULTICULTURAL SOCIETY

Marlies GALENKAMP

1. INTRODUCTION

In Western European multicultural societies in the last few years, rights collisions have become daily practice. Especially the right to freedom of religion and freedom of expression are the talk of the town. Are discriminatory statements on homosexuals under the banner of the freedom of religion acceptable?[1] Does the right to freedom of expression also imply the right to offend, a question that was raised in the debate on the Danish cartoons.[2] Does the right to freedom of religion also legitimate that an orthodox Islamic employee may refuse to shake hands with someone of the opposite sex?[3]

In Dutch constitutional law circles, the answers to these questions tend to be in the affirmative. Rights such as the two aforementioned are commonly viewed as the most fundamental ones in a liberal-democratic state. By restricting them too easily, one would endanger rule of law fundamentals. Consequently, these rights are commonly seen as rather absolute ones. It is up to the rights bearer himself to decide how to make use of these rights. In my contribution to this book, I will critically comment on this view. It seems to me that these two rights – fundamental though they may be – should always be exercised responsibly.

In order to elucidate this proposition, my point of view will be a legal-philosophical one. The examples will be taken from the Dutch legal setting. In section 2, the stage will be set up by providing some analytical clarification on the nexus between rights and responsibilities. In the next section, I will argue

---

1 In the Netherlands the criminal lawsuits on Van Dijke and El Moumni are paradigmatic. Respectively, HR 9 January 2001, *NJ* 2001, 203 (*Van Dijke*) and Hof's-Gravenhage, 18 November 2002, LJ-nummer AF0667 (*El Moumni*).

2 The question was answered in the affirmative by Hirsi Ali in her speech 'The Right to Offend', delivered in Berlin, 9 February 2006. See on the topic of the Danish cartoons J. Klausen, *The Cartoons That Shook the World*, New Haven/London: Yale University Press, 2009.

3 Equal Treatment Commission (Commissie Gelijke Behandeling), judgment 2006-202 and 2006-221. Both judgments concerned a case in which an orthodox Muslim (respectively a man and a woman) refused to shake hands with someone of the opposite sex.

that the current Dutch discourse commonly presupposes a rather absolute view of constitutional rights. In section 4, by way of comparison, I will sketch some developments in the private law doctrine on ownership. From an absolute and sacrosanct right in the 18th century, this right has gradually evolved into a right that is principally qualified by doctrines such as rights abuse. Likewise, we may argue that the rights to freedom of expression and of religion may not be abused. In section 5, the currently absolute interpretation of these rights will be critically assessed. In the next section, we will return to practice. The three rights collisions mentioned at the beginning of this chapter will be scrutinised in more detail. Were the rights to freedom of expression and of religion exercised responsibly here or can one speak of rights abuse? In section 7, some objections to a responsibility approach will be examined. In the final section, we will conclude by dwelling on the question what exactly our responsibilities should be within a multicultural society.

2. RIGHTS AND RESPONSIBILITIES

It is a truism that there are no rights without responsibilities. But what do we mean by this? In this section, the nexus between rights and responsibilities will be addressed. Two questions will be dealt with. What kind of responsibilities are we talking about? Who is the bearer of these responsibilities?

As to the first question, I shall restrict myself to those responsibilities that are linked to fundamental rights. This is already a considerable restriction of the concerned responsibilities. Take the duty of citizens to pay taxes or to comply with the law in any legal order. Or take the duties to the community that can be found in the Universal Declaration,[4] the two International Covenants[5] and the African Charter.[6] These kinds of duties will not be elaborated upon. We will focus on responsibilities that are intrinsically correlated to rights. A second question arises then. Who is the bearer of these responsibilities? Is it the state, other citizens or the rights bearer himself?

First of all, one could say that fundamental rights of individuals give rise to correlative duties of state authorities to respect, fulfil and protect these rights. This viewpoint is the predominant one within the human rights framework.

4 Art. 29(1) of the *Universal Declaration of Human Rights* (1948) runs as follows: 'Everyone has duties to the community in which alone the free and full development of his personality is possible.'

5 The fifth preambular paragraph of both the *International Covenant on Civil and Political Rights* (1966) and the *International Covenant on Economic, Social and Cultural Rights* (1966) contains a statement that reads: 'the individual, having duties to other individuals and to the community to which he belongs.'

6 Art. 27(1) of the *African Charter on Human and Peoples' Rights* (1981) reads: 'Every individual shall have duties towards his family and society, the State and other legally recognized communities and the international community.'

As noted by Hammarberg[7] in his report on duties: 'The main approach of the Universal Declaration of Human Rights is to define the rights of individuals and to make fulfillment of those rights a responsibility of governmental authorities.' He concludes: 'Linked to human rights is a State obligation.' Within human rights instruments a lot of duties and obligations of state authorities are already recognised. One mostly distinguishes between negative duties of states – prohibitions on acting in a certain manner – and positive duties, that is, requirements to act in a certain way. In my contribution, I will not take this analysis as my starting point. For if one were to focus on duties and responsibilities of states with regard to the protection of individual rights, there would be nothing new under the sun.

Secondly, the responsibility could be argued to bear upon other citizens. That is, the exercise of one's rights creates responsibilities on the part of fellow citizens to respect these rights. This viewpoint also seems to be quite a familiar one within the human rights doctrine. This conclusion can be inferred from several articles of the Universal Declaration and of the two International Covenants.[8] These articles grant the individual the fundamental right to be accorded the dignity of a human being and they put an obligation on everyone to respect this dignity. Notice that this linkage of rights and responsibilities seems to lie at a moral level. In the last few decades it has been acknowledged that fundamental rights do not only create a moral responsibility on the part of other citizens to respect these rights, but also a legal obligation. This topic will be dealt with below.

Last but not least, one could connect rights and responsibilities by ascribing them to one and the same person. Anybody is the bearer of fundamental rights, but at the same time of responsibilities with regard to the proper exercise of these rights. In my article, I shall focus on this third, rather neglected approach. An example of this approach can be found in the Universal Declaration of Human Responsibilities that was proclaimed by the InterAction Council in 1997 at the fiftieth anniversary of the Universal Declaration.[9] The thought underlying this declaration was that the current tendency of maximisation of one's personal freedom – without consideration of others and even at the expense of others – is as problematic as having no rights at all. It seems to me that this 'rights and responsibilities' view is commonly overlooked in the Dutch debate on constitutional rights. This is due to a rather absolute interpretation of these rights.

---

[7] T. Hammarberg, 'Preface', in International Council on Human Rights, *Taking Duties Seriously: Individual Duties in International Human Rights Law. A Commentary,* Switzerland, 1999.

[8] Take, for example, Arts. 2 and 6, 29 and 30 of the *Universal Declaration* (1948) and the fifth preambular paragraph of both *International Covenants* (1966).

[9] See further on this declaration and on some criticisms section 7.

3. THE ABSOLUTISM OF FUNDAMENTAL RIGHTS IN DUTCH DISCOURSE

From the outset it should be noted that by using the adjective of 'absolutism', I depart from the standard phraseology within the human rights doctrine. Commonly, a distinction is made between absolute and relative fundamental rights. As noted by Vande Lanotte and Haeck,[10] absolute fundamental rights are those rights that are principally not subjected to qualifications and state interventions and whereby no balancing with other rights or interests has to take place. The right to life is often seen as a paradigmatic absolute right. Most fundamental rights are, however, relative. Both the right to freedom of expression and the right to freedom of religion are commonly viewed to fall within this last category. That is to say, both rights can be subjected to restrictions and state interventions. Besides, it is generally acknowledged that in case of relative rights one should always balance these rights with concurring rights and interests.

So, what exactly do I mean by the absolute interpretation of fundamental rights? It seems to me that despite the current view in the legal doctrine on their relative outlook, in Dutch discourse both fundamental rights are generally conceptualised in absolute terms. Individuals are considered to have these rights in a rather unqualified way. It is up to the individuals themselves as autonomous actors to determine how to make use of their rights. More specifically, one can find six proofs of this absolutism.[11] These can be found respectively, within the historical background of fundamental rights; a currently predominant legal-philosophical viewpoint; Dutch doctrine of constitutional rights; European case law; Dutch case law; and Dutch political debates. In the next sections (from section 5 onwards), these elements will be critically assessed.

First, as we all know, historically seen, fundamental rights originated from the vertical relationship of the ruler with the ruled. These rights were seen as protective devices of relatively weak and powerless citizens against powerful and mighty states. In view of this context, it is not surprising that these rights are generally interpreted in absolute terms. For any restriction of these rights would strike at the roots of the constitutional state. Take for example the French Declaration of the Rights of Man and Citizen of 1789. In the preamble of this declaration, human rights are formulated as '*des droits naturels, inaliénables et sacrés de l'homme*'. That is, as natural, inalienable and sacred rights. Most scholars argue that this maximised conception of rights originated from the work of John Locke, one of the fathers of constitutional rights, or, as he called them, 'natural rights'.

---

10 J. Vande Lanotte and Y. Haeck, *Handboek*, vol. 1: Algemene beginselen EVRM (Handbook ECHR, Part 1. General Principles), Antwerp/Oxford: Intersentia, 2005, p. 92.

11 Parts of this section were derived from M. Galenkamp, 'Towards a Socialization of Fundamental Rights', in E. Brems (ed.), *Conflicts between Fundamental Rights,* Antwerp/Oxford/Portland: Intersentia, 2008, pp. 149–165.

But we do not have to go that far back in history. One of the currently most influential legal philosophers, Ronald Dworkin, in the seventies wrote a book called *Taking Rights Seriously.*[12] In this book, fundamental rights such as the right to freedom of expression are conceptualised as 'political trumps, held by individuals, over collective goals'.[13] It is evident that this trump-character presupposes a far-reaching absolutism, wherein, for example, the freedom of expression obtains a preferred position over other rights and interests.

Also in the Dutch doctrine on constitutional rights one can find some evidence of an extensive and absolute interpretation. Take for example Burkens' textbook on constitutional rights, one of the standard texts in this field: 'Actions by the authorities should always be limited and specific. Diametrically opposed to this, there is the freedom of the individual. The citizen is in relation to the authorities free to do what he likes … This freedom is guaranteed by the provision of constitutional rights. The way citizens make use of their fundamental rights is their own business.'[14] No doubt, seen from a legal-philosophical perspective, this viewpoint is quite understandable. Liberal-democratic states are always founded on the axiom of individual autonomy. Within those states, there seems to be – in the words of the legal philosopher Joel Feinberg[15] – 'a presumption in favor of liberty'. The father of liberalism, John Stuart Mill, already argued in the 19th century that 'the burden of proof is supposed to be with those who are against liberty, who contend for any restriction or prohibition … The *a priori* presumption is in favor of freedom'.[16] Hence, liberal argumentations always start from the assumption of freedom. There is no need at all for a justification hereof. Instead, the onus of justification is on civil authorities trying to limit this freedom. Constitutional rights are commonly seen as the legal expression of this axiomatic freedom.[17]

A cursory survey of the case law on freedom of expression of the European Court of Human Rights leads to the same observation. Over the last few decades, the Strasbourg jurisprudence has emphasised that the freedom of expression conferred in Article 10 of the European Convention is not to be seen as confined

12 R. Dworkin, *Taking Rights Seriously*, London: Duckworth, 1977.

13 Ibid., XI.

14 M.C. Burkens et al., *Beginselen van de democratische rechtsstaat. Inleiding tot de grondslagen van het Nederlandse staats- en bestuursrecht* (Principles of the Constitutional State. Introduction to the Fundamentals of the Dutch Constitutional and Administrative Law), Deventer: W.E.J. Tjeenk Willink, 2006, p. 123 (translation by the present author). See in the same vein R. De Lange, *Botsing van grondrechten voor de rechter* (Fundamental Rights Collisions and the Judiciary), Nijmegen: Ars Aequi Libri, 1994, p. 45.

15 J. Feinberg, *Harm to Others*; part I of the four-volume work on *The Moral Limits of the Criminal Law*, New York/Oxford: Oxford University Press, 1983, p. 9.

16 J.S. Mill, *On the Subjection of Women*, in J.S. Mill and H. Taylor Mill, *Essays on Sex Equality* (edited and with an Introductory Essay by A.S. Rossi), Chicago/London: The University of Chicago Press, 1970 (originally: 1869), pp. 126–127.

17 M. Galenkamp, 'Towards a Socialization of Fundamental Rights', in E. Brems (ed.), *Conflicts between Fundamental Rights*, Antwerp/Oxford/Portland: Intersentia, 2008.

to information or ideas that are favourably received or deemed inoffensive. Shocking or offensive speech should also fall under the zone of protection. In the ECHR judgment *Handyside v. United Kingdom* (1976)[18] one can find the famous quote that became one of the building blocks of the European doctrine on freedom of expression: 'Freedom of expression constitutes one of the essential foundations of a democratic society, one of the basic conditions for its progress and for the development of every man … It is applicable not only to "information" or "ideas" that are favorably received or regarded as inoffensive or as a matter of indifference, but also to those that offend, shock or disturb the state or any sector of the population. Such are the demands of that pluralism, tolerance and broadmindedness without which there is no "democratic society". This means … that every restriction imposed in this sphere must be proportionate to the legitimate aim pursued.' Following this line of thinking, we seem to be irrevocably driven to subscribe to Hirsi Ali's conclusion that the right to offend actually falls under the internationally guaranteed freedom of expression.

With regard to Dutch case law, let us start with the criminal case law. Take, for example, the well-known criminal lawsuits on El Moumni (imam from Rotterdam) and Van Dijke (a former member of parliament of an orthodox Christian political party). They both had, when interviewed, presented their critical views on homosexuality that were founded on their orthodox religious convictions. In both cases, the freedom of religion conflicted with non-discrimination clauses in the penal code. It is remarkable that both accused were discharged, and this on the basis of the primordial value of the freedom of religion. One gets the impression that in the Dutch legal setting the underlying dilemmas are solved by simple sticking to the rights discourse. That is to say, if fundamental rights are at stake, the discussion seems to have come to an end. The concerned right is proclaimed once more and that's it. By doing so, the judge is no longer obliged to get around to a balancing of competing interests. We can also refer to judgments of the Dutch semi-judicial Commission on Equal Treatment. In 2006, the commission gave two separate judgments on the issue of the refusal of orthodox Muslims to shake hands with someone of the opposite sex. The commission decided that by doing so these Muslims may legitimately appeal to their right to freedom of religion. Hence, also in these instances the religious freedom of the individual believer was conceptualised in absolute terms. Competing societal considerations such as the value of gender equality apparently fell beyond the scope of the Commission.

A final illustration of the absolute interpretation of fundamental rights can be found in Dutch political debates in the last decade. For example, in the parliamentary debate on the Danish cartoons in 2006 almost all political parties – both on the right and the left – emphasised the unqualified nature of the freedom of expression. As Nicolaï, the State Secretary of the Ministry of Foreign Affairs in

18 ECtHR, 7 December 1976, *Handyside v. UK*, 5493/72, para. 14.

those days, stated: 'The freedom of expression is simply indispensable, inviolable and crucial to the free world.'[19]

It will come as no surprise that such an absolute interpretation in all likelihood will give rise to more rights collisions. You may have your absolute and inviolable right to freedom of expression, but I from my side may stick to my right to freedom of religion and our homosexual neighbour may in his turn appeal to the right to non-discrimination.

4. LESSONS FROM OWNERSHIP: NO ABUSE OF RIGHTS

In view of this absolutism and the resulting growth of rights collisions, it seems to me that there are some striking parallels that can be drawn with the developments in the Dutch private law doctrine on ownership.[20] In the 19th century, ownership was generally seen as a pre-eminently absolute and sacred right. The owner was viewed to have the absolute and unconditional competence to decide in what way he should make use of this property. Gradually it turned out that by conceptualising ownership in this way, social life becomes intolerable since infinite conflicts with one's neighbours lie in wait. This was the birth of the doctrine on rights abuse. In the Dutch legal setting, the so-called *Watertorenarresten*[21] in the middle of the 20th century provided the groundwork for this doctrine. In these judgments it was ultimately determined that even a pre-eminently inalienable and sacred right such as ownership should be exercised in a responsible way, taking into account the rights and interests of one's neighbours. From then onwards, Dutch private law doctrine has been filled more and more with moral principles such as reasonability, fairness and carefulness in the exercise of ownership. In case this carefulness towards others is not taken into account, one can speak of rights abuse. As the French jurist Duguit states: 'Like *noblesse, propriété oblige*'.[22] Notice that this standard of carefulness towards others is not only to be found in the common private law, but also in statutory law. Take the provisions in the Dutch Civil Code on the prohibition of abuse of ownership or the ban on nuisance.[23]

---

19 *NRC Handelsblad*, 6 February 2006.

20 See on the topic of rights abuse from a civil perspective M. Galenkamp, 'Misbruik van recht volgens Scholten, Eggens en Meijers' (Rights Abuse from the Perspective of Scholten, Eggens and Meijers), in M.C. Foblets, M. Hildebrandt and J. Steenbergen (eds.), *Liber Amicorum René Foqué*, Brussels: Larcier, 2012, pp. 35–48.

21 HR 13 March 1936, *NJ* 1936: 415 (*Watertoren I*) and HR 2 April 1937, *NJ* 1937, 639 (*Watertoren II*).

22 Cited in the report of the Council of Europe, *Abuse of Rights and Equivalent Concepts: The Principle and Its Present Day Application*, Proceedings of the Nineteenth Colloquy on European Law, Strasbourg, 1990, p. 135.

23 These provisions are to be found, respectively, in Article 5:37 and 3:13 of the *Dutch Civil Code*.

Likewise, actual developments within our multicultural society necessitate the reconsideration of the too absolute connotations of the right to freedom of expression and of religion. In the last few decades most Western European societies have pluralised more and more. The old religions and philosophies of life (Christian, Jewish, humanist and atheist) and the new ones (Islamic, Hindu, Buddhist) are now close neighbours. By interpreting fundamental rights as too absolute, the resulting picture of society would be that of a mass of autonomous individuals sticking to their rights without giving their neighbours any elbowroom. So just like the former developments in Dutch private law, it can lead to a permanent polarisation and threatening escalation. In the famous words of the political philosopher Thomas Hobbes,[24] it may end up in a *bellum omnium contra omnes*, a war of all against all. It seems to me that in order to prevent a permanent civil war against one another, fundamental rights should always be exercised responsibly. That is to say, by using his rights a citizen should always take into account the rights and interests of others. If these responsibilities towards others are lost out of sight, rights abuse is lurking. As noted by Daes,[25] '[a]s the State is not permitted to abuse its power, so an individual is not entitled to abuse his freedom.'

In several human rights instruments, one can find clauses on the ban of fundamental rights abuse. Take, for example, the Universal Declaration (Articles 29(3) and 30); the two International Covenants (Article 5) and the European Convention on Human Rights (Article 17). This last article runs as follows: 'Nothing in this Convention may be interpreted as implying for any State, group or person any right to engage in any activity or perform any act aimed at the destruction on any of the rights and freedoms set forth herein or at their limitation to a greater extent than is provided for in the Convention.' In human rights documents further back in time, we can also find clauses on the ban of rights abuse. Take for example the aforementioned French Declaration of the Rights of Man and Citizen. In Article 11, we find quite a qualified freedom of expression: 'The unrestrained communication of thoughts and opinions being one of the most precious rights of man, every citizen may speak, write or publish freely, provided he be responsible for the abuse of this liberty, in the cases determined by law.' In the Dutch constitution, however, one searches in vain for such a standard.[26] In section 7 I will argue that the legal provision of such a standard seems to me indispensable.

---

24 T. Hobbes, *Leviathan*, Middlesex: Penguin Books Ltd, 1985 (originally 1651), chapter 13.

25 E-I.A. Daes, *Freedom of the Individual under Law. A Study on the Individual's Duties to the Community and the Limitations on Human Rights and Freedoms under article 29 of the Universal Declaration of Human Rights*, New York: UN, 1990, p. 129.

26 See further on this topic M. Galenkamp and R. Westrik, 'Naar een nieuw burenrecht. Grondrechten in een pluriforme samenleving' (Towards a New Neighbour's Law. Constitional Rights Within a Multiform Society) (2004) 2 *Nederlands Juristenblad* 67.

5. FUNDAMENTAL RIGHTS: FREEDOMS AND RESPONSIBILITIES

Thus far we have argued that rights are not to be equated with freedoms. Possessing fundamental rights does not imply full sovereignty of the individual. In the 21st century, it is not proper anymore to present oneself as an autarkic and egotistic monad, merely and continuously asserting one's rights. One's freedoms – even the most fundamental ones such as the freedom of religion and the freedom of expression – are not unqualified. They are restrained by one's responsibility towards neighbours and other fellow citizens. Let me elucidate this intrinsic linkage between freedom and responsibility by reconsidering the first four elements underlying the currently absolute interpretation (see section 3). An assessment of the fifth and sixth aspect will take place in section 6 and 8, respectively.

Historically, it is true that fundamental rights originated from the vertical relationship of the citizen and the state. Seen from this perspective, the provision of a maximal protection of a relatively weak individual against the powerful state by means of absolute human rights is understandable. However, nowadays it is commonly acknowledged that most fundamental rights can also have third party applicability in the sense that other citizens should respect these rights too. Seen from this perspective, the presumed absolutism must be commented upon. For it is not hard to see that permanent rights collisions are looming then. The appeal on Locke as one of the fathers of natural, inalienable and unqualified rights can also be put into perspective. A close reading of Locke's work makes clear that to him natural rights are principally embedded within and restricted by the so-called natural law, God-given moral maxims.[27] These maxims establish limits to the proper exercise of one's rights. One should always respect the rights and interests of others. For example, if someone should appropriate more than he may use under the pretext of his property right, according to Locke he would offend against the natural law. We have a moral duty to leave enough and as good for others.

Besides and related, in view of the currently widely accepted third party applicability of constitutional rights, Dworkin's trump thesis seems to lose its attractiveness.[28] In case of rights collisions one major problem arises: which right should trump the other competing right? On this topic Dworkin's theory does not provide a satisfactory answer.

In line with the foregoing, we can counter Burkens' absolute view of constitutional rights. In contradistinction to what he suggests, the way citizens

[27] See M. Galenkamp, 'Locke and Bayle on Religious Toleration' (2012) *Erasmus Law Review*, forthcoming.

[28] See for a critical perspective on this viewpoint M. Galenkamp, 'Taking Rights Not That Seriously', in E.T. Feteris, H. Kloosterhuis, H.J. Plug and J.A. Pontier (eds.), *Alles afwegende* (All Considered), Nijmegen: Ars Aequi Libri, 2007, pp. 131–140.

make use of their fundamental rights cannot and should not merely be their own business. Following Locke, we might argue that those rights should always be exercised in a responsible way, taking into account the rights and interests of one's fellow citizens.

With regard to European case law, we referred to the ECHR judgment *Handyside v. United Kingdom* as one of the paradigm cases on the freedom of expression. This judgment is commonly interpreted as providing a maximal zone of protection to all kinds of expressions, shocking, offending and disturbing ones included. Reading a bit further in the judgment one can find a considerable qualification of the seemingly absolute outlook of this right: 'From another standpoint, whoever exercises his freedom of expression undertakes "duties and responsibilities" the scope of which depends on his situation and the technical means he uses. The Court cannot overlook such person's "duties" and "responsibilities"'. On the basis thereof, Hirsi Ali's view of the legitimacy of the right to offend does not seem to me correct. Her view betrays a too extensively interpreted freedom of expression and a disregard of corresponding responsibilities.

6. BACK TO PRACTICE

Let me elucidate my thesis once more by returning to the practice of Dutch case law. How should we evaluate the aforementioned cases of religiously based discriminatory statements, the Danish cartoons and the refusal to shake hands with someone of the opposite sex? Were the rights to freedom of expression and of religion exercised in a responsible manner here? If not, can one speak of rights abuse? These are difficult questions to answer in the abstract and they give rise to further questions. Where exactly should we draw the boundary between the legitimate use and abuse of one's rights? What does responsibility *in casu* mean? It seems to me that a legitimate use of one's rights would imply that the rights bearer accounts for the impact of his rights exercise on the rights and interests of others. And on the reverse: one can speak of rights abuse in case the rights bearer exclusively focuses on his rights and interests, hereby not merely disregarding, but even maliciously riding roughshod over the rights and interests of others.

With regard to the three cases, some doubts arise. The emerging picture is of a rather selfish and egotistical rights bearer sticking to his freedoms to the exclusion of others. On the basis of my constitutionally guaranteed freedom of religion and of expression, no doubt I can present my religiously inspired disapproving views on homosexuality or publish Muslim-offending cartoons. And of course, in our Western European and liberal societies an orthodox Muslim may choose for abstaining from all earthly temptations by refusing to shake hands with someone of the opposite sex. But is this really the societal harmony we are seeking? I do not think so. Orthodox beliefs – in whatever form: Christian,

Islamic or other – might be fine as providers of rules that can guide our private and inner lives. These beliefs lose their attractiveness however if they are given the role of providing societal and political guidelines.[29] In the words of Grimm,[30] '[t]he secular state does not oblige any religion to renounce its claim to be the only true one. But it does prevent every religion from imposing its truth on society as a whole.' In view of our pluralised societies in the 21st century, we cannot afford this anymore. Other, concurring and even antithetical beliefs live nearby us and have become our neighbours. In view of this, we cannot but live together. Already this empirical fact necessitates the willingness to abide by standards of civility and to move up a bit. As Grimm[31] concludes with regard to the freedom of religion: 'Peaceful coexistence of mutually exclusionary beliefs is not possible without limitations on religious freedom.' These qualifications can be elucidated in more detail now by focusing on the three cases once more.

First of all, the issue of the religiously based discriminatory statements by Van Dijke and El Moumni. As I said before, both accused were acquitted on the basis of the primordial importance and – I would say – unqualified and too absolute interpretation of the freedom of religion. By presenting these criminal cases in this manner, judges did not even get around the issues of balancing the competing interests. For example, nowhere in the verdicts can one find the consideration that both accused had to account for the impact of their sayings on homosexual fellow citizens. As Loenen[32] notes, the Dutch legal system up till now seems to be quite generous to religious opinions and religion-based behaviour. Referring to these criminal lawsuits, I would say there is too much generosity. Reframed in terms of this book, it seems to me that in judgments such as these the responsibility side of the rights-coin has mistakenly been lost out of sight.

In the worldwide debate on the Danish cartoons, the competing rights – right to freedom of artistic expression versus right to freedom of religion – were both presented as absolute. Consequently, as we all will remember, the debate polarised and escalated at high speed. Up until now there has not been any case law on the Danish cartoons in the Dutch legal setting. But if the Dutch judge were to decide on this issue, no doubt the right to freedom of expression would have prevailed. The right to freedom of expression is mostly seen as one of the cornerstones of a liberal-democratic society. As long as one's expressions contribute to societal debates – something that the Danish cartoons indubitably did! – they should go free and should not be restricted. The relevant provisions in the Dutch penal

29 See in the same vein I. Buruma, *Taming the Gods. Religion and Democracy on Three Continents*, Princeton: Princeton University Press, 2010.

30 D. Grimm, 'Freedom of Speech in a Globalized World', in I. Hare and J. Weinstein (eds.), *Extreme Speech and Democracy*, Oxford: Oxford University Press, 2009, p. 18.

31 Ibid., p. 18.

32 T. Loenen, *Geloof in het geding. Juridische grenzen van religieus pluralisme in het perspectief van de mensenrechten* (Beliefs in Issue. Legal Limits To Religious Pluralism From the Perspective of Human Rights), The Hague: Sdu Uitgevers, 2006, p. 55.

code – such as the ban of scornful blasphemy[33] – are currently interpreted very restrictively. But once again, we are witnesses to an imbalance here. The right to freedom of expression seems to have been prioritised, and this at the cost of other considerations, such as the protection of vulnerable religious minorities. The newspapers that published the cartoons can be blamed for not having accounted enough for the rights and interests of Muslim citizens. Even more, the publication of the cartoons was explicitly meant as a test case in order to determine the extent and limits of the right to freedom of expression. In such a case, it is practically impossible to evade a deliberate riding roughshod over the rights and interests of others.

Finally, the debate on the refusal of some orthodox Muslims to shake hands with someone of the opposite sex. It seems to me that here the Dutch Equal Treatment Commission went too far in the recognition of religious claims, hereby overlooking other competing considerations, such as the value of gender equality and of respectful treatment. It seems to me that the right to freedom of religion is neither absolute, nor should it be elevated – by means of these semi-judicial judgments – to a nearly absolute status. The necessary conditions for living together peacefully are at stake.

To sum up: it remains to be seen whether in the cases above we can really speak of rights abuse. Further research on this topic is needed. What is clear however is that in all cases the intrinsic linkage between rights and responsibilities was disregarded, not only by the rights-bearer himself, but also by the (semi-) judge. A reappraisal of the responsibility side of the rights discourse is called for.

7. THE DARK SIDES OF RESPONSIBILITY

But is a reappraisal of responsibilities all rosy? Or has the duty discourse its dark sides too? In this section, I will give an overview of the critical remarks that have been raised in the literature.[34] Four kinds of criticisms can be distinguished: (a) vagueness; (b) redundancy; (c) potentially dangerous outlook; and (d) seemingly too moralistic outlook. Since the first two criticisms were already

[33] Article 147 of the *Dutch Penal Code.*

[34] I will mainly focus on the criticisms that were raised in Dutch legal circles on the *Universal Declaration of Human Responsibilities.* Among others: P. Baehr, 'Greater Respect for Human Rights Rather Than for Human Responsibilities is What is Needed' (column) (1998) 16(2) *Netherlands Quarterly of Human Rights* 119–120; M. De Blois, 'De universele verklaring van de verantwoordelijkheden van de mens: enige kanttekeningen' (The Universal Declaration of Human Responsibilities: Some Caveats) (1998) 23(8) *NCJM-Bulletin* 1037–1052; G. Van der List, 'Over mensenrechten en plichten' (On Human Rights and Duties) (1998) *Volkskrant*, 11 September; 'NJCM-Commentaar universele verklaring van de verantwoordelijkheden van de mens' (NJCM-Commentary on the Universal Declaration of Human Responsibilities) (1998) 23(8) *NJCM-Bulletin* 1103–1111 and the special issue 'Verklaring Plichten van de Mens ter discussie' (Universal Declaration of Human Responsibilities under Discussion) (2000) 39(1)&(2) *Civis Mundi*, March.

examined and assessed in section 2, I will focus on the third and fourth criticism, respectively.

To start with, one might argue that by reappraising the duty terminology individual human rights might be at danger. They can lose their unconditional outlook. For the legitimate exercise of one's fundamental rights might become dependent on one's responsible behaviour as a citizen. More specifically, the 'responsibility' frame can redirect our attention from fundamental and unconditional rights towards quite an outdated and incompatible duty-based approach. Individuals would be subjected to and disciplined again by the social control by the community and the state. Instead, human rights discourse originated in order to act as a bulwark against a disproportionately powerful state. It was exactly this discourse that gave the individual human being an independent and autonomous status. In the words of the legal-philosopher Joel Feinberg: 'Having rights enables us to "stand up like men", to look others in the eye, and to feel in some fundamental way the equal of anyone. To think of oneself as the holder of rights is not to be unduly but properly proud, to have that minimal self-respect that is necessary to be worthy of love and esteem of others.'[35] More specifically, human rights advocates have warned that the duty frame might be abused in order to suppress fundamental rights. Besides, there is the so-called slippery slope argument.[36] When we start compromising on individual's autonomy, at the end of the day we may have arrived at a situation where there is no autonomy left at all. Related to this, one might argue that by adopting a duty framework, the false impression is being made that the former liberal age of human rights is over and that we are entering a new and totalitarian era wherein the citizen is relegated to a mere duty-bearer.

In view of these dangers, the allergic reaction to the duty discourse that can sometimes be found in human rights circles is understandable. So the main question is whether and – if so, how – we can rectify a too individualistic and egotistic way of thinking without losing human rights discourse as such. I think this is possible by sticking to the fundamental rights discourse as our main starting point. More specifically, the intrinsic nexus of rights and responsibilities should be seen as a one-way traffic. The possession of rights gives rise to responsibilities with regard to the proper way these rights are to be exercised, but it is not the other way around. Rights are not to be derived from our duties that should be fulfilled beforehand. To say it in yet other words, within a constitutional state based on rule of law requirements, fundamental rights of citizens are pre-eminent and should also be predominant.

Finally, one could ask whether moral notions such as duties and responsibilities can be protected by legal instruments. Aren't we introducing overly moralistic

35 J. Feinberg, 'The Nature and Value of Rights', (1970), *The Journal of Value Inquiry*, 4, 252.

36 I. Hare and J. Weinstein, 'General Introduction: Free Speech, Democracy and the Suppression of Extreme Speech Past and Present', in I. Hare and J. Weinstein (eds.), *Extreme Speech and Democracy*, Oxford: Oxford University Press, 2009, p. ix.

overtones within the legal debate? Don't we have to distinguish between law and morality? No doubt, law and morality should be distinguished. We should beware of filling up the legal sphere with purely moralistic admonitions. For example, a reappraisal of the Golden Rule – 'do to others what you would like to be done to you' – can be fine, but ultimately this is not the law's business. This distinction between law and morality should be qualified as well, however. As we already saw in section 4, currently Dutch private law doctrine abounds with moral principles such as reasonability, fairness and carefulness in the exercise of one's ownership. They are no longer merely moralistic recommendations. They have become part and parcel of the Dutch statutory private law. It seems to me that the same kind of development would be quite welcome in the field of Dutch constitutional rights doctrine. Surely a law order cannot compel individuals to hold benevolent attitudes towards others or to act from altruistic motives. But it can prohibit particular forms of objectionable external conduct. Applied to the topic under review, we arrive at the following conclusion. Although the legal system may not be able to enforce a responsible exercise of fundamental rights, it can provide for some mechanisms that may prevent rights abuse. Seen from this perspective, the legal provision of a ban on rights abuse – for example in our constitution[37] – could function as a minimal, though indispensable legal standard.

8. FREEDOM OF EXPRESSION AND FREEDOM OF RELIGION WITHIN A MULTICULTURAL SOCIETY

Let me finish my contribution by dwelling on the question what exactly should be our (rights-based) responsibilities within a multicultural society. This question will be answered by focusing on the rights to freedom of expression and of religion. Both rights are currently still at the centre of Dutch political debate.

No doubt, the protection of one's freedom of expression is of key importance to a liberal-democratic legal order. Fundamental though it is, it should not be seen as an absolute right. I would like to subscribe to the view that can be found in the so-called *Pre-draft Declaration on Human Social Responsibilities* of 2002. Herein the freedom of expression is laid down in Article 22: 'Every person who lives in a heterogeneous society has the duty to promote the harmonious coexistence of the diverse human groups with which they coexist, in particular, to abstain from sponsoring or condoning excuses for national, religious, racial, etc. hatred, from uncritically spreading such opinions and from engaging in practices that generate or increase insecurity, rancour or conflicts between them.' In other

[37] See for a text suggestion, M. Galenkamp and R. Westrik, 'Naar een nieuw burenrecht. Grondrechten in een pluriforme samenleving' (Towards a New Neighbour's Law. Constitional Rights Within a Multiform Society) (2004) 2 *Nederlands Juristenblad* 67.

words, hate speech is not allowed. This kind of speech transgresses one of the basic ground rules of public discourse. As Heyman[38] notes: 'Hate speech may be regarded as a form of abuse that violates the rules of order that make democracy possible. ... The aim of hate speech is to dominate and subordinate others.' So the mutual respect of free and equal citizens is at stake here. More specifically, one's freedom of expression does not allow a person to slander or libel a fellow citizen. No doubt, these qualifications will raise new questions. For example: how to identify the boundary between legitimate public discourse and objectionable hate speech? Although this question is a difficult one, it is not an unanswerable one. Practically all Western European criminal legal doctrines, but also several international human rights conventions[39] forbid hate speech. In those systems – in contradistinction to the absolute (First Amendment) protection within the US – hate speech does not fall under the protected freedom of expression, and, to me, rightly so. The main virtue of hate speech regulations seems to me that a minimal standard of respect is provided. It is acknowledged that there can be expressions that are beyond the realm of legitimate public debate and hence fall outside the protection zone. This is also in line with recent Strasbourg jurisprudence. In the last few years hateful expressions have commonly been treated as falling outside the protective ambit of Article 10,[40] either because of the derogatory provisions of Article 10(2)[41] or, more fundamentally, under the banner of Article 17.

The same kind of qualifications can be applied to the right to freedom of religion, however. One may not abuse this right by proclaiming one's own religious convictions and living one's religious life to the full, without accounting for the way the expression of these convictions might harm or unduly interfere with the rights and interests of fellow citizens and without recognising their equal right to freedom of religion. We seem to have arrived at the norm of reciprocity here. Human rights should always be exercised with due respect for the rights of others. It seems to me that the inclusion of reciprocity in the Dutch constitutional law doctrine – as a precondition to be fulfilled in order to speak of the legitimate exercise of one's rights – would really make a difference. This standard was

---

38 S.J. Heyman, 'Hate Speech, Public Discourse and the First Amendment', in I. Hare and J. Weinstein (eds.), *Extreme Speech and Democracy*, Oxford: Oxford University Press, 2009, p. 176.

39 Take for example Art. 20(2) of the International Convention on Civil and Political Rights: 'Any advocacy of national, racial or religious hatred that constitutes incitement to discrimination, hostility or violence shall be prohibited by law.'

40 For example: ECtHR, 16 July 2009, *Féret v. Belgium*, *NJ* 2009, 412; ECtHR, 20 April 2010, *Le Pen v. France*, 18788/09, and ECtHR, 16 November 2004, *Norwood v. United Kingdom*, 23131/03.

41 'The exercise of these freedoms, since it carries with it duties and responsibilities, may be subject to such formalities, conditions, restrictions or penalties as are prescribed by law and are necessary in a democratic society, in the interests of national security, territorial integrity or public safety, for the prevention of disorder or crime, for the protection of health or morals, for the protection of the reputation or rights of others, for preventing the disclosure of information received in confidence, or for maintaining the authority and impartiality of the judiciary.'

already formulated in the aforementioned and much criticised *Universal Declaration of Human Responsibilities*. Herein it was argued – and to me, rightly so – that religious groups in pressing for their religious freedom should have the responsibility to respect the freedom of others. Article 15 of this declaration runs as follows: 'While religious freedom must be guaranteed, the representatives of religions have a special responsibility to avoid expressions of prejudice and acts of discrimination towards those of different beliefs. They should not incite or legitimize hatred, fanaticism and religious wars, but should foster tolerance and mutual respect between all people.'

The foregoing can also be reformulated and summarised in the proposition that fundamental rights should be seen as a package deal. So-called 'selective shopping' in the supermarket of constitutional rights is not allowed. For example, the appeal of the Dutch SGP (an orthodox Christian party) on its right to freedom of religion and of assembly does not sound that convincing in view of its exclusionary perspective on women and on Islam. This norm of reciprocity should not only apply to religious citizens and authorities, but to other citizens as well. If one appeals to fundamental rights, one should grant fellow citizens the same measure of rights protection. If you ask for toleration, please practice it yourself.

FROM *LAWLESS* TO A HUMAN RIGHTS APPROACH IN THE FIGHT AGAINST TERRORISM

The Council of Europe Standards

Martin KUIJER*

> 'Against the call for so-called "tough measures", few political leaders can find the strength and wisdom or indeed the support to fight terrorism while preserving the established human rights protective system. Repressive sirens will always call for "new" harsh measures to meet these "new" challenges from terrorism and few leaders have the toughness to "hold the fort" in such circumstances.'
>
> *ECtHR Judge John Hedigan*

1. INTRODUCTION

The fight against terrorism is high on the domestic and international political agenda. Over the past years, various governments in Europe (and elsewhere) have approved numerous laws to amend domestic law in order to fight the so-called 'War on Terror' more effectively. This contribution looks at this security legislation from a human rights perspective, focussing on the applicable standards developed within the framework of the Council of Europe in which the case law of the European Court of Human Rights (ECHR) plays a prominent role. In doing so, this chapter aims to identify certain trends. Its aim is not to present an exhaustive overview of all relevant case law of the ECHR.

When examining the standards developed within the framework of the Council of Europe, the dual responsibility for national authorities emerges. On the one hand, one may expect a state to uphold fundamental rights of terrorist

* This chapter is partly based on M. Kuijer, *Van* Lawless *naar een rechtmatige bestrijding van terrorisme*, Nijmegen: Wolf Legal Publishers, 2005. Final revision of this chapter took place in 2012.

suspects. On the other hand, states have the responsibility (also from a human rights perspective) to offer protection to their citizens. By way of introduction the 'Gibraltar judgment' of the ECHR is discussed (section 2), after which some more general comments are made concerning terrorism being a 'new' threat (section 3) and the clash between the responsibility to uphold civil liberties and the duty to protect (section 4). Attention then shifts to the need for proper procedural guarantees (section 5). Two specific issues in this regard are highlighted: the problematic use of information from intelligence agencies in judicial proceedings (section 6) and the tendency of domestic legislators to create a separate legal space for terrorism (section 7).

2. THE GIBRALTAR CASE

'The shooting took place on a fine Sunday afternoon' could be the opening sentence of an Ernest Hemingway novel, but is in fact to be found in the *McCann* judgment of the European Court of Human Rights.[1] In 1988, the United Kingdom, Spanish and Gibraltar authorities became aware that the Irish Republican Army (IRA) was planning a terrorist attack on Gibraltar. More specifically, the assembly area south of Ince's Hall where the Royal Anglian Regiment usually assembled to carry out the changing of the guard every Tuesday at 11.00 hours. The attack would be carried out by McCann, Farrell and Savage, most probably by using a car bomb. McCann and Farrell had previously been convicted for terrorist activities; Savage was a known explosives expert. Members of the SAS (Special Air Services) were sent to Gibraltar to foil the attempt. On Sunday 6 March 1988, two days prior to the changing of the guard, the three alleged IRA members were spotted in Gibraltar. Savage parked his car in the vicinity of the likely target and was then seen in the company of McCann and Farrell. The SAS considered the possibility that the car contained a bomb that could be detonated from a distance. It was decided that the situation had become too dangerous for bystanders and that an arrest had to be effected. The SAS agents were ordered to arrest the three suspects. When McCann made a 'sudden and aggressive' movement, the SAS agents decided to open fire. McCann was hit by five bullets. Farrell who had been walking beside McCann grabbed for a handbag and was hit by eight bullets. When the two other SAS agents tried to arrest Savage, he 'spun round and his arm went down towards his right hand hip area'. The agents believed he was going for a detonator. Savage was shot a total of 16 times. According to the pathologist who conducted the post-mortem, Savage was 'riddled with bullets'. Some of which were most likely fired into Savage's head as he lay on the ground. No weapons were, however, found on McCann, Farrell and Savage. The car that Savage had parked a few hours before did not contain any explosives. Two days later a car was discovered in a basement

[1] ECtHR, 27 September 1995, *McCann et al. v. United Kingdom* (Series A-324), para. 68.

car-park in Marbella. It contained over 60 kilos of Semtex explosive. A horrible terrorist attack had been prevented.

What remains to be determined is whether the British authorities, i.e. the SAS operation, dealt with the terrorist threat in an appropriate manner consistent with human rights standards. On 28 April 1988 Thames Television broadcasted its documentary entitled 'Death on the Rock', during which a reconstruction was made of the events in Gibraltar on that fine Sunday afternoon. The documentary sparked off a public debate on the immediate use of lethal force by the SAS agents. In September 1988, an inquest by the Gibraltar Coroner into the killings was opened. In those proceedings the families of the deceased were represented. The inquest lasted nineteen days during which seventy-nine witnesses were heard. At the conclusion of the inquest, the jury returned verdicts of lawful killing by a majority of nine to two. After equally unsuccessful actions in the High Court of Justice in Northern Ireland against the Ministry of Defence, the families of the deceased lodged a complaint with the European Court of Human Rights invoking Article 2 ECHR (the right to life).

In its judgment the European Court held Article 2 ECHR to be violated. Article 2 ECHR sets out the circumstances when deprivation of life may be justified. An essential condition is that the use of lethal force needs to be 'absolutely necessary'. In the present case the Court was not convinced of this. In order to reach that decision it examined four different aspects:

- the relevant domestic law regulating the use of force;
- the planning, preparation and organisation of the operation;
- the execution of the operation by the State agents; and
- the *ex post facto* investigation into the lawfulness of the operation.[2]

Those four aspects need to be in conformity with the Strasbourg standards of the European Court of Human Rights. I will not deal with the Court's judgment in detail. Having said that, there are some more general aspects of the judgment I would like to emphasise.

Firstly, the Court produced a detailed and elaborate reconstruction of the facts. High Contracting Parties better get used to the idea that their anti-terrorist operations are subject to thorough supervision on the international level. In other Strasbourg judgments the European Court left Contracting States a wide margin of appreciation in the event that considerations of national security were at stake,[3] but that line of reasoning is definitely not adopted by the Court in the present case where it concerned a 'core' right enshrined in the Convention. By

[2] See more elaborately M. Kuijer, 'Geweldgebruik door de politie en de jurisprudentie van het Europees Hof voor de Rechten van de Mens' (The use of force by police officers in light of the case law of the European Court of Human Rights), in Borgers, Duker and Stevens (eds.), *Politie in beeld*, Nijmegen: Wolf Legal Publishers, 2009.

[3] For example, ECtHR, 28 October 1994, *Murray v. United Kingdom* (Series A-300-A), para. 47.

now, it is settled case law of the Court to examine the facts of an anti-terrorist operation leading to a death in detail.[4]

Secondly, the Court seems very aware of the difficulties encountered by domestic authorities when confronted with a terrorist threat. It acknowledged that it is well aware that States may face immense difficulties in protecting their citizens from terrorist violence. Accordingly, national authorities have a 'duty to protect the lives of the people of Gibraltar including their own military personnel' (paragraph 192). The use of lethal force, if 'absolutely necessary', can therefore be justified under Article 2 ECHR. Even if the intelligence on the basis of which the operation was executed turns out to be false. Inevitably, the security authorities are not in possession of the full facts and are obliged to formulate their policies on the basis of incomplete hypotheses (paragraph 193). The Court is prepared to assume the good faith of the national authorities in that regard.

Thirdly, the considerations of the Court with regard to the *preparation of the operation* are noteworthy. The Court believes that the use of lethal force became almost inevitable after the authorities decided to let the three suspects enter Gibraltar. Why were the three suspects not arrested at the border immediately on their arrival in Gibraltar? Why did the authorities not prevent them from entering Gibraltar if they were believed to be on a bombing mission? The answer is simple. Because the authorities wanted to collect as much evidence as possible in order to secure a criminal conviction. And this is an inherent dilemma in the fight against terrorism: the necessity of preventing terrorist attacks as much as possible versus the desire to secure a criminal conviction of a terrorist suspect. My wording of the dilemma already indicates that I personally believe the prior interest will always outweigh the latter interest.

Finally, the violation found by the Court was partly based on the manner of the *execution of the operation*. The Court disapproves with the 'automatic recourse to lethal force'. The Court disapproves of a 'licence to kill' policy.

The Court's judgment that the SAS operation had been in breach with the requirements of the Convention was not welcomed with great enthusiasm in the United Kingdom. The British tabloids characterised the judgment as a victory of the IRA; 'Europe' was frustrating an effective fight against terrorism. Prime Minister John Major described the judgment as 'irresponsible and defying common sense'.[5] Vice-Prime Minister Hesseltine announced 'not to take the slightest notion of this ludicrous decision'.[6] The British government wrote a memo in which the Court was severely criticised and in which proposals were

---

4 See for example, ECtHR, 20 December 2011, *Finogenov et al. v. Russia* (appl. no. 18299/03), para. 198.

5 *The Independent*, 28 September 1995.

6 See R.A. Lawson, 'Artikel 2 EVRM en de bestrijding van terrorisme; Britse wrevel over het Hof' (Article 2 ECHR and the fight against terrorism: British resentment vis-à-vis the Court) (1996) 4 *NJCM-Bulletin*, 537–561, 553.

made to amend the election procedure of members of the Court.[7] In my opinion, the violent reaction of the British authorities is unjustified. The Court did not undermine the effective fight against terrorism. The British response to the *McCann* judgment demonstrates that emotions can run high in cases of issues related to the fight against terrorism. The politically sensitive nature of anti-terrorism measures may be understandable to a certain extent, but it is exactly for this reason why international supervision by a human rights tribunal is of such great importance. It offers a more objective system of checks and balances in order to ensure that national authorities – stirred up by emotions – continue to respect fundamental right and freedoms.

The case also demonstrates that as far as Europe is concerned, terrorism did not start on 11 September 2001.

3. TERRORISM AS A 'NEW' THREAT

The horrific events of '9/11' had a tremendous impact on public debate on the issue of the fight against terrorism. Media, politicians and international organisations were quick to respond on this 'new' threat to international stability and security. On the one hand, this response may be understandable. For the first time non-Americans executed successfully a terrorist attack on American territory. The American administration was clearly shocked by the realisation that its national security was not inviolable. Its reaction was consequently a very strong one. That is my polite qualification of the interrogation techniques and detention circumstances in Abu Ghraib and Guantánamo Bay, and the (permanent) withholding of the right of access to an ordinary court. I believe that in the American hearts and minds '9/11' was the beginning realisation of the existence of a 'new' threat. In view of the position of the United States in international politics, its reaction had a global impact in other parts of the world. There are other considerations to be taken into account. The nature of the terrorist attacks seems to have changed. Terrorists no longer primarily seem to target governmental, infrastructural, industrial or military objects. Attacks nowadays seem to target as many as possible innocent civilians, at random, aimed at creating as much as possible fear under the population, disrupting ordinary life. Another consideration is the global nature of modern (religiously motivated) terrorism, whereas terrorism used to be nationally orientated.

Whereas it may be understandable to a certain degree that modern forms of terrorism are considered as a 'new' threat, it is good to realise that many European democracies have been confronted with terrorist movements (albeit nationally

7 *Financial Times*, 3 April 1996. See also: M. Kuijer, *The Blindfold of Lady Justice – Judicial Independence and Impartiality in Light of the Requirements of Article 6 ECHR*, Nijmegen: Wolf Legal Publishers, 2004, p. 253.

orientated) for many decades: the *Rote Armee Fraktion* (RAF) in Germany, the Irish Republican Army (IRA) in the United Kingdom, the PKK in Turkey, and the Basque separation movement ETA in Spain to name a few. This also means that the debate on the tension between anti-terrorist measures and human rights standards started a few decades ago. The very first judgment of the European Court of Human Rights in 1961 in the *Lawless* case[8] dealt with a person who was arrested and kept in administrative detention because he was a member of the IRA and was suspected of being engaged in activities prejudicial to the conservation of public peace and order or to the security of the state. The administrative detention lasted five months. During this period Lawless was not brought before a court. The Strasbourg Court held that the administrative detention was therefore in breach with the requirements of Article 5 ECHR. I fully realise that the United States administration is in no way bound by the case law of the European Court of Human Rights. But it is interesting to realise that an international human rights tribunal already ruled on the compatibility of withholding alleged terrorists access to court with human rights standards more than fifty years ago.

So, for fifty years the European Court has had to examine the strained relationship between anti-terrorist measures and fundamental rights and freedoms, trying to strike a balance between both interests in order to silence those who argue that human rights are a hindrance in the fight against terrorism.

4. THE STRIKING OF A BALANCE

Some would argue that protecting a state against the scourge of terrorism outweighs the protection of individual rights and freedoms. A state based on the Rule of Law including the protection of human rights can only exist if the integrity of the state as such is guaranteed. The integrity of a state and the corresponding national security is a *conditio sine qua non* for the existence of any state. The fight against terrorism, which is considered a direct attack on the integrity and stability of a state, is in this view of the most fundamental nature. More fundamental than the protection of individual rights and freedoms. In short: the interests of the collective outweigh the interests of the individual, the preservation of the state outweighs the preservation of the state based on the Rule of Law, security outweighs the protection of human rights. Personally, I am not convinced by this line of reasoning. A victory over terrorism can no longer be considered a victory when human rights are sacrificed, the constitutional state is eroded and the '*Streitbare Demokratie*' is merely '*streitbar*'. Peter Schieder, former

[8] ECtHR, 1 July 1961, *Lawless v. Ireland* (Series A-3). See also: A.H. Robertson, 'The First Case before the European Court of Human Rights: Lawless v. the Government of Ireland' (1960) *British Yearbook of International Law* 343–354.

chairman of the Parliamentary Assembly of the Council of Europe, stated the following during a conference in St Petersburg in March 2002:

> 'The perpetrators of the attacks on 11 September 2001 tried to provoke an uncontrolled reaction. A reaction which would blur the boundary between right and wrong, and throw the world into chaos, into a war of religion against religion, of culture against culture ... A war against terrorism, which neglects human rights, is perpetuating the threat. In the long term, terrorists will be quick to exploit any human rights abuse or violation of justice as an argument to further their cause ... They prosper under oppression, because it provides a fertile ground for their recruitment. They thrive on injustice, because they can exploit it to argue their cause. They profit from censorship, because their lies do not have to compete with the truth. They fervently believe in capital punishment, because it transforms murderers into martyrs. What they are afraid of is justice and human rights.'

At the same time, one should not forget that the fight against terrorism is to a certain degree also recognised as a human right.[9] In its case law, the European Court of Human Rights acknowledged that States have a positive obligation to protect the life of their citizens.[10] They should do all that could be reasonably expected from them to avoid a real and immediate risk to life of which they have or ought to have knowledge. In that sense the right to security has long been 'codified' as a human right in the Strasbourg case law. In my opinion, this doctrine is equally applicable to life-threatening situations as a result of a terrorist threat. This seems to have been confirmed in various soft law documents. The preamble to the *Guidelines on Human Rights and the Fight against Terrorism* which the Committee of Ministers of the Council of Europe adopted on 11 July 2002 refers to 'the *imperative* [emphasis added] duty of States to protect their populations against possible terrorist acts'. The same consideration can be found in the *Guidelines on the Protection of Victims of Terrorist Acts*, adopted by the Committee of Ministers of the Council of Europe on 2 March 2005.[11]

Therefore, States have to balance competing human rights interests, that is the protection of its population against terrorist threats and the fundamental rights of individuals, including persons suspected or convicted of terrorist activities. On the basis of the specific facts of the case, one has to determine which human right has to yield. In the case of so-called *notstandsfeste* human rights, like the absolute prohibition of torture, one may assume that the protection of

9 In that respect I recall that Freedom from Fear is one of the Four Freedoms mentioned in Roosevelt's famous speech in 1941.

10 ECtHR, 28 October 1998, *Osman v. United Kingdom* (Reports 1998, 3124); ECtHR, 19 February 2009, *A. et al. v. United Kingdom* (appl. no. 3455/05), and more recently ECtHR, 20 December 2011, *Finogenov et al. v. Russia* (appl. no. 18299/03), paras. 208–209.

11 In the Preamble sub f: 'Underlining in particular the states' obligation to take the measures needed to protect the fundamental rights of everyone within their jurisdiction against terrorist acts, especially the right to life'.

the fundamental rights of the individual outweighs the fight against terrorism. However, with regard to other human rights (such as privacy, freedom of religion, freedom of expression, freedom of assembly) the balancing exercise may have a different outcome. The European Court of Human Rights has always emphasised that the Convention is a 'living instrument' that needs to be interpreted according to present day conditions.[12] If our societies change substantially as a result of modern terrorism, the possibility can not be ruled out that the Court interprets certain provisions differently. This could theoretically even result in a certain lowering of standards.[13]

5. MAKING ANTI-TERRORISM MEASURES HUMAN RIGHTS-PROOF

As a reaction to the threat of terrorism, States have adopted various new anti-terrorism measures. In view of the diverse nature of the various anti-terrorism measures, it is impossible to come up with a uniform approach of ensuring the compatibility of these measures with human rights standards. However, a few more general comments can be made.

When introducing a new legislative measure, national authorities have a duty to properly motivate the necessity of the new measure. This entails demonstrating the real nature and extent of the phenomenon which the measure is intended to target, the manner in which the new measure will be *effective* in the fight against that phenomenon, and why *new* measures are necessary on top of already existing measures. Too often new legislative measures are proposed without properly answering these fundamental questions.

When assessing the proportionality of an anti-terrorism measure, the existence of proper procedural guarantees is essential. In my view, access to court and judicial control should always be guaranteed, not only *ex post facto* at a trial against a suspected terrorist, but also, in the case of human rights intrusive measures (whether of an investigative nature or of a preventive character), prior to their application. We should confront terrorism *within* our legal framework. As a matter of principle suspected terrorists should receive the same level of procedural guarantees as other suspected criminals. Withholding terrorists the system of

[12] See for example ECtHR, 6 September 1978, *Tyrer v. United Kingdom* (Series A-26), para. 31. Former President of the European Court of Human Rights Rolv Ryssdal stated: 'Democratic society and its underlying values move on, and so, accordingly, should the Convention if it is not to loose contact with the forces that invest it with legitimacy' (R. Ryssdal, 'Rudolf Bernhardt at the European Court of Human Rights', in U. Beyerlin (ed.), *Recht zwishen Umbruch und Bewahrung (Festschrift für Rudolf Bernhardt)*, Berlin: Springer, 1995, p. 2.

[13] See also the former Netherlands judge at the European Court of Human Rights Egbert Myjer in: T. Barkhuysen, M. Kuijer and R. Lawson, 'Voorzichtig met Straatsburg! Interview met onze nieuwe rechter Egbert Myjer' (Cautious with Strasbourg! An interview with the new Judge Egbert Myjer) (2004) 7 *NJCM-Bulletin*, 903–904.

judicial control strikes at the roots of our legal order and it merely provides a fertile ground for radicalisation (claiming that the democratic societies based on the Rule of Law impose dual standards).

6. (UN)ACCOUNTABILITY OF INFORMATION FROM INTELLIGENCE AGENCIES IN JUDICIAL PROCEEDINGS

In the previous section I made some remarks concerning the issue of *access to court*. Equally important is the issue of evidence, i.e. the use of information from intelligence agencies in judicial proceedings and its impact on the right to adversarial proceedings and the equality of arms principle.[14] Counterterrorism measures are often based on confidential information from intelligence services. In view of that fact, an absolute prohibition on using information available to intelligence services in judicial proceedings would be undesirable and make it all but impossible to fight terrorism effectively in the courtroom. Furthermore, the public would regard it as inexplicable if a public authority in possession of highly relevant evidence did not share this evidence with the courts because of the confidential nature of the work of intelligence services. It would be equally undesirable to require an intelligence service to disclose in full the manner in which certain information is collected. That would interfere with its ability to do its work effectively in an unacceptable way.

This tension is recognised in the Court's case law. In the Al-Nashif case, the Court states: 'Where national security considerations are involved certain limitations on the type of remedies available to the individual may be justified ... Article 13 requires a remedy "as effective as it can be"'.[15] One could also refer to the 2002 Guidelines of the Committee of Ministers of the Council of Europe on human rights and the fight against terrorism, which state that 'the imperatives of the fight against terrorism may ... justify certain restrictions to the right of defence, in particular with regard to: ... (ii) the arrangements for access to the case-file'.[16]

---

14 According to Strasbourg case law the right to adversarial proceedings implies the opportunity for the parties to a trial to have knowledge of and comment on all evidence adduced or observations filed (ECtHR, 20 February 1996, *Vermeulen v. Belgium* (appl. no. 19075/91), para. 33). According to the equality of arms principle 'each party must be afforded a reasonable opportunity to present his case – including evidence – under conditions that do not place him at a substantial disadvantage vis-à-vis his opponent' (ECtHR, 27 October 1993, *Dombo Beheer v. the Netherlands* (appl. no. 14448/88), para. 33).

15 ECtHR, 20 June 2002, *Al-Nashif v. Bulgaria* (appl. no. 50963/99), para. 136.

16 Adopted on 11 July 2002 at the 804th session of the Council of Europe Committee of Ministers, Principle IX, para. 3.

The Court gave a further clarification in the *A. and others* case[17] in which the applicants complained about a violation of Article 5(4) ECHR; they argued that they did not have a proper chance to challenge the lawfulness of their (administrative) detention since they had only limited knowledge of the case against them as a result of the classified evidence for reasons of national security. The Court made it clear that three factors were of major importance: (a) the fact that an independent court would be able to examine all relevant evidence, both confidential and public evidence, so that it could ensure that no material was unnecessarily withheld from the suspect; (b) the fact that the suspect was provided under domestic law with a special advocate empowered to examine confidential materials after prior security clearance; and (c) the fact that the allegations contained in the public material had been sufficiently specific for the applicant to provide his representatives and the special advocate with information with which to refute them.

Perhaps the use of confidential information from intelligence services in open judicial proceedings is unavoidable, but domestic authorities do need to ensure that some form of accountability of that information is provided for. In Dutch law similar constructions are to be found.

In Dutch administrative law proceedings (which in the Netherlands include expulsion proceedings), the materials in the possession of the intelligence service can be considered in arriving at a judicial decision, after the independent court has had an opportunity to examine the underlying documents at the offices of the AIVD and form an opinion about them.[18] However, the other party (in this case, the applicant) must give its consent before the court can use the documents in arriving at its judgment, without counsel being permitted to examine them. The system therefore offers limited accountability at the expense of an equally limited form of the right to adversarial proceedings.

The compatibility of this system with Convention standards was at the heart of the case of *A. v. the Netherlands*,[19] even though the Court reiterated that it is not its task to review *in abstracto* the compatibility of the relevant law and practice with the Convention. Furthermore, it is important to note that the applicant in this particular case invoked Article 3 of the Convention (the prohibition of torture). The applicant was declared an undesirable alien after the General Intelligence and Security Service had considered the applicant to constitute a danger to national security. The applicant, however, alleged that his expulsion to Libya would violate his rights under Article 3 of the Convention. When interpreting Article 13 of the Convention (the right to an effective remedy), the Court explicitly referred to the

17 ECtHR, 19 February 2009, *A. et al. v. United Kingdom* (appl. no. 3455/05).

18 *Cf.* para. 137 of the aforementioned Al-Nashif judgment: 'the guarantee of an effective remedy requires as a minimum that the competent independent appeals authority must be informed of the reasons grounding the deportation decision, even if such reasons are not publicly available.'

19 ECtHR, 20 July 2010, *A. v. the Netherlands* (appl. no. 4900/06).

factual context of the case: 'Given the irreversible nature of the harm that might occur if the alleged risk of torture or ill-treatment materialised and the importance which the Court attaches to Article 3, the notion of an effective remedy under Article 13 requires (i) independent and rigorous scrutiny of a claim that there exist substantial grounds for believing that there was a real risk of treatment contrary to Article 3 in the event of the applicant's expulsion to the country of destination, and (ii) the provision of an effective possibility of suspending the enforcement of measures whose effects are potentially irreversible' (paragraph 157). The Court then specifically referred to the use of the AIVD report in the judicial proceedings: 'the Court notes that with the parties' consent these materials were disclosed to the provisional-measures judge of the Regional Court of The Hague which in the Court's view has not compromised the independence of the domestic courts involved in the proceedings concerned and neither can it be said that these courts have given less rigorous scrutiny to the applicant's Article 3 claim. Furthermore, the Court notes that this report and the underlying materials did not, as such, concern the applicant's fear of being subjected to ill-treatment in Libya but whether he was posing a threat to the Netherlands national security' (paragraph 160).

In criminal law proceedings similar difficulties exist.[20] Fairly unproblematic is the use of official reports of the General Intelligence and Security Service as starting information for a criminal investigation. More problematic is the use of such reports as evidence at a criminal trial in order to secure a conviction.[21] In the latter scenario it is particularly important that the reliability of the data contained in such reports can be tested. On 1 November 2006 an amendment to the Code of Criminal Procedure (protected witnesses, *afgeschermde getuigen*) entered into force in order to improve the practicability of such reports in criminal proceedings.[22] The law provides for an isolated hearing of an official active for the intelligence and security service as a witness by the examining magistrate. The defence retains the right to hear the witness. However, the examination of the witness in open court by the defence is only possible in highly exceptional

[20] There was a lively debate in Dutch literature. See, among others, M. Alink, 'AIVD-informatie als bewijs in het strafproces' (The use of intelligence in criminal proceedings), in P.D. Duyx and P.D.J. Van Zeben (eds.), *Via Straatsburg – Liber Amicorum Egbert Myjer*, Nijmegen: Wolf Legal Publishers, 2004, pp. 155–179; Y. Buruma and E.R. Muller, 'Wet Terroristische Misdrijven in perspectief' (The Crimes of Terrorism Act in perspective) (2003) *Nederlands Juristenblad*, 2144 and L. Van Wifferen, 'Intelligence in het strafproces' (Intelligence in criminal proceedings) (2003) *Nederlands Juristenblad*, 617.

[21] E. Prakken, 'Terrorisme en het strafproces' (Terrorism and the criminal trial) (2004) *Strafblad*, 228–236.

[22] See the explanatory memorandum to the bill (Parliamentary Papers, House of Representatives 2003–2004, 29 743, no. 3). The legislative proposal coincided with some court rulings in which the issue of the use of information from intelligence agencies was discussed: a ruling by the Regional Court of Rotterdam of 18 December 2002 (LJN AF2141; see www.rechtspraak.nl) and a ruling by the Court of Appeal of The Hague of 21 June 2004 (LJN AP2058; see www.rechtspraak.nl).

circumstances in light of state security considerations. Therefore, in most instances the defence will only be able to check the reliability of the witness by submitting questions to the examining magistrate who will serve as an intermediary. The statement of a protected witness heard in this way shall be included in a report to be drawn up by the examining magistrate, after having ascertained that the text laid down in the report does not damage state security. Because ultimately only the intelligence service can fully assess whether disclosure of certain information laid down in the record of the witness examination would damage state security, the report shall only be admitted to the proceedings subject to approval of the witness. An additional guarantee is that a conviction may not be solely or to a decisive extent be based on the report. Sentencing based mainly on the report as only evidence is not possible.

Even though the European Court of Human Rights prefers a direct confrontation with a witness at a public hearing, it has allowed the use of anonymous witnesses under certain specific circumstances in its case law. The Court has acknowledged that considerations of state security may justify a limitation of the right to question witnesses.[23] In its *Edwards and Lewis* judgment,[24] the Court stated:

> 'The entitlement to disclosure of relevant evidence is not … an absolute right. In any criminal proceedings there may be competing interests, such as national security or the need to protect witnesses at risk of reprisals or keep secret police methods of investigation of crime, which must be weighed against the rights of the accused. In some cases it may be necessary to withhold certain evidence from the defence so as to preserve the fundamental rights of another individual or to safeguard an important public interest. Nonetheless, only such measures restricting the rights of the defence which are strictly necessary are permissible under Article 6 § 1. Furthermore, in order to ensure that the accused receives a fair trial, any difficulties caused to the defence by a limitation on its rights must be sufficiently counterbalanced by the procedures followed by the judicial authorities'.

Finally, reference should be made to the judgment of the Grand Chamber in the case of Al-Khawaja and Tahery in which the Court laid down the leading guidelines when dealing with absent witnesses in criminal proceedings.[25] The Court reiterated that normally, all evidence against an accused must be presented in his presence at a public hearing with a view to adversarial argument. The Court

[23] ECtHR, 24 June 2003, *Dowsett v. United Kingdom* (appl. no. 39482/98), para. 42.

[24] ECtHR, 22 July 2003, *Edwards and Lewis v. United Kingdom* (appl. nos. 39647/98 and 40461/98), para. 53. See also ECHR, 16 February 2000, *Fitt v. United Kingdom* (appl. no. 29777/96), para. 45.

[25] ECtHR, 15 December 2011, *Al-Khawaja and Tahery v. United Kingdom* (appl. nos. 267766/05 and 22228/06).

indicated that it would only allow exceptions if: (a) there was a good reason for admitting the evidence of an absent witness (for example, if a witness had died or was absent owing to fear attributable to the defendant or those acting on his behalf, or if the defendant had waived his rights under Article 6(3)(d) of the Convention); (b) the conviction was not solely or to a decisive degree based on the statement of an absent witness (even though this is not an absolute rule for the Court which should be applied in an inflexible way); and (c) there had been sufficient counterbalancing factors, including the existence of strong procedural safeguards.

There are various 'counterbalancing measures' provided for in domestic law. Most importantly, the hearing of the protected witness is handed over to the independent courts. From the *Edwards and Lewis* judgment it can be concluded that the European Court of Human Rights is of the opinion that if certain information is withheld from the defence, the deciding body may not take note of that information either. Therefore, the questioning of the protected witness is left to the examining judge, and not (one of) the judges hearing the case. Equally important is the fact that the defence must have an adequate and proper opportunity to challenge and question the witness, directly or on his behalf. The law on protected witnesses deliberately copies the legal framework which is in place for 'ordinary' anonymous witnesses which is strongly influenced by Strasbourg case law[26] and which has (eventually) been found in conformity with Strasbourg standards.[27] As I mentioned before, in most instances the defence will only be able to check the reliability of the witness by submitting questions to the examining magistrate who will serve as an intermediary. In my opinion, practice will have to be as 'interactive' as possible in order to ensure compatibility with ECHR standards. Another safeguard was already mentioned before: a conviction may not solely or to a decisive extent be based on the report. Yet again this safeguard is copied from Strasbourg case law.[28] Other guarantees include: the requirement that the examining magistrate must be able to inform himself of the full identity of the witness, the requirement that the witness be sworn in, and the obligation for the judge to carefully motivate the use and reliability of the evidence.[29] Taking into account the various safeguards in the new law, I do not share the opinion of those who argue that the law as such is in breach of

---

26 ECtHR, 20 November 1989, *Kostovski v. the Netherlands* (appl. no. 11454/85); ECtHR, 27 September 1990, *Windisch v. the Netherlands* (appl. no. 12489/86); and ECtHR, 23 April 1997, *Van Mechelen et al. v. the Netherlands* (appl. nos. 21363/93, 21364/93, 21427/93 and 22056/93), paras. 50–55.

27 ECtHR (admissibility), 4 July 2000, *Mink Kok v. the Netherlands* (appl. no. 43149/98).

28 For example, ECtHR, 20 November 1989, *Kostovski v. the Netherlands* (appl. no. 11454/85).

29 *Cf.* ECtHR, 27 January 2004, *Lorsé v. the Netherlands* (appl. no. 44484/98) and ECtHR, 27 January 2004, *Verhoek v. the Netherlands* (appl. no. 54445/00). In both cases this proved to be an important element in the assessment whether a trial could be deemed a fair trial in the sense of Article 6 ECHR.

Strasbourg requirements. However, much will depend on the manner in which a judge handles a specific case.[30]

I find both (administrative and criminal) legislative measures intriguing because they symbolise the difficulties when 'striking the balance'. Undoubtedly, both legal regimes raise human rights concerns. In both instances, the legislator was conscious of those human rights concerns, but equally aware of the undesirability to prohibit the use of information from intelligence agencies in judicial proceedings in absolute terms. In both instances, the legislator arrived at a solution which it would not consider desirable in 'normal' circumstances. This raises the more general question whether it is desirable to create a separate legal space for the handling of terrorism.

7. THE CREATION OF A SEPARATE LEGAL SPACE FOR TERRORISM

I would differentiate between issues concerning additional investigative powers for the authorities and issues concerning procedural protection offered to a suspect.

With regard to the latter category, I do not – in general – favour the creation of a separate legal regime applicable to cases related to terrorism. As I stated above, I believe that, as a matter of principle, suspected terrorists should receive the same level of procedural guarantees as other suspected criminals. Withholding terrorists the system of judicial control strikes at the roots of our legal order. In general, fair trial guarantees, as they have been interpreted by the Court on the basis of Articles 5 and 6 ECHR, should fully apply in judicial proceedings in the context of terrorism. National courts (and the European Court of Human Rights) have been confronted with 'striking the balance' situations before. Most of them were related to organised crime and its distinguishing characteristics. It is therefore already standing case law of the Strasbourg Court that most procedural rights are not absolute (for example, the right to adversarial proceedings, the right to a public trial, etc.). Restrictions on these rights have been accepted by the Court with regard to ordinary criminal offences. Member States can now apply this standing case law vis-à-vis the phenomenon of terrorism. Apart from that, one may look at the practice of some European countries which have been confronted with violent movements on their territory for many years. Turkey had until recently two procedures, one for ordinary crimes, and another for terrorist

30 See also paragraph 4.2 of the report 'Nederlandse antiterrorismeregelgeving getoetst aan fundamentele rechten' conducted by Professor P.H.P.H.M.C. Van Kempen and J. Van de Voort in December 2010 commissioned by NCTb and WODC. This report was presented to Parliament by letter of 28 January 2011 as an annexe to the evaluation of anti-terrorism measures in The Netherlands carried out by the Minister of Security and Justice ('Antiterrorismemaatregelen in Nederland in het eerste decennium van de 21e eeuw').

offences. On top of ECHR-related problems, this dual system did not prove to be as effective as planned and therefore it was abolished in the new criminal procedure code.

With regard to issues concerning additional investigative powers, I do favour separate legal regimes for ordinary crimes and terrorist offences in order to avoid 'contamination' of ordinary criminal law. I believe there is a natural tendency for authorities to fully use existing investigative powers, even though the investigative method was originally intended to serve a more limited purpose.

This brings me to my final remark. A separate legal regime can also be the result of an increased use of non-criminal measures, which seems to be happening in the fight against terrorism. Terrorism is not exclusively addressed by the legislator using criminal law measures. Instead, the legislator turns more and more often to administrative measures. To a certain degree this is not surprising. Criminal law is an outstanding example of an *ex post facto* instrument. Criminal law is ordinarily activated *after* an event has taken place. Of course, national authorities will try to prevent criminal acts from occurring. This is even more true with regard to terrorist acts which could potentially have a devastating impact on the lives of many people. Two legislative methods can be discerned in order to tackle this issue: firstly, pushing the moment when criminal law provisions may be activated forward (the most striking example is the criminalisation of preparatory acts);[31] and, secondly, introducing administrative measures. The possibility cannot be totally excluded that the 'popularity' of administrative measures is partly due to a desire to 'circumvent' the high procedural guarantees of criminal proceedings. However, if an administrative measure can be qualified as a 'criminal charge' in the autonomous sense of Article 6 ECHR, a legislator needs to offer procedural protection to the person concerned that is comparable to a suspect in criminal proceedings. The implications for domestic administrative law are tremendous; it follows that safeguards usually to be found only in criminal law have to be introduced in administrative law, for example the right to remain silent or the *nemo tenetur* principle.

8. LAWLESSNESS?

The very first judgment of the Strasbourg Court, in the case of *Lawless*, dealt with the fight against terrorism. Many judgments were to follow in which the Court had to rule on the conformity of various kinds of anti-terrorism measures with ECHR standards. From IRA terrorism in the *Lawless* case, via the Turkish cases

[31] This was also done in Dutch criminal law (Law of 27 January 1994 amending the Criminal Code in order to criminalise preparatory acts, *Staatsblad* 1994, 60). See in this respect among others P.L. Bal, 'Remoralisering van het strafrecht: een discourstheoretische benadering' and D. Roef, 'Strafrechtelijke verantwoordelijkheid in de risicomaatschappij', both in P.L. Bal, E. Prakken and G.E. Smaers (eds.), *Veiligheid of Vergelding?*, Deventer: Kluwer, 2003, pp. 3–57.

relating to the PKK to the more recent judgments against the Russian Federation concerning operations in Chechnya. In all these instances, emotions ran high, mainly because state security and terrorism were at stake. In that sense, the European Court of Human Rights provides a safety net. It offers a more objective system of checks and balances in order to ensure that national authorities – stirred up by emotions – continue to respect fundamental right and freedoms. Thereby, from its *Lawless* judgment, the Court has contributed greatly to avoid a state of lawlessness in the fight against terrorism. Having said that, 'striking the balance' between the *rights* of terrorist suspects and the *duty* of the state to protect its population, remains a difficult challenge, even after more than fifty years. The use of information from intelligence agencies in judicial proceedings will undoubtedly lead to new Strasbourg case law, as will some of the newly adopted legislative measures.

CHILDREN'S RIGHTS AT A DIGNITARIAN HORIZON OF RESPONSIBLE PARENTHOOD

Jan C.M. Willems

'We have national debates about industrial relations, education, water, nuclear power. But we have no national debates about our most valuable asset, our children and their protection ... We still have no national standards for child protection, no federal children's minister, no national policies or legislation, no national definitions, no federal system of children's commissioners, no independent scrutiny of child protection, and no reliable national data.'
Chris Goddard and Joe Tucci[1]

1. INTRODUCTION

All over the world, children, especially infants and pre-school children, are treated as the property of their parents rather than as legal subjects, entitled to the empowerment of their parents, to healthy development and to preparation for responsible life, including responsible parenthood. A strong libertarian tradition of formal parental autonomy (that is, autonomy as a legal fiat or fiction, as opposed to real or psychological autonomy) does not seem to leave much room for a child rights based evolution towards a more dignitarian construct of reproductive rights and parental responsibilities. In this chapter, this theme is preliminarily explored and attempts are made for its further development. In section 2, a helicopter view of the theme is presented. In section 3, the concept of responsible parenthood is explored on the basis of a pedagogical model of the principle of the best interests of the child, as well as of an overview of parental responsibilities and related state obligations under the Convention on the Rights of the Child (CRC, 1989).

---

1 C. Goddard and J. Tucci (quoting Goddard and Mudali, 2006), 'Foreword' in Max Liddell *et al.*, *The State of Child Protection: Australian Child Welfare and Child Protection Developments 2005*, Caulfield East, National Research Centre for the Prevention of Child Abuse, Monash University, September 2006 www.nrcpca.monash.org/assets/files/childprotection.pdf.

2. A HELICOPTER VIEW

2.1. LIBERTARIAN AND DIGNITARIAN TRADITIONS

In human rights law, a libertarian and a dignitarian stand or tradition may be discerned.[2] Whereas the former emphasises individual freedoms, especially against state intervention, and formal individual autonomy (negative liberty, individualism), the latter tries to clarify the aspect of duties and responsibilities in relation to rights, and to integrate freedom, equal opportunities and solidarity (justice, or even love)[3] into its concept of human dignity (positive liberty, personal development and global citizenship). Not so much 'respect' as a claim against others but the combination of self-respect and respect for others, as a core value or virtue, underlies this concept.[4] However, self-respect and the ensuing respect for others are not simply a matter of virtue, but also of mental health and psycho-education. Especially children's rights are closely connected with mental health and psycho-education, both of parents, who are supposed to give their children affection-based guidance and direction,[5] and of children themselves, who are supposed to be – guided in a manner consistent with their evolving capacities – actors in their own healthy physical, emotional, social, moral, intellectual, spiritual and cultural development.[6] Children's rights, therefore,

---

2 See M.A. Glendon, 'Rights from Wrongs', in H.J. Steiner and P. Alston (eds.), *International Human Rights in Context; Law, Politics, Morals*, Oxford: Oxford University Press, 2000, p. 153. Glendon opposes 'the older, more individualistic and "libertarian" rights tradition of the Anglo-American nations' to 'dignitarian traditions [which] accord an equally high priority to freedom, but it is a freedom grounded in dignity and linked with solidarity.'

3 As the NGO Ius Primi Viri (www.iusprimiviri.org) puts it: 'Every human being on our planet, wherever he/she is born, has the possibility to develop awareness and conscience of his/her own dignity, of the value of freedom, of the sense of justice, and of the search for pleasure, that must be transformed into love for him/herself and for every existing form of life.' (E/CN.4/2005/NGO/151, 4 March 2005).

4 See J.C.M. Willems, chapters 5–6 of *Developmental and Autonomy Rights of Children; Empowering Children, Caregivers and Communities*, 2nd ed., Antwerp/Oxford: Intersentia, 2007, pp. 114–117, 148–152. For an in-depth analysis, see A. Honneth, *The Struggle for Recognition; The Moral Grammar of Social Conflicts*, Cambridge: Polity Press, 1995.

5 See sixth preambular paragraph ('love') in conjunction with Article 5 (direction and guidance), and Article 18(1) (best interests) of the Convention on the Rights of the Child (CRC; UNGA 20 November 1989). Both affection and guidance and direction are part and parcel of the best interests of the child. The CRC does not mention the word 'affection', but it does refer to a child-rearing 'atmosphere of happiness, love and understanding.' By stating, in its preamble, 'that the child, for the full and harmonious development of his or her personality, should grow up in a family environment, in an atmosphere of happiness, love and understanding', the CRC is the only UN human rights treaty that contains the word 'love'.

6 Healthy (holistic, harmonious) child development may be seen as the object and purpose of the CRC. Holistic, a term used by the Committee on the Rights of the Child, refers to both physical – first of all early brain – development and mental development. The latter includes emotional development (first of all a secure attachment development in infants and young children), intellectual (or cognitive) development, and social, moral, spiritual and cultural development (see Articles 27(1), 29(1)(a), 23(3) and 32(1) CRC). The interaction between – rather than the sum or combination of – all these aspects determines holistic development.

have to endeavour to achieve two things at the same time: *responsibilisation*, that is specifying parental duties and responsibilities, as well as related duties and responsibilities of professionals, others adults, and of the state; and *empowerment*, that is empowering children, adolescents and young adults as parents-to-be, empowering parents, and empowering professionals (such as teachers, social workers, etc.) and others within the community. Empowerment implies ending discrimination and exclusion, especially through the promotion of income distribution (ending material poverty), of general and psycho-education (ending mental and emotional poverty), and of physical and mental health (ending material and emotional poverty). Responsibilisation and empowerment are two sides of the same dignitarian coin: specifying duties and responsibilities implies empowering people to fulfil them. Most national legal systems, however, do not specify parental duties and responsibilities, in spite of the many specifications in the Convention on the Rights of the Child,[7] nor even consider the empowerment implications thereof. Libertarian attitudes and views still prevail in most democratic states.

2.1.1. *Dignitarian Developments*

Recently, several international and European human rights bodies or actors seem to be moving away from libertarian individualism by putting forward and elaborating dignitarian aspects of human rights, especially children's rights. To mention the main actors, and outcomes, in the field: the Committee on the Rights of the Child, and its General Comment 8, 2006;[8] the Parliamentary Assembly of the Council of Europe, and its Recommendation 1666, 2004;[9] the European Committee of Social Rights, and its Conclusions and Decisions regarding Article 17 of the European Social Charter, 2003 to present;[10] and the

The conditions that have to be met in order to achieve holistic development are precisely those which constitute the principle of the best interests of the child (on which see section 3, below). Child participation, to be sure, both inside and outside the family, is an inherent dimension of both. It should certainly not be seen as the opposite of the best interest's concept. Holistic development without child participation is unthinkable. To state that the commitments of Article 3 CRC, that is, the best interests principle, are 'protectionist and paternalistic,' as opposed to those of Article 12 CRC, that is, the child participation principle, as Archard does (D. Archard, 'Preface', in F. Ang *et al.*, *Participation Rights of Children*, Antwerp/Oxford: Intersentia, 2006, pp. v–viii, viii), caricatures, in my opinion, both Articles.

7 See J.C.M. Willems, 'Het kindbeeld in het Verdrag inzake de Rechten van het Kind' (2005) 5 *Justitiële verkenningen* 94–112, 102–104. I will come back to this in the second part of this chapter.

8 General Comment No. 8 (2006): The right of the child to protection from corporal punishment and other cruel or degrading forms of punishment (Articles 19, 28(2) and 37, *inter alia*), www.ohchr.org, Human Rights Bodies, Committee on the Rights of the Child, General Comments.

9 Recommendation 1666 (2004): Europe-wide ban on corporal punishment of children, www.coe.int, Institutions/Parliamentary Assembly, Documents/Adopted texts.

10 See www.coe.int, Activities/Human rights: European Social Charter, European Committee of Social Rights, conclusions, decisions.

Commissioner for Human Rights of the Council of Europe, and his Issue Paper 1, 2006.[11] The focal point of these quasi- or proto-legislative documents is the right of the child not to be hit and humiliated, but the implementation strategies these documents propose – law reform to ban parental privileges in this regard (such as the criminal law excuse of reasonable chastisement), awareness raising, school human rights and child rights education, parenting education and parenting support, as well as child participation – have everything to do with mental health and psycho-education. This opens up new horizons for human rights and new hopes for our future: more children who will grow up as – and grow up to become – self-respecting and respectful citizens. These documents, therefore, shed light on future democratic societies, based on four, rather than only one or two, dignitarian building blocks. These four building blocks are:

(1) Ethnic-cultural and socio-economic integration and global citizenship – that is, a sense of public responsibility as a citizen not only of one's society but of the world – as opposed to prejudice, xenophobia, antisemitism, and racism.
(2) Equal treatment of and equal opportunities for men and women, as opposed to patriarchy and sexism (or rather gender discrimination, including homophobia and transphobia).
(3) The best interests, including the full participation, of the child, as opposed to *parentiarchy* and *transism* (transgenerational discrimination), also called juvenile ageism, or childism.[12] *Parentiarchy* refers to *de jure* or formal parental autonomy abstracted from and unconnected with real or psychological autonomy, thus relegating children to a *de facto* status of parental property, that is, of total dependence on their parents' mental health and socio-emotional resources. More specifically, it refers to the privilege of 'unprepared parenthood,' that is, of automatic parental rights upon child birth.[13] *Transism*, or transgenerational discrimination, refers to a state's

11 Issue Paper 2006/1: Children and corporal punishment: 'The right not to be hit, also a children's right', www.coe.int, Institutions/Commissioner for Human Rights, Documents/Documents index, Issue Papers.

12 In this chapter, the terms *transgenerational discrimination* or the shortened form *transism*, will be used. The term *juvenile ageism* was coined by Westman, see J.C. Westman, *Parent Power: The Key to America's Prosperity*, North Charleston, South Carolina: CreateSpace/Amazon, 2013, pp. 69–118. On the term, or rather the concept of *childism*, see E. Young-Bruehl, *Childism: Confronting Prejudice Against Children*, New Haven/London: Yale University Press, 2012. Childism, juvenile ageism (or juvism), and transgenerational discrimination (or transism) are related to the concept of adultism (or adultocentrism). The fact that most children's rights researchers are not familiar with these terms and concepts may be due to denialism with respect to children, on which see J.G. Dwyer, 'Speaking truth for and with children', keynote speech, Conference on Denialism and Human Rights, Maastricht University, 23 January 2015 (not yet published, for an abstract see www.maastrichtuniversity.nl/web/Faculties/FL/Theme/research_law/conferences_research_law/Past2015/DenialismAndHumanRights/ConferenceProgramme.htm).

13 See J.C.M. Willems, 'Kindisme en anti-kindisme na Korczak: Kinderrechten tussen vooroordeel en SMECC-model', in H. Brouwers and T. Cappon (eds.), *Het verlangen naar een betere wereld:*

not adequately addressing socio-economic and, especially, socio-emotional differences between parents (e.g. in relation to parenting knowledge, parental awareness, reparation of own childhood trauma, mental health, emotional stability and maturity, sensitivity, social network, social integration, and so on and so forth), thus contributing to widespread transgenerational transmission of poor mental health or other forms of emotional poverty, of poor parenting and of social (socio-emotional and/or socio-economic) exclusion.[14]

(4) School curricula which fully implement Article 29(1) of the Convention on the Rights of the Child,[15] as opposed to school curricula in which psycho-education (personal, social and health education), education on global and democratic citizenship[16] (citizenship education and global citizenship education), and education on child rights-based – or positive[17] – parenting (parenthood education) are absent.

2.1.2. Dignitarian Individualism

These four building blocks may at the same time be seen as the dignitarian cornerstones of international human rights law. Four UN human rights treaties, with specific state obligations to deal with discrimination, exclusion and related material, mental and emotional poverty, are the legal reinforcement of these cornerstones: the International Convention on the Elimination of all forms of Racial Discrimination (ICERD, 1965), the International Covenant on Economic, Social and Cultural Rights (ICESCR, 1966), the Convention on the Elimination of all forms of Discrimination Against Women (CEDAW, 1979), and the Convention on the Rights of the Child (CRC, 1989).[18] ICESCR's Articles 10 (family, mothers, children: protection and assistance), 11 (adequate family standard of living), 12

Een hoopvol perspectief voor kinderen en opvoeders in moeilijke situaties, Amsterdam: Janusz Korczak Stichting, 2012, pp. 37–55, http://arno.unimaas.nl/show.cgi?fid=25623.

14 For state responsibility and accountability in relation to transism, see J.C.M. Willems, *Wie zal de Opvoeders Opvoeden? Kindermishandeling en het Recht van het Kind op Persoonswording* (Who will Educate the Educators? Child Abuse and the Right of the Child to Become a Person) (with a summary in English), PhD Maastricht University, 1998, T.M.C. Asser Press, The Hague, 1999, pp. 629–991.

15 See also General Comment No. 1 (2001): The aims of education (Article 29(1)), www.ohchr.org, Human Rights Bodies, Committee on the Rights of the Child, General Comments.

16 On 'democracy and democratic citizenship as the final goals of human rights education,' see L. Cattrijsse, 'Participation and human rights education: a Gordian knot?', in F. Ang *et al.*, *Participation Rights of Children*, Antwerp/Oxford: Intersentia, 2006, pp. 199–229, 221–224.

17 'Positive parenting refers to parental behaviour based on the best interests of the child that is nurturing, empowering, non-violent and provides recognition and guidance which involves setting of boundaries to enable the full development of the child.' See Rec (2006)19 of the Committee of Ministers to member states on policy to support positive parenting, Appendix(1), www.coe.int, Institutions/Committee of Ministers, Documents/Adopted texts, Recommendations of the Committee of Ministers to Member States, All Recommendations.

18 As interpreted by their respective treaty bodies: see www.ohchr.org, International Law and Human Rights Bodies (Treaty Bodies, General Comments), respectively.

(physical and mental health, healthy development of the child), and 13 (education directed to the full development of the human personality, participation in a free and tolerant society, and world peace) may be seen as (again, four) early dignitarian landmarks. In the near fifty years after its adoption, however, libertarian individualism, over-emphasising – and rather abstractly and individualistically interpreting – civil and political rights, would prevail. But change may be on its way.

To be sure, individualism is here to stay, but a more dignitarian individualism may be laying ahead of us. That is, if national societies, and states, wholeheartedly follow the trend set by the human rights bodies or actors mentioned above. Co-incidentally, if mental health issues and psycho-education (especially on human relations, interpersonal communication, child development and child rights based parenting) are addressed in a more systematic manner, well before families are founded, far less state intervention in families is to be expected. After a century of intrusive and paternalistic, and rather unsuccessful, child protection, dignitarian individualism may be the best, if not the only, alternative for growing state power.

In the Netherlands, for instance, a law specifying parental authority (Article 1:247 of the Dutch Civil Code) in such a way as to ban corporal punishment and other forms of humiliation of children was unanimously adopted by both the Second and the First Chamber of parliament.[19] The law was signed by the Queen on 8 March 2007 (to become effective as of 25 April 2007): exactly twelve years after the Netherlands had become a party to the CRC (on 8 March 1995). The Netherlands seems to be breaking away from its libertarian tradition of formal parental autonomy. But will the outcome be more than symbolic? Will the ban on corporal punishment mark the beginning of more dignitarian human rights policies in relation to parents and children, including the responsibilisation and empowerment of all concerned – as expounded by international bodies and actors? Will it, eventually, turn out to have been a major step towards a more dignitarian interpretation of reproductive and parental rights, that is, an interpretation that takes the duties and responsibilities that come with making and raising a child fully into account? Including, once again, the empowerment and responsibilisation obligations of states that are the intrinsic and urgent message of children's rights.

Before turning back to these issues, let us first have a closer look at the meaning of the term 'dignitarian' (as opposed to 'libertarian').

---

[19] See www.overheid.nl, Officiële publicaties, Staatsblad, 2007, No. 145.

2.2. DIGNITARIAN VERSUS LIBERTARIAN ATTITUDES AND VIEWS

As Glendon observes:[20]

> 'Within the libertarian tradition, the rights-bearer tends to be imagined as an independent, autonomous, self-determining being. Dignitarian personhood also pays tribute to the uniqueness of each individual, but recognizes that we are constituted in important ways by and through our relations with others.'

And she goes on to say:

> 'The danger of confusing freedom with the absence of restraint has been known since ancient times. In its personal dimension, it has been nicely captured in the old saying: "A man has as many masters as he has vices." In public life, when freedom unravels into license, politics becomes a war of all against all.'

Apart from libertarianism ('radically autonomous man'), also utilitarianism ('economic man') and relativism ('plastic man') may be opposed to dignitarianism in Glendon's view. In my opinion, radically autonomous – or individualistic – man, economic man and plastic man are close relatives, contrary to dignitarianism's free-and-responsible man, if I may label him or her that way. Of course, these men have old ancestors. Libertarian man reminds us of Hobbes's (1588–1679; *Leviathan* 1651) man as a wolf to his fellow man (*homo homini lupus*), originally – as Glendon sees it, ultimately – engaged in a war of all against all (*bellum omnium contra omnes*). Whereas dignitarian man reminisces Grotius's (1583–1645; *De Jure Belli ac Pacis* 1625) man as a social animal endowed with reason. In other words, an animal with moral, that is, social-and-rational potential. This, in my view both dignified and emancipatory image of man, is reflected in Grotius's definition of natural law (*De Jure Belli ac Pacis* I.1.10:1): a dictate of conscientious reason (*dictatum rectae rationis*) which points out that an act is either moral or immoral because it is in conformity with or contrary to man's rational and social nature. From this definition, it may be concluded that a person who acts reasonably and socially lives up to his or her human potential and is more in tune with his or her humanity than a person who acts unreasonably and anti-socially. In the Prolegomena of his book (paragraphs 6–17), Grotius says that man's desire for organised life with his fellow men, according to his rational talents – his *appetitus societatis* ('social appetite') as Grotius calls it – makes him care for his

---

20 Statement by Dr Mary Ann Glendon (1996), see www.holyseemission.org, Search: Glendon; www.academiavita.org/_pdf/documents/pav/evangelium_vitae_and_law.pdf. See also C. Emerson Welch, 'A World Made New: Eleanor Roosevelt and the Universal Declaration of Human Rights', and 'The Universal Declaration of Human Rights: Origins, Drafting and Intent' (review) (2002) *Human Rights Quarterly* 287–290.

community (*societatis custodia*). And ultimately, one may hope and expect, for the society of all mankind (*magna humani generis societas*). Grotius's man, therefore, may be seen as someone who feels himself responsible for his community, and sees himself as a responsible member of the human family. Grotius's dignitarian man of 1625, it appears to me, looks very much like the world's dignitarian man of 1948. The Universal Declaration of Human Rights, adopted by the General Assembly of the UN on December 10, 1948, seems to combine dignitarian and libertarian traditions in its first preambular paragraph, which speaks of both the 'inherent dignity' and the 'equal and inalienable rights' of all members of the human family. This is repeated in Article 1: man is born free and equal in dignity and rights. The Article then goes on, however, to state that man is endowed with reason and conscience, and stipulates that man should act towards his fellow man in a spirit of 'brotherhood' (solidarity, as we would say today; as I see it, a rational passion somewhere in between justice and love of one's fellow-man). To which spirited words Article 29(1) of the Universal Declaration adds that man has duties to the community in which alone the free and full development of his personality is possible.

2.2.1. Definitions

After 1948, the pendulum swung far in the libertarian direction, maybe to swing back to the Universal Declaration's arguably mixed, but in Glendon's (and my) view predominantly dignitarian anthropology, in the years ahead. However, discussing anthropologies in relation to human rights is not what I intend to do in this chapter.[21] Therefore, I will limit myself now – against the background of Glendon's observations – to present some examples of what I conceive as libertarian versus dignitarian attitudes and (legal or juridical) views. As these examples will show, I attach positive connotations to the term dignitarian: prosocial, empathetic, respectful, thoughtful, sensitive, caring; and negative connotations to the term libertarian: individualistic, egocentric, or even antisocial, reckless or myopic. Obviously, this does injustice to their original and more nuanced meaning. But it is hoped that these examples will illustrate the usefulness for human rights discourse of the distinctions made, even if in reality things are not always that black and white. Let me first, then, clarify the terms dignitarian and libertarian as I intend to use them.

Dignitarian refers to human dignity in the sense that no one is the property or the instrument of others. It thereby refers to respect for others, but a dignified or authentic respect, that is, respect that comes from within. In other words, respect

[21] For a more in-depth analysis of the issues concerned, especially as they relate to children's rights, see J.C.M. Willems, J.C.M. Willems, *Wie zal de Opvoeders Opvoeden? Kindermishandeling en het Recht van het Kind op Persoonswording* (Who will Educate the Educators? Child Abuse and the Right of the Child to Become a Person) (with a summary in English), PhD Maastricht University, 1998, T.M.C. Asser Press, The Hague, 1999, pp. 51–289, 635–670, and *passim*.

for others on the basis of self-respect. To this I add that the origins of self-respect (self-esteem, emotional stability) are to be found in secure emotional attachments of infants and young children to their carers (see Textbox 1: Attachment security). Sustained messages of inclusion, belonging and participation by adults and society at large to children and adolescents may then further enhance self-respect, resilience and sense of responsibility. For dignitarians, both dignity and liberty include responsibility. In other words, dignitarian man is not just endowed with rights, but with rights, duties and responsibilities.

Libertarian refers to rights seen as mere claims, privileges or powers, and liberty seen as freedom from (state or other) intervention rather than freedom from fear (emotional and mental poverty: poor mental health, superstition, ignorance) and freedom from want (material and mental poverty: low income, poor education). In other words, libertarian freedom is linked to abstractions and procedures rather than to context and values.

Textbox 1: Attachment security

'For a normative population, it is reported that about 62% of infants are classified as secure, 15% as insecure-avoidant, 8% as insecure-ambivalent and 15% as disorganized. Secure attachment is considered a protective factor as it has been associated with better developmental outcomes in areas such as self-reliance, self-efficacy, empathy and social competence in toddlerhood, school-age and adolescence. Infants with insecure attachment have been shown to be at risk for later adaptation problems such as conduct disorder, aggression, depression and anti-social behaviour. Children with disorganized attachment are at the highest risk for psychopathology. There is a high percentage of attachment disorganization among children who have been victims of maltreatment. An array of parental behaviours has been linked to infant disorganization. These include affective communication errors (such as contradictory responses to infant signals), parental withdrawal, negative-intrusive responses, role-confused responses, disoriented responses and frightened or frightening behaviours. Negative life events (such as divorce) can compromise attachment security, but differences in attachment security result primarily from the children's interactions with their social environment during the first few years of life. Parenting therefore plays a crucial role. For this reason, preventive interventions in early childhood have enormous potential to alter behavioural and developmental trajectories, especially in high-risk families.'

Source: Centre of Excellence for Early Childhood Development.[22]

22 Centre of Excellence for Early Childhood Development, Online *Encyclopedia on Early Childhood Development*, Synthesis on attachment, www.excellence-earlychildhood.ca, Attachment; www.child-encyclopedia.com/Pages/PDF/synthesis-attachment.pdf.

2.2.2. Some Examples

Let me present some examples of dignitarian-libertarian distinctions, or dignitarian versus libertarian emphases, in relation to individuals, the state, and lawyers. An individual with a dignitarian attitude would always try to balance rights and duties, he or she would optimise this balance rather than minimise his or her responsibilities as a parent, a family member, a worker, a citizen, a student, and so on. A state with a dignitarian perception of its international commitments would implement its human rights obligations to the maximum extent of its resources rather than minimise, or even evade its responsibilities. Dignitarian lawyers would disagree with libertarian lawyers on issues such as soft law, e.g. General Comments by treaty bodies (binding and important, versus non-binding and irrelevant); democracy (based on human rights, versus based on majority rule only);[23] the principle of equality (substantive, versus formal only); and the freedom of opinion (implying a duty not to unnecessarily shock or offend, versus implying a right to offend for the sake of offending). In relation to the CRC, dignitarian and libertarian lawyers would differ on the (high versus low) impact and significance of, in my – dignitarian – opinion core CRC obligations, such as:

- prioritising the principle of the best interests of the child: Article 3(1) seen as a central, versus a marginal 'primary consideration' in domestic policy and foreign relations;
- incorporating the pedagogical aims of education in school curricula: Article 29(1) seen as a state's duty (something a state must do) versus a state's power (something a state may do);
- improving universal and selective prevention of child abuse and neglect:[24] Articles 18(2) and 27(3) in conjunction with Articles 19(2) and 39, taken

[23] See J.C.M. Willems, 'Staat dient op te treden tegen "pedopartij"; Pedofilie, democratie, transisme en het belang van het kind' (2007) 3 *Ars Aequi* 218–224; earlier online version available at http://arno.unimaas.nl/show.cgi?did=9216, e1-e9 (27 October 2006).

[24] On child abuse and neglect (CAN) in relation to the CRC, see J.C.M. Willems, *Wie zal de Opvoeders Opvoeden? Kindermishandeling en het Recht van het Kind op Persoonswording* (Who will Educate the Educators? Child Abuse and the Right of the Child to Become a Person) (with a summary in English), PhD Maastricht University, 1998, T.M.C. Asser Press, The Hague, 1999, pp. 457–627, as well as the CAN classification in Appendix 3, 1038–1062. On (combined) universal and selective prevention, or a continuum of care, and the related IFOI system (Inform all parents, Filter out good enough parents, Offer all others parenting support, and Intervene if help does not work), see chapter 4 of *Developmental and Autonomy Rights of Children; Empowering Children, Caregivers and Communities*, 2nd ed., Antwerp/Oxford: Intersentia, 2007, pp. 79–82. Combined universal and selective prevention were, to a certain degree, introduced in the Dutch so-called RAAK regions (www.raak.org or www.stopkindermishandeling.nl), on which see chapter 5 of *Developmental and Autonomy Rights of Children; Empowering Children, Caregivers and Communities*, 2nd ed., Antwerp/Oxford: Intersentia, 2007, pp. 132–137. At present, the RAAK care continuum is formally introduced in the Netherlands (see K. Kooijman, *Niets doen is geen optie! Verder met de aanpak van kindermishandeling*, Utrecht: Nederlands Jeugdinstituut, 2011). For a comprehensive preventative model, the so-called SMECC model, which includes a professional care

together, and seen as a duty to transform the traditional system of child protection into an integrated system of combined medical, social, psychological and protective services for children and families, versus anything but structural reform (see Textbox 2: Child maltreatment can be prevented).

Textbox 2: Child maltreatment can be prevented

'According to the recently released UN Secretary-General's Study on Violence Against Children [available at <www.violencestudy.org>], much of the violence endured by children aged 0–14 years occurs in the home at the hands of parents, caregivers, and family members. The consequences of this violence hinder children's health and development and can last well into adulthood, negatively affecting health and increasing the risks of further victimization and becoming a perpetrator of violence. ... Research shows that child maltreatment can be prevented. The need to increase investment in prevention is urgent and global. Promising strategies include reducing unintended pregnancies; improving access to high-quality pre- and post-natal care; reducing harmful levels of alcohol and illicit drug use during pregnancy and by new parents; providing home visitation services by nurses and social workers to families at risk of maltreatment, and training parents on child development, non-violent discipline and problem-solving skills. ... "For too long now the response to child maltreatment has been dominated by systems for reacting to cases once maltreatment has already started. The scientific evidence for preventing physical, sexual and psychological abuse from occurring in the first place is already quite strong, and the time is ripe for a paradigm shift from reaction to prevention," said Dr. Anders Nordström, WHO Acting Director General.'

Source: World Health Organization.[25]

Although in relation to lawyers or legal views, libertarianism should not be confused with legal positivism, both are probably equally predominant in present-day legal discourse. This is one of the reasons why I think it is important to bring dignitarian developments, as I see them, to the forefront. It is my conviction that both libertarianism (individual rights disconnected from interpersonal or social responsibilities) and legal positivism (the study and practice of law whereby rules

continuum, see J.C.M. Willems, 'Principles and Promises in the Convention on the Rights of the Child and the Convention on the Rights of Persons with Disabilities', in G. Quinn, L. Waddington and E. Flynn (eds.), *European Yearbook of Disability Law Volume 3*, Antwerp/Oxford: Intersentia, 2012, pp.59–100; or the extended online version: J.C.M. Willems, 'It takes a SMECC to raise a child: Meeting basic developmental needs of newborn persons', http://arno.unimaas.nl/show.cgi?fid=25622.

25 World Health Organization, 'World Health Organization says violence against children can and must be prevented', Geneva, 16 October 2006, www.who.int/mediacentre/news/releases/2006/pr57/en/print.html.

and court decisions rather than principles and values, including human rights and human dignity, are decisive) are in need of corrections. Of course, it is up to the reader to decide whether my endeavours in this respect deserve a better fate than being put aside as wishful thinking.

3. RESPONSIBLE PARENTHOOD

3.1. DIGNITARIAN LANGUAGE AND REPRODUCTIVE RIGHTS

The use of the words responsibility, responsible or responsibilities in an international instrument is a sure sign if not of dignitarian intent then at least of dignitarian potential. But also reference to the best interests of the child and to state obligations to empower and 'responsibilise' caregivers could, indeed should be seen as dignitarian. CEDAW, the 1979 Convention on the Elimination of all forms of Discrimination Against Women, contains several examples of this dignitarian language:

- in its 13th preambular paragraph, it is said that 'the upbringing of children requires a sharing of responsibility between men and women and society as a whole';
- Article 5(b) speaks of 'the common responsibility of men and women in the upbringing and development of their children, it being understood that the interest of the children is the primordial consideration in all cases';
- Article 11(2)(c) urges states 'to enable parents to combine family obligations with work responsibilities and participation in public life';
- Article 16(1)(c) urges states to give men and women the 'same rights and responsibilities during marriage and at its dissolution';
- Article 16(1)(d) urges states to give men and women the 'same rights and responsibilities as parents, irrespective of their marital status, in matters relating to their children; in all cases the interests of the children shall be paramount';
- Article 16(1)(e) urges states to give men and women the 'same rights to decide freely and responsibly on the number and spacing of their children and to have access to the information, education and means to enable them to exercise these rights'; and
- Article 16(1)(f) urges states to give men and women the 'same rights and responsibilities with regard to guardianship, wardship, trusteeship and adoption of children … in all cases the interests of the children shall be paramount.'

Article 16(1)(e) CEDAW was preceded by, *inter alia*, the following two declarations. The 1974 Bucharest World Population Plan of Action proclaims:[26]

> 'All couples and individuals have the basic right to decide freely and responsibly the number and spacing of their children and to have the information, education and means to do so; the responsibility of couples and individuals in the exercise of this right takes into account the needs of their living and future children, and their responsibilities towards the community.'

Twenty years later, the 1994 Cairo ICPD (International Conference on Population and Development) Programme of Action repeats and elaborates this theme:

> 'Principle 8. ... All couples and individuals have the basic right to decide freely and responsibly the number and spacing of their children and to have the information, education and means to do so. ... In the exercise of this right, they should take into account the needs of their living and future children and their responsibilities towards the community. The promotion of the responsible exercise of these rights for all people should be the fundamental basis for government- and community-supported policies and programmes in the area of reproductive health, including family planning.'

On top of this, several paragraphs make explicit mention of responsible parenthood:

> 'Special efforts should be made to emphasize men's shared responsibility and promote their active involvement in responsible parenthood, sexual and reproductive behaviour, including family planning ... Male responsibilities in family life must be included in the education of children from the earliest ages. Special emphasis should be placed on the prevention of violence against women and children.'
>
> 'Countries ... should take necessary steps to ... [ensure] educational strategies regarding responsible parenthood and sexual education.'
>
> 'All countries should strive to make accessible through the primary health-care system, reproductive health to all individuals of appropriate ages as soon as possible and no later than the year 2015. Reproductive health care in the context of primary health care should ... include: ... information, education and counselling ... on ... responsible parenthood.'

---

26 World Population Plan of Action, adopted by consensus of the 137 countries represented at the United Nations World Population Conference at Bucharest, August 1974 (UN Doc. E/CONF.60/19)(1)4.f, www.population-security.org; www.population-security.org/27-APP1.html.

Commenting on reproductive rights before and after CEDAW, Brems remarks:[27] 'The CEDAW provisions aside, reproductive human rights have not yet been included in other legally binding documents.' This may be the case, to be sure, for the libertarian part of reproductive rights ('to decide freely'). But a different conclusion may be reached for the dignitarian part ('to decide responsibly' and to be empowered, through information, education and other means, to exercise one's rights). As I intend to point out in this section, the 1989 Convention on the Rights of the Child has a great deal to say on the latter. I am afraid Brems' remark illustrates how strongly libertarianism holds grip on most lawyers. In my – dignitarian – opinion, responsible parenthood should be seen as an integral part of reproductive rights and health. From the perspective of children's rights and the CRC, responsible parenthood refers to three things which are closely related. First of all, the concept and principle of the best interests of the child. Secondly, parental duties and responsibilities as they are (all) related to the child's best interests. And thirdly, state obligations to empower parents to fulfil their duties and responsibilities, including empowerment through responsibilisation, that is, specifying and clarifying these duties and responsibilities in the national legal system. Let us first have a look at the concept and principle of the best interests of the child, and then turn to parental responsibilities and state obligations under the CRC.

3.2. THE BEST INTERESTS OF THE CHILD

According to Article 3(1), the best interests of the child are 'a primary consideration' for the state, its organs and its public and private social welfare institutions. According to Article 18(1) CRC, the best interests of the child are 'the basic concern' of both parents. The Committee on the Rights of the Child deems the best interests of the child to be one of the four cornerstone principles of the CRC, the other three being non-discrimination (although the Committee does not seem to be aware of concepts such as transgenerational discrimination, juvenile ageism, or childism),[28] participation ('respect for the views of the child'), and life, survival and development (Articles 3, 2, 12, and 6, respectively).[29]

---

27 E. Brems, 'Protecting the rights of women', in R. Pierre Claude and B.H. Weston, *Human Rights in the World Community; Issues and Action*, 3rd ed., Philadelphia: University of Pennsylvania Press, 2006, pp. 120–133, at 128.

28 See note 12.

29 See General guidelines regarding the form and content of initial reports to be submitted by States Parties under Article 44(1)(a), of the Convention, CRC/C/5 (1991), General principles, paragraph 13: 'Relevant information, including the principal legislative, judicial, administrative or other measures in force or foreseen, factors and difficulties encountered and progress achieved in implementing the provisions of the Convention, and implementation priorities and specific goals for the future should be provided in respect of: (a) Non-discrimination (Article 2); (b) Best interests of the child (Article 3); (c) The right to life, survival and development (Article 6); (d) Respect for the views of the child (Article 12).' See

Neither the CRC nor, thus far, the Committee present a definition, however, of the best interests principle.[30] In order to clarify the best interests concept, the developmental psychological and pedagogical model of Kalverboer and Zijlstra (2006) will be used.[31] This model consists of fourteen conditions or elements, seven to be met (mainly) within the family, and seven to be met (mainly) within the community or society at large. For mnemonic reasons, I have translated and rearranged these seven-plus-seven conditions so as to let their first letters form the acronyms saccade (in the family) and fressen (in society), respectively. *Saccade* means (according to dictionary.com): '1. the series of small, jerky movements of the eyes when changing focus from one point to another (ophthalmology); 2. the act of checking a horse quickly with a single strong pull of the reins.' In a metaphorical sense, we might understand the word saccade as referring to (examples of) affection and direction in child rearing: (1) looking at one's baby and trying to read his or her face; (2) protecting one's child from danger or stopping one's child from misbehaving by means of non-punitive physical action.

Fressen is a German word, well known from the saying: *Zuerst kommt das Fressen und dann die Moral* (food comes first, then morality). Since in human rights law, the relationship between food and morality may be somewhat more complex – or closer – I leave it to the reader to attach a metaphorical sense to the word *Fressen* and its use as an acronym in 'the best interests of the child.' The fourteen *Saccade* and *Fressen* conditions, then, are:

Saccade 7:

1. security (physical security: no physical dangers, toxic influences, domestic violence, corporal punishment, maltreatment, chronic marital conflicts);
2. affection (secure attachment; emotional security);
3. care (breast, bread, bed, bath; health, housing, heating, hygiene; no poverty stress);
4. continuity in child rearing (enabling secure attachment and basic trust, as well as creating perspective; including knowledge of one's biological origins);

---

also the revised General guidelines for periodic reports (Article 44(1)(b) CRC), CRC/C/58/Rev.1 (2005), General principles, paragraph 21. Both available at www.ohchr.org, Human Rights Bodies, Committee on the Rights of the Child, Initial/Periodic Reports.

30 See, however, for a recent clarification by the Committee, General Comment No. 14 (2013): The right of the child to have his or her best interests taken as a primary consideration (Art. 3(1)), www.ohchr.org, Human Rights Bodies, Committee on the Rights of the Child, General Comments. For denialism (see n. 12) in relation to this principle, that is, the gap between this principle and national practice in child protection, see, e.g., CEDAW/C/58/D/47/2012, Communication No. 47/2012, *González Carreño v. Spain*, Decision of 16 July 2014, http://tbinternet.ohchr.org/_layouts/treatybodyexternal/Download.aspx?symbolno=CEDAW/C/58/D/47/2012&Lang=en.

31 M. Kalverboer and E. Zijlstra, *Het belang van het kind in het Nederlands recht; Voorwaarden voor ontwikkeling vanuit een pedagogisch perspectief*, Amsterdam: SWP, 2006. For a version in English, see the Appendix in M.E. Kalverboer, A.E. Zijlstra and E.J. Knorth, 'The developmental consequences for asylum-seeking children living with the prospect for five years or more of enforced return to their home country' (2009) 11(1) *European Journal of Migration and Law* 41–67.

5. attention (parents' sincere interest in each individual child);
6. direction and guidance consistent with evolving capacities (in the terminology of Article 5 CRC);[32] including disciplining without violence and humiliation (according to General Comment 8);[33]
7. examples (that is, parents set good examples);

Fressen 7:
1. friends (peer interaction);
2. respect (active respect for the child in society, school, community);[34]
3. education (school, vocational training; including sports, music, et cetera);[35]
4. security (in society, school, community; no physical and extreme virtual violence);
5. stability (no abrupt, unexplained change; social perspective);
6. examples (friends and adults set good examples);
7. network (a social network of people to whom the child may turn for help).

The *Saccade* condition 'direction and guidance consistent with evolving capacities' is taken literally from Article 5 CRC. The model itself speaks of a supportive and flexible pedagogical structure, for which six sub-conditions have to be met:

- regularity (daily rhythm and routine of feeding, sleeping and hygiene);
- realistic demands (stimulating and instructing the child based on realistic demands);
- rules (or limits, which are explained to the child);
- room (to experience, experiment, negotiate);
- responsibilities (participation in family and community responsibilities);
- supervision.

32 The model's terminology (and sub-conditions) follows directly below.

33 General Comment No. 8 (2006): The right of the child to protection from corporal punishment and other cruel or degrading forms of punishment (Articles 19, 28(2) and 37, *inter alia*), paragraphs 13, 28, 39 (www.ohchr.org, Human Rights Bodies, Committee on the Rights of the Child, General Comments). In paragraph 11, the Committee defines corporal (or physical) punishment as 'any punishment in which physical force is used and intended to cause some degree of pain or discomfort, however light.' To which the Committee adds: 'In addition, there are ... non-physical forms of punishment that are also cruel and degrading and thus incompatible with the Convention. These include, for example, punishment which belittles, humiliates, denigrates, scapegoats, threatens, scares or ridicules the child.'

34 Meeting – I would add – the primarily participatory and primarily protective pedagogical aims (or general protective purposes) of, respectively, Articles 12–17, and Articles 7–11, 14(2), 17(e) 20–23, 25, 26, 28(2), 30 and 32–40 CRC. And including school or other disciplining without violence and humiliation (see General Comment 8, quoted above).

35 Meeting – I would add – the pedagogical aims mentioned in Article 29(1) – on which see General Comment 1, 2001: The aims of education (www.ohchr.org) – and implied in Article 31 CRC.

Of course, direction and guidance should be affection-based. As the sixth preambular paragraph of the CRC puts it: 'the child, for the full and harmonious development of his or her personality, should grow up in a family environment, in an atmosphere of happiness, love and understanding.' This should not be seen as overly romantic. Other than the able-bodied man's 'pursuit of happiness' in the American Declaration of Independence, happiness in the CRC refers to the well-being of the (vulnerable) child. The CRC's love and understanding are evenly child-specific. Affection, seen as the combination of love and understanding, is the beating heart of the child's best interests. No wonder, then, that happiness and love ('love and understanding') appear in no other UN human rights treaty. At the same time, we may conclude – reading Article 5 CRC in the light of the sixth preambular paragraph – that the CRC favours a parenting style which adequately combines affection (responsiveness, warmth) and direction (demandingness, control). Such a style is called authoritative parenting. Authoritarian (or autocratic) parents are also demanding but not very responsive. Permissive parents are responsive but not at all demanding. Parents who are neither demanding nor responsive are neglectful (or unengaged). Article 18(1) CRC proclaims the best interests of the child to be both parents' basic concern. It may, therefore, be argued that authoritative parenting is (not just favoured but) required by the CRC.[36] Authoritative parenting, I would add, is positive and sensitive parenting: it is non-violent and non-humiliating, and sensitive to the child's needs not only for attention and affection but also for structure and limits, guidance and direction. As The National Society for the Prevention of Cruelty to Children (NSPCC) in the UK puts it:[37]

> 'All children need acceptance, love, encouragement, discipline, consistency and positive attention from their parents. Children who are denied these things often grow up thinking they are deficient in some way and that they somehow deserved to be treated badly. Sadly, when they become parents themselves they may emotionally deprive their own children because they don't have a positive model of parenting to draw on.'

The more the *Saccade* and *Fressen* conditions are met, the higher the likelihood that the child will develop a personality which is optimally rational, moral and authentic,[38] and that he or she will develop the seven adult abilities which may

36 See L. Bornstein and M.H. Bornstein, 'Parenting styles and child social development', in R.E. Tremblay *et al.* (eds.), *Encyclopedia on Early Childhood Development* [online], Centre of Excellence for Early Childhood Development, Montreal, Quebec, 2007, e1-e4, www.excellence-earlychildhood.ca/documents/BornsteinANGxp.pdf; www.child-encyclopedia.com/parenting-skills/according-experts/parenting-styles-and-child-social-development.

37 See www.nspcc.org.uk, search: Children's emotional needs (26 August 2007).

38 On optimal (and minimal) personality development (becoming a person) in relation to the CRC, see J.C.M. Willems, *Wie zal de Opvoeders Opvoeden? Kindermishandeling en het Recht van het Kind op Persoonswording* (Who will Educate the Educators? Child Abuse and the Right

be identified – in my translation and adaptation from the Dutch[39] – by use of the acronym 'IPIPIPI': (1) ability to maintain *intimate* relationships (adult attachment capacity, self-esteem); (2) ability to maintain *personal* relationships (friends, colleagues); (3) ability to live by *internalised* values and norms (mature conscience formation); (4) ability to keep *promises* (to be responsible for oneself and others); (5) ability to control *impulses*; (6) ability to solve *problems*; and (7) ability to (develop one's capacities in order to) earn an *income*.

Of course, one may expect that meeting the conditions of the 'best interests of the child' will produce healthier personalities and reduce personality disorders.[40] Here, reference may be made to a – final – acronym, one that is well known in the literature on personality and the so-called Big Five personality traits, namely 'OCEAN'.[41] OCEAN refers to the following psychologically well-established traits ('versus' should be read as: on a scale or continuum from one extreme to the other): (1) *openness* to experience (versus closedness to experiences); (2) *conscientiousness* (versus lack of conscientiousness); (3) *extraversion* (versus introversion); (4) *agreeableness* (versus disagreeableness); and (5) (emotional stability versus) *neuroticism*.

All these traits may be associated with a dignitarian ('what can I do to fulfil my responsibilities?') versus a libertarian attitude ('what can I do to evade my responsibilities?'), although conscientiousness is likely to be the most influential trait in this regard. This is speculation on my part, however. Whether personality development on the basis of the fourteen best interests' conditions leads to better personality-Big Five outcomes, falls outside the scope of this chapter. However, going by the Adverse Childhood Experiences Study (see Textbox 3: Adverse childhood experiences), better physical and mental health are certainly to be expected (see Textbox 4: ACE Study findings). Obviously, especially neuroticism and mental health are closely related.

---

of the Child to Become a Person) (with a summary in English), PhD Maastricht University, 1998, T.M.C. Asser Press, The Hague, 1999, pp. 291–455.

39 M. Kalverboer and E. Zijlstra, *Het belang van het kind in het Nederlands recht; Voorwaarden voor ontwikkeling vanuit een pedagogisch perspectief*, Amsterdam: SWP, 2006, p. 34 (referring to Weterings and Van den Bergh, 2005).

40 Cf. W.E. de Boever and T.W. van Driel, *FACT-grafiek, blauwdruk van de menselijke geest*, Syntyche: Dordrecht, 2006, www.syntyche.nl.

41 See e.g. http://wilderdom.com/personality/traits/PersonalityTraitsBig5.html; www.personality research.org/bigfive.html.

Textbox 3: Adverse childhood experiences

Adverse Childhood Experiences (ACEs) are: 'Growing up (prior to age 18) in a household with: recurrent physical abuse; recurrent emotional abuse; sexual abuse; an alcohol or drug abuser; an incarcerated household member; someone who is chronically depressed, suicidal, institutionalized or mentally ill; mother being treated violently; one or no parents; emotional or physical neglect.' – 'ACEs are surprisingly common. They happen even in "the best of families." They have long-term, damaging consequences.' – 'The ACE Study reveals a powerful relationship between our emotional experiences as children and our physical and mental health as adults, as well as the major causes of adult mortality in the United States. It documents the conversion of traumatic emotional experiences in childhood into organic disease later in life. How does this happen, this reverse alchemy, turning the gold of a newborn infant into the lead of a depressed, diseased adult? The Study makes it clear that time does not heal some of the adverse experiences we found so common in the childhoods of a large population of middle-aged, middle class Americans. One does not "just get over" some things, not even fifty years later.'

Source: The Adverse Childhood Experiences Study.[42]

Textbox 4: ACE Study findings

'Childhood abuse, neglect, and exposure to other traumatic stressors which we term *adverse childhood experiences* (ACEs) are common. Almost two-thirds of our study participants reported at least one ACE, and more than one in five reported three or more ACEs. The short- and long-term outcomes of these childhood exposures include a multitude of health and social problems. The ACE Study uses the ACE Score, which is a count of the total number of ACE respondents reported. The ACE Score is used to assess the total amount of stress during childhood and has demonstrated that as the number of ACEs increase, the risk for the following health problems increases in a strong and graded fashion: alcoholism and alcohol abuse; chronic obstructive pulmonary disease (COPD); depression; fetal death; health-related quality of life; illicit drug use; ischemic heart disease (IHD); liver disease; risk for intimate partner violence; multiple sexual partners; sexually transmitted diseases (STDs); smoking; suicide attempts; unintended pregnancies; early initiation of smoking; early initiation of sexual activity; adolescent pregnancy.'

Source: Centers for Disease Control and Prevention.[43]

42 The Adverse Childhood Experiences Study, www.acestudy.org and www.cdc.gov/violenceprevention/acestudy. For a video series on the ACE Study, see http://cavalcadeproductions.com/ace-study.html. For videos for adult survivors of child abuse ('30-minute videos containing … interviews with adult survivors of child abuse, as well as therapist discussion related to client issues'), see http://cavalcadeproductions.com/adult-survivors.html.

43 Centers for Disease Control and Prevention, Adverse Childhood Experiences (ACE) Study, Major Findings, www.cdc.gov/nccdphp/ace/findings.htm; www.cdc.gov/violenceprevention/

3.3. PARENTAL RESPONSIBILITIES AND STATE OBLIGATIONS

Article 3(2) CRC establishes a *trias pedagogica* of children, parents and the state.[44] It reads as follows:

> 'States Parties undertake to ensure the child such protection and care as is necessary for his or her well-being, taking into account the rights and duties of his or her parents, legal guardians, or other individuals legally responsible for him or her, and, to this end, shall take all appropriate legislative and administrative measures.'

As we have seen, the best interests of the child are concerns of both the state (Article 3(1)) and parents (Article 18(1) third sentence). According to the whole concept of children's rights, and especially according to Article 12: child participation as a general principle, the child is also an actor in his or her own best interests, that is, in his or her own healthy holistic (physical-emotional-social-moral-intellectual)[45] development and the pursuit of the other pedagogical aims of the Convention, mentioned in Article 29(1). Taken together, these aims may be summarised as holistic development and preparation for democratic and global citizenship. And the latter may be construed – on the basis, *inter alia*, of Articles 18(1) second sentence (primary responsibility of parents for the development of the child), and 29(1)(d) (preparation of the child for responsible life) – as including preparation for responsible parenthood. Thus, three actors are involved in child development: the state, parents, and the child him- or herself. All these actors have rights, duties and responsibilities, which, according to their fundamental character, should be constitutionalised, but at any rate should be specified – and clarified – in the national legal system.

Two of the most outstanding state obligations, in my opinion, in the CRC are to be found in Articles 27(3) and 18(2) which require the state to empower, that is to facilitate, educate, assist and support parents, in socio-economic and socio-emotional ways, respectively. Specifying and clarifying parental duties and responsibilities, as they appear in the CRC, is also a very important state

acestudy/findings.html. It is important to add to the information on this site that not all ACEs are avoidable, no matter how empowered parents may be. Also, ACEs do not mean that one is predestined to develop all kinds of health and social problems later in life. They are serious risk factors. Moreover, traumatisation may be overcome, later in life or already during childhood. This underlines the enormous importance of Article 39 CRC, because of its potential to prevent – through child trauma reparation (on which see www.childtrauma.org) – transgenerational transmission of trauma.

44 On this *trias pedagogica* (defined below), see chapters 4–6 of *Developmental and Autonomy Rights of Children; Empowering Children, Caregivers and Communities*, 2nd ed., Antwerp/Oxford: Intersentia, 2007.

45 See note 6.

responsibility, however. Such a specification and clarification provide us with an essential yardstick for parenthood education in schools and parenting education for parents and parents-to-be. As such, they are an integral part of preparation for parenthood and empowerment of children, parents and other carers and the community (neighbours, relatives, professionals, volunteers, bystanders, etc.). Therefore, specification and clarification of parental duties and responsibilities should be considered as an implied state obligation. Furthermore, it may be argued that specifying and clarifying parental duties falls within the scope of the 'appropriate legislative and administrative measures' called for by Article 3(2) to ensure the child's care and protection with positive regard to parental duties. Responsibilisation is the term we use to denote, *inter alia*, the state's obligation to specify and clarify parental duties and responsibilities in the national legal system. The combination of CRC provisions and state obligations mentioned above enables us to present the following definition of (a children's rights-based) *trias pedagogica*.

Trias pedagogica means the national or constitutional relationship between the state, parents and children, based on children's rights and other human rights and, therefore, implying state obligations in relation to the healthy holistic development of children, including the participation of the child and his or her preparation for democratic (and global) citizenship and responsible parenthood, and, more specifically, to the responsibilisation and empowerment of parents and other caregivers, professional and otherwise.

Even though the CRC may not make it possible to exactly define the concept of responsible parenthood, it does stipulate the core conditions that have to be met by parents and the state. Apart from CRC Articles 18(2) and 27(3) (and a few other provisions), however, it does so in a rather implicit way. Most implicit, of course, are the conditions that have to be distilled out of the principle of the best interests of the child, as we have seen above. But also parental duties and responsibilities, and related state obligations to enact these and enable their fulfilment, require careful reading of the Convention.

3.3.1. *Fifty-Plus-One Parental Duties*

The following responsibilisation Articles, and ('fifty-plus-one') parental duties and responsibilities to be legislated and promulgated by the state on the basis of these Articles, may be discerned in the CRC. This list should not be seen as exhaustive, however. It should also be kept in mind that the degree of specification and the details of clarification in national legislation is subject to national democratic process and discretion.

Article 18(1) CRC contains three closely related parental duties:
– 1. *both* parents (whatever their gender and marital status) have *common* responsibilities for the upbringing and development of the child;

– 2. parents have the *primary* responsibility for the upbringing and development of the child (the state having the *ultimate* responsibility, *see* Article 3(2) CRC);
– 3. the best interests of the child will be their *basic concern*. – The 'best interests' principle consists of fourteen conditions, one of which consists of six subconditions, according to the model of Margrite Kalverboer & Elianne Zijlstra, discussed above. Based on this model, parents have the duty:
– 3.1 to provide physical security;
– 3.2 to provide physical care;
– 3.3 to provide loving care and emotional security;
– 3.4 to provide a supportive and flexible pedagogical structure ('direction and guidance consistent with evolving capacities'), for which six sub-conditions have to be met: (1) regularity ('routines, rituals and rules'); (2) realistic demands (stimulating and instructing the child based on realistic demands); (3) room (to experience, experiment, negotiate); (4) responsibilities (participation in family and community responsibilities); (5) rules (boundaries or limits, which are explained to the child); and (6) supervision;
– 3.5 to provide continuity in child-rearing;
– 3.6 to give personal attention to each individual child;
– 3.7 to set good examples;
– 3.8 to see to their child's education (school, vocational training; including sports, music, etcetera);
– 3.9 to see to their child's physical and emotional security in school and community;
– 3.10 to stimulate their child's interaction with peers;
– 3.11 to stimulate their child's access to a social support network;
– 3.12 to devote themselves to active respect for (the human dignity, personal integrity and equal developmental opportunities of) children in school, community and society;
– 3.13 to contribute to good adult examples in community and society;
– 3.14 to contribute to stable living conditions in community and society.
Taken together (and in conjunction with the ninth – 'before as well as after birth'– preambular paragraph), the three main duties of Article 18(1) imply a fourth duty:
– 4. both parents have to prepare themselves and actively seek information and support from family, community, and the state before their child is born. – Pre- and perinatal (preparation, or rather preparation-and-reparation) responsibilities may be said to include:
– 4.1 a physically and mentally healthy lifestyle (*cf.* ninth preambular paragraph and Article 24);
– 4.2 a healthy, stable relationship (*cf.* ninth preambular paragraph and Article 18(1) first sentence: 'both parents');
– 4.3 a stable family income (*cf.* ninth preambular paragraph and Article 27(2));
– 4.4 parenting education (*cf.* ninth preambular paragraph; Article 18(1) third sentence: 'best interests basic concern'; and Article 24);

– 4.5 mental health counselling (own childhood trauma reparation, psychotherapy; *cf.* ninth preambular paragraph and Articles 18(1); 19(1); and 24).
Article 5, in conjunction with the sixth – 'love and understanding'– preambular paragraph, contains the duty of parents:
– 5. to provide affection-based direction and guidance, consistent with the child's evolving capacities.
This duty implies the duty:
– 6. to acquire knowledge on child rearing and child development in general, and
– 7. to seek specific information, advice, feedback and counselling on the rearing and development of their child.
It may even imply the duty:
– 8. to seek psychotherapy in case of relational or psychological problems, or unresolved childhood trauma of parents themselves.
Article 27(2) (in conjunction with (1)) contains the duty of parents:
– 9. to provide a standard of living adequate for the holistic development of their child.
If this is not 'within their abilities and financial capacities' (Article 27(2)), another duty is implied, namely:
– 10. to actively seek family, community and state assistance.
It may also imply the (civic) duty:
– 11. to mobilize parents' organizations, trade unions, child rights NGOs, political parties and the media with a view to improving parenting allowances, benefits and credits.
Taken together, Articles 18(1) (*both* parents; best interests *basic concern*) and 27(2) contain the duty of parents:
– 12. to prudently combine work and care, and seek high-quality child-care services.
This duty implies the (civic) duty:
– 13. to mobilize parents' organizations, trade unions, child rights NGOs, political parties and the media if national policies are lacking or inadequate in this regard.
Article 19(1) in conjunction with General Comment 8, contains the duty of parents:
– 14. not to use any form of violence, including humiliation, in child rearing.
This duty implies the duty:
– 15. to acquire knowledge on positive parenting and non-violent child rearing (positive discipline), and
– 16. to seek advice, feedback and counselling if this causes any problems or difficulties.
Article 24(1) in conjunction with Article 39, contains the duty of parents:
– 17. to seek the best available physical and mental health care for their child.
This duty implies the (civic) duty:
– 18. to mobilize parents' organizations, trade unions, child rights NGOs, political parties and the media, or go to court, if health care is lacking or inadequate.

Article 24(3) contains the duty of parents:
– 19. not to resort to and to abandon any harmful child-rearing practices and traditions.
This duty implies the (civic) duty:
– 20. to mobilize parents' organizations, trade unions, child rights NGOs, political parties and the media if the state is not doing enough to ban such practices and to support parents in child rights based parenting and positive discipline.
Article 28(1) contains the duty of parents:
– 21. to send their child to school and see to their child's education and vocational training.
This duty implies the (civic) duty:
– 22. to mobilize parents' organizations, trade unions, child rights NGOs, political parties and the media, or go to court, if schools are lacking or school education is inadequate.
Article 29(1) in conjunction with the seventh – 'fully prepared and brought up' – preambular paragraph, as well as in conjunction with Articles 18(1) (best interests *basic concern)*, and 19(1) (no mental violence), contains the duty of parents:
– 23. not to harm and confuse their child, and compromise his or her loyalty, by raising him or her contrary to the CRC's holistic development and democratic and global citizenship aims of education.
Article 17 contains the two-sided duty of parents:
– 24. to stimulate the child's use of media that contribute to his or her holistic development and physical and mental health, including his or her democratic and global citizenship education; and
– 25. to protect the child from harmful material.
These duties imply the (civic) duty:
– 26. to mobilize parents' organizations, trade unions, child rights NGOs, political parties and the media themselves if the state and/or the media are not meeting the standards of Article 17.
Article 30 in conjunction with Article 29 contains the duty of parents who belong to an ethnic, religious or linguistic minority:
– 27. to promote their child's and their family's integration in society on the basis of their own cultural identity.
Article 31(1) in conjunction with Articles 18(1) (best interests *basic concern*), and 24, contains the duty of parents:
– 28. to provide age-appropriate play and recreational and cultural activities for their child.
This duty implies the (civic) duty:
– 29. to mobilize parents' organizations, trade unions, child rights NGOs, political parties and the media if national policies or community facilities in this respect are lacking or inadequate.
Article 7(1) contains two duties of parents:
– 30. to register their child at birth, and

– 31. to inform the child about his or her biological origins.
Article 8(1) contains the duty of parents:
– 32. not to deprive their child of his or her personal identity (the knowledge of his or her origins).
Article 9(3) contains the two-sided duty of divorced or separated parents:
– 33. to enable their child to maintain personal relations and direct contact with both parents on a regular basis, and
– 34. to prevent contact if it is contrary to the child's best interests.
Article 2 in conjunction with Article 18(1) (best interests *basic concern*) contains the duty of parents:
– 35. not to discriminate between boy and girl children, and
– 36. not to favour one child above the other.
Article 12, in conjunction with Articles 18(1) (best interests *basic concern*) and Articles 5 and 29, contains the duty of parents:
– 37. to stimulate their child to form his or her own views and to freely express him- or herself, and
– 38. to stimulate their child, and to provide direction and guidance in this respect, to bear his or her own responsibilities in family, school, community and country.
Article 13, in conjunction with Article 18(1) (best interests *basic concern*) and Articles 5, 17 and 36, contains the duty of parents:
– 39. to respect and promote their child's freedom of expression and freedom to seek, receive and impart information and ideas, and to provide direction, guidance and protection in this respect.
Article 14(1) in conjunction with Article 18(1) (best interests *basic concern*) and Articles 5, 14(2) 17 and 36, contains the duty of parents:
– 40. to respect and promote their child's freedom of thought, conscience and religion, and to provide direction, guidance and protection in this respect.
Article 15, in conjunction with Article 18(1) (best interests *basic concern*) and Articles 5, 17 and 36, contains the duty of parents:
– 41. to respect and promote their child's freedom of association and peaceful assembly, and to provide direction, guidance and protection in this respect.
Article 16 in conjunction with Article 18(1) (best interests *basic concern*) contains the duty of parents:
– 42. to respect their child's privacy and personal integrity.
Article 20(3) in conjunction with the ninth – 'before as well as after birth'– preambular paragraph, Article 18(1) (best interests *basic concern*) and Article 24 contains the duty of parents:
– 43. to (prenatally) seek foster care or adoption if they are unable to raise the child themselves.
Article 23, in conjunction with Article 18(1) (best interests *basic concern*) and Article 24, contains the duty of parents:

– 44. to seek special care and opportunities for their physically, mentally and/or emotionally disabled child.
This duty implies the (civic) duty:
– 45. to mobilize parents' organizations, trade unions, child rights NGOs, political parties and the media if national policies or community facilities in this respect are lacking or inadequate.
Article 32, in conjunction with Article 18(1) (best interests *basic concern*) and Article 24, contains the duty of parents:
– 46. to stimulate their child to work for as many hours as – and to prevent their child from working for more hours than – are beneficial for his or her holistic development.
Article 33, in conjunction with Article 18(1) (best interests *basic concern*) and Article 24 contains the duty of parents:
– 47. to prevent their child (in cooperation and coordination with other parents and social partners) from smoking, using illegal drugs and abusing alcohol.
Article 34, in conjunction with Articles 17, 18(1) (best interests *basic concern*), 24 and 29, contains the duty of parents:
– 48. to see to their child's sexual education and to prevent their child (in cooperation and coordination with other parents and social partners) from falling victim to sexual exploitation and sexual abuse by peers, predators and paedophiles.
Article 36, in conjunction with Articles 17, 18(1) (best interests *basic concern*), 24 and 29, contains the duty of parents:
– 49. to see to their child's financial, consumer and 'screen' or 'electronic' (TV, PC, MSN, video games, internet, mobiles, etcetera) education and to prevent their child from falling victim to commercial, 'electronic' and any other exploitation.
This duty implies the (civic) duty:
– 50. to mobilize parents' organizations, trade unions, child rights NGOs, political parties and the media if national policies are lacking or inadequate in this regard.
Article 42 in conjunction with Article 18(1) (best interests *basic concern*) and Article 29 contains the duty of parents:
– 51. to educate their child on his or her rights and to see to their child's child rights education in school (and community).

3.3.2. Empowerment Obligations

The following empowerment articles, divided into two sections (*A* and *B*, relating to parents and to children as parents-to-be, respectively), may be discerned in the CRC. This list should not be seen as exhaustive either. Also, it should be kept in mind that the state has several obligations which indirectly empower parents, for instance in relation to health care (Article 24), education (Articles 28 and 29), quality of institutions and supervision of professionals (Article 3(3)), the mass media (Article 17), children's play, sport and cultural activities (Article 31), disabled children (Article 23), foster care (Article 20), and so forth and so on.

Empowerment Articles (A)

The CRC may be said to contain the following positive obligations for states to facilitate, educate, assist and support parents:

- Article 18(2) contains the obligation of the state to provide parenting assistance (assistance in the performance of child-rearing responsibilities) and support (institutions, facilities and services for the care of children).
- Article 18(3) in conjunction with Article 3(3) contains the obligation of the state to provide sufficient and high-quality child-care services and facilities.
- Article 24(2)(d), (e) and (f) contains the obligation of the state to provide pre- and postnatal care; to provide information, education and support for parents, children and all others on child health and nutrition, breastfeeding, hygiene etcetera; and to develop preventive health care, guidance for parents and family planning education and services.
- Article 27(3) (in conjunction with (1)) contains the obligation of the state to provide material (financial, fiscal and other) assistance and support for parents so that families may have a standard of living adequate for the child's holistic development.
- Article 27(3) in conjunction with Article 18(1) (*both* parents) and (2) (parenting assistance), imply a state obligation to (at least) facilitate paid parental leave.

Empowerment Articles (B)

The CRC may be said to contain the following positive obligations for states to empower children as citizens and parents-to-be:

- Article 29(1) contains the obligation of the state to see to it that school education be directed to the holistic development of the child and his or her preparation for democratic and global citizenship (including responsible parenthood).
- Article 31(2) contains the obligation of the state to promote child participation in cultural, recreational and leisure activities.
- Article 39 contains the obligation of the state to promote child trauma reparation (and thus prevent transgenerational transmission of trauma and end cycles of violence, insecure attachment, poor mental health, child abuse and neglect, delinquency, etcetera).

In relation to the empowerment list (*A* and *B*) above, it is important to highlight three CRC Articles, namely Article 3(3) containing the obligation of the state to empower, that is, to ensure the quantity and quality of, and to supervise institutions and professionals working with parents and/or children; and

Articles 4 and 6(2) containing the obligation of the state to invest in children's rights and child development to the maximum extent of its resources. On the basis of these three Articles, and the various Articles in the lists above – of parental duties and responsibilities and of states' empowerment obligations – we may safely conclude that responsible parenthood, whatever its precise meaning as a dignitarian human rights concept, at any rate refers to responsibilised-and-empowered parenthood as required and indicated by the CRC.

4. CONCLUSION

Even in the wealthiest of states we see large-scale violations of basic needs and rights of children to emotional security, secure attachment and healthy development of personality and identity, caused by a lack of parental awareness in their families. In these families, children are born in conditions of serious emotional, mental or material poverty. Material poverty refers to a lack of adequate income or (income related) time to raise a child. Mental poverty refers to a lack of knowledge of child rearing, or of capacity to acquire such knowledge. Emotional poverty refers to poor mental health, caused by or related to addictions, psychiatric conditions, unresolved adverse childhood experiences or other unresolved trauma, severe stress and so on. These forms of poverty illustrate that extreme inequalities still exist, even in wealthy democracies. Especially in relation to adults with child-rearing responsibilities, these inequalities are unacceptable – and no longer excusable. Addressing these forms of poverty and inequality, well before children are born, should be on the top of the agenda of governments and children's rights NGOs in wealthy states. Libertarian concepts of reproductive and parental rights, and related state non-intervention in the family, rather than dignitarian concepts of children's rights, parental responsibilities, and related positive obligations of states to responsibilisation and empowerment of (future) caregivers still prevail, however, in most if not all states of the world. Traditional systems of child protection and foster (and adoptive) care are by definition not equipped to prevent violations of children's rights: they are – often seriously flawed – instruments of intervention after grave violations have occurred. In spite of many dignitarian calls for action by the Committee on the Rights of the Child and the Council of Europe, these traditional systems seem to stand in the way of, rather than to contribute to responsible parenthood. For dignitarian reform, we will have to look elsewhere. But even children's rights researchers and activists appear to be largely absent in this debate. Nonetheless, references to responsibilities in international instruments, whether binding as strict or soft law, are not just moral appeals to people of good will, easy to put aside for libertarians and legal positivists alike. They imply obligations of states to empower people, first of all those with child-rearing responsibilities. Legal specifications and clarifications both of parental responsibilities and of the best interests of the child are urgent dignitarian steps for governments to take. But they are certainly not the only ones. Responsibilisation will only open the road to empowerment if it is part and parcel of policies of provision, prevention and participation. Children's rights, and women's rights for that matter, will not mean very much until responsibilisation-and-empowerment are put at the heart of reproductive rights and their corollary: parental responsibility. As we proceed on the road to empowerment, a dignitarian horizon of responsible parenthood will come into sight. The question is: when will we truly embark on this road?

INDIVIDUALS' DUTIES IN THE AFRICAN HUMAN RIGHTS PROTECTION SYSTEM

Challenges and Prospects

Mumba Malila

The African human rights protection system is the youngest of the three established regional human rights systems, the other two being the European and the Inter-American systems. The defining differences between the African human rights framework and the other two regional human rights systems stem from the desire on the part of the African people to preserve traditional African values. This desire is evidenced by the special importance attached to the protection of the family, the preservation of moral values and the definition of both rights and duties of individuals. The purpose of this article is to provide an insight into the actual and potential role of the concept of individual duties in the African Charter on Human and Peoples' Rights (the African Charter or the Banjul Charter).[1]

This contribution attempts to pigeonhole and analyse the duties under the African Charter to show that not all duties have the same efficacy and should be treated in the same way. While some individual duties have legally binding value, others are merely supererogatory moral obligations, devoid of legal effect; while some are quite clear in their import, others are plainly vague; and while some have a content which can be ascertained, others do not.

The chapter is divided into three main parts. The first part examines the historical background to the establishment of the African Charter. This historical overview is necessary to set the discussion into context. After all, as Sloth-Nielsen and Mezmur advise, '[i]n order to understand the 'language of duties' in the African human rights system, one needs to have an informed view of the general conception of human rights in Africa.'[2] The second part focuses on the distinguishing attributes of the African Charter and, in particular, those aspects

[1] Organization of African Unity, *African Charter on Human and Peoples' Rights* (Banjul Charter), adopted on 27 June 1981, OAU Doc. CAB/LEG/67/3 rev. 5; 1520 *UNTS* 217.

[2] J. Sloth-Nielsen and B.D Mezmur, 'A Dutiful Child: The Implication of Article 31 of the African Children's Charter' (2008) 52(2) *Journal of African Law* 159–189, 164.

which are generally perceived as its main weaknesses. This section essentially highlights the main differences between the African human rights system and the other major human rights systems. The third and final part considers the duties pertaining to individuals listed in the African Charter. An analysis will be made as to why the inclusion of duties in the Charter in the manner it was is generally considered at least somewhat problematic, but also why this can be regarded as an opportunity for the African continent and, by extension, for the global human rights framework to redefine itself.

1. THE HISTORICAL BACKGROUND TO THE ESTABLISHMENT OF THE AFRICAN HUMAN RIGHTS SYSTEM

In an effort to promote political, social and economic change as well as to foster unity and a sense of belonging, African countries established the Organization of African Unity (OAU) in 1963. The principal aims were to promote solidarity, peace and international cooperation and to eradicate colonialism throughout the continent.[3] In 1981, the eighteenth Assembly of Heads of State and Government of the OAU[4] adopted the African Charter. It entered into force on 21 October 1986 upon ratification by a simple majority of Member States of the OAU.[5]

The African human rights protection system became the latest of the three established regional human rights systems; the other two being the European and the Inter- American systems. The defining differences between the African human rights protection system and the other two regional human rights systems emanate from the desire on the part of the African people to preserve traditional African values, as is evidenced by the special importance attached to the protection of the family, preservation of moral values and the definition of rights and duties of the individual. These considerations are set out in a legal context in the African Charter.

It is probably fair to state that what contributed to the urgency for the need for an African human rights instrument was the heightened sensitisation of the international public opinion to the severe human rights abuses committed in Africa in the mid-1970s by dictatorial governments, and which created a huge outrage in the international fraternity. The leadership of Africa was naturally

3 Article 2 of the OAU Charter sets out the objectives of the OAU as being the promotion of unity and solidarity of African states, the coordination and intensification of cooperation and efforts to achieve a better life for the people of Africa, defending the sovereignty, territorial integrity and independence, eradication of colonialism and the promotion of international cooperation.

4 The meeting was held in the Kenyan capital, Nairobi, in June 1981.

5 Article 63 provides that the Charter was to enter into force three months after the reception by the Secretary General of the instrument of ratification or adherence of a simple majority of the Member States of the OAU.

concerned about this perception and had to do something about it. Mutua points out that the atrocities committed by these dictators and others and the resulting international outcry forced the leadership of Africa to:

> 'reclaim international legitimacy and salvage its image. In 1979, shaken by these perceptions, the OAU Summit in Monrovia, Liberia, appointed a committee of experts to prepare a draft of an African human rights charter. It was ironic that virtually none of the men, the Heads of State and Government, were freely and fairly elected. Without exception, they presided over highly repressive states. It was virtually the same club of dictators who adopted the African Charter in Nairobi, Kenya in 1981. Thus was born the African human rights system.'[6]

Fombad equally observed that:

> '[a]s democratization swept through the continent, it generated expectations of a new dawn and the end of an era of corrupt, authoritarian and incompetent dictatorships that had earned the continent notoriety for political instability, civil wars, famine, disease and similar ills.'[7]

Human rights had, furthermore, around the same period become a legitimate and important subject of international discourse, as exemplified by the adoption of the Final Act of Helsinki and the entry into force of the two United Nations Covenants.[8] Above all, a new trend in the foreign policy of some Western states was to link economic aid to the human rights record of the recipient country. The United States under the Jimmy Carter administration is a case in point.

The following twenty years after the Lagos Law, in the 1960s and 1970s, saw the organisation of several conferences in Africa, either by the United Nations or by non-governmental organisations, to discuss the need for an African regional system to promote and protect human rights.[9] The combination of all these developments acted as a catalyst which induced the post-colonial African States to demonstrate to the international community that they were concerned not only with the situation of human rights in the restrictive context of anti-colonial

6 M. Mutua, 'The African human rights system in a comparative perspective: the need for urgent reformulation', paper presented at the Third Afro-America-the Americas and Europe held in Strasbourg, France, 15–19 June 1992.

7 C.M. Fombad, 'Challenges to constitutionalism and constitutional rights in Africa and the enabling role of political parties: lessons and perspectives from Southern Africa' (2007) 55(1) *American Journal of Comparative Law* 2.

8 These are the International Covenant on Civil and Political Rights and the International Covenant on Economic Social and Cultural Rights, both of 1966.

9 For a brief drafting history of the African Commission on Human Rights see B.G. Ramcharan, 'The *Travaux Préparatoires* of the African Commission on Human Rights' (1992) 13 *Human Rights Law Journal*.

human rights struggle and apartheid in South Africa, but also by the violations occurring in their own countries.

The International Commission of Jurists concentrated its efforts in Francophone Africa. It organised two meetings in Dakar in 1967 and 1978 respectively. On each of these occasions, the participants reiterated their idea of a regional human rights instrument, and this became an urgent request addressed to the OAU. In 1978, the United Nations, through its Commission on Human Rights, renewed its concern and called upon pan-African organisations to establish a regional Commission for Human and Peoples Rights.

Noting that the symposiums and conferences convened earlier had not ended in strict commitments, the participants of the 1978 symposium set up a 'follow-up' Committee composed of four African personalities for the follow-up of the implementation of the conclusion and recommendations that they adopted. This Committee was to make many trips to African countries and was to explain to the Heads of State and other political authorities of such countries, that it was necessary and urgent for Africa to have a Human Rights Commission. After the visit to Dakar by the Committee, the then President of the Republic of Senegal, President L.S. Senghor, accepted to present at the next meeting of the Heads of State and Government of the OAU, a resolution for the creation of an African Commission on Human and Peoples' Rights. This resolution was established on the basis of the decision of the Conference of Heads of State and Government of the OAU in its 16th Ordinary Session.[10] At the invitation of Senegal, the Secretary General of the OAU organised a conference in Dakar from 28 November to 8 December 1979, re-grouping under the Chairmanship of Judge Keba Mbaye. Twenty African experts coming from sixteen countries attended the meeting.

The Committee did a remarkable job and, in a short time, succeeded in writing up a text, taking into account the political diversity of the Member States of the OAU, and focusing on the principles on which rest the African traditions. The document that was written was to be submitted at the Conference of Ministers.[11] Unfortunately, the meeting did not take place due to lack of a quorum. This lack of quorum, far from being accidental, was a manifestation of the hostility of some governments who were not able to express their position openly about their disfavour of the adoption of a human rights charter by the OAU, fearing that this might be the beginning of liberalism which they did not want to be introduced in Africa. The first attempt of the Secretary-General of the OAU to call for the adoption of the text on human rights ended up in failure. Following this first failure, the Secretary-General of the OAU then decided to ask one of the countries in Africa perceived then to be very democratic and where human rights were

10 AHG/115 (XVI). The conference was held in Monrovia (Liberia) on 17–20 July 1979. That decision called upon the Secretary General of the OAU to: 'Set up a Committee of top level African experts, who will be responsible to prepare a draft for the African Charter on Human and Peoples' Rights, designed mainly as a mouthpiece for the promotion and protection of human and peoples' rights'.

11 This meeting was held in Addis Ababa on 24 March 1980.

most respected, The Gambia, to invite the OAU to hold its Ministerial Meeting in Banjul, with a view to adopting the draft Charter drawn up in Dakar by the Committee of Experts. The President of the Republic of the Gambia welcomed the idea with enthusiasm, and invitations were extended instead to the Council of Ministers of Justice of the OAU to meet in Banjul. The meeting was convened in Banjul on 9 June 1980. From the beginning of the deliberations of the Council of Ministers, it appeared that the representatives of certain countries suspected that the Committee of Experts chosen in Dakar had adopted an unbalanced (one sided) draft project, since the Committee had not taken into account certain concerns and had also opted for capitalist ideas. The deliberations went on in an extremely tense atmosphere with the discussions suffering several setbacks. At the end of the meeting, the experts had only discussed the preamble and eleven articles. A second meeting was to be held to continue the discussions. This far the Charter future was uncertain.

It was on the occasion of the ordinary session held in Freetown in June 1980 that the OAU, through its resolution,[12] requested that the second session of the Ministerial Conference of Banjul do its best to complete the discussion of the draft Charter in order to submit it to the 18th Ordinary Session of the Conference of Heads of State and Government of the OAU, which was to be convened in Nairobi in June the following year. In order to implement the aforementioned resolution, the Secretary-General of the OAU convened a meeting in Banjul from 7 to 19 January 1981. The text was submitted to the Conference of Heads of State and Government of the OAU. The text was adopted during the meeting held in Nairobi, Kenya in June, 1981. A deserved homage was rendered to The Gambia for the role it played in the formative process of the African human rights charter. At the end of the last session, the meeting unanimously voted for a resolution which requested that the Charter be entitled the 'Banjul Charter'. Later, Banjul was designated to seat the headquarters of the African Commission on Human and People's Rights.

2. THE BANJUL CHARTER

2.1. AN INNOVATIVE LEGAL INSTRUMENT

The question one may legitimately ask is whether it was indeed useful, from a legal point of view, to create a new legal instrument in the field of human rights. After all, there were already human rights legal standards applicable to the African continent, i.e. those contained in the International Bill of Human Rights, that is, the Universal Declaration of Human Rights[13] and the two 1966 United

[12] CM/Res.792 (XXXV) of 23/61980.

[13] UN General Assembly, Universal Declaration of Human Rights, adopted on 10 December 1948 by GA Res. 217A (III), UN Doc A/810 at 71 (1948).

Nations Covenants.[14] This question, in the author's view, should be answered in the affirmative. This is notwithstanding the fact that the creation of regional mechanism for the protection of human rights raised questions, particularly to the United Nations, on the understanding by these regional bodies of the issue of universality of human rights. Some scholars[15] have asserted, quite fittingly, that norms developed within a regional system may, to some extent, go against the principle of universality.

The reasons that favoured the creation of a regional human rights protection system for the African region were not different from those that justified the creation of other regional human rights systems, which are considered as more effective than the universal or global system. Among these are, first, that the universal human rights promotion and protection system, spearheaded by the United Nations, provides the lowest denominator which could be improved upon in a regional arrangement. For example, the universal system does not have a court for the enforcement of these human rights norms. Shelton argues that:

> 'Regional systems are indispensable to achieving effective compliance with international human rights; performing as they do the necessary intermediary function between state domestic institutions that violate or fail to enforce human rights and the global system which is incapable of providing redress to individual victims of human rights violations. They have the necessary ability and flexibility to change as conditions around them change, yet are applied in response to regionally-specific problems; they achieve equilibrium between enforcement of global norms and regional diversity.'[16]

Second, countries are likely to respond more positively to the homogeneity of a region. Governments are more likely to agree to implementation of human rights treaties if they are adopted in a regional setting, where cultural, legal and intellectual traditions are similar and where some form of peer pressure or persuasion will matter. People in countries from the same or similar regions tend to have 'shared interest in the protection of human interests and influence each other in a manner the international community may not be able to do.'[17] Heyns and Viljoen explain that:

> '[w]hile international systems for the protection of human rights lack the benefit of enforcement which domestic systems have, regional systems for the protection of

[14] The Covenant on Economic Social and Cultural Rights and the Covenant on Civil and Political Rights.

[15] C. Heyns, D. Padilla and L. Zwaak, 'A schematic comparison of regional human rights systems: an update' (2006) 4 *International Journal on Human Rights* 163–171, 163.

[16] D. Shelton, 'The Promise of Regional Human Rights Systems', in B. Weston and S. Marks (eds.), *The Future of International Human Rights,* 1999, pp. 351, 353–398.

[17] C. Heyns, D. Padilla and L. Zwaak, 'A schematic comparison of regional human rights systems: an update' (2006) 4 *International Journal on Human Rights* 163–171, 163.

> human rights arguably have some advantage over the global or UN system. They can give more authentic expression to the values and historical peculiarities of the people of a particular region, resulting in more spontaneous compliance, and due to the geographical proximity of the states involved, regional systems under the right conditions, have the potential of stronger pressure being exerted against neighbours in case of violations. Peer pressure is easier to exert in a smaller circle of friends. An effective regional system can consequently supplement the global system in important ways.'[18]

Heyns *et al* make an important point when they observe that regional bodies are more flexible and adaptive. Some ways of enforcement may find wide and easy acceptance in some regions while that might not be the case in the international system where the same mechanism and standard is applicable irrespective of the region.[19] Hansungule makes the same point when he says that:

> '[r]egional systems are particularly important for the opportunity to reflect local values that cannot be reflected under the international law system in being preoccupied with values of the universe as such. The preoccupation of universal values, though important, can lead to a de-emphasis of certain peculiarities that are nonetheless basic to some societies. In a regional system states have the opportunity of recalling their values for inclusion in the system. In addition to what may be borrowed from other systems. This is why regional systems have been found necessary in Africa, Americas and Europe.'[20]

The approach adopted by the African Commission on Human and Peoples' Rights bears eloquent testimony to this. In *Social and Economic Rights Action Centre and the Centre for Social and Economic Rights v. Nigeria*,[21] the African Commission brought forth into notice the singularity or 'uniqueness' of the African situation and the 'special qualities' of the African Charter that make it necessary for the international human rights bodies to be specially perceptive to the unique needs of the African people. Thus, as the Commission noted, 'collective rights, environmental rights, economic and social rights are essential elements of human rights in Africa' and the various African states that are a member to the African Charter have a 'duty to respect, protect, promote, and fulfil' as well as

18 C. Heyns and F. Viljoen, 'Regional Protection of Human Rights in Africa: An Overview and Evaluation', in P.T. Zelaza and P.J. McConnaughay, *Human Rights, The Rule of Law and Development in Africa,* Philadelphia: University of Pennsylvania Press, 2004, pp. 129, 131.

19 C. Heyns, D. Padilla and L. Zwaak, 'A schematic comparison of regional human rights systems: an update' (2006) 4 *International Journal on Human Rights* 163–171, 164.

20 M. Hansungule, 'Protection of Human Rights under the Inter-American System: An Outsider's Reflection', in A. Gudmundur *et al.* (eds.), *International Human Rights Monitoring Mechanisms: Essays in Honour of Jacob Th. Moller,* The Hague: Martinus Nijhoff Publishers, 2001, pp. 679, 684.

21 Communication No. 155/1996, para. 68.

make effective by different measures all the obligations as outlined by the African Charter.

Third, there are also practical considerations. It is more convenient and cost effective to have to attend to regional human rights implementation machinery than to a centrally positioned global system. This view, however, is self-defeating when one considers that belonging to a regional human rights protection system does not exempt Member States from their global obligation assumed by their membership to the United Nations.

Fourth, there is also the view founded on conventional wisdom that two heads are better than one, so that, in addition to the universal system of human rights protection, it is better to have an additional international system, preferably at the regional level. There is no harm in duplicating the international effort at protecting human rights at the regional level. If anything, duplicity would only work to render protection more thorough. Mugwanya, like Shelton, thus observes that:

> '[r]egional systems have served to fill the gaps in the global system's mechanism. They have successfully complemented the global system by impacting on and influencing domestic human rights practice in member states. Regional systems are flexible and have the ability to change, as conditions change, and sometimes quickly.'[22]

The foregoing partly explains why regionalism in human rights protection has become an important – if not indispensable – phenomenon in the whole human rights movement. Take the European region in the 1950s, for example. The European Convention on Human Rights established a court and launched a resounding regional human rights movement. In the American region, in 1978, the American Convention on Human Rights set up a court and incorporated into the convention system the previously created Inter-American Commission on Human Rights. Not perhaps surprisingly therefore, in the African region, the African Charter on Human and Peoples' Rights set up the African Commission on Human and Peoples' Rights,[23] and more recently an African Court of Human and Peoples' Rights. There have been significant movements towards the establishment of regional human rights bodies in the Middle East and North Africa[24] and for the Asia-Pacific region too.[25]

---

22 G.W. Mugwanya, 'Realising Universal Human Rights Norms through Regional Human Rights Mechanism: Reinvigorating the African System' (1999) 10(1) *Indiana International and Comparative Law Review* 40–41.

23 The Commission became operational in 1986, the Charter itself having been adopted in 1981.

24 For example, the Arab Charter on Human Rights was adopted by the League of Arab States in 1994. An amended version of it entered into force on 16 March, 2004. It establishes the Arab Human Rights Committee.

25 A. Durbach, C. Renshaw and A. Byrnes, '"A tongue but no teeth?"': The emergence of a regional human rights mechanism in the Asia Pacific region' (2009) 31 *Sydney Law Review* 211.

2.2. AFRICAN VALUES

Human rights norms, as universal as they are, naturally tend to be viewed in a slightly different light from one region to another. There is no doubt that the whole concept of human rights has taken on a different 'flavour' when adopted or incorporated into the vocabulary of traditions other than the Western liberal one, in which the modern notion of human rights originated. The African Charter was conceived as an instrument aimed at complementing the International Bill of Human Rights, tailored to the specific needs of African societies. The idea was to create a regional legal instrument which would take into account the peculiar history and the specificities of Africa.

It is interesting to note in this respect that the group of African experts drafting the African Charter rejected the initially proposed convention adopted at the Monrovia Seminar on the establishment of an African regional human rights commission.[26] The reason advanced for the rejection was that the Convention simply proposed standards embodied in other international conventions and declarations and showed no influence of African cultural traditions and values or of the African reality at that time. First of all, it was felt, there was the perceived existence in the whole continent of a very strong feeling of community, with the social African structures giving more importance to the group than to the individual. Second, there was the economic underdevelopment of the African countries, which brought with it its own set of human rights needs and questions.

When finally the Banjul Charter was drafted, the drafters not only drew heavily on universal human rights instruments but they also emphasised that it was important to incorporate an African conception of human rights into the Charter. The final document thus paid special attention to such concepts as 'peoples' rights' and 'duties' and the importance of the role of the individuals in the community and the family. This special 'African focus' is clearly reflected in the preamble of the Banjul Charter, which explicitly refers to

> 'the virtue of [the Member States'] historical tradition and the values of African civilization which should inspire and characterize [the] reflection [of the African States] on the concept of human and peoples' rights'.[27]

It was believed that the concept of human rights, viewed through an African prism, would take on African emphases and, with this missing piece of the puzzle added to the global human rights framework, would become truly universal.

---

26 See R. Gittleman 'The Banjul Charter on Human and Peoples, Rights: A Legal Analysis', in C. Welch and R. Meltzr (eds.), *Human Rights and Development in Africa*, Albany: State University of New York Press, 1984.

27 Banjul Charter, preambular paragraph 4.

Writing on what he thought the establishment of the African Charter meant for Africa, Kunig opined that:

> 'The African Charter on Human Peoples Rights is a significant piece of law by young states. It represents the heritage of the Universal Declaration of Human Declaration of Human Rights and also follows the United Nations Conventions on Human Rights, but does not assert rights which are either not yet realizable or have few roots in African traditions ... All in all the Charter thus demonstrates an independent approach by comparison with other regional conventions on human rights, which also reflect its provisions on the sources of law; customary law practiced by states and general principles of law contained in their nations' legal systems are emphasized without rejecting universal international law in principle.'[28]

The Banjul Charter presented at the time the most promising regional human rights implementation system. Chris Maina Peter made the following comment which typifies the optimism that greeted the establishment of the African Charter.

> 'The adoption of the African Charter on Human and Peoples' Rights was an epoch-making event, not only to the over millions Africans but to peace loving and democratic minded people the world over. It was the crescendo of sporadic and sometimes uncoordinated attempts by different interest groups in Africa to create a legal mechanism that would guarantee fundamental rights and freedoms to the common people. For many Africans the Charter had created high expectations especially regarding the restoration of human dignity, which had been totally violated by some African leaders.'[29]

While drawing heavily on the existing universal human rights instruments, the Banjul Charter thus also emphasised its uniqueness. The importance of individual duties is stressed from the outset. Preambular paragraph 6 states that:

> 'Considering that the enjoyment of rights and freedoms also implies the performance of duties on the part of everyone ...'[30]

The African Charter sought to create a regional human rights system, which was intended to run on similar lines as that of the American and European human rights systems. Its uniqueness derives mainly from its cultural component and

---

28 P. Kunig, 'The Protection of Human Rights by International Law in Africa' (1982) 25 *German Yearbook of International Law* 138, 167.

29 C.M. Peter, *Human Rights in Africa: A Comparative Study of the African Charter on Human and Peoples' Rights and the New Tanzanian Bill of Rights,* New York: Greenwood, 1990, p. 7.

30 The Banjul Charter was adopted on 27 June 1981, OAU Doc. CAB/LEG/67/3 rev. 5; 1520 *UNTS* 217, preambular paragraph 6.

the question of African development, as embodied in the guidelines submitted to the Committee of Experts that drafted the Charter, namely that the Charter 'should reflect the African conception of human rights, [and] should take as a pattern the African philosophy of law and meet the needs of Africa.'[31]

Normatively speaking, the African Charter is, therefore, an original and innovative legal instrument in comparison to other 'traditional' instruments aimed at the international protection of human rights.[32] With its focus on the preservation of African traditions and its emphasis on individual duties, the Charter 'substantially departs from the narrow formulations of other regional and universal human rights instruments'.[33]

2.3. THREE GENERATIONS OF RIGHTS IN ONE CHARTER

The Banjul Charter consists of 68 articles. In as far as its substantive content is concerned, perhaps one of the first and most striking features of the African Charter is that it includes three 'generations' of human rights in a single instrument, i.e. civil and political rights (the so-called first generation human rights); economic, social and cultural rights (the so-called 'second generation' human rights); and group and peoples' rights (the so-called third generation human rights). The African Charter is the only international human rights instrument to do so.[34] Murray states that the inclusion in one document of all rights treating them as indivisible and the drafting of provisions relating to duties of the individual in considerable detail defines the uniqueness of the Charter and led some to claim that it is the most interesting of the regional instruments.[35]

The generations of rights under the Charter are treated on an equal footing. The preamble of the African Charter stresses the importance of the right to development – a third-generation right – and expressly states that civil and political rights shall not take precedence over the guarantee of economic, social and cultural rights:

> 'it is henceforth essential to pay a particular attention to the right to development and that civil and political rights cannot be dissociated from economic, social and cultural rights in their conception as well as universality and that the satisfaction

31 See Amnesty International, *The Organisation of African Unity and Human Rights,* AI Index IOR 03/04/87 at 8.

32 See M. Mutua 'The African human rights system: A critical evaluation', http://hdr.undp.org/sites/default/files/mutua.pdf, p. 5.

33 Ibid.

34 The classification of human rights into categories is no longer fashionable since all human rights are universal, interrelated, indivisible and interdependent. Indeed, the Vienna Declaration and Programme of Action 1993 affirmed this position.

35 R. Murray, *Human Rights in Africa: From the OAU to the African Union,* Cambridge: Cambridge University Press, 2004.

> of economic, social and cultural rights is a guarantee for the enjoyment of civil and political rights.'[36]

As far as the second-generation rights are concerned, the African Commission has indeed confirmed that civil and political rights should be treated on the same level as social, economic and cultural rights. It held that:

> 'Internationally accepted ideas of the various obligations engendered by human rights indicate that all rights-both civil and political rights and social and economic-generate at least four levels of duties for a State that undertakes to adhere to a rights regime, namely the duty to respect, protect, promote, and fulfil these rights. These obligations universally apply to all rights and entail a combination of negative and positive duties.'[37]

It then continued by stating that the order in which the Commission would deal with these rights 'in no way should it imply the priority accorded to them'.[38] Furthermore, the so-called 'third generation rights' also take in an important place in the Banjul Charter. This category of rights includes, for instance, the rights of peoples to political self-determination and the right of peoples to freely dispose of their wealth and natural resources.

It should be noted that the African Charter tries to promote what could be labelled a 'global approach' to the question of human rights. The 'right of people to development' is of particular importance in this context. This right should be understood mainly as a claim regarding the long-awaited new international economic order. This 'global' or all-embracing approach to the problem of human rights advocated in the African Charter is not new. As a matter of fact, by providing for the right to development, the African Charter was in a way reflecting one of the concerns of the Universal Declaration of Human Rights, whose Article 28 states that '[e]veryone is entitled to a social and international order in which the rights and freedoms set forth in this declaration can be fully realized'.[39] In the African context, however, the right to development takes on the specific meaning of a claim for more economic justice from the developed countries. From a strictly legal point of view, providing for such a right in the African Charter is, however, largely meaningless. The right of the African peoples to development nevertheless can be said to give a strong political dimension to the African Charter. How this right can be realised and against whom it can be claimed remains, nevertheless, rather unclear.

---

36 Banjul Charter, preambular paragraph. 7.

37 African Commission on Human and Peoples' Rights, *The Social and Economic Rights Action Center and the Center for Economic and Social Rights v. Nigeria*, Comm. No. 155/96 (2001), 30th Ordinary Session, held in Banjul, The Gambia, 13–27 October 2001, paragraph 44.

38 Ibid.

39 Universal Declaration of Human Rights, Art. 28.

2.4. WEAKNESSES

A number of important weaknesses, however, can be identified in the Charter. I will discuss four of them, before continuing with a discussion of the inclusion of individual duties in the Charter, a fact which, as we shall see, is a weakness as much as it is an opportunity.

2.4.1. Unmentioned Rights

A first problem pertains to the omission of certain important first-generation rights. The Banjul Charter mentions a number of civil and political rights, i.e. the right to equality (Article 3), the right to life and integrity (Article 4), the right to dignity and the prohibition of slavery and cruel inhuman and degrading treatment or punishment (Article 5), the right to liberty and security (Article 6), the right to a fair trial (Article 7), the freedom of conscience and religion (Article 8), the freedom of speech and the right to receive information (Article 9), the freedom of association and of assembly (Articles 10 and 11), the freedom of movement and residence, the right to seek asylum, the prohibition of mass expulsion of non-nationals (Article 12), the right to participate in the government of one's country (Article 13) and the right to property (Article 14). Specific mention is also made of the protection of the family and of women, children, the aged and the disabled. However, the Banjul Charter omits certain human rights which are in fact quite important, especially in the African context. Among the rights not guaranteed by the African Charter are the right to form and join trade unions, the right to equal protection of all children whether born in or out of wedlock, the right to marry with the full and free consent of the intending spouse and the freedom to change one's religion. Moreover, unlike the American and European Convention systems, the African Charter does not contain a provision on capital punishment and does not provide for the right of nationals not be expelled or the prohibition of forced labour – the latter which, as we shall see, also poses an extra threat in view of the individual duties listed in the Charter.

2.4.2. Vague Formulation of Rights

Second, aside from the omission of certain rights, there is also a considerable amount of vagueness in the formulation of those civil and political rights which are guaranteed by the African Charter. A case in point is provided by the fair trial provisions in the Charter. A number of important components of the right to a fair trial are omitted. For instance, the African Charter does not provide for the right of a detainee to be informed of the reasons of his or her detention or the charges brought against him or her, the right to have recourse to a court in order to review the lawfulness of the detention, the right to a public hearing or the right to appeal the judgement to a higher court. Yet these are very important components of the right to a fair trial that are clearly elaborated on in other human rights instruments. The African Commission on Human and Peoples' Rights later attempted to remedy this deficit in the Charter by elaborating on the right to fair trial in what is known as the Dakar Declaration.[40] This Declaration was later adopted by the African Commission[41] which, in turn, led to a set of principles on fair trial.[42] The Charter also deals with the right to work under equitable and satisfactory conditions just as it deals with freedom of conscience and free practice of religion. However, the scope of those rights in the Charter is not as well defined as is the case in international or other regional human rights instruments. An example is provided by the provision dealing with freedom of association (Article 10), which guarantees this freedom for an individual only 'provided that he abides by the law' and 'subject to the obligation of solidarity provided for in Article 29'. As we shall see, it is exactly Article 29 which lists a number of – often vague – individual duties. Hence, the scope of protection offered by Article 10 ultimately remains quite unclear.

2.4.3. No Derogation Clauses

A third problem is that the African Charter does not provide for derogation clauses. Unlike is the case with the Covenant on Civil and Political Rights (Article 4), the European Convention (Article 15) and the American Convention

40 African Commission on Human and Peoples' Rights in collaboration with the African Society of International and Comparative Law and Interights, *Dakar Declaration and Recommendations on the Right to a Fair Trial in Africa*, adopted on 11 September 1999, Dakar, Senegal, www.chr.up.ac.za/images/files/documents/ahrdd/theme17/fair_trial_dakar_declaration_1999.pdf. The Dakar Declaration was adopted at a seminar organised by the African Commission on Human and Peoples' Rights in collaboration with the African Society of International and Comparative Law and Inter-Rights on the Right to a Fair Trial. This seminar brought together a wide range of experts, scholars, human rights activists, lawyers and judges, including from the International Court of Justice, the European Court of Human Rights, the Inter-American Court of Human Rights, the African Commission on Human and Peoples' Rights, the office of the U.N. High Commissioner for Human Rights and International NGOs. Various issues relative to the right to a fair trial were considered and extensively discussed, including, *inter alia*, the independence and impartiality of the judiciary, military courts and special tribunals, legal aid, women and fair trial, children and fair trial, etc. The seminar recommended that the African Commission consolidate and expand all its pronouncements on the right to fair trial into a coherent body of principles.

41 African Commission on Human and Peoples' Rights, *Resolution 41(XXVI)99: Resolution on the Right to Fair Trial and Legal Aid in Africa*, adopted on 15 November 1999, Kigali, Rwanda. Under this resolution, a Working Group on Fair Trial was constituted to prepare a draft of the general principles and guidelines on the right to a fair trial and legal assistance under the African Charter and submit it to the 27th Ordinary Session of the Commission.

42 African Commission on Human and Peoples' Rights, *Principles and Guidelines on the Right to a Fair Trial and Legal Assistance in Africa*, adopted on 29 May 2003, Niamey, Niger. These general principles include, *inter alia*, an explanation of the meaning attached by the Commission a fair hearing, the right to habeas corpus, the right to be detained in a place recognised by law, the right to humane treatment, the right to counsel and the right to an interpreter.

(Article 27), there is no provision in the Charter which allows a State party to derogate from its obligations in times of war, public danger or other national emergency. As the African continent is certainly not free from emergencies, this lacuna begs the question how African governments will deal with situations in which complex balancing of rights and societal interests are required.

2.4.4. Clawback Clauses

Rather, and this is the fourth weakness, the Banjul Charter does contain a number of clawback clauses, i.e. qualifications that have the potential to take away the fundamental rights and freedoms listed elsewhere in the Charter. These are provisions such as 'subject to law and order', 'except for reasons and conditions previously laid down by law', 'within the law,' etc. As a matter of fact, all the civil and political rights guaranteed by the African Charter shall be exercised either 'within the law', 'in accordance with the law', or 'in accordance with the provisions of appropriate laws.'[43] There is no precise qualification of those limitations as is the case, for example, in the two United Nations Covenants or the American and European Conventions, all of which provide that limitations of rights should be proportionate and necessary in a democratic society, in the interest of national security, public safety, public order, the protection of public health or morals or the protection of rights and freedom of others. The reference to the concept of democratic society in those limitation clauses can be considered as a 'limitation of the limitation' and is therefore protective of the rights and freedom of the individuals. States parties to the African Charter could in the worst case rely on the vague limitation clauses of the Charter to empty the rights of their whole substance.[44] In *Legal Resources Foundation v. Zambia*, the African Commission therefore reiterated that clawback provisions in the Charter cannot be used by

---

43 Article 6 of the Banjul Charter, for example, guarantees the right of every individual to liberty and security of his person. However, the Charter adds that '[n]o one may be deprived of his freedom except for reasons and conditions previously laid down by law. In particular, no one may be arbitrarily arrested or detained.' Article 8 guarantees freedom of conscience 'subject to law and order', while Article 10 gives every individual the right to free association 'provided that he abides by the law'. Likewise, the right to assemble freely with others must, under Article 11, be exercised 'subject only to necessary restrictions provided for by the law, in particular those enacted in the interest of national security, the safety, health, ethics and rights and freedoms of others.'

44 African Commission on Human and Peoples' Rights, *Legal Resources Foundation v. Zambia,* Comm. 211/98 (2001), 29th Ordinary Session, held in Tripoli, Libya, from 23 April to 7 May 2001. In this case, Zambia had sought to rely on the limitation provisions of the right against discrimination contained in its own republican constitution. Article 23 of the Zambian Constitution prohibits discrimination of all kinds on any ground. However Article 23(5) allows for derogation of the right against discrimination. It argued that the right against discrimination was according to Zambian law restricted in certain respects and therefore that there was no breach of the provisions of the Charter which clearly recognised that the enjoyment of the rights under the Charter must be in accordance with the law.

a state to avoid its international obligation under the Charter. The Commission stated that:

> '[it] has argued forcefully that no State Party to the Charter should avoid its responsibilities by recourse to the limitations and "claw-back" clauses in the Charter. It was stated following developments in other jurisdictions, that the Charter cannot be used to justify violations of sections of it. The Charter must be interpreted holistically and all clauses must reinforce each other. The purpose or effect of any limitation must also be examined, as the limitation of the right cannot be used to subvert rights already enjoyed. Justification, therefore, cannot be derived solely from popular will, as such cannot be used to limit the responsibilities of the State Parties in terms of the Charter'.[45]

Notwithstanding this finding by the Commission, however, there is no doubt that clawback provisions have the potential, in some cases, of negating or watering down the substantive human rights provisions in the Charter. It is fair to state that these clawback provisions in the Charter can have the effect of limiting in a very severe way the enjoyment of the rights guaranteed by the Charter.

3. DUTIES PROVISIONS IN THE AFRICAN CHARTER

The specific characteristics of the Charter set out above carry in them the potential to pose a threat to human rights protection. This risk is further increased by the interplay with another unique feature of the Charter, namely the references made in some of its provisions to individual duties.

Indeed, this emphasis on the duties of each and every individual is probably the most distinguishing feature of the African Charter. The Charter devotes a whole chapter to the duties of the individual members of the African society. In three articles namely, Articles 27, 28 and 29, and in no less than eleven paragraphs, the Charter sets out the duties of the individual.

3.1. DUTIES NORMALLY BELONG TO STATES

The inclusion of duties of the individual in the Charter was quite revolutionary considering that the whole human rights regime is based on the concept of state responsibility, with state responsibility itself being an enduring principle of international law. International law, on the other hand, has long been regarded

45 Ibid, paragraph 70.

as the exclusive province of state actors under which States are bound by those norms that are known as customary law or those that they explicitly consent to through treaties. Treaties, which are regarded as the primary instruments of international law, are concluded between sovereign states to regulate and govern relations between those states. Traditionally, therefore, it is States which have been recognised as the primary subjects of international law. Flowing from this traditional view is the argument that at the level of international law, individuals may be holders of rights while states are the principal, if not the exclusive, holders of duties. This notion is grounded on the premise that the state is the ultimate guardian of its population's welfare and, therefore, has the responsibility of guaranteeing human rights since it alone is capable of doing so.

3.2. ANTECEDENTS IN INTERNATIONAL DOCUMENTS

The creation and imposition of duties on private individuals – at least in a general way – by international human rights instruments or treaties is, however, not a new phenomenon, nor was it first encapsulated in the African Charter on Human and Peoples' Rights. The Universal Declaration of Human Rights already stated in 1948 that:

> 'The General Assembly proclaims this Universal Declaration of Human Rights as a common standard of achievement for all peoples and all nations, to the end that *every individual and every organ of society* ... shall ... promote respect for these rights and freedoms'.[46]

Moreover, it states in Article 29(1) that:

> 'Everyone has duties to the community in which alone the free and full development of his personality is possible.'

The American Declaration of the Rights and Duties of Man also clearly spells out private duties. It provides that:

> 'the fulfillment of *duty by each individual* is a prerequisite to the rights of all.'[47]

46 Eighth preambular paragraph, Universal Declaration of Human Rights (emphasis added).

47 Second preambular paragraph, Ninth International Conference of American States, American Declaration on the Rights and Duties of Man, 1948, Bogotá, Colombia, OAS Res. XXX, reprinted in Basic Documents Pertaining to Human Rights in the Inter-American System, OAS/Ser.L/V/I.4 Rev. 9 (2003); 43 *AJIL Supp.* 133 (1949).

Even the twin covenants, the International Covenant on Civil and Political Rights and the International Covenant on Economic Social and Cultural Rights, reaffirm the obligation of individuals when they state that:

> 'the individual, having duties to other individuals and to the community to which he belongs, is under a responsibility to strive for the promotion and observance of the rights recognised in the present Covenant.'[48]

Besides these stipulations, it cannot be ignored that international law has in many instances contemplated and prescribed duties for non-state actors such as individuals. For example, international treaties which outlawed piracy and slavery[49] targeted private individuals. Even the Genocide Convention of 1948 clearly imposes duties on individuals, for instance, when it states that:

> 'persons committing genocide ... shall be punished, whether they are constitutionally responsible rulers, public officials or private individuals'.[50]

Yet, the style in which the duties of the individual under the Charter are formulated and packaged raises significant questions which justify a completely separate *tour d'horizon*. As appears clearly from the above, the main difference between the African Charter and other international instruments is that it lays down not only a *general* principle that individuals have duties, but also 'special' duties.[51] As Ouguergouz notes, other instruments can leave the possibility of States imposing special duties on individuals, but the African Charter is specific in that it elevates these duties to the rank of 'African civic obligations'.[52]

3.3. DUTIES AS A REFLECTION OF AFRICAN CULTURE

The relationship between the individual and the society he or she lives in is said to be different in African society than in other parts of the world. This was certainly so in pre-colonial times, but the difference in approach arguably continues up to this day. Nguema distinguishes the prevalent African conception of a 'human

---

48 See common preambular paragraph 5, International Covenant on Civil and Political Rights and International Covenant on Economic, Social and Cultural Rights.

49 See League of Nations, *Slavery, Servitude, Forced Labour and Similar Institutions and Practices Convention of 1926,* adopted on 25 September 1926, 60 *LNTS* 253.

50 Article IV, United Nations General Assembly, Convention on the Prevention and Punishment of the Crime of Genocide, adopted by Resolution 260 (III) A on 9 December 1948, 78 *UNTS* 277.

51 F. Ouguergouz, *The African Charter on Human and Peoples' Rights. A Comprehensive Agenda for Human Dignity and Sustainable Democracy in Africa*, The Hague: Martinus Nijhoff Publishers, 2003, p. 420.

52 Ibid.

person' from the Western notion, which he refers to as 'abstract, mechanical, static and materialist'.[53] Contrary to the human person within traditional African ancestral society, who was valued within an ethnic group – a notion which, due to globalisation, can be extended to the world community today – the western person, Nguema argues, is valued in function of the role he or she plays in the machinery of economic production.[54] Moreover, in the Western conception, the legal personality of a person exists merely between birth and death, while in African thought these bounds are far more fluid.[55] These differences explain, for example, why the fate of a European person of old age is that of one cast aside in an old age home once he or she is no longer economically productive, while in the African conception old age is considered, on the contrary, a source of veneration.[56]

With the foregoing background in mind, the writers of the African Charter believed in the position that without duties, none of the rights had any meaning and the two simply translate into each other. If one closely scrutinises the African Charter one finds that, unlike any other international human rights treaty, it does not segregate rights and duties. These are closely entwined with each other and almost inseparable, and can be both easily placed under one heading 'obligations'. As the well-known Indian religious and nationalist leader Mahatma Gandhi once famously said:

> '[t]he true source of rights is duty. If we discharge all our duties, rights will not be far to seek. If leaving duties unperformed we run after rights, they will escape us like a will-o'-the-wisp. The more we pursue them, the further they will fly.'[57]

The element of duty, as El-Obaid and Appigyei-Atua[58] argue, underlies the concept of rights in the African community. The community assists the individual to exercise his or her rights and the individual for his part ensures his contribution to the general development of the community. The notion of duty in the Charter entrenches positive African cultural and traditional values which existed in pre-colonial Africa, and which complement rights. The African Charter broke new ground by elaborating duties more fully than other international and regional instruments. The position awarded to individual duty in the Banjul Charter is

53 I. Nguema, 'Universalité et spécificité des droits de l'homme en Afrique' (1989) juillet-octobre (3&4) *RJPIC* 341, 345. Nguema writes that: '*En d'autres termes, la conception de la personne humaine dans la pensée occidentale est une conception abstraite, mécanique, statique, matéraliste. La personne n'acquiert de valeur qu'en function du role qu'elle joue dans le fonctionnement de l'appareil de production économique.*'

54 Ibid., pp. 344–345.

55 Ibid.

56 Ibid., p. 345.

57 Cited in F. Ouguergouz, *The African Charter on Human and Peoples' Rights: a comprehensive agenda for human dignity and sustainable democracy in Africa*, The Hague: Martinus Nijhoff Publishers, 2003, p. 382.

58 E.A. El-Obaid and K. Appigyei-Atua, 'Human Rights in Africa – A New Perspective on Linking the Past to the Present' (1996) 41 *McGill Law Journal* 819, 845–846.

decidedly different from that adopted in other major human rights instruments. It clearly sets the African human rights system apart from the other regional systems and in this regard the Charter can be said to make a conscious statement by 'protecting values and virtues of solidarity and community which other peoples have lost'.[59] In particular, as Nmehielle held, '[t]he duties enshrined in the Charter could be read as intended to recreate the bonds of the pre-colonial era among individuals and between individuals and the State.'[60] Mutua also observes that:

> 'The duty/rights conception in the African Charter could provide a new basis for individual identification with compatriots, the community and the state. It could forge and instil a national consciousness and act as the glue to unite individuals and different nations within the modern state and at the same time set the upper limits of conduct by state officials. The motivation and purpose behind the concept of duty in pre-colonial societies was to strengthen community ties and social cohesiveness, creating a shared fate and common destiny. This is the consciousness that the impersonal modern state has been unable to foster. It has failed to shift loyalties from the lineage and community to the modern state, with its mixture of different nations.'[61]

In Africa, therefore, an individual can only realise him or herself *in and through society*. Individual rights only acquire meaning from an African perspective when they are exercised in communion with other members of society. This conception of rights implies solidarity and therefore also individual duties.[62] Ahanhanzo therefore speaks of rights and duties as a 'diptych'.[63] In the same vain, Mbaye notes that traditional African law considers duties to be the flipside of subjective human rights. Duties and rights are therefore naturally intimately intertwined.[64] The essence and the reality of the respect for human rights is nothing else but

---

59 M.G. Ahanhanzo, 'Introduction à la Charte Africaine des Droits de l'Homme et des Peuples (Organisation de l'Unité Africaine)' in *Droit et Libertés à la fin du XXe Siècle: Influence des données économiques et technologiques. Études offertes à Claude-Albert Colliard*, Paris: Pedone, 1984, pp. 511, 525. Ahanhanzo writes: '*Il s'agit de sauvegarder des valeurs et vertus de solidarité et de communauté que d'autres peuples ont perdues.*'

60 V.O. Orlu Nmehielle, *The African Human Rights System. Its Laws, Practice, and Institutions*, The Hague: Martinus Nijhoff Publishers, 2001, p. 163.

61 M. Mutua, 'The Banjul Charter and the African Fingerprint: An Evaluation of the Language of Rights and Duties' (1995) 35 *Virginia Journal of International Law* 339–380, 368.

62 M.G. Ahanhanzo, 'Introduction à la Charte Africaine des Droits de l'Homme et des Peuples (Organisation de l'Unité Africaine)', in *Droit et Libertés à la fin du XXe Siècle: Influence des données économiques et technologiques. Études offertes à Claude-Albert Colliard*, Paris: Pedone, 1984, pp. 524–525.

63 Ibid., p. 524 ('*La Charte africaine des droits de l'Homme et des Peuples présente le diptyque droits et devoirs de l'Homme*').

64 K. Mbaye, *Les droits de l'homme en Afrique*, Paris: Pedone & Commission Internationale de Juristes, 1992, p. 38. Mbaye writes: '*Le droit africain traditionnel considère les devoirs comme l'autre face des droits subjectifs de l'homme. Les uns et les autres sont intimement mêlés.*'

the expression of the duty of all individuals towards rights-holders.[65] Individual rights do not make sense if they are looked at 'in a social and political vacuum'.[66] A conception of individual duties is therefore deemed essential.

The view that emphasises the notion of duties as corresponding with rights is perhaps more interesting. According to Quasigah,[67] the complementarity of rights and duties seems to have some prominent emphasis in African traditional society and this brings to the fore the Hohfeldian analysis of rights and duties as co-relatives. In his view, the African Charter generally emphasises the Hohfeldian concept of rights as corollary of duties and the interrelatedness of human rights in society. In this regard, one sees Quasigah's view point as being identical to that of M'baye and Ndiaye who propounded their thesis thus:

> 'In Africa, the individual, completely taken over by the archetype of the totem, the common ancestor or the protective genius, merges into the group ... In traditional Africa, rights are inseparable from the idea of duty. They take the form of a rite which must be obeyed because it commands like a "categorical imperative". In this, they tie in, through their spiritualism, with the philosophy of Kant.'[68]

Theoretically, the argument that is made here is very attractive. It is, however, difficult to agree entirely with this postulation given the worries that are associated with the duties provisions, as will be shown in the part dealing with the analysis of the duties provisions in the African Charter. Quasigah, nonetheless, makes the pertinent point that under Chapter II of the African Charter, although the primary duty holder is the individual, it is not beyond conjecture to argue that the state becomes the secondary duty carrier in that respect.[69]

3.4. CHARTER ARTICLES RELATING TO DUTIES

In no less than eleven paragraphs in the three Articles, namely 27, 28 and 29, the Banjul Charter sets out the duties of the individual elaborating in detail and in very simplistic terms the duties each individual holds. Identified with regard

---

65 Ibid., p. 39: '*Mais il ne faut pas oublier non plus que l'essence même et la réalité du respect de ces droits ne sont autre chose que l'expression d'un devoir: devoirs des personnes privées ou publiques vis-à-vis du bénéficiaire des droits.*'

66 M. Mutua, 'The Banjul Charter and the African Fingerprint: An Evaluation of the Language of Rights and Duties' (1995) 35 *Virginia Journal of International Law* 339–380, 340–341.

67 K. Quashigah, 'Scope of Individual Duties in the African Charter', in M. Ssenyonjo (ed.), *The African Regional Human Rights System: 30 years after the adoption of the African Charter on Human and Peoples' Rights*, Leiden: Martinus Nijhoff Publishers, 2011, pp. 119–134, 127.

68 K. M'baye and Ndiaye, 'The Organisation of African Unity', in K. Vasak (ed.), *The International Dimension of Human Rights*, vol. 2, Westport: Conn. Greenwood Press, 1982, p. 583.

69 K. Quashigah, 'Scope of Individual Duties in the African Charter', in M. Ssenyonjo (ed.), *The African Regional Human Rights System: 30 years after the adoption of the African Charter on Human and Peoples' Rights*, Leiden: Martinus Nijhoff Publishers, 2011, pp. 119–134, 124.

to whom they are owed, these duties can be grouped in five clusters as follows: (a) duties to the family; (b) duties to the society; (c) duties to the state; (d) duties to other legally recognised communities; and (e) duties to the international community.

An article by article analysis of the duties provisions in the African Charter reveals gaps and ambiguities and raises legitimate questions that cannot be easily wished away as we attempt to make practical sense of the African Charter in the vindication of individual rights and freedoms. It must be appreciated in the first place that the duties as listed in Articles 27–29 of the African Charter may try to create an individual who takes responsibility, has some duties to perform towards his family, community and the state and is a willing member of society who conforms to its rules. I now turn to analyse the Charter duties provisions individually.

3.4.1. *Article 27: Duties to the Family, the International Community and other Legally Recognised Communities*

Article 27 of the African Charter proclaims individual duties in its two sub-articles. In Article 27(1) it speaks very broadly about the individual duties towards his family, the international community and other legally recognised communities as follows: '*[e]very* individual shall have duties towards his family and society, the State and other legally *recognised* communities and the international community'. At first glance this appears to be a general statement made to remind the citizens of their moral obligations towards their country/nation. There is no specification as to what exact duties the individual must perform, or what is expected of the individual in performing this duty. The provision of Article 27(1) is quite general and can therefore be said not to have any great legal significance.[70] It does not lay down any specific duties, and can therefore be regarded merely as a 'framework provision'.[71]

Not without serious misgivings could one perhaps attempt to figure out one's duties to the family, but one would probably fail to do so as regards duties to the state and other legally recognised communities.

It would appear though that Article 27 tries to instil a sense of respect for the international laws and moral values. Umozurike tells us that this duty towards the international community as a whole 'could also play down extreme nationalism and national jingoism'.[72]

70 F. Ouguergouz, *The African Charter on Human and Peoples' Rights: a comprehensive agenda for human dignity and sustainable democracy in Africa*, The Hague: Martinus Nijhoff Publishers, 2003, p. 413.

71 Ibid.

72 U. Umozurike, *The African Charter on Human and Peoples' Rights*, The Hague: Martinus Nijhoff Publishers, 1997, p. 74.

The individual may be uncertain as to the entity the duty is owed to; what family is it – the nucleus or the extended? What is a legally recognised community in this context? As much as an individual would, with difficulty, suppose what he must do and what he must avoid doing to comply with the duties envisioned in Article 27(1), there is also an associated difficulty in trying to effectuate the duty. How would anyone be held accountable for failure to observe the duty?

Article 27(2) says: '[t]he rights and freedoms of each individual shall be exercised with due regard to the rights of others, collective security, morality and common interest'. What this article appears to intend to do is to impose a direct duty on the individual. It places a limitation on the exercise of rights by an individual for the protection of the rights of others, and in the interest of collective security, morality and security of others. Here the individual is probably being enjoined to reflect on how the exercise of his rights might adversely affect the rights of others or the community at large. The duty here is premised on the assumption that the full development of individual's rights is only possible where individuals care about how their actions would impact others. Thus, one will have to exercise his rights with a certain amount of responsibility. So here the African Charter rejects selfish individualism and asks the citizen to take into account their neighbours and other community members as they exercise their rights.

The placing by Article 27(2) of a limitation on the exercise of rights by individuals for the protection of the rights of others, and in the interests of collective security, morality and interests of others, reflects the normal position that obtains everywhere else that no rights are absolute. After all, human rights can never be regarded in isolation of other people's rights and therefore this provision can be said to reflect a 'normal fact of life'.[73] Article 27(2) therefore merely 'raises the level of care owed to neighbors and the community'.[74]

In three communications[75] brought before it, the African Commission on Human and Peoples' Rights reiterated that Article 27(2) constitutes the only legitimate reasons for limitations to the rights and freedoms protected by the African Charter. The interpretation placed on Article 27(2) by the African Commission has been interpreted by Heyns and Killander as now giving the said article the status of a general limitation clause.[76]

However, what is meant by collective morality and common interest intended in that Article is potentially contentious. With the silence of the African Charter

[73] V.O. Orlu Nmehielle, *The African Human Rights System. Its Laws, Practice, and Institutions*, The Hague: Martinus Nijhoff Publishers, 2001, p. 163.

[74] Ibid.

[75] *Constitutional Rights Project, Civil Liberties Project and Another v Nigeria* (Communication Nos. 140/94, 141/95), 13th Activity Report 1999–2000; *AHRLR* 200; *Constitutional Rights Project and Others v Nigeria* (2000) *AHRLR* 227; and *Interights and Others v Mauritania* (Communication No. 242 of 2001), 17th Activity Report, 2003–2004; (2004) *AHRLR* 87.

[76] C. Heyns and M. Killander, 'The African Regional Human Rights System', in F. Gomez Isa and K de Feyter (eds.), *International Protection of Human Rights: Achievements and Challenges*, Bilbao: University of Deusto, 2006, p. 520.

as to what exactly are the prescribed moral values and common interests, Article 27(2) remains open to different and conflicting interpretation although its general purpose may be common ground.

The vague wording could – in theory at least – cause some problems, as there is no requirement of legality included in order for the restrictions to be imposed.[77] Article 27(2) could, therefore, be considered to be a general limitation or clawback clause, as the limitation of the exercise of individual rights and freedoms is conceivable without these restrictions being subject to the requirement of legality.[78] However, this is not necessarily a problem in this case, as the Banjul Charter, at least most of the time, requires limitations to be established by law. All in all, Article 27(2) can be seen as a relatively 'safe' provision, i.e. one protecting human rights, as it could even be said that the provision, at least to some extent, 'marks out' the freedom afforded to States to impose restrictions on individual rights.[79]

It is axiomatic that the limitation on individual rights envisioned in Article 27(2) is so significant that it is recognised by many States parties to the African Charter. Consequently, many African countries do know a duty provision similar to the African Charter duty under Article 27(2). The Constitution of Ghana, for example, enjoins 'every citizen' a negative, implied duty 'to respect the rights, freedoms and legitimate interests of others, and generally to refrain from doing acts detrimental to the welfare of other persons'. The Ugandan Constitution,[80] too, provides for duties in Article 17, including the duty to have regard to the rights and freedoms of others. Under section 24 of the Nigerian Constitution duties incumbent on citizens include those of respecting the dignity of citizens and the rights and legitimate interests of others and living in unity and harmony and in the spirit of common brotherhood.[81] In addition to constitutional provisions, subsidiary legislation in many countries is replete with instances where duties are imposed on individuals.[82]

77 F. Ouguergouz, *The African Charter on Human and Peoples' Rights: a comprehensive agenda for human dignity and sustainable democracy in Africa*, The Hague: Martinus Nijhoff Publishers, 2003, p. 402.

78 Ibid., p. 413.

79 Ibid., p. 414.

80 Adopted on 8 October 1995, this is Uganda's fourth constitution since independence in 1962.

81 These examples of African constitutions represent neither an exhaustive nor definitive survey but merely a sample of the prevalent thought regarding duties on the African continent.

82 F. Viljoen, *International Human Right Law in Africa*, New York: Oxford University Press, 2007, states that domestic legislation routinely impose individual duties on individuals either explicitly or implicitly. He cites section 6 the Uganda Children's Act Chapter 50 of the laws of Uganda which casts on parents or guardians the responsibility to maintain their children as an example of an explicit imposition of duty. For implicit imposition, he gives the example of laws that require payment of taxes and those criminalising certain conduct. Other examples that can be cited are the Malawian Child Care, Protection and Justice Act 2010 which creates duties and responsibilities for parents and guardians towards their children, and equally creates in section 4 duties for children to respect their parents, to serve the community, etc.

However, although many African countries do have duties provisions in their constitutions[83] which may in some respects mirror those set out in Article 27(2) of the African Charter, they are regarded as a purely domestic affair between the state and the individual, making the African Charter and its provisions rather far removed from them. The state here is clearly identifiably the beneficiary of the majority of those duties. Once a state has made provision of duty similar to those of Article 27(2) of the Charter, the individual's obligations henceforth become one of observing the national laws and no reference will be made to the Charter provisions either by the individual or by the state.

3.4.2. *Article 28: Duties of Respect, Non-Discrimination, Mutual Respect and Tolerance*

Under Article 28 of the African Charter:

> '[e]very individual shall have the duty to respect and consider his fellow beings without discrimination, and to maintain relations aimed at promoting, safeguarding and reinforcing mutual respect and tolerance.'

The duty of non-discrimination between individuals which is entailed in this provision is especially relevant considering the ethnic diversity of African States.[84] Apart from the reference to non-discrimination, which is capable of enforcement by way of a constitutional and or legislative provision, as is in fact the case in many African countries,[85] this Article has a very general note that does not suggest or import any legal implications. It uses a very commonplace tone that speaks of pleasant 'neighbourliness' without proposing solidarity in strong terms, or hinting that it is one's general duty to help others.[86] It translates into more

83 For example, Article 17 of the Uganda constitution includes the duty to defend Uganda and render national service when necessary and cooperate with lawful agencies in the maintenance of law and order; pay taxes; register for electoral and other lawful purposes; combat corruption and misuse of wastage of public property and create and protect a clean and healthy environment. Furthermore, under Article 17(2) it is the duty of all able bodied citizens to undergo military training for the defence of the constitution and the protection of the territorial integrity of Uganda whenever called upon to do so. Under the Nigerian constitution section 24 of the Nigerian Constitution duties incumbent on citizens including defending Nigeria and rendering such national service as may be required; respecting the dignity of citizens and the rights and legitimate interests of others and living in unity and harmony and in the spirit of common brotherhood; making positive and useful contributions to the advancement, progress and well-being of the community and paying taxes promptly. Article 113 of the Zambian Constitution lists duties of the citizen which include the duty of loyalty to the country; to foster unity and live in harmony with others; to promote democracy and the rule of law; to vote; to pay taxes; and to provide defence and military service when called upon.

84 Ibid., p. 402.

85 For example Article 27(5) of the Kenyan Constitution, Article 20 of the Constitution of Malawi Chapter 4 and Article 21 of the Ugandan Constitution.

86 Ibid., p. 403.

or less a general code of conduct, without any legal implications, thus making it impossible for States parties to the African Charter to prosecute an individual who fails to perform this duty. The duties here are clearly those that would in W.D. Ross' ethical theory[87] be *prima facie* duties of beneficence and maleficence, totally devoid of enforcement.

Legally speaking, the provision as formulated is too vague to have any (negative) impact on the enjoyment of individuals' rights and freedoms. An individual must respect another person's rights, but aside from that he has no precise legal obligations; only moral ones could be deduced from this provision.[88] In conclusion, while lacking any real legal significance, the provision does have a symbolic importance, as it represents those values which act as 'a lubricant that oils the wheel of social interaction'.[89]

3.4.3. Article 29(1): Duties to Preserve the Harmonious Development, Cohesion and Respect for the Family, etc.

According to Article 29(1) of the Banjul Charter an individual has a duty to

> 'preserve the harmonious development of the family and to work for the cohesion and respect of the family; to respect his parents at all times, to maintain them in case of need.'

There are two distinct duties outlined here: one towards the family and the other towards the parents. While it is arguable that the duty towards parents implies a reciprocal right on the part of the parents to be accorded respect and maintenance from the individual, it is doubtful that one can talk of any meaningful right to anything by the family as an entity. Equally it is easy to appreciate the significance of the duty to one's parents in the African context. Owing to the poor economic conditions that most African states find themselves in, they cannot run along the lines of the Western welfare states. And so, the elderly, the needy and the poor must necessarily be taken care of. Their own families shoulder the first line of responsibility in this regard. This duty, which has its roots in the pre-colonial social order when one lived under strong communitarian rules (when abandoning parents or for that matter any elderly community members, was completely unthinkable), has become a complete necessity today, even though that old social order does not exist anymore. These old rules where a family is held sacred is an age-old tradition and cannot be dispensed with so easily even under significant influence of Western individualism and liberal human rights laws. The other part of the duty is also more or less a moral sermon, and according to traditional

87 W.D. Ross, *The Right and the Good* (reprinted), Oxford: Oxford University Press, 2002.
88 Ibid., p. 415.
89 V.O. Orlu Nmehielle, *The African Human Rights System. Its Laws, Practice, and Institutions*, The Hague: Martinus Nijhoff Publishers, 2001, p. 163.

values an African will find it natural to look after his parents. It does not clearly specify as to what the individual must do to look after his parents and whether he needs to look after all his other blood relations too. These outlined obligations are so vague that the legal implications for any of these duties will be found to be varied and multidimensional. This will make it very difficult for the state to decipher their normative contents and take some measures to implement them.

It would seem that from a traditional African point of view, there is nothing extraordinary about this provision. As Orlu Nmehielle notes, '[t]here is nothing wrong for an individual to be reminded that he or she ought to respect his or her parents and to provide them with necessary care and maintenance.'[90] Article 29(1) in this view merely reflects the – otherwise somewhat elusive notion of – 'positive African cultural value'.[91]

According to Article 18 of the African Charter, the family forms the 'natural unit and basis of society' and, since the family by tradition forms the natural unit of society, the individual will observe this duty without any need for outside enforcement if it is clearly identified. However, the African Charter does not clarify the scope and nature of the duties to be observed by an individual towards his family. It also does not clarify and define what was meant by the word 'family', whether it refers to just a couple and their children as in modern nuclear families, or refers to the traditional form of African families, which are large and extended. Even the notion of 'parents' could be interpreted more broadly than the typical Western connotation, although Ouguergouz proposes to interpret the notion *stricto sensu*.[92] Is this duty limited to support of parents only, or does it include grandparents, uncles, aunts, brothers and sisters? Again, one is inclined to conclude that the duty to the family is what Ross calls a *prima facie* duty of beneficence, that is to say the duty to do good to others: to foster their health, security, wisdom, moral goodness, or happiness which 'rests upon the fact that there are other beings in the world whose condition we can make better in respect of virtue, or of intelligence, or of pleasure'.[93]

It is probably fair to say that the duties entailed in Article 29(1) towards family and parents are in fact not heavier than those which are in any case already included in the various domestic legislations.[94] The provision therefore merely reiterates what is already widely known, and accepted, in African society. As Ouguergouz observes, the duty of individuals to parents and their children is

90 Ibid., p. 164.

91 Ibid.; Orlu Nhemielle even becomes somewhat lyrical when he states that: 'It is the joy of the African parent to toil and train his or her child, with a great expectation that when that child becomes "somebody" that child would take care of him or her.'

92 F. Ouguergouz, *The African Charter on Human and Peoples' Rights: a comprehensive agenda for human dignity and sustainable democracy in Africa*, The Hague: Martinus Nijhoff Publishers, 2003, pp. 405–406.

93 W.D. Ross, *The Right and the Good* (reprinted) (Oxford: Oxford University Press, 2002), pp. 21–22.

94 Ibid., p. 416.

normally sanctioned by domestic criminal and civil law.[95] This point is also alluded to by Viljoen[96] when he cites section 6 of the Ugandan Children's Act Chapter 50 which casts on parents or guardians the responsibility to maintain their children, as an example of an explicit imposition of duty. One could go further and cite the Ethiopian Constitution and its Criminal Code which contain duties of the individual in the manner they are formulated in the Charter. Seychelles too, has individuals' duties imposed by its Constitution and other subsidiary laws such as the Civil Code of Seychelles Act.[97] Malawi has the Child Care, Protection and Justice Act 2010 which creates duties and responsibilities for parents and guardians toward their children, and equally creates duties and responsibility for children towards their parents.[98] For implicit imposition, he gives the example of laws that require payment of taxes and those criminalising certain conduct.

What Article 29(1) of the African Charter does is to give ambiguous directions to the individual to preserve harmonious development and cohesion and respect of the family. The point is that enforcement mechanisms are usually not specified, nor is what triggers enforcement of these statutes clear. If the reason for having familial support duties is to strengthen the family, it is more likely that bringing criminal charges or other legal action with domestic legislation which give effect to the duty provisions in the African Charter would create disharmony in the family. Indeed the elderly person needing the support of their adult children would almost surely be loath to seek enforcement of their rights if it meant putting their children in the criminal justice system.

3.4.4. Article 29(2): Duty to Serve National Community and Deploying Physical and Intellectual Abilities

Article 29(2) requires the individual '[t]o serve his national community by placing his physical and intellectual abilities at its service.' It is unclear from this provision the extent to which the duty of an individual towards his society and state can, for instance, be solicited to stem the process of brain drain from Africa. Trained professionals in Africa find it more worthwhile to go and work in foreign states, owing to the better conditions of service they receive there, even though it means their own country suffers from the lack of professional man power. Medical personnel trained in Africa prefer to go and work abroad owing to the poor wage scale in Africa, though their services are really required by their own countrymen.

95 F. Ouguergouz, *The African Charter on Human and Peoples' Rights: a comprehensive agenda for human dignity and sustainable democracy in Africa*, The Hague: Martinus Nijhoff Publishers, 2003, p. 416.

96 F. Viljoen, *International Human Right Law in Africa*, New York: Oxford University Press, 2007.

97 Article 205 of the Civil Code of Seychelles Act 1/01/1975, laws of Seychelles 1996 provides that the child shall be bound to maintain their father and mother or other ascendants who are in need. Article 2006 of the same law extends this duty to other relatives.

98 Section 4 of the Act.

According to the Centre for Global Development, for example, there were 883 Zambian health professional emigrants in the year 2006 notwithstanding the dire need for these professionals locally.[99]

Article 29(2) has been attacked as dangerous, as it could justify obstacles to freedom of movement of nationals.[100] Can a country legislate against professional emigration on the basis that it is enforcing the duty under Article 29(2) of the African Charter? There is a theoretical risk that this provision might be invoked to limit an individual's freedom of movement, but according to Ouguergouz this risk is minimal, as Article 12(2) is quite strict in this regard.[101] Nmehielle refers to the provision as reflecting 'the essence of community service' which 'has been a long standing practice in the African past.'[102]

The bottom line however, is that the full import of the duty imposed on the individual by Article 29(2) is far from clear.

3.4.5. Article 29(3): Duty not to Compromise National Security

Article 29(3) requires of an individual not to compromise national security. Together with Article 29(4) and (5), it requires an individual to serve his country and nation by working towards its unity, solidarity and maintaining its independence. Thus these articles have been written keeping in mind the years of captivity, slavery and human rights abuse at the hands of the European colonial powers. These duties are used as armour against future foreign occupation. The duty to promote African unity has been described as 'an especially critical role given arbitrary balkanisation by colonial powers and the ethnic animosity fostered within and between states.'[103]

In Article 29(3) it is the duty of the African individual '[n]ot to compromise the security of the State whose national or resident he is.' While the African Charter talks of 'compromising of the security of the State', it does not enlighten us as to what actions can be taken as a breach of a state's security. An authoritarian state may translate this duty and force its citizens to give up their freedom of expression or the freedom of political association, under the guise of protecting state security. Since the rights and duties are very closely inter-related in the Banjul Charter and cannot in some instances be easily divorced from each other, a manipulative

---

99 Centre for Global Development, *A new database of health professional emigration from Africa*, Working Paper 95, http:/www.cgdev.org/content/publications/detail/9267.

100 W. Benedek, 'People's Rights and Individual's Duties as Special Factors of Human by International Law: The Emerging African System' (1955) *Nomis Verlagsgesellschaft* 59, 89.

101 F. Ouguergouz, *The African Charter on Human and Peoples' Rights: a comprehensive agenda for human dignity and sustainable democracy in Africa*, The Hague: Martinus Nijhoff Publishers, 2003, p. 417.

102 V.O. Orlu Nmehielle, *The African Human Rights System. Its Laws, Practice, and Institutions*, The Hague: Martinus Nijhoff Publishers, 2001, p. 164.

103 M. Mutua, 'The Banjul Charter and the African Fingerprint: An Evaluation of the Language of Rights and Duties' (1995) 35 *Virginia Journal of International Law* 339–380, 368, 371.

state may indeed construe these unclear duties to force individuals to give up their basic rights. It seems though that this duty finds it origin in pre-colonial communities.[104] As Mutua notes, writing at the beginning of the 21st century, '[i]f anything, there exists a heightened need today, more than at any other time in recent history, to fortify communal relations and defend national solidarity.'[105] Nmehielle, too, and writing around the same time, refers to the situation in Liberia, Somalia, Rwanda and Sierra Leone to argue that '[t]he maintenance of social and national solidarity ... is of utmost importance in present day Africa where many modern States have collapsed or failed.'[106] Now, even almost halfway through the second decennium of this century, we unfortunately cannot but agree with these authors.

3.4.6. *Article 29(4): Duty to Preserve and Strengthen Social and National Solidarity*

Under Article 29(4) the individual is enjoined to '[t]o preserve and strengthen social and national solidarity, particularly when the latter is threatened.' The meaning of Article 29(4) is extremely vague and, in reality, makes almost no sense. Perhaps a better way to frame it would have been to say that it is the duty of all individuals 'to protect and strengthen social and national solidarity' and the next part should have been that this duty is all the more exigent when there is an imminent threat to the nation and society.

It would appear though that here the duty outlined is simply one that existed, albeit in a slightly different form, amongst the community members of a pre-colonial social organisation. It asks the individual to work towards building national unity. Many post-colonial states which have failed to instil this feeling of solidarity have encountered difficulties.[107] So like the state, the individual too bears the responsibility of keeping the community and state together. Chege[108] observes that the maintenance of social and national solidarity is of utmost importance in present day Africa, where many modern states have collapsed and failed.

While Article 29(4) is without doubt formulated in a vague way, suggesting perhaps even excessive requirements could be demanded from the individual in the name of solidarity, the underlying principle is of such importance to African society today, and surely also in the future, that it warrants mentioning, at least

104 M. Mutua, *Human Rights. A Political and Cultural Critique*, Philadelphia: University of Pennsylvania Press, 2002, p. 87.

105 Ibid.

106 V.O. Orlu Nmehielle, *The African Human Rights System. Its Laws, Practice, and Institutions*, The Hague: Martinus Nijhoff Publishers, 2001, p. 164, footnote 613.

107 One would argue that countries like Somalia, Liberia and Rwanda, are examples of countries that may not have handled the issue of national solidarity well.

108 M. Chege, 'Between Africa's Extremes' (1995) 6 *Journal of Democracy* 44, 45.

as a 'didactic' provision 'stimulating individuals' spirit of solidarity',[109] among the duties listed in the Charter.

3.4.7. *Article 29(5): Duty to Preserve and Strengthen National Independence and Territorial Integrity and to Contribute to its Defence*

Article 29(5) reminds Africans of 'the need to preserve their hard-won independence'[110] and can be considered to be connected to the right of self-determination of the African peoples. As such, this principle acts 'as a shield against foreign occupation'.[111] Many African countries reflect a similar duty in their constitutions. Under Article 17 of the Ugandan Constitution there is a duty on every individual to defend Uganda and render national service when necessary and cooperate with lawful agencies in the maintenance of law and order, while under Article 17(2) it is the duty of all able bodied citizens to undergo military training for the defence of the constitution and the protection of the territorial integrity of Uganda whenever called upon to do so. Under the Nigerian constitution section 24 of the Nigerian Constitution duties incumbent on citizens include defending Nigeria and rendering such national service as may be required. Article 113 of the Zambian Constitution[112] lists duties of the citizen which include the duty to provide defence and military service when called upon.

3.4.8. *Article 29(6): Duty to Work to the Best of One's Ability and Competence, and to Pay Taxes*

Under Article 29(6) of the African Charter, it is the duty of the individual to work to the best of his ability and competence, and to pay taxes imposed by law in the interest of the society. This article entails the duty 'to work to the best of his abilities and competence' and 'to pay taxes imposed by law in the interest of the society'. The first part of this provision, i.e. the one dealing with work, is without doubt one of the more problematic ones in the Charter. The background of this provision is quite clear, as it must be seen in light of the chronic economic under-development of the African continent.[113] The 'total deprivation' found in large parts of Africa, in spite of economic progress of the last decennia, can arguably justify 'participation' as an obligation on members of African societies.[114] The problem, however, is that Article 5 of the Banjul Charter does not prohibit forced

---

109 F. Ouguergouz, *The African Charter on Human and Peoples' Rights: a comprehensive agenda for human dignity and sustainable democracy in Africa*, The Hague: Martinus Nijhoff Publishers, 2003, p. 407.

110 Ibid.

111 M. Mutua, 'The Banjul Charter and the African Fingerprint: An Evaluation of the Language of Rights and Duties' (1995) 35 *Virginia Journal of International Law* 339–380, 371.

112 Constitution of 1991 as amended in 1996.

113 Ibid., p. 408.

114 Ibid.

labour, creating the risk that authoritarian governments may invoke Article 29(6) to justify such forced labour of their citizens. There are, nevertheless, other guarantees against such abuses, for example through ILO Convention No. 105, which can act as a counterweight.[115] The second part of this provision, i.e. the duty to pay taxes, is far less spectacular, as it can reasonably held that it is the duty of any citizen in any county where taxation is organised to pay such taxes.[116]

3.4.9. Article 29(7): Duty to Preserve and Strengthen Positive African Cultural Values

Article 29(7) enjoins the individual '[t]o preserve and strengthen positive African cultural values in his relations with other members of the society, in the spirit of tolerance, dialogue and consultation and, in general, to contribute to the promotion of the moral well-being of society'. This article can be related to the implementation of the African Cultural Charter.[117] As Ouguergouz notes, the provision entails a general duty and is quite vague. The notion 'preserve and strengthen positive African, cultural values' was actually new, even to the African legal terminology, so it is unclear what is meant by it.[118]

Here the African Charter specifies a certain code of conduct without actually clarifying as to how it should be effected in daily lives. Charter provisions on duties such as the duty of the individual to preserve and strengthen positive African cultural values in his relations with other members of the society, in the spirit of tolerance, dialogue and consultation and, in general, to contribute to the promotion of the moral wellbeing of society[119] are, to say the least, of very doubtful meaning. This is so in light of the absence of pointers or indicators of what may amount to 'positive African cultural values.' To speak of preserving positive aspects of African culture in a continent which is such an elaborate a mosaic as Africa, may be equally absurd.

The African Charter also fails to define what it means by 'moral well-being of society' or 'positive African cultural values'. So a state trying to make legal implications will be completely confused. African cultural values are many and not all of them are positive, as for example the practice of female circumcision which has been present in the African tradition for centuries. The African Charter remains silent on such traditional practices, which are certainly not 'positive'. This is a question that had to be addressed some years later under the Protocol to the

---

115 Ibid., p. 417; International Labour Organization, *Convention concerning the Abolition of Forced Labour*, C105, adopted on 25 June 1957, Geneva, Switzerland.

116 V.O. Orlu Nmehielle, *The African Human Rights System. Its Laws, Practice, and Institutions*, The Hague: Martinus Nijhoff Publishers, 2001, p. 164.

117 F. Ouguergouz, *The African Charter on Human and Peoples' Rights: a comprehensive agenda for human dignity and sustainable democracy in Africa*, The Hague: Martinus Nijhoff Publishers, 2003, p. 407.

118 Ibid., p. 415.

119 Article 29(4) of the African Charter on Human and Peoples' Rights.

African Charter relative to women's rights in Africa. Udombana however, argues that one possible interpretation is that the African Charter favours African rights to the extent that they do not collide with universal principles.[120] So one wonders as to what are the 'positive' cultural values which the African Charter talks about, but fails to clarify. The point has already been made about African cultural values.

Here some scholars point out that these duties are a little ambiguous in nature, and that the state may misinterpret them and advocate the patriarchal social order that was prevalent during the pre-colonial times, leading to gender bias. The Charter does overtly condone these age-old acts of bias against women when it says a family is 'the custodian of morals and traditional values recognized by the community'. Ouguergouz deplores that the Charter provision in this regard is not adequately protective of women and could be used to abuse women's rights.[121] However, Article 29(3), provides for the protection of women against any bias and directs the state to work for 'the elimination of every discrimination against women and also ensure the protection of the rights of women and the child as stipulated in international declarations and conventions.' In this regard, it can equally be argued that the Charter leaves no scope for misinterpretation of any sort. Mutua sees the criticism of Article 29(2) as exaggerated, because a progressive and liberal interpretation of the African Charter should leave no room for discrimination of women.[122] According to Mutua, the Charter should be read in reference to traditional values that enhance the dignity of the individual and emphasise the dignity of motherhood and the importance of the female as the central link in the reproductive chain.[123]

3.4.10. Article 29(8): Duty to Contribute to the Promotion and Achievement of African Unity

Article 29(8), which deals with the 'promotion of African unity', is probably the only real duty towards the international community[124] in the list of duties. However, the 'international community' here is limited to the 'African' community, and this provision can therefore be linked directly to the Charter of the Organisation of African Unity.[125] A duty like this is clearly in origin more of a duty incumbent on States than on individuals. When it pertains to individuals,

---

120 N.J. Udombana, 'Between promise and performance: Revisiting states obligations under the African Charter' (2004) 40 *Stanford Journal of International Law*, 105, 111.

121 F. Ouguergouz, *La Charte Africaine des Droits de l'Homme et des Peuples Historique, Portée juridique et contribution à la protection des droits de l'homme en Afrique,* Paris: Presses Universitaires des France, 1993, p. 252.

122 M. Mutua, 'The Banjul Charter and the African Fingerprint: An Evaluation of the Language of Rights and Duties' (1995) 35 *Virginia Journal of International Law* 339–380, 372.

123 Ibid., pp. 371–372.

124 As mentioned in Article 27(1) of the Banjul Charter.

125 F. Ouguergouz, *The African Charter on Human and Peoples' Rights: a comprehensive agenda for human dignity and sustainable democracy in Africa,* The Hague: Martinus Nijhoff Publishers, 2003, pp. 410–411.

it can therefore not be more than a duty to refrain, for instance, from propaganda for war or 'national, racial or religious hatred'.[126]

There appears to be a great deal of merit in the reasoning that Hansungule employs when he comes to the conclusion that the duties of the individual in the African traditional and cultural set-up are generally not enforceable. They are mere moral and supererogatory directives which fall short of being legal claims. He gives the example of a person who does not look after his grandmother. While such a person cannot be taken to court for his failure, it is believed that 'his ancestors would laugh at him', that is to say that he would not live long.'[127]

According to Hansungule, one way in which duties should be considered is through reliance on one another. He posits that:

> 'A young man needs the assistance of his uncle to pay his bride price when marrying which will not be forthcoming if he did not respect him, help him in his endeavours or was regarded by the community to be truant or disrespecting. The question of locus standing for these duties does not arise because they have their own method of enforcement in culture. Other duties however can be legally enforced. For example, the duty to pay tax has clear legal implications. Similarly the duty to contribute to the defence of one's country may include military service, which can be provided for in national legislation.'[128]

None of the provisions under Article 29, except for the ones related to duties towards the family, signify any legal implications. Their commonplace tones, lack of specific clarifications and a general air of an ethical or a moral code of conduct, makes it very difficult for the state to translate them into specific normative provisions and makes it even harder to implement them as duties which are legally binding and hence unavoidable for an individual. Only the duties towards the family do have some sort of legal implication and can come under the jurisprudence of the domestic national laws.

3.5. EVALUATION

As regards criticisms directed specifically at duties provisions, Sloth-Nielsen and Mezmur[129] observe that 'a more general charge against the imposition of duties on the individual is that they would override individual rights.' And this is precisely

126 Ibid., p. 411.

127 M. Hansungule, 'The African Charter on Human and Peoples' Rights: A Critical Review' (2008) 8 *African Yearbook of International Law* 265–331, 294.

128 Ibid., p. 294.

129 J. Sloth-Nielsen and B.D Mezmur, 'A Dutiful Child: The Implication of Article 31 of the African Children's Charter' (2008) 52(2) *Journal of African Law* 159–189, 167.

the point made by Cohen who is sceptical about the wisdom in subjugating rights to duties because:

> '[i]f the state has a collective right and obligation to develop the society, economy, and polity (Article 29), then as an instrument it can be used to defend coercive state actions against both individuals and constituent groups to achieve policies rationalised as social and economic improvements.'[130]

Rhoda Howard and Jack Donnelly also think the mixing up of rights and duties in the modern state is to risk eventual complete disappearance of the rights. In their words 'all duties will be aimed towards the preservation of the state and of the interests of those who control it.'[131] Another scholar calls these duties to be 'little more than formulation, entrenchment, and legitimation of state rights and privileges against individuals and peoples.'[132]

There is expressed fear amongst experts that the concept of duty towards the state may be translated into a coercive force in the hands of a dictator, which may be used to force people into giving up their rights in the name of obligation towards the state. On this basis the concept of individual duties has been vehemently opposed by many Western scholars like Buergenthal and Haysom. They have opined that duty towards the state can be easily manipulated and turned into an authoritarian rule. Buergenthal maintains that the inclusion of duties in the African Charter is nothing but an invitation for the imposition of an unlimited restriction on the enjoyment of rights.[133] Heysom's fear is that the concept of duties in the Charter could be used to suppress the rights guaranteed in the Charter. He considers that the interpretation of a duty towards the community as meaning a duty towards the state lends itself to an autocratic style of government.[134] One point that ought to be made is that, although the duties posture in the African Charter has been subject to criticism, with some critics being concerned that it would be a basis for States parties to the African Charter to perpetrate human rights violations, many of these duties as seen in the classification of duties are not of such a nature that they could be tied to particular rights which a state would in turn use as a tool for the violation of rights.

---

130 R. Cohen, 'Endless Teardrops: Prolegomena to the study of Human Rights in Africa', in R. Cohen, G. Hyden and W.P. Nagan (eds.), *Human Rights and Governance in Africa*, Gainesville: University Press of Florida, 1993.

131 R.E. Howard and J. Donnelly (eds.), *International Handbook of Human Rights*, New York: Greenwood Press, 1987, p. 25.

132 See H. Okoth-Ogendo, 'Human and peoples' rights: what point is Africa trying to make', in R. Cohen *et al.*, *Human Rights and Governance in Africa*, 1993, pp. 78–79.

133 T. Buergenthal (1995), p. 175.

134 N.R.L. Hysom, 'African Charter: Inspirational Document or False Start?', paper presented at the Bill of Rights Conference, Victoria Falls, Zimbabwe, 14 December 1994, p. 6.

Besides the traditional points of criticism of the African Charter, there are other basic points of discomfort that may be raised in relation to the African Charter.

First of all, there is the question of what the legal value is of the duties mentioned in the Charter. A first problem appears to be that the provisions dealing with individual duties in the African Charter impose obligations on the *individual*, yet the Charter as a document in international law is regarded as a treaty concluded between the parties to it, i.e., *States*. The special importance of the law of treaties in international law does not require any emphasis. A treaty remains the best medium available for imposing binding rules of precision and detail in new areas of expansion for international law and of course, for codifying or clarifying customary law as it already exists. Consequently, the law on treaties provides that only parties to the treaty are bound by its provisions. This is stated clearly in Article 26 of the Vienna Convention on the Law of Treaties[135] which states that every treaty in force is binding upon the parties to it and must be performed in good faith. As a general rule, a treaty therefore cannot impose obligations or confer rights upon a third party without that party's consent. In any event, while State duties can be legally enforced through the African regional mechanisms, individual duties cannot.[136]

In this regard, however, it needs to be noted that the African Charter does not only list individual duties, but also imposes complementary duties on States. This fact does not solve the legal question about the imposition of duties upon individuals, but it does point at a rather holistic approach regarding the human rights issues dealt with by the Charter. It could be said that individual and state duties in fact form a comprehensive whole. Article 18, for instance, lists the duties of the States towards the family when it holds:

> 'The family shall be the natural unit and basis of society. It shall be protected by the State which shall take care of its physical health and moral.
> 1. The State shall have the duty to assist the family which is the custodian of morals and traditional values recognized by the community.
> 2. The State shall ensure the elimination of every discrimination against women and also ensure the protection of the rights of women and the child as stipulated in international declarations and conventions.
> 3. The aged and the disabled shall also have the right to special measures of protection in keeping with their physical or moral needs.'

135 United Nations, *Vienna Convention on the Law of Treaties*, adopted on 23 May 1969, UN Doc. A/Conf.39/27, 1155 *UNTS* 331.

136 V.O. Orlu Nmehielle, *The African Human Rights System. Its Laws, Practice, and Institutions*, The Hague: Martinus Nijhoff Publishers, 2001, pp. 164–165.

Similarly, Articles 25 and 26 impose duties on the State:

> '25. State Parties to the present Charter shall have the duty to promote and ensure through teaching, education and publication, the respect of the rights and freedoms contained in the present Charter and to see to it that these freedoms and rights as well as corresponding obligations and duties are understood.'
>
> '26. State Parties to the present Charter shall have the duty to guarantee the independence of the Courts and shall allow the establishment and improvement of appropriate national institutions entrusted with the promotion and protection of the rights and freedoms guaranteed by the present Charter.'

Second, a state cannot bring an individual violator of the provisions of the Charter to the African Commission or the African Court. The whole system was structured with state violations of Charter rights in mind. As one reads the civil, political, economic, social and cultural rights provided for in the African Charter, and simultaneously goes through the duties imposed on the individual and the state, one cannot but raise the question how these duties can be imposed on individuals who are neither party to the Charter, nor can in any way be brought either before the African Commission or the African Court for violation of those duty provisions. While indeed provision is made for the state and other non-state institutions like NGOs to officially file a complaint with the African Commission if they feel that there has been a breach of conduct by a Member State in regard to any of the rights and duties listed in the African Charter, there is no provision for similar complaints towards individuals who fail to perform their duties. This is eloquent testimony to the fact that the Charter is premised on the traditional view that in international law individuals may be holders of rights while states are the principal, if not the exclusive, holders of duties. This notion is grounded on the premise that the state is the ultimate guardian of its population's welfare and, therefore, has the responsibility of guaranteeing human rights since it alone is capable of doing so. It falls upon the state to instil a sense of duty within its citizens, and not necessarily punishment for each wrongdoing by an individual.

The duties in the African Charter, even those that are not merely supererogatory or beneficent such as the duty to pay taxes and to defend the territorial integrity and security of the state, still lack legal efficacy for as long as they only remain in the African Charter.

Third, it is unclear what these duties require of the individual to do or not to do in order to conform to them. Fourth, there are no sanctions prescribed or contemplated under the African Charter for individuals violating their duties.

It is, however, plausible to hold that individual duties in the African Charter are dependent on some positive action on the part of the state to enact legislation and/or take other measures to ensure that the individual's duties are carried into effect. Many African states in fact reflect in their constitution or indeed in subsidiary legislation the notion of duty to the same extent as entailed in the African Charter. A survey by Heyns and Kaguogo[137] shows that many constitutions of African countries include provisions on duties.[138] As a matter of fact, Heyns and Kaguongo found that the notion of duties was at the time of their review, present in forty African constitutions.[139] If approached from the perspective that the duties provisions in the African Charter are only capable of being given meaning and effect after a state has passed domestic legislation, the whole picture changes. And this is where one would situate Quasigah's point that the state becomes the secondary duty carrier in respect of Charter duties. Once the state is implicated in the manner suggested, that is to say, by legislating or making provisions in its constitution of the duties reflected in the African Charter, the state carries, as it were, the first responsibility to act through passing enabling legislation. The Charter duty will therefore remain, for all purposes and intents, on paper only. And once the state imposes equivalent duties on the individual, such duties no longer remain Charter-based duties – they will be duties sanctioned by the enabling legislation under specific states, so that it henceforth becomes idle to insist that an individual is observing a duty because of the African Charter provisions on duties and not because of local legislation. Even then, only a handful of duties suggested by the African Charter for the individual are capable of being the subject of implementing legislation. Many of these duties do elude even the very notion of regulation. Those that can be the subject of legislation and regulation are both positive and negative and include the duty to have regard for the general rights of others; the duty against discrimination; the duty to maintain parents in times of need; the duty not to compromise the security of the state; and the duty to pay taxes. In fact, although these duties are a feature of many African constitutions and domestic legislation today, there is never any suggestion that they are African Charter-based, or African Charter-instigated, or African Charter-likened duties. Once these are set out in local constitutions or laws, they are treated purely as a domestic affair and are not referable in any way to the African Charter.

As for those duties whose gamut is a matter of surmise or conjecture because of either their flawed formulation or their normative content, is it is difficult to think of a piece of legislation that would define or prescribe their standard. For example, it would seem inherently difficult to determine or define the content or import of the duty of mutual respect and tolerance or cohesion of a family, or the duty to strengthen positive African cultural values.

137 C. Heyns and W. Kaguongo, 'Current Developments: Constitutional human rights law in Africa' (2006) 22 *South Africa Journal of Human Rights* 673–717, 712.

138 See C. Heyns, 'Where is the voice of Africa in our Constitution?', Centre for Human Rights, Pretoria, Occasional Paper 8. He cites the Constitutions of Algeria (Article 60), Cape Verde (Article 80(2)), Congo (Article 56), Ghana (Article 41), Sao Tomé e Principe (Article 20), Sierra Leone (Article 13(e)), Tanzania (Articles 29(5), 30(1) and (2) and Zimbabwe (Article 11).

139 See C. Heyns and W. Kaguongo, 'Constitutional Human Rights Law in Africa' (2002) 22 *South African Journal of Human Rights*.

The criticisms levelled against the notion of duties in the African Charter are sometimes perceived as overstated. Proceeding from the premise that the duties provisions are a rather unique dimension of the Charter, entrenching positive African cultural and traditional values which existed in pre-colonial Africa and which complement rights, arguments have been made that any perceived weaknesses of the Charter provisions are not fatal. Okoth-Ogenda argues that it is not always correct to speak against the duties enlisted in the African Charter because in most cases 'the state is the villain against which human rights law is the effective law' and it is towards this villainous state only that 'individuals should not be called upon to discharge any duties.'[140] The despotic rule of some dictators, or misguided political leaders who misuse old traditions to justify their oppressive/suppressive measures in violation of individual rights, should not be the reason for uniformly denouncing the entire set of rights and duties under the Banjul Charter. Pityana argues that, far from seeing duties as creating an environment allowing a gratuitous interference with rights, these duties should be understood as reinforcing rights.[141] To claim that the African system is weak is one thing. It is quite another to dismiss it as totally unworkable. To do so, as Odinkalu puts it, would be 'ill informed, ignorant or both.'[142] Elsewhere, Odinkalu posits that any dismissive view of the African Charter system can even justifiably be said to be clouded by a taint of afro-pessimism.[143] On balance, however, the weaknesses of the African Charter provisions, especially with regard to individual duties, are well-acknowledged, and it would be totally unjustified to pretend that this is an issue of little consequence.

4. CONCLUSION

It is evident from what has been reflected in this contribution that there are certain sterling qualities that the Banjul Charter possesses. Possibly the most innovative feature of the Charter is the insertion of the rights and duties in one human rights document, and the fact that they were made complementary to each other. The human rights approach which at least attempts to reconcile duties and rights could

140 H. Okoth-Ogenda, 'Human Rights in Africa: what point is African trying to make?', in R. Cohen *et al.*, *Human Rights and Governance in Africa*, Gainesville: University Press of Florida, 1993, p. 79.

141 N.B. Pityana 'The Challenges of Culture for Human Rights in Africa: The African Charter in a comparative context', in M.D. Evans and R. Murray (eds.), *The African Charter on Human and Peoples' Rights: The system in practice, 1986–2000*, Cambridge: Cambridge University Press, 2002.

142 C.A. Odinkalu, 'Individual Complaints Procedure of the African Commission on Human and Peoples' Rights: A Preliminary Assessment' (1988) 8 *Transnational Law and Contemporary Problems* 359, 402.

143 C.A. Odinkalu, 'Analysis of Paralysis or Paralysis by Analysis? Implementing Economic, Social and Cultural Rights under the African Charter on Human and Peoples' Rights' (2001) 23 *Human Rights Quarterly* 327.

perhaps, as Mutua wishes, provide 'a new basis for individual identification with compatriots, the community, and the State.' This way '[i]t could forge and instill a national consciousness and act as the glue to reunite individuals and different nations within the modern State, and at the same time set the proper limits of conduct by State officials.'[144] The Charter clearly implies that without certain duties towards the state, the community and one's family, individual rights will become completely muffled. The basic belief that rights cannot function in a vacuum, created by the absence of social and political duties, makes this Charter very unique and different from any other international human rights treaty. Yet the Banjul Charter is also exceptional in the sense that it managed to move away from the normal narrow formulations of rights in international and regional human rights treaties and that it includes all three 'generations' of rights.

A review of the concept of rights and duties as outlined in the African Charter, however, reveals beyond doubt that there are issues both as regards the conception and formulation of these rights and duties which should cause concern. The verbiage in many parts of the African Charter appears significantly flawed and quite incomprehensible. For example, if one looks at Article 18, the Charter makes it a duty for the state to 'assist the family which is the custodian of morals and traditional values recognized by the community.' It equally imposes a duty on the African individual under Article 29 to promote and protect positive aspects of African culture and morals. Yet nowhere does the Charter clarify what these specified moral and traditional values that the state has to protect are. This makes it difficult for the state to interpret the unstated part, and to create measures to be able to fulfil this particular duty. The absence of clarity, especially when the Banjul Charter outlines duties to be performed by both the state and the individual, may lead to a misconception that provisions on duties impose only a non-binding form of obligation. In combination with the other weaknesses, i.e. the lack of certain rights and vague formulation of others, and the existence of clawback provisions, these duties could be misused to justify unwarranted infringements of individuals' rights. The other institutions of the African human rights system have a role to play in clarifying the scope of both rights and duties.

The Banjul Charter's insistence on observing and preserving African tradition and culture is capable of sending mixed signals as to the real intention, at face value, of the Charter. Taken to extremes, this insistence on African culture and traditions can cause serious disharmony to the universality of human rights, and may be used to perpetuate values that may undermine human dignity. It could also cause undue contradictions between some rights. More importantly, the mistaken claim that certain things are African and other are not, may well be based on an essentialist assumption that African is a homogeneous entity and also that African culture and tradition are static. The reality, however, is that Africa is

144 M. Mutua, *Human Rights. A political and Cultural Critique*, Philadelphia: University of Pennsylvania Press, 2002, p. 369.

an elaborate mosaic of traditions and cultures which are forever changing. Thus, the pleonasm of the Charter with respect to rights and duties may give the wrong impression of sanctioning some violations of rights.

Most of the Charter duties directed at the individual are of a general nature and seem to be more of a moral sermon with an advisory tone than intended to have legal consequences. There are no clear definitions of the terms used, nor are there any clarifications on what some of the enlisted duties expect the individual and the state to do. This again is capable of spelling confusion for the state as to what it should do when the duties are directed not at the state itself, but at an individual.

One is inclined to agree with Mutua that a valid criticism of the language of duties should focus on their precise meaning, content, conditions of compliance and application. In this sense, more needs to be done in terms of clarifying the status of the duties in the Charter, as well as establishing their moral and legal dimensions and implications for enforcement.[145] The shortcomings in the language employed in the Charter are seen throughout the Charter in the rights and duties chapter of the Charter and are consistently present in the chapters that deal with the mandate and functioning of the African Commission.

On the whole, however, the duties included in the Banjul Charter represent a unique attempt to complement the international human rights framework based on traditional African thought, in a way which may eventually also be an inspiration to the global human rights framework and to other regions. As such, these duties can be considered as 'an embodiment of the positive dimension of African cultural philosophy, which the Charter tries to codify for the benefit of posterity.'[146] If it could achieve even a fraction of these ambitions in the future, the Banjul Charter would truly become an example for – and a unique complement to – the international human rights framework. Until then, the document surely can be a source of inspiration as to how to reconceptualise our contemporary notion of human rights even if, at least from a legal perspective, some caution regarding potential abuses will remain necessary.

---

145 M. Mutua, 'The African human rights system in a comparative perspective: The need for urgent reformulation' (1993) 5 *Legal Affairs* 7.

146 V.O. Orlu Nmehielle, *The African Human Rights System. Its Laws, Practice, and Institutions*, The Hague: Martinus Nijhoff Publishers, 2001, p. 165.

DECLARATION OF HUMAN DUTIES AND RESPONSIBILITIES

ADOPTED BY A HIGH-LEVEL GROUP CHAIRED BY RICHARD J. GOLDSTONE UNDER THE AUSPICES OF THE CITY OF VALENCIA AND UNESCO INITIATED AND ORGANISED BY THE VALENCIA THIRD MILLENNIUM FOUNDATION, 1998

Preamble

The High-Level Group,

Reaffirming that respect for the dignity and equal rights of all human beings as enshrined in the Universal Declaration of Human Rights is the inalienable foundation for peace, democracy, human security, freedom, justice and development in the world,

Reiterating the universal significance, global reach and indivisibility of the rights enunciated in the Universal Declaration of Human Rights, the International Covenant on Civil and Political Rights and the International Covenant on Economic, Social and Cultural Rights and other international human rights instruments,

Concerned that, fifty years after the adoption of the Universal Declaration of Human Rights, and subsequent to the adoption of other human rights instruments, disregard and gross violations of human rights and fundamental freedoms continue to outrage the conscience of humankind,

Aware that the effective enjoyment and implementation of human rights and fundamental freedoms is inextricably linked to the assumption of the duties and responsibilities implicit in those rights,

Reaffirming that States, both in their individual capacity and as the constituent members of inter-governmental organisations, continue to exercise the primary duty and responsibility for the promotion and enforcement of human rights and fundamental freedoms,

Recognising the important contribution that non-governmental organisations, citizen associations and human rights defenders have made and continue to make to the promotion and protection of human rights and fundamental freedoms,

Conscious of the increasing power and influence exercised by private and public corporations in the global order,

Recognising that all collectives within the global community are composed of individuals and that individuals share an obligation to respect, promote and implement human rights and fundamental freedoms,

Recalling that Article 29 of the Universal Declaration of Human Rights recognises that individuals have duties and responsibilities towards their communities, and therefore

*E*mphasising that the assumption of the duties and responsibilities implicit in human rights and fundamental freedoms rests upon all members of the global community, including States, international, regional and sub-regional inter-governmental organisations, the private and public sectors, non-governmental organisations, citizen associations, other representatives of civil society as well as all individual members of the human family,

*S*tressing the significant relationship between the effective implementation of human rights and fundamental freedoms, human security, a healthy and stable environment, the freedom of the media and the arts, and a culture of peace, and therefore

*R*eaffirming that respect for human rights, fundamental freedoms and the rule of law, the meeting of basic human needs through the principle of sustainable human development, promotion of a healthy and stable environment, and the achievement of social equity are as important to global peace and human security as are collective security arrangements and disarmament,

*C*oncerned by the great disparities in wealth, socio-economic, scientific and technological development between economically more endowed States and economically less endowed States, as well as their uneven participation and roles in global decision-making,

*R*ecognising that international co-operation, broad based participation and the equitable sharing of resources and the benefits of scientific and technological progress are all necessary for the achievement of an equitable global order in which human rights, fundamental freedoms, the meeting of basic human needs and the security of all humankind can be achieved,

*M*indful that new and evolving local, national, sub-regional, regional and global mechanisms will be required to implement and enforce human rights, fundamental freedoms and human security in all circumstances,

*R*ecognising the changes that new technologies, scientific development and the process of globalisation have brought about, and aware of the need to address their impact upon and potential consequences for human rights and fundamental freedoms,

*B*earing in mind that managing globalisation requires equitable global and regional solutions based on the precepts of both joint and individual responsibility and solidarity,

*R*ecognising the contribution of all cultures, traditions and civilisations within the framework of universal and indivisible human rights and fundamental freedoms,

*A*ffirming that there is an abiding responsibility to promote and protect diversity in the human family and to respect the rights of minorities,

*F*urther recognising that the rights and identity of indigenous peoples of the world, in particular in relation to their culture, traditions and relationship to their lands, must be upheld,

*S*tressing that women's rights are human rights and that substantive equality must be achieved for women in every aspect of national and international life and that effective steps must be taken to eradicate violence against women in all its manifestations,

*A*sserting the special and conscious need to protect and enforce the rights of the child, the elderly and those suffering from a physical or mental disability,

*C*onvinced of the need for all members of the human family to strive for the realisation of human rights and fundamental freedoms enshrined in the Universal Declaration of Human Rights, the International Covenant on Civil and Political Rights and the

International Covenant on Economic, Social and Cultural Rights and other international human rights instruments,

Hereby adopts the text of a Declaration of Human Duties and Responsibilities, and

*R*equests its Chairman, Justice Richard J. Goldstone, to present it to the Director-General of the United Nations Educational, Scientific and Cultural Organisation (UNESCO).

Chapter 1
General Provisions

Article 1
Definition of Duties and Responsibilities

For the purposes of this Declaration, unless the context indicates otherwise:

(a) "duty" means an ethical or moral obligation;

(b) "responsibility" means an obligation that is legally binding under existing international law;

(c) "global community" means States – including their governments, legislatures and judicial institutions –, international, regional and sub-regional intergovernmental organisations, non-governmental organisations, public and private sector corporations, including transnational corporations, other entities of civil society, peoples, communities and individuals taken as a collective.

Article 2
Bearers of Duties and Responsibilities

1 Members of the global community have collective, as well as individual duties and responsibilities, to promote universal respect for and observance of human rights and fundamental freedoms.

2 States have a duty and a responsibility to adopt all legislative, administrative, policy and other steps necessary to ensure respect, and to enforce and proactively promote, within their territory or under their jurisdiction, human rights and fundamental freedoms in all circumstances, including situations of armed conflict.

3 States have a further duty to take appropriate action, within the framework of the principles of international law, to promote the implementation of the human rights and freedoms of all humankind in all circumstances, including situations of armed conflict.

4 Competent inter-governmental organisations have a duty, in accordance with their mandates, to promote awareness of and to respect human rights and fundamental freedoms; to monitor compliance by States and other entities with a responsibility to respect and enforce human rights and fundamental freedoms; to assist States in the implementation of human rights and fundamental freedoms, and to use advocacy to help enforce human rights and fundamental freedoms.

5 Relevant non-governmental organisations have a duty to respect and promote, as best they are able, awareness of human rights and fundamental freedoms; to monitor compliance by States and other entities; to assist States and inter-governmental

organisations in the monitoring and implementation of human rights and fundamental freedoms; and to use advocacy to help enforce human rights and fundamental freedoms.

6 Public and private corporations, especially transnational corporations, have a duty to respect, promote and implement human rights and fundamental freedoms in all spheres of their activities.

7 As the holders of human rights and fundamental freedoms, all individuals, peoples and communities in the exercise of their rights and freedoms, have the duty and responsibility to respect those of others, and a duty to strive for the promotion and observance thereof.

Chapter 2
The Right to Life and Human Security

Article 3
The Duty and Responsibility to Protect Life and Ensure the Survival of Both Present and Future Generations

1 Members of the global community have collective, as well as individual duties and responsibilities, to take appropriate action to protect the right to life of every member of the human family, and shall ensure the survival of present and future generations -unencumbered by war and violent conflict, gross and systematic human rights violations, extreme poverty, hunger, disease and environmental destruction.

2 States have the primary duty and responsibility to respect and ensure the right to life of all within their territory and under their jurisdiction. In accordance with this duty and responsibility States shall take all necessary measures to prevent the deprivation of life by the State and its officials, and shall take positive and effective measures to protect and enforce the right to life.

3 Individuals and non-State actors have a duty and a responsibility to respect life, and have a duty to take reasonable steps to help others whose lives are threatened, or who are in extreme distress or need.

Article 4
The Duty and Responsibility to Promote Collective Security and a Culture of Peace

1 Members of the global community have collective, as well as individual duties and responsibilities, to promote a culture of peace by taking appropriate action to prevent war and foster international peace, collective security and co-operation.

2 States have a duty and a responsibility to refrain from acts of war, aggression, the use of force or the threat of force in their international relations in accordance with the Charter of the United Nations, and have a duty and a responsibility to promote global security through collective security arrangements and mechanisms established in accordance with the United Nations Charter.

3 Competent inter-governmental organisations have a duty and responsibility to promote conflict prevention and promote peaceful means of resolving inter-State and intra-State conflicts or disputes in accordance with the Charter of the United Nations. In particular, the Security Council of the United Nations has a duty and a responsibility to

set up a standing peacekeeping force as provided for in Chapter 7 of the United Nations Charter. Regional and sub-regional entities endowed with the necessary powers should be encouraged to enhance their peacekeeping capabilities and play an active peacekeeping role in their regions.

4 States have a duty to build and/or enhance mediation, conflict prevention and post-conflict peace-building mechanisms and should contribute to and strengthen local, sub-regional, regional and international conflict resolution and peacekeeping capacities.

5 States, competent inter-governmental organisations, and relevant non-governmental organisations and other entities of civil society have a duty to promote a culture of peace by encouraging people, especially children and young people to establish friendly relations with other peoples, and to educate them in methods for the peaceful resolution of conflicts.

Article 5

The Duty to Promote Disarmament in the Interests of Peace

1 Members of the global community have collective, as well as individual duties and responsibilities, to take appropriate action to promote rapid and effective disarmament in the interests of peace.

2 States have a duty to reduce military expenditure in order to increase the resources available for human development, and should actively reorient the composition and role of their military establishments towards professional armies mandated with greater peacekeeping, peace-building and civic responsibilities.

3 States and non-State actors have a duty, and in accordance with emerging norms of international law, a responsibility, to promote and carry out effective nuclear disarmament under strict international controls with a view to the total elimination of nuclear weapons.

4 States and non-State actors have a duty, and a responsibility, to cease the development, improvement, production, procurement, proliferation, and use of all chemical and biological weapons and other weapons of mass destruction, and shall destroy all such weapons under strict international controls.

5 States and non-State actors have a duty, and in accordance with emerging norms of international law, a responsibility, to cease the development, production, procurement and use of landmines and should destroy all stockpiles of landmines.

6 States have a duty to exercise restraint in the production and stockpiling of conventional weapons, including small arms. In accordance with this duty, States should ensure that their production and acquisition of arms do not exceed their legitimate self-defence and security requirements.

7 States have a duty to maintain strict legal and physical controls over the trade and transfer of conventional weapons and weapons related technology. Such controls should ensure that:

(a) no conventional weapons are traded/transferred in violation of international law;

(b) no conventional weapons are traded/transferred in circumstances where the trade/transfer of weapons will endanger peace, security and stability, or stimulate local arms races, or prolong ongoing wars;

(c) no conventional weapons are traded or transferred to recipients who support or carry out terrorism;

(d) no conventional weapons are traded or transferred to recipients responsible for human rights violations, or in circumstances where the acquisition of weapons may contribute to human rights violations;

(e) no conventional weapons are traded or transferred to persons who participate in armed conflicts for private gain;

(f) no conventional weapons fall into the hands of unauthorised recipients or contribute to the illegal trade/transfer of weapons.

8 States have a duty to participate in the United Nations Register of Conventional Arms and to generally promote transparency with respect to conventional weapons transfers at both the international and the national levels. In accordance with this duty States should enhance the capacity of competent international organisations and relevant non-governmental organisations to monitor arms transfers.

9 Individuals and non-State actors have a duty and a responsibility to cease any participation or involvement in the illegal trade of conventional weapons, and shall strictly comply with national and international laws regulating the development, production, possession, procurement, stockpiling, trade and use of conventional weapons.

10 The global community has a duty and responsibility to prevent the establishment and activities of mercenaries and private military organisations.

11 Competent international, regional and sub-regional intergovernmental organisations or agencies have a duty to take all steps within their powers to advocate, monitor and enforce State compliance with their duties and responsibilities towards disarmament and arms control.

Article 6

The Duty to Intervene to Prevent Gross Human Rights Violations

1 Members of the global community have collective, as well as individual duties and responsibilities, to take appropriate action to prevent the commission of genocide, crimes against humanity, war crimes and other gross or systematic human rights abuses in all circumstances, including situations of armed conflict.

2 States have the primary duty and responsibility for the prevention of gross and systematic human rights abuses and for punishing such conduct. In accordance with this duty States should implement, in conjunction with competent inter-governmental organisations and relevant non-governmental organisations, effective, transparent and reliable early warning mechanisms.

3 Where individual States fail to act effectively to prevent the commission of gross or systematic human rights abuses, other States have a collective duty to intervene, after due warning has been given, or to support appropriate intervention, irrespective of considerations of national sovereignty, to prevent or stop such abuses.

4 The United Nations Security Council, under the United Nations Charter, has primary responsibility in this regard and should fulfill its responsibility in accordance with Chapter 7 of the United Nations Charter to establish a standing peacekeeping force which could be used for such purposes. Regional or sub-regional entities endowed with necessary powers should regard themselves as guardians of human rights in their regions, and should carry out such interventions as are necessary if gross human rights violations

occur. For that purpose, these entities should be supported by the global community, in particular through the provision of requisite resources.

Article 7

The Duty and Responsibility to Respect International Humanitarian Law during Times of Armed Conflict

1 Parties to an armed conflict have a duty and a responsibility to respect international humanitarian law unconditionally and in all circumstances, whether in the course of an international or an internal armed conflict. In particular, government forces and insurgents, military or paramilitary forces, have an obligation to refrain from committing:

(a) acts of genocide;

(b) crimes against humanity;

(c) war crimes such as

(i) mass killings, torture or other forms of cruel, inhuman or degrading treatment or punishment;

(ii) hostage-taking, rape and other forms of sexual violence against women and children;

(iii) forced and illegal displacement of people, such as ethnic cleansing;

(iv) indiscriminate attacks against civilians;

(v) denying elementary humanitarian assistance to the civilian population;

(vi) using child soldiers; and

(vii) non-respect of the elementary rights of persons in occupied territories.

2 Parties to an armed conflict have a duty and a responsibility to authorise humanitarian relief for persons in need, and to grant humanitarian relief organisations access to affected areas and to ensure the safety of their personnel.

3 States have a duty and a responsibility to disseminate international humanitarian law, in particular to the armed forces and the police, and to ensure that its violations, in particular war crimes, are prosecuted, and that the perpetrators of such crimes are punished.

Article 8

The Duty and Responsibility of Humanitarian Assistance and Intervention

1 Members of the global community have collective, as well as individual duties and responsibilities, to take appropriate action, without discrimination, to ensure the right to life, through the provision of food, shelter, health care and other essential requirements for survival, of refugees and internally displaced people fleeing war, internal conflict, gross human rights abuses and other human made or natural disasters.

2 The primary duty and responsibility to provide humanitarian assistance to those in need lies with States, and in the case of internal armed conflicts where insurgents exercise control over territory, with such insurgents. In carrying out that duty and responsibility States and insurgents should facilitate the involvement and assistance of recognised and competent inter-governmental and non-governmental organisations.

3 Competent inter-governmental organisations have a duty to provide humanitarian assistance to populations under the control of States or insurgents on whose territory there are large refugee populations or internally displaced people.

4 To the extent that they are able, relevant non-governmental organisations have a duty to assist in the provision of humanitarian assistance.

5 Inter-governmental and non-governmental organisations have a duty to carry out their mandates effectively based on the best available assessment. To this end, all such agencies should, where appropriate, co-operate and co-ordinate their activities.

6 Where a State or insurgent fails to provide humanitarian assistance to internally displaced people or refugees, other States have a collective duty to support appropriate intervention to provide such assistance. The United Nations Security Council, under the United Nations Charter, has primary responsibility in such instances. Regional or sub-regional entities endowed with necessary powers have a duty to play a role in their respective regions and should be encouraged and empowered to do so by the global community.

Article 9

The Duty and Responsibility to Protect and Promote a Safe, Stable and Healthy Environment

1 Members of the global community have collective, as well as individual duties and responsibilities, to respect, protect and preserve the uniqueness and diversity of all forms of life, and to preserve and promote an environment suitable for sustaining all forms of life.

2 To this end:

(a) States, relevant non-State actors, including the private sector, and individuals have a duty to protect and preserve the stability and quality of the global, regional and local environment and to utilise natural resources in a manner which ensures the preservation and protection of bio-diversity.

(b) States, relevant non-State actors, including the private sector, and individuals have a duty to conserve natural resources and to prevent the degradation and destruction of the environment through misuse and excessive exploitation and consumption.

(c) States, inter-governmental organisations, all other relevant non-State actors, including the private sector, and individuals have a duty to provide for and promote a free flow of basic scientific information about the environment, and shall promote and enable research and analysis necessary for the development of appropriate new methods and models for the preservation and promotion of a safe, stable and healthy environment.

Chapter 3
Human Security and an Equitable International Order

Article 10

The Duty and Responsibility to Promote an Equitable International Order

1 Members of the global community have collective, as well as individual duties and responsibilities, to take appropriate action to promote an equitable international order in which all States, peoples and individuals can enjoy sustainable human, economic, social,

cultural, political, scientific and technological development and can participate equitably in international institutions and decision-making processes.

2 States have the primary duty and responsibility for the economic, social, cultural and political development of their peoples and to this end shall pursue economic and social policies designed to achieve sustainable human development and well-being as well as economic and financial stability.

3 States have a duty and responsibility to recognize the interdependence of all States in a global community and shall avoid any measure which may cause substantial injury or harm to other States.

4 States have a duty to take appropriate steps in co-operation with relevant international organisations to prevent public or private manipulation of national, regional or global markets to the prejudice of the stability of States.

5 To overcome extreme poverty and to achieve higher levels of economic and social justice, economically more endowed States have a duty to contribute to the economic and social development of lesser endowed States. International financial and development organisations have a like duty to contribute.

6 Economic policies and development should not be pursued at the expense of human rights or social development. The promotion of human rights, and in particular the rights and interests of those most disadvantaged sectors of the population, including those living in extreme poverty, children, women and rural communities, shall form an integral part of the planning and implementation of economic, monetary and fiscal policies by all States, governmental, inter-governmental organisations and non-governmental organisations.

7 Economic and social development shall not be pursued at the expense of the environment and natural resources. The principle of sustainable human development, whereby the priorities of development are guided by the need to preserve the environment, conserve resources and protect the interests and options of future generations, should form an integral part of the planning and implementation of economic and social development policies by all States, inter-governmental, non-governmental organisations, public and private corporations and any other relevant non-state actors.

8 As sovereign and equal members of the international community, all States have the right to participate fully, equitably and effectively in international and global institutions and decision-making processes and they must be afforded equal opportunities to do so.

Article 11

The Duty to Alleviate Usurious Debt

1 Members of the global community have collective, as well as individual duties and responsibilities, to ensure that levels of debt and interest payments by States do not reach usurious levels which grossly exceed their repayment capacity and which endanger human lives and impede economic and social development.

2 For their part, debtor nations have a duty and responsibility to adopt and pursue policies in accordance with the highest standards of efficiency, social equity and integrity.

Article 12

The Duty and Responsibility to Promote Safe, Responsible and Equitable Scientific and Technological Development

1 Members of the global community have collective, as well as individual duties and responsibilities, to promote responsible scientific and technological development for the equal benefit of all humankind.

2 States have the primary duty to promote their own scientific and technological development for the benefit and upliftment of their peoples.

3 Scientifically and technologically more advanced States, and competent inter-governmental organisations, have a duty to contribute to the strengthening and development of the scientific and technological capacity of lesser scientifically advanced States.

4 States have a duty to cooperate at the international level to promote a free flow and equitable sharing of scientific and technological information and knowledge. Such cooperation should ensure a balance between national and individual interests and the need to establish equitable global access to technological developments and scientific knowledge.

5 States have a duty to regulate scientific and technological research activities conducted within their jurisdiction in order to ensure that the results of such research are not used for the purpose of threatening peace and security, or in a manner which infringes upon human rights and fundamental freedoms.

6 The research and scientific communities have a duty to act with full respect for the life and welfare of every human being and to take all necessary measures, including the adoption of a code of ethics, to prevent the results of scientific and technological research being used for the purpose of threatening peace and security, or in a manner which infringes upon human rights and fundamental freedoms.

7 Individual researchers and scientists have a duty at all times to conduct their research in accordance with strict ethical practices and to inform the public of any unethical or potentially dangerous research of which they become aware.

Article 13

The Duties and Responsibilities of Public and Private Sector Corporations

1 Private and public corporations have a duty and a responsibility to respect the sovereignty of the host State in which they conduct business and shall comply with the laws of host States, unless those laws constitute an infringement of human rights and fundamental freedoms, including universally accepted labour standards.

2 Private and public corporations have a duty to contribute to the development and capacity development of host communities through training and empowerment, provision and transfer of technology, fair sharing or other appropriate measures.

3 Private and public corporations have a duty to respect and promote the enforcement of human rights and fundamental freedoms within their spheres of influence, and should adhere to universally accepted labour standards, in particular those concerning the use of universally condemned forms of exploitation, including the exploitation of children, women, enforced labour and discrimination.

4 Private and public corporations have a duty to adhere to and enforce sound environmental management and conservation measures. Such corporations should ensure meaningful and transparent consultations with all those who might be affected by their activities and provide full and timely disclosure of all relevant information.

5 Private and public corporations have a duty to ensure that the activities of contractors, suppliers and distributors are consistent with the principles referred to in paragraphs 3 and 4 above.

Article 14

The Duty and Responsibility to Prevent and Punish International and Organised Crime

1 Members of the global community have collective, as well as individual duties and responsibilities, to take appropriate action to prevent, punish and eradicate international crime.

2 States have a duty to take effective steps to prevent, investigate, and prosecute international crimes or crimes which have international implications. Such steps should include:

(a) co-operating with one another or with international law enforcement agencies in the combating of international crimes, transnational crimes and organised crime;

(b) where, in accordance with international law a State has jurisdiction, prosecuting or extraditing persons responsible for committing international crimes,

(c) co-operating with and assisting international criminal tribunals.

3 Competent intergovernmental organisations, non-governmental organisations and, where appropriate, other non-State actors have a duty to cooperate with and assist States and international criminal tribunals in the prevention, investigation and prosecution of international crimes, transnational and organised crime.

4 Individuals and non-State actors have a duty and responsibility not to condone, support or participate in any manner in the commission of crime, and where appropriate, have a duty and responsibility to co-operate with and assist governments or international criminal tribunals in the prevention, investigation, or prosecution of crime.

5 All States have a duty to ratify or accede to the Convention establishing the Permanent International Criminal Court and the global community has a duty to support the establishment, effective operations and activities of the Court.

Article 15

The Duty and Responsibility to Eradicate Corruption and Build an Ethical Society

1 Members of the global community have collective, as well as individual duties and responsibilities, to promote an ethical society free from endemic corruption.

2 States have a duty to take effective measures to prevent, detect, punish and eradicate corruption in both the public and private sectors. Such measures should include:

(a) implementing codes of conduct for all public officials, and proper systems of control within organs of state and public institutions;

(b) implementing training programmes designed to educate public officials about their duties and responsibilities as public officials;

(c) establishing effective independent mechanisms to enforce accountability and transparency within public institutions and by public officials, including the establishment of an ombudsperson and auditor-general;

(d) providing protection for those providing evidence of corruption in the public and private sectors;

(e) criminalising corruption, and providing effective penal and civil remedies;

(f) promoting public awareness of the harm caused by corruption and providing for complaints procedures which are both effective and which adequately protect the complainants.

3 States have a duty to promote and establish mechanisms for the effective participation of civil society in efforts to eradicate corruption. In particular, they should encourage public discussion of ethical issues involving government, political parties and civil society, including the media and relevant non-governmental organisations.

4 States have a duty to cooperate and coordinate at the international level to prevent, detect, punish and eradicate corruption. In particular, they have a duty to provide assistance for the effective tracing, freezing and seizing of property illicitly acquired by public officials from other states.

5 Private sector organisations have a duty, in partnership with government, to develop an ethical commercial environment designed to ensure open and fair competition. They have a duty to refrain from participating in, promoting or condoning any corrupt or restrictive business practices.

6 Intergovernmental organisations and non-governmental organisations have a duty to act accountably and should refrain from promoting or condoning any corrupt practices. They also should ensure the integrity of their own projects.

7 Civil society, including relevant non-governmental organisations and individuals, have a duty to promote awareness about the importance of containing corruption and of the harm that it inflicts on the lives of all, governance and sustainable human development. All have a duty to expose corruption in both the public and private sectors.

Chapter 4
Meaningful Participation in Public Affairs

Article 16
The Duty and Responsibility to Ensure Meaningful Participation in Public Affairs

1 Members of the global community have collective, as well as individual duties and responsibilities, to take appropriate action to respect, promote and ensure the right of individuals to meaningfully participate in local, national and global governance, and to ensure that the authority of government is based upon the will of the people and the rule of law.

2 States have the primary duty and responsibility to take measures to ensure the right to meaningful participation in governance. Such measures shall include:

(a) ensuring the right of citizens to vote in periodic, genuine and free local and national elections based on universal and equal suffrage and a secret ballot. In particular States have a duty to ensure that there is a level playing field for all political parties during the run up to elections and during elections; that there are adequate controls over the financing of political campaigns so as to prevent any unfair influence by the public or private sector or any other interest group; that voters are free from intimidation and harassment, and that there are adequate and effective judicial remedies for any complaints concerning the freeness and fairness of elections. Where necessary States should establish independent electoral commissions charged with the duty of ensuring the freeness and fairness of elections;

(b) ensuring equal access to the public service, information and a free and independent media;

(c) wherever possible and appropriate, encouraging active participation by civil society in governance.

3 Competent intergovernmental and relevant non-governmental organisations have a duty, in full respect of the principle of state sovereignty, to promote and assist the development of participatory governance at all levels of society. In particular, they should work with States to ensure that elections are free, fair and transparent and should promote active participation by civil society at all levels of governance.

4 Individuals have a duty to participate in public affairs.

Chapter 5
Freedom of Opinion, Expression, Assembly, Association and Religion

Article 17
The Duty and Responsibility to Respect and Ensure Freedom of Opinion, Expression, and the Media

1 Members of the global community have collective, as well as individual duties and responsibilities, to respect, protect and ensure freedom of opinion and expression and a free and independent media, all of which are necessary for the protection and promotion of democratic values and pluralism, and in the fight against corruption, abuse of power and other threats to human rights and fundamental freedoms. This duty is based on underlying universal values and responsibilities. In particular, there is a duty and a responsibility to:

(a) ensure that the pursuit of truth is unhindered. This applies equally to information and communications technologies;

(b) ensure that citizens have accurate and unbiased information that will enable them to participate effectively in decision-making;

(c) avoid any degrading treatment of individuals and the presentation of violence as entertainment;

(d) protect individual self-fulfillment, autonomy and privacy.

2 The media and journalists have a duty to report honestly and accurately and to avoid incitement of racial, ethnic or religious violence or hatred.

Article 18
Duties and Responsibilities Concerning Information and Communications Technologies

1 Members of the global community have collective, as well as individual duties and responsibilities, to ensure universal access to basic communication and information

infrastructure and services that will enable all States and members of civil society to access data, information and knowledge and to engage in networking activities.

2 States and the private sector have a duty to promote the fulfillment of the potential of information and communications technologies by providing equitable and affordable access to a wide range of communication media and by ensuring the open flow of information among all individuals and institutions.

3 States and the private sector have the duty to ensure a range of means for individuals and institutions to engage in civic dialogues and to obtain the education and skills necessary for participation in the information society.

4 States have a duty to prevent any misuse of these communications technologies and systems, especially as regards the propagation of hate and of material compromising the well-being of children.

5 States have the duty to take measures to protect communications security, privacy and reliability.

6 States, civil society, private corporations and individuals have a duty:

(a) to establish, access and use available information systems and services in ways that do not result in harm to that system or its users;

(b) to make use of the systems and services in ways that are consistent with the common good;

(c) to foster truthfulness and honest disclosure;

(d) to respect the rights of others to dissent.

7 States, the private sector and other relevant actors of civil society have the duty to collect only information concerning individuals when relevant, necessary and socially acceptable. Whenever possible, such information should be collected directly from the individual concerned, otherwise information collectors have the duty and responsibility to operate in a transparent manner and to apprise the individuals concerned with a notice of information collection practices.

8 Information collectors have the duty to provide individuals, upon request, with a copy of any information gathered concerning those individuals. They also have the duty to assure the accuracy and security of the information gathered, including allowing individuals to see and correct their personal data.

9 States have a duty to establish rules about the collection, maintenance, use, disclosure and correction of information together with suitable mechanisms to implement those rules, such as administrative processes, professional standards, civil actions, criminal penalties, ombudspersons and other means.

10 The global community has a duty to set rules providing for the sharing of innovation and patents relevant for the creation, establishment and operation of information systems and services based on an equitable intellectual property regime.

11 The global community has a duty to design equitable rules and arrangements governing the access to and use of cyberspace.

Article 19

The Duty and Responsibility to Respect and Ensure Freedom of Assembly and Association

States have a duty and a responsibility to take all necessary steps to ensure the substantive realisation of the rights to free assembly and freedom of association.

Article 20

The Duty and Responsibility to Respect and Ensure Freedom of Religion, Belief and Conscience

1 Members of the global community have collective, as well as individual duties, to take appropriate action to respect, protect and ensure freedom of religion, belief and conscience.

2 States have the primary duty and responsibility to respect, protect and ensure the freedom of religion, belief and conscience of all within their territory or under their jurisdiction. In accordance with this duty and responsibility States should:

(a) respect and ensure the right of all individuals to have and adopt, or not to have, a religion or belief of their choice;

(b) respect and ensure the right of individuals to manifest that religion or belief, in worship, observance, practice and teaching, either individually or in community with others, in private and in public.

3 Religious leaders have a duty to promote tolerance of and respect for other religions and their adherents, and have a duty and responsibility not to incite religious hatred or violence.

4 All religions and their adherents have a duty to exercise religious tolerance and have a duty and a responsibility to respect the rights of other religions or beliefs and their adherents or non-believers.

5 All religions and their adherents have a duty and responsibility to respect human rights and fundamental freedoms in the practice or manifestation of their religion.

Chapter 6
The Right to Personal and Physical Integrity

Article 21

The Duty and Responsibility to Respect and Ensure Physical and Personal Integrity

Members of the global community have collective, as well as individual duties and responsibilities, to take appropriate action to respect and ensure the physical, psychological and personal integrity of all members of the human family in all circumstances, including in situations of armed conflict.

Article 22

The Duty and Responsibility to Respect and Ensure the Right to Personal Liberty and Physical Security

1 States have the primary duty and responsibility to take all necessary measures to respect and ensure the rights to personal liberty and physical security of all within their territory or under their jurisdiction. Such measures should include:

(a) taking all necessary steps to prevent arbitrary arrest and detention by the State or its officials and ensuring that deprivations of liberty only take place in accordance with a law which is consistent with universally recognised grounds necessitating such deprivations;

(b) ensuring that all arrests and detentions by the State or sanctioned by the State are carried out in accordance with universally recognised standards of fairness and due process. In particular, anyone arrested or detained shall be promptly informed of the reasons for the arrest and detention, shall be entitled promptly to bring proceedings before a judicial officer to determine the lawfulness of the arrest or detention, and where charged with a criminal offence shall promptly be brought before a judicial officer, be entitled to apply for her/his release subject to reasonable conditions if the interests of justice permit, be entitled to legal assistance of her/his choice, and be entitled to a trial within a reasonable time;

(c) taking effective measures to protect and ensure the physical security of all persons within its jurisdiction.

Article 23

The Duty and Responsibility to Prohibit and Prevent Slavery and Institutions and Practices Similar to Slavery

1 States have the primary duty and responsibility to take all necessary measures to protect all within their territory or under their jurisdiction from, and to prevent, slavery and slave-like practices including child prostitution, child exploitation, enforced prostitution, debt bondage, serfdom, and other forms of enforced labour inconsistent with international law. Such measures should include:

(a) declaring criminal and punishing such practices;

(b) instituting effective controls at relevant points of entry to and exit from their territory, to prevent the illegal trafficking of persons;

(c) taking steps to cooperate at the sub-regional, regional and international levels to prevent and halt such practices, including cooperation between law enforcement agencies to dismantle national, regional and international networks in trafficking;

(d) instituting training programmes designed to create greater awareness concerning slavery-like practices amongst law enforcement officials and other relevant officials;

(e) creating greater public awareness through education and public programmes of the human rights abuses associated with such practices.

2 Individuals and non-State actors have a duty and a responsibility not to condone, support or in any manner participate in practices of slavery or slavery-like practices.

3 Competent inter-governmental organisations and relevant non-governmental organisations have a duty to monitor compliance by States with their duties and responsibilities to prevent and punish slavery and slavery like practices, and should promote public awareness of such practices.

Article 24

The Duty and Responsibility to Respect and Ensure Freedom from Torture, Cruel, Inhuman and Degrading Treatment or Punishment

1 States have the primary duty and responsibility to condemn torture and to take all necessary measures to prevent torture, cruel, inhuman and degrading treatment or punishment from being practised within their jurisdiction. Such measures should include:

(a) declaring criminal and punishing all acts of torture, cruel and inhuman and degrading treatment or punishment, whether by State officials, political movements or insurgents, other non-state actors or private persons with the acquiescence or complicity of the State, committed within their jurisdiction;

(b) enforcing strict controls over places and conditions of custody of persons deprived of their liberty and interrogation methods and practices;

(c) enforcing strict supervision of all law enforcement officials responsible for persons taken into State custody;

(d) ensuring that training programmes for all law enforcement personnel and other relevant public officials include adequate training concerning the prohibition of torture, cruel and inhuman and degrading treatment and punishment.

2 Individuals and non-State actors have a duty and a responsibility not to condone, support or participate in any manner in the commission of acts of torture, cruel and inhumane and degrading treatment or punishment.

3 Competent intergovernmental organisations and relevant non-governmental organisations have a duty to monitor the compliance by States with their duties and responsibilities to prohibit, prevent and punish torture and cruel and inhuman and degrading treatment, and have a duty to publicise and denounce all such treatment.

Article 25

The Duty and Responsibility to Prevent and Eradicate Enforced Disappearances

1 States have the primary duty and responsibility to condemn and to take all necessary measures to prevent forced disappearances from occurring within their territory. Such measures should include:

(a) declaring criminal and punishing all acts of forced disappearances committed within their territory or jurisdiction;

(b) ensuring that persons deprived of their liberty are only held in officially recognised places of detention, and that they have adequate access to judicial officers, legal representation, medical personnel and family members during the course of their detention;

(c) ensuring that a current register is kept of all persons taken into custody, and that the information contained therein is made available to all judicial authorities, legal representatives and family members concerned with the whereabouts of detained persons;

(d) ensuring strict supervision of all law enforcement personnel and other public officials responsible for persons taken into the custody of the State;

(e) taking steps to cooperate at the sub-regional, regional and international levels to prevent and halt the practice of forced disappearances.

2 Individuals and non-State actors have a duty and a responsibility not to condone, support or participate in any manner in the commission of enforced disappearances.

3 Competent inter-governmental and relevant non-governmental organisations have a duty to monitor States compliance with their duties and responsibilities to prohibit, prevent and punish disappearances, and have a duty to publicise and denounce such treatment.

Chapter 7
Equality

Article 26
The Duty to Respect and Ensure Equal Treatment and Non-Discrimination

Members of the global community have collective, as well as individual duties and responsibilities, to take appropriate action to respect, ensure and promote the right to equal treatment and to eradicate discrimination in all its forms.

Article 27
The Duty and Responsibility to Respect and Ensure Equality

States have the primary duty and responsibility to take adequate measures to respect and ensure the substantive equality of all persons within their territory or under their jurisdiction. Such measures should include:

(a) ensuring equality before the law for all and ensuring equal protection and benefit of the laws for all;

(b) not discriminating on the grounds of race, color, sex, age, gender, sexual orientation, language, religion, political or other opinion, national, ethnic or social origin, disability, property, birth or other similar such grounds;

(c) taking positive action to prevent direct or indirect discrimination by private persons, corporations or organisations in the sphere of employment, education and in relation to the right of access of any person to places or services intended for use by the general public, such as transport, hotels, restaurants, cafes, theatres and parks;

(d) taking positive action to promote the substantive equality of persons or groups of persons who continue to suffer the effects of past and present discrimination.

Article 28
The Duty and Responsibility to Ensure Racial and Religious Equality

In accordance with their duty and responsibility to ensure substantive racial and religious equality States should:

(a) ensure the effective enjoyment of all human rights and fundamental freedoms without discrimination on the basis of race, religion or ethnicity;

(b) take positive measures to:

(i) condemn all forms of racial and religious discrimination and respect racial, ethnic and religious diversity;

(ii) promote the adequate representation of racial, ethnic and religious groups suffering the effects of past and present discrimination at all levels of public and political life;

(iii) ensure equal opportunities for education for all racial, ethnic and religious groups;

(iv) promote the economic empowerment of racial, ethnic and religious groups suffering the effects of past and present discrimination;

(v) promote access to the mass media and information technology by all racial, ethnic and religious groups;

(vi) declare illegal and prohibit organisations and activities designed to promote racial, ethnic or religious violence or hatred.

Article 29

The Duty and Responsibility to Ensure Sex and Gender Equality

1 In accordance with their duty and responsibility to ensure sex and gender equality and the recognition of women's rights as human rights every State should:

(a) ensure the effective enjoyment of all human rights and fundamental freedoms without discrimination on the basis of sex or gender;

(b) take positive measures to:

(i) promote the equality of women in the representation and participation of women at all levels of public and political life;

(ii) condemn and eradicate cultural, religious and social practices which discriminate against women;

(iii) promote the economic empowerment of women;

(iv) ensure equal rights to property and inheritance for women;

(v) ensure the full legal capacity of women;

(vi) ensure equality with respect to marriage and its proprietary and personal consequences for women;

(vii) ensure the equal parental and guardianship rights of both women and men to their children;

(viii) ensure the protection of the reproductive rights and bodily integrity of all women;

(ix) promote the right to health of women, including equal access to healthcare;

(x) promote effective access to and participation by women in the mass media and the use of all forms of information technology;

(c) take effective measures to eradicate violence and abuse of women in all its forms. In particular States should:

(i) condemn all acts of violence or abuse of women in both times of peace and in situations of armed conflict;

(ii) refrain from any acts of violence against women and take effective measures to prevent, investigate and punish acts of violence or abuse perpetrated by the State or private persons;

(iii) provide women who have been subjected to violence or abuse adequate civil, administrative and penal remedies, including access to forensic medical procedures that are effective and provided in a manner which is sensitise to women victims;

(iv) ensure that the law enforcement process is sensitive to the needs of women victims of violence and abuse;

(v) ensure that law enforcement officials and other public officials responsible for the implementation of laws and policies to prevent, investigate and punish violence against and abuse of women receive adequate training to sensitize them to the needs of women victims;

(d) take effective measures to protect women against and punish acts or practices of slavery, enforced prostitution and other forms of sexual exploitation of women.

2 States and intergovernmental organisations have a duty to ensure equality in the representation and active participation of women in international organisations and international affairs.

3 Intergovernmental organisations have a duty to ensure that the promotion and implementation of the human rights of women are prioritised and addressed regularly and systematically by their relevant organs.

4 Relevant non-governmental organisations have a duty to create awareness of the human rights of women and issues affecting the rights of women, and should co-operate with States and inter-governmental organisations in the promotion and implementation of women's human rights.

Article 30

The Duty and Responsibility to Ensure the Equality of Persons with a Disability

1 In accordance with their duty to facilitate and encourage the substantive equality of persons with a disability States should:

(a) ensure the enjoyment and exercise of all human rights and fundamental freedoms without discrimination on the basis of disability;

(b) take positive measures to:

(i) ensure that persons with a disability have a right of effective participation in decisions at all levels of government which affect their rights or interests;

(ii) raise awareness through education and public awareness programs of the rights and needs of persons with a disability;

(iii) ensure the right to rehabilitation, adequate medical care and support services for persons with a disability;

(iv) take and enforce measures of reasonable accommodation to adapt the physical environment to the needs of persons with a disability;

(v) ensure equality in education for persons with a disability in an integrated schooling system, unless their specific needs require special schools;

(vi) ensure equality in employment opportunities for persons with a disability in both the public and private sectors;

(vii) ensure the right to dignity and physical and personal integrity of persons with a disability.

2 States and competent inter-governmental organisations have a duty to co-operate at the international level to contribute to the development and implementation of disability policy.

3 Competent intergovernmental organisations have a duty to ensure that the promotion and implementation of the human rights of persons with a disability are prioritised and addressed regularly and systematically by their relevant organs.

4 Relevant non-governmental organisations should assist governments and intergovernmental organisations with the development and implementation of disability policy and should help to promote awareness of the rights and needs of persons with a disability.

Chapter 8
Protection of Minorities and Indigenous Peoples

Article 31
The Duty and Responsibility to Respect and Protect the Rights of Minorities

1 Members of the global community have collective, as well as individual duties and responsibilities, to take appropriate action to respect and protect the existence, identity and rights of national, ethnic, religious and linguistic minorities.

2 States have the primary duty and responsibility to take measures to respect and protect the rights of national, ethnic, religious and linguistic minorities within their territory or under their jurisdiction. Such measures should include:

(a) respecting and protecting the right of such minorities to freely express, manifest, preserve and develop their cultural, religious, ethnic and linguistic identity if they so choose;

(b) respecting and protecting the right of such minorities to establish and maintain their own associations and institutions for the preservation, maintenance and development of their own identity if they so choose;

(c) taking positive action, where necessary, to ensure the effective enjoyment and full exercise of all human rights and fundamental freedoms by national, ethnic, religious or linguistic minorities without discrimination;

(d) ensuring that such minorities have a right of effective participation in decisions at all levels of government which affect their rights or interests;

(e) co-operating with one another in promoting the rights of national, linguistic, religious and ethnic minorities.

3 Competent intergovernmental and relevant non-governmental organisations have a duty to promote and contribute to the full realisation of the rights and interests of national, ethnic, religious and linguistic minorities.

Article 32
The Duty and Responsibility to Respect, Protect and Promote the Rights of Indigenous Peoples

1 Members of the global community have collective, as well as individual duties and responsibilities, to take appropriate action to respect and ensure the existence and rights of indigenous peoples, in particular their right to preserve, maintain and develop their distinct identities and characteristics and to protect their means of livelihood.

2 States have the primary duty and responsibility to take measures to respect and ensure the rights of indigenous peoples within their territory or under their jurisdiction. Such measures should include:

(a) refraining from any action or measures which are aimed at or which will have the effect of destroying the existence of or distinct identity of indigenous peoples;

(b) ensuring the right of indigenous peoples to preserve, maintain, manifest and develop, their own indigenous political, social, cultural, religious and economic systems if they so choose;

(c) ensuring for indigenous peoples the right to enjoy the benefits of traditional lands, territories, waters or other resource traditionally owned or occupied by such peoples and a right to restitution of or compensation for land, territories, waters or other resources from which they were dispossessed or forcibly removed;

(d) ensuring the right of indigenous peoples to exercise autonomy with respect to their own affairs, including control of land, culture, religion, environment, education, health, housing, economic activities, resource management and social welfare if they so choose;

(e) ensuring the right of indigenous peoples to establish, maintain and develop their own indigenous as well as other institutional structures necessary for the exercise of their cultural autonomy if they so choose;

(f) ensuring the full and effective enjoyment by indigenous peoples and their members of all human rights and fundamental freedoms without discrimination on the basis of indigenous origins or identity;

(g) taking positive measures to ensure the economic and social empowerment and improvement of indigenous populations;

(h) facilitating the voluntary participation of indigenous peoples in the political, economic, social and cultural life of the State where they live.

3 Competent inter-governmental organisations have a duty to facilitate the effective participation of indigenous peoples in their activities, in particular in activities concerning the rights and interests of indigenous peoples or which will impact upon such rights or interests.

4 Competent inter-governmental organisations have a duty to work towards the continued promotion and realisation of the rights of indigenous peoples.

5 Relevant non-governmental organisations have a duty to promote continued awareness and implementation of the rights and concerns of indigenous peoples and should assist States and inter-governmental organisations in the realisation of the rights of indigenous peoples.

Chapter 9
Rights of the Child and the Elderly

Article 33
The Duty and Responsibility to Respect, Protect and Promote the Rights of the Child

1 Members of the global community have collective, as well as individual duties and responsibilities, to take appropriate action to protect, respect and ensure the rights of the child.

2 States have the primary duty and responsibility to take measures to protect, respect and ensure the rights of all children within their territory or under their jurisdiction. Such measures should include:

(a) taking special care to ensure the survival and well being, through adequate nutrition, health care and other necessities of life, of all children, and ensuring an adequate standard of living for all children;

(b) protecting, and wherever possible, ensuring the right of children to grow up in the care of and under the responsibility of their parents, family, or a similar caring and nurturing environment;

(c) ensuring special protection and assistance, including health care and social security, to mothers both before and after birth;

(d) preventing and protecting children from all forms of abuse, exploitation or illicit trafficking, including:

(i) neglect and maltreatment;

(ii) physical and mental/psychological violence or injury and sexual abuse;

(iii) economic, sexual and social exploitation;

(iv) illicit use by children of narcotic drugs and the use or involvement of children in the illicit production, dealing in and trafficking of such substances;

(v) illegal trafficking in children for the purposes of sexual exploitation, forced adoption or any other purpose;

(e) ensuring the establishment of adequate and well monitored institutions, facilities, services and arrangements for the protection, maintenance, care, well-being and, where necessary rehabilitation, of children in need of the special care, assistance and protection of the State;

(f) ensuring the protection of children during times of war, including:

(i) respecting and enforcing the rules of international humanitarian law applicable to the protection of children in situations of armed conflict;

(ii) taking necessary measures to ensure that children are not permitted to join the armed forces or participate either directly or indirectly in hostilities;

(g) respecting the rights, duties and responsibilities of parents, family and/or legal guardians to care and provide for their children, and give direction and guidance to their children in accordance with the children's best interests;

(h) respecting and ensuring the rights of children to participate, in accordance with their evolving capacities based on age and maturity, in decisions and matters concerning their rights and interests. In particular, States have a duty and a responsibility to ensure the right of children to hold and express their opinions freely in all matters affecting them;

(i) ensuring that the criminal justice system provides special protection to children in accordance with recognised universal human rights standards, in particular, ensuring that children are only institutionalised as a last resort and only where children have committed acts of violence, and ensuring humane conditions in correctional institutions when children are incarcerated;

(j) ensuring the full and effective enjoyment of all human rights and fundamental freedoms by all children without discrimination on any basis, including their parents' race, colour, sex, age sexual orientation, gender, language, religion, political or other opinion, national, ethnic or social origin, marital or any other status.

3 Parents, or as the case may be, legal guardians have the primary responsibility for the care, well-being and healthy upbringing of their children and have a duty and a responsibility to promote the full and harmonious development of their children.

4 States have a duty to ratify the Convention on the Rights of the Child of 1989.

5 States have a duty to promote international cooperation for the full realisation of the rights of the child and have a duty to assist developing States in the implementation of the rights of the child.

6 Competent inter-governmental and relevant non-governmental organisations have a duty to promote and contribute to the full realisation of the rights of the child.

Article 34

The Duty and Responsibility to Promote and Enforce the Rights and Well-being of the Elderly

1 Members of the global community have collective, as well as individual duties and responsibilities to take appropriate action to respect, promote and ensure the rights and well-being of the elderly.

2 States have the primary duty to take measures to respect, promote and ensure the rights of all the elderly within their territory or under their jurisdiction. Such measures should include:

(a) ensuring the full and effective enjoyment by elderly people of all human rights and fundamental freedoms without discrimination on the basis of age

(b) respecting and ensuring the well-being, dignity and physical and personal integrity of the elderly;

(c) ensuring the establishment of adequate and well monitored institutions, facilities, services and arrangements for the maintenance, care and well-being of elderly persons in need of the special care and assistance of the State;

3 States and competent inter-governmental organisations have a duty to cooperate at the international level to contribute to the development and implementation of the rights of the elderly, and should promote and contribute to the full realisation of the rights of the elderly.

4 Relevant non-governmental organisations have a duty to assist governments and inter-governmental organisations with the development and implementation of the rights of the elderly and should help to promote awareness of the rights and needs of elderly persons.

Chapter 10
Work, Quality of Life and Standard of Living

Article 35

The Duty and Responsibility to Promote the Right to Justly Remunerated Work

1 Members of the global community have collective, as well as individual duties and responsibilities, to take appropriate action to respect, protect and promote the right to justly remunerated work.

2 States have the primary duty and responsibility to use every possible endeavour to ensure the right to work of all persons within its territory or under its jurisdiction. Such measures should include:

(a) adopting policies designed to promote productive work;

(b) ensuring employment security, in particular protection against arbitrary or unfair dismissal;

(c) ensuring equality of opportunity and conditions of work, without discrimination on the basis of race, color, sex, sexual orientation, gender, language, religion, political or other opinion, national, ethnic or social origin, disability, property, birth or other similar such grounds;

(d) ensuring just remuneration and favorable conditions of work.

3 The private sector has a duty to promote and create employment opportunities, and, wherever possible and feasible to prevent the loss of jobs.

4 States have a duty to co-operate with one another to promote employment opportunities, especially in developing nations.

5 Competent inter-governmental organisations have a duty to assist States in the development of policy to promote employment, and should monitor and enforce compliance by governments of their duties under this article.

Article 36

The Duty and Responsibility to Promote Quality of Life and an Adequate Standard of Living

1 Members of the global community have collective, as well as individual duties and responsibilities to take appropriate action to respect, protect and ensure the right to an adequate quality of life and standard of living for all.

2 States have the primary duty and responsibility to take measures to ensure, to the maximum extent possible, that all persons within its territory or under its jurisdiction are free from hunger and have access to adequate food and clean water necessary for a healthy, normal and active existence. Such measures should include:

(a) ensuring efficient production and distribution of food supplies;

(b) ensuring dissemination of knowledge about nutrition;

(c) providing assistance to persons who are unable to provide adequate food for themselves or their families;

3 States have a duty to cooperate to ensure the full realisation of the right to be free from hunger and the right to adequate food for all. In particular, they should cooperate to prevent and alleviate famine, and to ensure an equitable distribution of food supplies in accordance with the principle of need.

4 Competent inter-governmental organisations should work towards the continued promotion and realisation of the right of everyone to be free from hunger.

5 States have the primary duty and responsibility to take measures to ensure, to the maximum extent possible, that everyone within its territory or under its jurisdiction has access to adequate, affordable housing and that their access is sufficiently protected. Such measures should include:

(a) ensuring the provision of adequate, affordable housing in accordance with need;

(b) providing assistance to those unable to secure for themselves or their families affordable housing through their own resources;

(c) ensuring security of tenure, including protection from arbitrary and unlawful forced evictions, and harassment.

6 States have a duty to cooperate to ensure the full realisation of the right to adequate housing for all. In particular, steps should be taken to ensure that a sufficient amount of financial and other international assistance is dedicated to the provision of adequate housing.

7 Competent intergovernmental organisations should work towards the continued promotion and realisation of the right of everyone to adequate housing.

8 States should take measures to ensure, to the maximum extent possible, that everyone within its territory or under its jurisdiction has access to the highest attainable state of health. Such measures should include:

(a) ensuring the provision of adequate, equitable health care facilities and services, especially preventative and primary health care facilities;

(b) taking adequate steps to promote a healthy environment and eliminate causes of ill health;

(c) preventing, controlling and treating epidemic, endemic and occupational diseases;

(d) providing health education and promoting individual responsibility for good health;

(e) ensuring health care for all according to need, irrespective of income or wealth;

(f) ensuring the right to the highest attainable state of health of children.

9 States have a duty to cooperate to promote the highest attainable state of health for all. In particular, States should cooperate to prevent, control and treat epidemic and endemic diseases, and should equitably share the benefits of medical research and technology.

10 Competent inter-governmental organisations have a duty to work towards the continued promotion and realisation of the right of everyone to the highest attainable state of health.

11 States have the primary duty to take measures to ensure, to the maximum extent possible, adequate social security to all those in need, including the unemployed, sick, disabled, old, or anyone else unable to secure an adequate livelihood for themselves or their family through circumstances beyond their control.

12 Employers have a duty to provide for and contribute to adequate social insurance, including old age, disability and sickness benefits for employees.

Chapter 11
Education, Arts and Culture

Article 37
The Duty and Responsibility to Promote and Enforce the Right to Education

1 Members of the global community have collective, as well as individual duties and responsibilities, to take appropriate action to promote, respect and enforce the right to education for all.

2 States have the primary duty and responsibility to take measures to respect, promote and ensure, to the maximum extent possible, the right to education of all within its territory or under its jurisdiction. Such measures should include:

(a) developing, maintaining or providing for an adequate system of schools and other educational institutions;

(b) ensuring access to educational institutions at all levels without discrimination on the basis of race, color, sex, age, sexual orientation, gender, language, religion, political or other opinion, national, ethnic or social origin, disability, property, birth or other such similar status, and ensuring equality of opportunity and treatment in education;

(c) ensuring the right to free and compulsory primary education for all children;

(d) making secondary and tertiary education available and accessible to the maximum extent possible;

(e) protecting the academic freedom of teachers;

(f) respecting the right of individuals and other legal entities to establish and maintain their own private educational institutions;

(g) promoting vocational and technical training;

(h) promoting adult education and more particularly adult literacy.

3 Parents have a duty and a responsibility to encourage and facilitate the education of all their children, and have a responsibility in this regard not to discriminate between male and female children. States have a responsibility to ensure this.

4 States have a duty to ensure that all levels of education are directed towards the full development of the human personality without discrimination in particular on the basis of sex or gender; respect for and understanding of human rights and a culture of peace, and enable all persons to participate meaningfully in a democratic society based upon tolerance, understanding and respect for racial, ethnic, religious, and cultural diversity.

5 Academic institutions, teachers and academics have a duty to promote and develop human rights education and awareness, as well as education designed to promote and develop a democratic and peaceful culture based on respect for racial, religious, ethnic and cultural diversity.

6 Competent inter-governmental organisations have a duty to promote and contribute to developing the educational capacity of States, in particular developing countries.

7 Competent inter-governmental organisations have a duty to promote international cooperation in the development and implementation of human rights education, and education designed to instil and develop a democratic and peaceful culture based on respect for racial, religious, ethnic and cultural diversity.

8 Non-governmental organisations have a duty to work with States and inter-governmental organisations in the promotion of the right to education and, in particular human rights education, and shall develop and implement their own human rights education programs.

Article 38

The Duty and Responsibility to Foster Arts and Culture

1 Members of the global community have collective as well as individual duties to provide a framework for and to foster the arts and culture.

2 States have a duty and responsibility to respect, protect and promote freedom of artistic expression, the right to culture and cultural diversity. In accordance with this duty and responsibility they should:

(a) ensure free access to the arts and culture on a non-discriminatory basis;

(b) encourage creativity and protect innovations and artistic works through intellectual property laws at the national and international levels;

(c) ensure and promote, within the framework of universal human rights and fundamental freedoms, the right of individuals to enjoy their culture in community with others.

3 Competent intergovernmental organisations have a duty to promote international collaboration and exchanges among artists from various cultures, to disseminate

knowledge and information about different cultures and to take appropriate steps to protect and preserve the cultural heritage of humankind.

Chapter 12
Right to a Remedy

Article 39
The Duty and Responsibility to Provide for and Enforce Effective Remedies

1 States have a duty and responsibility to provide for effective national judicial, administrative, legislative and other remedies where a human right or fundamental freedom is threatened or has been violated.

2 States have a duty and a responsibility to ensure that such remedies are effectively carried out.

3 States have a duty and a responsibility to co-operate at the sub-regional, regional and international levels to provide effective regional and international enforcement mechanisms for the prevention of and remedies for the violation of human rights and fundamental freedoms.

4 Existing national, sub-regional, regional and international human rights enforcement mechanisms have a duty and a responsibility to use their enforcement powers effectively to enforce human rights and fundamental freedoms.

Article 40
The Duty to Monitor and Implement the Declaration of Human Duties and Responsibilities

1 States and competent intergovernmental organisations have a duty to give effect to this Declaration by establishing tripartite councils composed of

State, civil society and private sector representatives who will be tasked with establishing a precise plan of action to promote (including early warning co-operation), implementation of the duties and responsibilities set forth in this Declaration.

2 Such tripartite councils shall also be entrusted with monitoring compliance with the duties and responsibilities set forth in this Declaration and, together with States, relevant civil society organisations, national, regional and international inter-governmental organisations, shall publicise their record of compliance.

Article 41
Non-Derogation Clause

1 Nothing in this Declaration shall be interpreted as impairing or restricting the rights contained in the Universal Declaration of Human Rights and other international and regional human rights instruments, nor shall any derogation from or restriction of any human right or fundamental freedom existing in any international human rights instrument or domestic law be admitted on the pretext that the present Declaration does not recognise such rights or that it recognises them to a lesser extent.

2 Nothing in this Declaration shall be construed as implying that any State, organisation, entity, community, people or individual has the right to engage in any activity

or to perform any act which violates the rights set forth in the Universal Declaration of Human Rights or other international or regional human rights instruments.

Participants who intervened in the drafting of the document

Chairman
Richard J. Goldstone (South Africa)
Judge of the Constitutional Court; former Chief Prosecutor of the United Nations War Crimes Tribunal.

Representative of UNESCO
Barbara Barry de Longchamp
Director, Partnerships for the Twenty-first Century.

City of Valencia
Rita Barberá Nolla (Spain)
Mayor of Valencia; President, Foundation "Valencia Tercer Milenio".
Rafael Ripoll (Spain)
Advisor to the Mayor.

Foundation "Valencia Tercer Milenio"
Francisco Villanueva (Spain)
Director of the Foundation "Valencia Tercer Milenio".
Rosa María Rodríguez Magda (Spain)
Cultural Director of the Foundation "Valencia Tercer Milenio"; Writer; Philosopher.

Adc Nouveau Millénaire Partners
Lucio Attinelli (Italy)
Partner, ADC Nouveau Millénaire; former Director of Public Relations and Special Events Division, UNESCO; former Acting Coordinator of Integral Study of the Silk Road, Roads of Dialogue, UNESCO; Journalist; Writer.
Fernando Caruso (Italy)
Partner, ADC Nouveau Millénaire; former Director, Italian Cultural Institute, Paris.
Léon Davico (Yugoslavia)
Partner, ADC Nouveau Millénaire; Special Advisor to Director-General of UNESCO; former Director of Public Information, UNESCO and UNHCR.

Participants
Marieclaire Acosta Urquidi (Mexico)
President, Mexican Commission for the Defence and Promotion of Human Rights.
Ednan Agaev (Russia)
Former Director, Department for Policy Analysis, Ministry of Foreign Affairs; Ambassador to Colombia; Member of Advisory Board to UN Secretary-General for Disarmament Studies.

Lluis Álvarez (Spain)
Professor at the Department of Aesthetics of the University of Oviedo; Member, Academy of the Asturian Language.
Chief Emeka Anyaoku (Nigeria)
Secretary-General of the Commonwealth; former Foreign Minister.
Jesús Ballesteros (Spain)
Professor of Philosophy of Law, University of Valencia.
Enrique Barón Crespo (Spain)
Member of the European Parliament.
Michel Bonnot (France)
Ministry for Public Health.
Michael Brozska (Germany)
Head of Research, Bonn International Center for Conversion.
Joaquín Calomarde (Spain)
Writer and philosopher; former Member of Parliament.
José Casas Pardo (Spain)
Chair of Applied Economics, University of Valencia.
Jacqueline Cassette (South Africa)
Lawyer, Constitutional Court of South Africa.
Luciana Castellina (Italy)
Member of European Parliament; Chair of Commission for External Policy.
Miguel Chamorro (Spain)
Director, Executive Office of the Secretary-General, Interpol; International Criminal Police Organisation, Lyon.
Diego Cordovez (Ecuador)
Former Foreign Minister; Special Representative of UN Secretary General for Cyprus; former UN Under-Secretary-General for Special Political Questions.
Jean Daniel (France)
Editor, Le Nouvel Observateur.
Adama Dieng (Senegal)
Secretary-General, International Commission of Jurists.
Peter Eigen (Germany)
Chairman, Transparency International
Souheil El-Zein (France/Lebanon)
Director, Legal Affairs, Interpol.
Emmanuel A. Erskine (Ghana)
General; former Commander of Ghana Army and Force Commander, United Nations Interim Force in Lebanon (UNIFIL).
Miguel Ángel Estrella (Argentina)
Pianist; Founder of Musique Espérance; UNESCO Goodwill Ambassador.
Richard A. Falk (United States)
Albert G. Milbank Professor of International Law and Practice, Center of International Studies, Princeton University.
Charles Firestone (United States)
Director, Aspen Institute – Communications and Society Programme.
Baya Gacemi (Algeria)

Former Editor-in-Chief, La Tribune.
Antonio Garrigues Walker (Spain)
International Lawyer; President, Spanish Section of UNHCR.
Hans-Peter Gasser (Switzerland)
International Committee of the Red Cross; Editor, International Review of the Red Cross.
José Manuel González Páramo (Spain)
Professor Emeritus at the Complutense University of Madrid; Co-founder of the Cánovas del Castillo Foundation.
Mário da Graça Machungo (Mozambique)
Former Prime Minister and Finance Minister; President, Banco Internacional do Mozambique; Chairman, Africa Leadership Forum.
Ahmed Haggag (Egypt)
Ambassador; Assistant Secretary-General, Organisation for African Unity.
Wakako Hironaka (Japan)
Member of the House of Councillors; former Director General, Environmental Protection Agency.
Lord Frank Judd (United Kingdom)
Former Minister for Development Co-operation; former Director, Oxfam UK; Member, House of Lords.
Sergei Kapitsa (Russia)
Professor; Member, Russian Academy of Sciences.
Rushworth Kidder (United States)
Director, Institute for Global Ethics; former Correspondent, Christian Science Monitor.
Bernard Kouchner (France)
Minister for Health and Humanitarian Action; Founder, Médecins sans Frontières.
Vladimir Lomeiko (Russia)
Special Advisor to Director General of UNESCO; former Ambassador to UNESCO and spokesman for Foreign Minister.
Ruud Lubbers (The Netherlands)
Former Prime Minister; Professor for Globalisation.
Errol P. Mendes (Canada)
Director, Human Rights Research and Education Centre, University of Ottawa.
Guy Mettan (Switzerland)
President, Swiss Press Club, Geneva; former Editor-in-chief, La Tribune de Genève.
Stuart Mole (United Kingdom)
Director, Private Office of the Commonwealth Secretary-General.
Patricia Morales (Argentina)
Assistant to Ruud Lubbers (The Netherlands), former Prime Minister.
Chandra Muzaffar (Malaysia)
Professor; President, International Movement for a Just World (Pergerakan Keadilan Sedunia).
Dragoljub Najman (Yugoslavia)
Former Assistant Director General, UNESCO.
Luis Núñez Ladevéze (Spain)
Chair of Journalism at the Complutense University of Madrid.
Hans d'Orville (Germany)

Director, Information Technologies Development Programme, United Nations Development Programme (UNDP).
Augusto Ramírez Ocampo (Colombia)
Former Foreign Minister; former Assistant Administrator for Latin America, UNDP.
Elisabeth Rehn (Finland)
UN Under-Secretary-General and Special Representative of the UN Secretary-General in Bosnia and Herzegovina.
Joseph Rotblat (United Kingdom)
Nobel Peace Laureate 1995 and Albert Einstein Prize 1992; Professor Emeritus of Physics, University of London; Co-ordinator, Pugwash Conferences on Science and World Affairs.
Michel Serres (France)
Writer and philosopher; Professor and Member of the French Royal Academy (Académie Française).
Farooq Sobhan (Bangladesh)
Executive Chairman, Board of Investment, Prime Minister's Office; former Foreign Secretary and Ambassador/High Commissioner to China, Malaysia, India and UN.
Wole Soyinka (Nigeria)
Nobel Laureate for Literature.
Serge Spitzer (United States)
Artist/sculptor.
Tan Sri Ghazali Shafie (Malaysia)
Former Foreign and Interior Minister; Member of South Commission.
Thorvald Stoltenberg (Norway)
Ambassador to Denmark; former Foreign and Defence Minister.
José María Tomás y Tío (Spain)
Dean of Judges of Valencia; President of the Foundation for Justice.
Jakob von Uexküll (Sweden)
Director and founder, The Right Livelihood Award.
Jan Urban (Czech Republic)
Publisher, Transitions; former Editor, Lidove Noviny.
Amelia Valcárcel (Spain)
Chair of the Department of Philosophy of Law, Ethics and Politics, University of Oviedo.
Miguel Veyrat (Spain)
Deputy Director, RNE; Writer and journalist.
Joanne Weschler (Poland)
United Nations Representative, Human Rights Watch.
Baroness Shirley Williams of Crosby (United Kingdom)
Professor, Harvard University, JFK School of Government; former Minister of Education; Member, House of Lords.
George Woodwell (United States)
President, Woods Hole Institute; Member, National Academy of Sciences.
Martin Woollacott (United Kingdom)
Foreign Policy Columnist and Assistant Editor, The Guardian.
Sheng Yu (China)
Professor; Advisor to Economic and Social Council of the National People's Congress.
Norton Zinder (United States)

Professor for Genetic Biology, Rockefeller University, New York; former Chairman, Program Advisory Committee on the Human Genome.

Personalities who participated in the debates and congresses of the programme 'Human Duties and Responsibilities in the Third Millennium'

José Luis Abellán (Spain)
Chair of Philosophy at the Complutense University of Madrid.
María José Alcón (Spain)
Councillor for Culture, Valencia City Council.
Adrián Alemán de Armas (Spain)
Dean of the Faculty of Information Science at the University of La Laguna.
Pedro Altares (Spain)
Journalist, RNE.
Consuelo Álvarez de Toledo (Spain)
Audience ombudswoman at Antena 3.
Angelo Azzi (Italy)
Director of the Institute of Biochemistry and Molecular Biology of the University of Bern.
Lluís Bassets (Spain)
Assistant Director of El País.
Ignacio Bel (Spain)
Professor of Information Law at the Complutense University of Madrid and President of the Executive Committee of the Foundation for Social Communication.
Marisa Berenson (Italy)
Actress; Goodwill Ambassador, UNESCO.
Francisco Camps (Spain)
Secretary of State for Public Administration; former Councillor for Culture of the Valencian Government.
Pablo Capilla (Spain)
Professor at the Department of Journalism of the Faculty of Information Science at the Ramon Llull University of Barcelona.
Juan Carlos Carbonell Mateu (Spain)
Dean of the Faculty of Law at the University of Valencia.
Rodolfo Castro (Spain)
Director of the Faculty of Journalism at CEU-San Pablo, Valencia.
Antonio Colomer Viadel (Spain)
Professor of Constitutional Law, University of Valencia.
Jesús Conill (Spain)
Professor of Ethics, University of Valencia.
Adela Cortina (Spain)
Chair of Philosophy of Law, Ethics and Politics, University of Valencia.
Luis Escobar de la Serna (Spain)
Dean of the Faculty of Humanities at CEU-San Pablo, Madrid.
José María Espinosa (Spain)
Director of CEU-San Pablo, Valencia.

Joaquín Espinosa Carbonell (Spain)
Chair of Italian Philology at the University of Valencia.
Antonio Ferrandis (Spain)
Actor.
Joaquín Ferrandis (Spain)
President of the Association of Valencian Journalists.
Dario Fo (Italy)
Nobel Prize Laureate for Literature.
Vicente Garrido Malloll (Spain)
Secretary General, Juridical Advisory Council of the City of Valencia.
Baltasar Garzón (Spain)
Senior Judge of the National Criminal Court of Spain.
Ángel Gómez-Hortigüela (Spain)
Historian and philosopher; Specialist in the work of Juan Luis Vives.
Santiago Grisolía (Spain)
Professor and Director, International Programme for the Human Genome; President of the Valencia Council of Culture; President, Foundation for Advanced Studies.
Henry Kamm (United States)
Former editorialist of The New York Times.
Guillermo Kirkpatrick (Spain)
Ambassador of Spain to the European Council.
Manuel Lombau (Spain)
News Editor at TVE.
Josep Carles Laínez (Spain)
Writer and publisher; Editor, Círculo Cero.
Xosé López García (Spain)
Dean of the Faculty of Information Science at the University of Santiago de Compostela.
Juan José López Ibor (Spain)
Psychiatrist.
Javier de Lucas Martín (Spain)
Professor of the Department of the Philosophy of Law, Morals and Politics at the University of Valencia.
José Antonio Marina (Spain)
Philosopher and writer.
Margarita Mariscal de Gante (Spain)
Minister for Justice.
Jorge Martínez "Aspar" (Spain)
World Motorcycling Champion.
Federico Mayor Zaragoza (Spain)
Director General of UNESCO.
Juan Antonio Mesa (Spain)
Secretary of the National Commission of UNESCO.
Marcela Miró (Spain)
Councillor for Social Welfare of the Valencian Government
Manuel Montero García (Spain)
Dean of the Faculty of Information Science at the University of the Basque Country.

Vicente Navarro de Luján (Spain)
Director of CEU-San Pablo, Valencia.
Franco Nero (Italy)
Actor.
Luis del Olmo (Spain)
Director programme "Protagonistas" Onda Cero.
Leoluca Orlando (Italy)
Mayor of City of Palermo, Sicily; Member of the European Parliament; Professor of Law, University of Palermo.
Carlos Ortega (Peru)
Director, Diálogo, a UNESCO publication.
Marcelo Palacios (Spain)
President of the Spanish Bio-ethics Foundation and of the International Society of Bio-ethics.
Franca Rame (Italy)
Actress.
Manuel Reyes Mate (Spain)
Former Director of the Institute of Philosophy of the Higher Council for Scientific Research.
Carlos Robles Piquer (Spain)
President of the Cánovas del Castillo Foundation; Member of the European Parliament.
Concha Roldán (Spain)
Institute of Philosophy, Higher Council for Scientific Research.
Mort Rosenblum (United States)
Editor, Herald Tribune.
Piero Sanavio (Italy)
Writer and journalist.
Antonio Sánchez Bravo (Spain)
Chair of the Faculty of Journalism at the Complutense University; President of the Communications Working Group of the Spanish Commission for Co-operation with UNESCO.
José Sanmartín (Spain)
Chair of the Philosophy of Science at the University of Valencia; Director of UIMP-Valencia and the Reina Sofía Centre for Studies on Violence.
Fernando Savater (Spain)
Chair of Ethics at the Complutense University of Madrid.
Antonio Szigriszt Laca (Spain)
Area Manager for National News of RNE.
Manuel Tarancón Fandos (Spain)
Councillor for Culture of the Valencian Government; former President of the Diputación de Valencia
Francisco Torrent Guasp (Spain)
Cardiologist; Researcher on heart structure.
Leyla Umar (Turkey)
SIPA and GAMMA Agencies; Journalist at Sabah.

Eduardo Vallejo de Lejúa (Spain)
Mayor of Gernika.
Bernardo Valli (Italy)
Editorialist at La Repubblica.
Gianni Vattimo (Italy)
Philosopher; Chair at the Department of Philosophical Hermeneutics at the University of Torino.

www.ingramcontent.com/pod-product-compliance
Ingram Content Group UK Ltd.
Pitfield, Milton Keynes, MK11 3LW, UK
UKHW051921100926
8556IPUK00021B/1307

9 789050 95886